Critical Studies in Media Commercialism

This book is dedicated to Everett Parker, whose life-long courageous struggle to compel the media to serve the public interest has most recently resulted in a new licensing agreement awarding community access to non-commercial, low-power FM radio broadcasting in the United States.

Critical Studies in Media Commercialism

Edited by

Robin Andersen and Lance Strate

OXFORD
UNIVERSITY PRESS

Great Clarendon Street, Oxford OX2 6DP

Oxford University Press is a department of the University of Oxford.
It furthers the University's objective of excellence in research, scholarship,
and education by publishing worldwide in

Oxford New York

Athens Auckland Bangkok Bogotá Buenos Aires Calcutta
Cape Town Chennai Dar es Salaam Delhi Florence Hong Kong Istanbul
Karachi Kuala Lumpur Madrid Melbourne Mexico City Mumbai
Nairobi Paris São Paulo Singapore Taipei Tokyo Toronto Warsaw

with associated companies in Berlin Ibadan

Oxford is a registered trade mark of Oxford University Press
in the UK and in certain other countries

Published in the United States
by Oxford University Press Inc., New York

British Library Cataloguing in Publication Data
Data available

Library of Congress Cataloging in Publication Data
Data available

ISBN 0-19-874277-0

1 3 5 7 9 10 8 6 4 2

Typeset in Minion
by RefineCatch Limited, Bungay, Suffolk
Printed in Great Britain
on acid-free paper by
Biddles Ltd.,
Guildford and King's Lynn

Acknowledgements

I WOULD like to thank all the authors in this volume for their contributions and congeniality. All the editors at Oxford were wonderfully professional and Everette Dennis offered needed support. I am grateful to the Paper Tiger Television collective, especially Heather Hendershot, Mike Simmons, Michael Eisenmenger, and Linda Iannacone, for their enthusiastic response to the critique of Sport Utility Vehicles, and their willingness to devote time and energy to producing the video-tape *Road to Ruin*. Their creativity and expertise helped develop the critique and resulted in an award-winning programme: I am grateful to Nancy Morris for keeping an eye out for news of SUVs. I am also indebted to Peter Hart from Fairness and Accuracy in Reporting (FAIR) and Paper Tiger TV for his up-to-the-minute faxes. Carol Bloom provided insightful comments about the business practices of America Online. She also made her VCR and comfortable sofa available so we could watch *Hercules*. Sameh Fakhouri opened a gateway to the Internet when mine failed, and Gwenyth Jackaway used campus mail to send me much-needed research material. Neil Hickey of the *Columbia Journalism Review* read the Introduction and offered valuable comments. Dan Weisberg's insights into the image and persona of presidential candidate Bob Dole, and our discussions with Darrin Arremony about the 1996 elections, were always fruitful. As usual, my Fordham students are keen observers of the commercial media terrain, and without them as a compass, I would be lost. As always, any missteps I have taken are all my own.

Robin Andersen

Contents

Introduction   1
Robin Andersen

Part I   **Human Need and the Commercial Imperative**

Introduction   25

1   **Advertising at the Edge of the Apocalypse**   27
Sut Jhally

2   **American Advertising**   40
Marshall McLuhan

3   **The Social Effects of Commercial Television**   47
Neil Postman

Part II   **Conglomeration, Synergy, and Global Media**

Introduction   57

4   **The Global Media Giants**   59
Robert W. McChesney

5   **Global Ethics in the Age of Behemoths**   71
Anthony Smith

6   **Sold American: US News Consultants and News Issues Abroad**   84
Craig Allen

7   **From Flick to Flack: The Increased Emphasis on Marketing by Media Entertainment Corporations**   101
Matthew P. McAllister

Part III   **Advertising and Culture**

Introduction   125

8   **US Voices on UK Radio**   127
Nancy Morris

9   **Intoxicating Consumptions: the Case of Beer Commercials**   145
Lance Strate

10   **Road to Ruin: the Cultural Mythology of SUVs**   158
Robin Andersen

11   **Starbucks Coffee: Cultivating and Selling the Postmodern Brew**   173
Katherine G. Fry

12   **Scalable Hype: Old Persuasions for New Technology**   186
Dan Weisberg

Part IV   **Commercial 'Diversity?'**

Introduction   201

13   **Image Culture and the Supermodel**   203
Delicia Harvey and Lance Strate

14   **Light Makes Right: Skin Colour and Racial Hierarchy in Television Advertising**   214
Robert M. Entman and Constance L. Book

15   **Talking Back to Calvin Klein: Youthful 'Targets' Confront their Commercial Image**   225
Lauren Tucker

Part V   **Politics, Citizenship, and Fragmentation**

Introduction   237

16   **Segmenting, Signalling and Tailoring: Probing the Dark Side of Target Marketing**   239
Joseph Turow

17   **The Commercial Politics of the 1996 US Presidential Campaign**   250
Robin Andersen

18   **Commercial Media and Corporate Presence in the K-12 Classroom**   264
Margaret Cassidy

19   **Commodity Fetishism: Symbolic Form, Social Class, and the Division of Knowledge in Society**   276
Paul Lippert

Part VI   **Resisting Persuasions**

Introduction   289

20   **KFC into India: a Case Study of Resistance to Globalization Discourse**   291
Melissa Wall

21 **Media Literacy and the Commercialization of Culture** 310
Norman Cowie

22 **The Public Interest in the Twenty-First Century** 324
Everett C. Parker

About the Authors 333

Index 337

Introduction

Robin Andersen

An amusing advertisement for the American cable movie channel HBO features Jane Goodall studying chimpanzees. She can't understand their strange behaviour, but we can, from our privileged perspective as viewers. The chimps are mimicking behaviour and stealing lines from characters in the movies *The God-father* and *Network*. At her desk, in a house surrounded by the forest habitat, writing that she is perplexed by their actions, Goodall ends her letter because *Braveheart* is soon to begin on HBO. The camera pulls back and we see the chimps perched before the windows also waiting for the movie to begin. HBO's slogan, 'It's not just TV, It's HBO', is spelled out as the commercial ends. *The X-Files* then returns to the Fox network channel.

We can't help but be entertained by this HBO ad. Everybody loves pictures of large furry mammals, especially primates, especially primates who talk like Marlon Brando in *The Godfather*. The ad is intertextual in its references to movie texts, its images of nature, and its celebration of Jane Goodall as a viewer of HBO. But if we look a little more closely, at the business practices of its production and distribution, at the attitudes and ambitions of its message, and consider them within the current state of media consolidation and ownership, it can also be read as a metaphor for the commercial transformations which have taken place in the world of advertising and the media. It is a contemporary myth that at once acknowledges and celebrates the structures and practices of this new ultra-commercialized media environment.

From spots to placement

The advertising economics of TV have had a particular trajectory over the twentieth century. After the battle over US broadcasting was won by commercial interests in the 1920s, advertising revenue was established as the sponsor of broadcast programming. Commercialism was to be the dominant force in the American media, the ramifications of which are only now, at the end of the century, being fully understood. What began as a one-sponsor, one-programme relationship in the 1950s gave way by the end of that decade (with a little help from the quiz-show scandals) to spot advertising (Barnouw 1975) like this for HBO. Spots that interrupt programming (the talking chimpanzees interrupted *X-Files*) are purchased by multiple advertisers at negotiated prices determined by a combination of ratings, programme demographics, time, and availability. In the 1980s, that model began to shift. Promotional messages are no longer restricted to spot advertising. In the age of deregulation, contemporary television now places products in just about every nook and cranny of airtime, turning much of television content into the once illegal and reproved format, the programme-length commercial (Andersen 1995; Jacobson and Mazur 1995). Although spot advertising is not going away, it now co-exists with *product placement*, a practice that embeds the promotion within the programme. With spot ads the pitch becomes harder, as ads become shorter, more frequent, and easier to zap. Viewers are media literate and wary of such overt persuasion. Celebrity endorsements help, but now celluloid and video stars pitch everything from aspirins to phone companies to HBO. Audiences have come to know that every endorsement has its price, making them a little less effective. But when stars use products in movies and TV programmes, it still appears to be the discourse of entertainment, not sales. In this strategic game of leapfrog, advertisers try yet another persuasive technique as the old one loses some of its punch.

Products become significant parts of TV shows, which themselves are carefully designed to appeal to particular consumer groups. Advertising demographics are essential in designing programmes carefully dovetailed with advertising messages. From *Friends* to *Frazier*, from *Rosie O'Donnell* to *Dawson's Creek*, entertainment embraces sales and unabashedly pitches the products that the stars notice, use, and even mock in a totalizing media universe propelled by promotions and marketing. Take, for example, the Time Warner entertainment product *Dawson's Creek*, a programme aired on the conglomerate's own WB network. With its ensemble cast of youthful characters negotiating love, relationships, parents, and infidelity, the melodramatic, angst-imbued series became a runaway hit with a huge teenage and young adult audience. Like many programmes on television today, *Creek* is represented by a product placement agency, the Vista Group, which also places products on such shows as *Friends* and *ER* (Patat 1999). Everything from boats to cars to kitchen appliances has made its commercial debut on *Creek*. But *Creek* has etched a special cross-promotional (McAllister 1996) relationship with J-Crew clothes and merchandise. The kids on *Creek* are dressed in the latest J-Crew fashions, and the cast was featured throughout the spring 1998 catalogue. On their web site the folks at Vista Group (1999) state, 'Products used in motion pictures or in television are perceived by the audience to be chosen by the star thus receiving an implied endorsement. Products shown on screen within a storyline have higher credibility than products in advertisements which the audience knows are paid announcements.' In fact, audience recall is two and a half times greater when products are submerged in TV programmes (Jacobson and Mazur 1995). Marketing strategies lead audiences to believe that the stars choose their own brand names. Through their purchases, young viewers can easily emulate the style and consumption patterns of their favourite television idols.

But for a more stunning example of this new television landscape, let's turn to a high-profile representative of women's culture on the commercial media, *The Rosie O'Donnell Show*. Every day Rosie jovially pitches dozens of products on her show. From Hot Tamales and Little Debbie's Desert Pies, to Devil Dogs and Listerine. And they are not mentioned casually, either. Rosie sings jingles for some, shows storyboards for others, throws product samples into the crowd, and recently had a six-pack of Pepsi One, a new soft drink, for every member of the audience. But that is not unusual either. On that show she popped open a can of the new product, tasted it, said it was great, and drank it throughout the show. She openly begs companies to supply her with more of her favourite products.

On the show Rosie promises the show's target audience, stay-at-home moms, that happiness and domestic harmony can be found through the purchase of a vast array of products. Rosie presents herself as, like her viewers, just another average mom, but one in desperate need of every kind of snack, product, and service. She describes how good it feels to consume a Drakes Devil Dog, but as ElHassan (1998: 5) notes, 'O'Donnell is keenly aware that most mothers are not in the same high-income bracket she is. To counterbalance the actual difference, she frequently refers to her modest upbringing. Hence, one is easily convinced that she is not pretending to prefer mid-range consumer products such as Junior Mints, YooHoo, or Reese's Pieces to the delicacies she could certainly purchase if she cared to indulge herself.'

It is not surprising that Rosie's nickname is 'the queen of everything'. The products promoted on the show are also featured on the pages of Rosie's web site. In addition, Rosie and her friend Penny Marshall appear in TV spots for K-Mart.

The commercialized *Rosie O'Donnell Show* contradicts just about everything that seems to be true of Rosie O'Donnell the person. As she is a single, working mother with an attitude, we might think she could offer alternatives to women. Rosie is a prominent leader in the 'size acceptance' movement, yet she reinforces the obsession with thinness by promoting the anorexic-sized Barbie Doll and congratulating her celebrity guests on their thinness. O'Donnell's lifestyle choices imply that she does not herself buy the one-dimensional framing of the traditional mother/caregiver, yet she reinforces the woman-as-consumer image for an hour every day. As a spectacular showcase for product promotion, the programme can never go beyond the marketing lifestyle imperatives of advertisers' demands for programming environments that augment their promotional messages. Outside a commercial frame, Rosie might be able to celebrate the accomplishments of women, applauding difference and helping create a cultural space for diversity and alternative life choices. Sadly, the programme's potential cannot even be remotely approached when asked to conform to the demands of product placement and commercialized media culture. But Rosie O'Donnell did not invent product placement. It came into its own as a major economic convention and financial force within the film industry during the 1980s (Miller 1990).

Films

When Michael J. Fox is retro-hurled into the 1950s in *Back to the Future*, he's called Calvin Klein because of the name branded on his underwear. No one would make that mistake today. Placing brands in films really took off after 1982 when Steven Spielberg's cute alien, ET, ate Reese's Pieces and candy sales rose by 300 per cent (Fuller 1997). Then, in 1983, Tom Cruise wore Wayfarer sunglasses in the movie

Risky Business. In one month Ray-Ban reported sales of 18,000, more pairs of that style sold than during the previous three years (Jacobson and Mazur 1995). Ray-Bans have shielded the eyes of stars in scores of movies since then, but they became more than simple props in the movie *Men in Black*. Only when Will Smith gets his Ray-Bans does he officially become partners with Tommy Lee Jones, so they can 'save the earth from the scum of the universe'. As part of the official uniform, the eye-wear got an extra boost in the companion MTV video also featuring Smith.

In the film *Jerry Maguire*, Tom Cruise plays a struggling sports agent and Cuba Gooding Jr plays the lovable football player Rod Tidwell, trying to make it big time. Products such as Coke, Visa and Reebok are plugged, but the film goes further, making a powerful statement in support of advertising. Tidwell's very success is measured by his popularity with advertisers. His career goal is to appear in a Reebok commercial, not on the late-night, low-budget waterbed pitches that are a sure sign of failure. Reebok's placement in the film led to contention about creative control, ultimately won by the shoe company. The director cut forty-seven seconds of Tidwell appearing in a Reebok commercial at the end of the movie. Reebok sued, and when the film was aired on the Showtime cable channel, the pitch had been reinserted. At this point advertisers have enormous control over motion-picture plot and dialogue, and, in this case, endings. The talented Gooding, by the end of 1998, was pitching Pepsi on TV spots, still in his Tidwell character.

Products now feature so prominently in films that they have come to upstage the movies themselves. Advertisements for the products used by Pierce Brosnan as James Bond came out well before anyone saw the movie. And films now serve to introduce major new products, their release timed to market debuts, as when *Jurassic Park: The Lost World*, featured the new Mercedes Sport Utility Vehicle.

Product placement is largely invisible to a generation raised on Saturday-morning cartoons, the vast majority of which became programme length commercials during the early 1980s, featuring toys and action heroes available at retail outlets (Engelhardt 1986). Now, movies targeted at the young often include inane dialogue about products that simply becomes the background chatter of this new media environment. *The Wedding Singer* stars Adam Sandler, an actor popular with youthful viewers already accustomed to watching such TV product vehicles as NBC's *Friends*. Sandler, playing the wedding singer, is lying in bed depressed after his fiancée has left him. A friend comes to visit, lies down on the bed with him and says, 'Hey, these sheets are soft. Do you use Downy?' Sandler replies, 'No, all-tempa-cheer. You can wash your clothes at any temperature and the colours don't run together.' There is no attempt at realism in the scene, as the actor is wearing all his clothes when he lies down and presumably would have no way of telling whether the sheets are soft or not. The segment is simply a commercial, inserted without pause into the text, providing the product with a place in the movie's dialogue spoken by the main character. It is so obvious it's funny, in the style of the hip cynicism that is the only plausible attitude available to a generation inundated by such cheesy hucksterisms (Nicholson 1998).

With product placement, commodities have come to define story lines, and function as essential plot elements. Characters are developed as commercial identities defined by the brand-name products they eat, use, and wear. At this point, the industry understands quite simply that to be persuasive there can be no difference between the entertainment and the ad. The entertainment is the promotion, and the viewers are the targets of ever-cleverer persuasions that hide their marketing motivations. In the Jane Goodall HBO spot, advertising and entertainment merge, but with product placement that merger constitutes a new set of commercial strategies, propelled by a long tradition, and only the latest in a historical trajectory racing towards ever-increasing market priorities. Ownership has had an enormous effect on the media's commercial priorities for the last quarter-century.

Media ownership: mergers, consolidation and 'tight diversification'

Let's return to the HBO spot. The cable movie service claims not to be television. If it's not TV, what is it? HBO is part of Time Warner's huge media empire, created by two historic media mergers. Fully to understand this escalating commercial media culture we need to examine the 'consolidation' craze itself. The mergers and acquisitions of the 1980s and 1990s took place in two significant waves. The first was 1989, 'the biggest year ever for media related deals' (Schatz 1997: 85). A total of 414 media deals worth over $42 billion were struck, the most notable, of course, being the 1989 $14 billion Time–Warner merger. In 1995 another record was set 'with 644 media mergers totalling an astounding $70.8 billion' (Schatz 1997: 85). Along with Disney's purchase of Cap Cities/ABC, Viacom's buyout of Blockbuster, and Westinghouse's merger with CBS, the already massive Time Warner bought Turner Broadcasting System Inc. (TBS) in a $7.3 billion deal. Among other things, CNN, TNT, and TBS gave the new company broadcast distribution for its vast range of media products. And they were vast, with TBS's numerous film and TV series holdings—'Time Warner now had the largest library in existence' (Schatz 1997: 89)—with 3,500 titles added to Warner Bros' holdings of 1,100 films. Bits and pieces from old movies turn up everywhere as the memory banks of media culture are mined for advertising and merchandising purposes, as demonstrated in the soundtrack for the HBO spot. Time Warner has also had spectacular marketing success, for example with vintage *Looney Toons*. Revenues for syndication and merchandising of Daffy Duck and his friends reached $3.5 billion in 1996. Tweety Bird and Sylvester can be seen on spot advertising entertaining babyboomers and convincing them that no one can eat a sandwich without Miracle Whip.

Media conglomeration has allowed Time Warner, along with Disney and a few others, to practise what some refer to as 'tight diversification', and economic 'synergy'. 'Synergy' is another key piece of this expanding commercial mosaic, a strategy in which corporations cross-promote their own stars, programmes and merchandise on their media outlets. Time Warner wanted to own the production and distribution of its TV shows, so it started its own TV network, WB. Returning to their big hit *Dawson's Creek* illustrates how synergy works. The people at Time

Warner understand that teenagers comprise the biggest consumer market in the music industry and they use *Dawson's Creek* to sell the songs and artists signed to Warner Bros record labels. Paula Cole's *I Don't Wanna Wait* became a top-ten single after being featured as the show's theme song. Numerous other songs and artists signed by Warner Bros can be found and purchased on *Creek*'s web site. The Warner Bros soundtrack of *Dawson's Creek* will soon be released.

Synergy has provided the economic fuel that propels the summer movie block-buster craze as a main financial media strategy. The primary requirement for synergy is capital, which only huge companies like Time Warner have, first to produce the blockbuster films that form the epicentre, then to provide the millions needed to drive the marketing machines behind them. These multi-purpose entertainment/marketing machines are vertically and horizontally diversified, allowing the media behemoths to create not simply films, but franchises. A movie is not just a summer blockbuster; as Schatz (1997: 74) notes, it is a 'two-hour promotion for a multimedia product line . . . which breeds movie sequels and TV series, music videos and sound track albums, video games and theme park rides, graphic novels and comic books, and an endless array of licensed tie-in and brand-name consumer products.' We have only to look at Disney's animated film *Hercules* for an illustration of synergy. In the film, when Hercules becomes a hero he also becomes an action figure. The cultural icons of his success are the vast array of tie-in merchandise, from Air-Hercules sandals to soft drinks, which are sold, of course, in their own branded, retail outlet. At the time of the movie's release, Disney made up the entrance to its store to look like the store in the film. The latest craze—the tie-in theme park—is also depicted in the movie itself. The movie's celebration of marketing synergy helps create a cultural attitude in its favour, finally erasing the distinction between cultural narratives, heroes, marketing, and merchandise.

Indeed, the first giant step forward in this direction was the *Batman* blockbuster. As others have pointed out, Warner is the Studio that *Batman* built. A Warner executive explained that *Batman* was 'the first time we utilized the whole machine of the company. The marketing, the tie-ins, the merchandizing, the international' (Schatz 1997: 93). In this media environment, we no longer have singular movie narratives; 'rather, they are related aspects or "iterations" of entertainment super-texts, multimedia narrative forms which can be expanded and exploited almost ad infinitum' (Schatz 1997: 75).

Batman the movie became *Batman* the industry, and that inspired the chain of Warner Bros retail stores, one of the most significant trends in all of this. These new entertainment/commodity facilities, or retail stores, feature 'branded' products, like those for Disney's *Hercules*. Tying products to the movies, programmes, networks, and cable services on which they appear gives media firms distinct brand identities that create new marketing horizons for a proliferating number of commodities. Cable channels and broadcast networks alike now strive to be regarded as brands, especially desirable to specific demographic groups targeted by advertisers, such as children who watch Disney and Nickelodeon. Disney now has 590 retail stores selling branded products and Time Warner is in hot pursuit with 160 stores. Viacom has also entered the branded retail marketing venture. It is this latest aspect of the merger/synergy craze which finally and completely erases the difference between movies and advertisements, programming and promotion, entertainment and shopping. As Michael Eisner, chief executive of Disney puts it, 'The Disney stores promote the consumer products, which promote the theme parks, which promote the TV shows. The TV shows promote the company. Roger Rabbit promotes Christmas at Disneyland' (Hazen and Winokur 1997: 46).

In this seemingly monolithic environment, one supernarrative after another becomes the vehicle for the vast enterprise of multiple promotion, crowding out a more diverse imaginative entertainment landscape. Entertainment products that 'work' under these conditions conform to a certain set of requirements, designed to target the highest-paying markets, the largest portion of which is teenagers who see movies more than once and buy the tie-in merchandise. The now standard and highly formulaic action-adventure narratives of the summer blockbusters, such as *Armageddon*, must be hyped with all the advertising that studio money can buy (Bart 1999). They are expensive to make, and expensive to advertise, and this is a major rationale for the media megacorporation, because only they can afford the risk and cost, and the 'risk–reward' quotient steadily increases as the stakes are raised. 'In 1990, the average cost of 169 major studio productions was $28.8 million, with another $11.6 million spent on marketing. In 1995, the average cost on 212 productions was $36.4 million, plus $17.7 million for marketing, pushing the total cost per feature over $50 million for the first time' (Schatz 1997: 96). The stakes are raised with the inflationary costs of production and promotion, crowding out smaller economic players with creative ideas instead of marketing vehicles. Because the 'buzz' created by advertising not only affects domestic revenues, but also accounts for the success of international marketing, spot advertising is now a huge expense for media firms themselves. A total of $1.94 billion was paid out in advertising by major studios for 1995 releases—an increase of 107 per cent on 1990.

Deregulation allowed TV programmes to become advertisements. Industry conglomeration created the synergy needed for transforming the rest of entertainment into merchandise. This paradigm shift in media economics did not happen overnight. It is, rather, a creeping ailment, like the black oil of *The X-Files*, that has seeped into every crevice of corporate media culture. As commentator Benjamin Barber put it, megamergers are manifestations of 'irresistible global and economic forces demanding integration and conformity. The fashionable term for all this vertical and lateral corporate integration is synergy, but synergy turns out to be just another word for monopoly . . . Do Americans simply want to be spectators and consumers of the synergy frenzy that is turning entertainment and media into a subsidiary of conglomerates like Disney?' (Hazen and Winokur 1997: 8).

Public discourse

In general, the dominance of the commercial ethos across the media spectrum serves to close down creative alternatives, offering only a narrowly acceptable range of content tied to corporate megaprofits. Such a range of discourse may be good for the bottom line, but it does not promote an open and democratic society. What happens to that most valuable commodity, information, in this increasingly commercial media environment? If advertisers demand that entertainment programming be designed to provide a positive environment for the sale of products, what about the news? Must it also be shaped to fit marketing parameters? What kind of pressures are brought to bear from the bottom-line managers of the media behemoths? What of information deemed lacking in ability to sell commodities or generate profits? What about media content that questions existing market priorities, a kind of content that does not evoke in viewers the desire to mimic, unquestioningly, what they see on TV, or HBO, or in the movies? What about democratic discourse?

Magazines

Industry demands for creative control through product placement (as noted above in the film *Jerry Maguire*) are not only a feature of the big screen. The pages of magazines are dominated by advertising, and escalating corporate demands. This has been a steady progression as well. Magazines provided adjacencies, then they included complimentary copy. Now the copy carries the brands, new styles, and commodities in the text itself—the magazine equivalent of product placement in film and TV. There are also advertorials and special advertising supplements formatted to look like feature journalism. Now magazine copy, much like the film script, is submitted to ad agencies, offering them the chance to find appropriate insertion points for their products. This merging of media content and product promotion has resulted in increasing demands by manufacturers and their agents that content conform to the themes, attitudes, and messages of the advertising. Chrysler publicly announced such *economic prior restraint* as corporate policy in January 1996. The company's advertising agency sent a letter to the magazines that carry its advertising, requiring them to submit articles to Chrysler for advance screening. If the company deemed any editorial content provocative or offensive, it warned, it would pull its advertising.

The American Society of Newspaper Editors prepared a response, and on 30 June 1997, sent out an appeal to editors to refuse to bow to such advertising pressure, and to reassert their right to have final authority over the editorial content of their magazines. Milton Glaser (1997: 7), a renowned graphic designer and co-founder of *New York* magazine, hearing of Chrysler's policies wrote:

Advertising in the right editorial environment has always been the prerogative of advertisers, but preemptive withdrawal is a new and repellent development . . . Censorship of this kind that acts to curtail the exchange of unpopular ideas is unacceptable for all those who care about human freedom and a healthy democratic society.

He added that such a practice 'violates our sense of fairness and our notion of how a free press works' (Glaser 1997: 7). Chrysler Corporation responded with surprise to the protest, saying it was only making public a policy that many other companies practise covertly, causing Glaser to note, 'It is curious that after the triumph of capitalism, American business is embracing the politburo practice of censoring ideas it deems unacceptable. The changes in our society that make it possible for a corporation to announce this sort of policy publicly and without embarrassment are difficult to understand. All of us, in and out of the media, have a great deal to lose if this insidious attack on the principles of a free press continues unchallenged' (Glaser 1997: 7).

Journalism under fire

In the fall of 1996 Roberta Baskin produced a hard-hitting investigative piece for CBS's *48 Hours*, exposing Nike's labour practices in Vietnam. The mistreatment, low wages, and long hours faced by Nike factory workers were substantiated by Nike's own commissioned report. Workers were paid $10 a week for sixty-five hours. They were exposed regularly to carcinogens, and 77 per cent had respiratory problems. Even though CBS submitted the report for an award, and executive producer Susan Zirinsky supported the piece, news head Andrew Heyward refused to rerun the piece or allow Baskin to do an update (Hentoff 1998). By that time Nike had become an official sponsor of the winter Olympic games being broadcast by CBS. Nike lawyers had written to CBS sales, complaining about Baskin's report.

This report and others like it have been done by the news magazines, and for this they should be applauded. However, hard-hitting investigation is becoming more rare in this media environment compelled continually to promote consumption. For such criticisms to be effective requires more frequency, but that would be a dangerous risk to the profits of manufacturers and broadcasters alike.

Corporate ownership and the news agenda

Advertising's increased influence on the press is only part of the corporate logic now being applied to news content. Non-fiction programming and content—news and information—has not been insulated from the consequences of megacorporate ownership and the increased commercialization of the media. HBO, for example, as part of Time Warner Inc., is a company which counts itself among the six largest broadcast corporations in the US, along with the General Electric Company (NBC), The Walt Disney Company (ABC), Westinghouse Electric Corporation (CBS), and Rupert Murdoch's News Corporation Ltd. (Fox), and Viacom, Inc. (cable). In 1996 these companies had a total of 81 directors who also held a combined total of 104 directorships on the boards of a number of Fortune 1,000 companies, such as 'Chase Manhattan Corp., J. P. Morgan & Co., PepsiCo, Inc., Columbia HCA Health-care Corp., Bank of America, Chevron Corp., Mobil Corp., Philip Morris Inc., and some 95 others' (Phillips 1998: 145). Many scholars have been documenting the rate of media mergers and acquisitions which have realigned our information and entertainment industries into global corporate structures with enormous power over democratic practices (Bagdikian 1997; Herman and McChesney 1997; Barnouw *et al.* 1997; Phillips 1998). Corporate owners have been asked to explain their management of the media.

The separation of church and state

It has long been argued that, even though the media are commercial, information and uninhibited public debate are so important for American democracy that they have been protected from commercial pressures. This is often referred to as 'the division between church and state'. At a symposium at Fordham University, the deputy general counsel for Time Inc., Nicholas Jollymore (1999), argued that there remains a strict separation within the Time Warner conglomerate between the editorial division, characterized as 'the church', and the rest of the company, referred to as 'the state'. He offered familiar arguments as to why news and editorial judgements remain distinct. First is the need to attract an audience, and so the perception of independence is paramount to continued profits. He also noted that journalists are professionals and resist pressure from the 'corporate chieftains'. After all, in the fall of 1998 *Time* magazine devoted an issue to the folly of corporate welfare. To prove his points he cited the negative reviews in a Time Inc. publication, *Entertainment Weekly*, of three Warner movies, *Jack Frost*, *Addicted to Love* and *Glimmer Man*; he read a long and devastating critique of the last-named.

But another panellist, Janine Jaquet (1999) from the Project on Media Ownership in New York, countered that for every case of independence there were many examples illustrating that the barrier between church and state is crumbling. She offered examples from NBC. The US government has taken legal action against NBC's parent company, General Electric (GE), because of PCB-related pollution. *NBC Nightly News* ignored such reports. With regard to corporate welfare, with the exception of one programme on *Nightline*, there was no coverage of the $70 billion giveaway of spectrum space to broadcasters for digital TV, characterized in public-interest circles as a huge corporate-welfare plan benefiting the media industry (Jaquet 1998).

With regard to journalists, they often resist pressures but their careers and incomes are on the line. Those who want to keep working know that controversial corporate stories are not welcome. Journalists are being socialized into the culture of self-censorship that now dominates news organizations (Phillips 1998). 'The people who constitute the conscience of broadcast news discipline—working journalists—now have less real influence on the daily news agenda then ever before, and they face harsh treatment from management if they speak out' (Kent 1998: 29). Gulf war correspondent Arthur Kent left NBC after a dispute over the network's lack of commitment to hard news. He challenged the GE-appointed NBC news managers in federal court, and, though the case was settled, it provided testimony from 'top executives, program makers, publicists and lawyers [showing] how the editorial autonomy of the news division had been systematically destroyed. "Bring down the barriers" between divisions was how entertainment president Warren Littlefield described his mandate, one given to him directly by Messrs. Welch and Wright' (Kent 1998: 29).

Let's turn to a case where journalists have asserted independence and challenged the corporate priorities of media owners. Television's Fox network (the one that aired the HBO spot) is owned by Rupert Murdoch's News Corporation. The company is being sued by two veteran journalists under Florida's whistleblower law. Investigative reporters Steve Wilson and Jane Akre were hired by Fox 13 in Tampa Bay in December 1996, to do hard-hitting local reporting. They quickly uncovered a story critical of Monsanto, the world's largest agrochemicals company, second largest seed company, and fourth largest pharmaceutical company, and a main advertiser on Fox Television nationally. Monsanto produces a synthetic bovine growth hormone (BGH) marketed under the name Prosilac. Prosilac is banned in Canada and Europe because of its links to cancers of the colon, breast and prostate, and the bacterial and antibiotic residues left in milk. Akre found that virtually all milk sold in Florida comes from cows injected with Prosilac, and even though labelling is required, to offer consumers a choice, consumers were not being informed. After two months of investigation, the reporters produced a hard-hitting story.[1]

But the story was pulled after Monsanto hired a lawyer to pressure the head of Fox News Network in New York. Monsanto is a client of Actmedia, an advertising firm also owned by Rupert Murdoch. After the story was pulled, the station's general manager reviewed the report's content, found it accurate and set another air date. The general manager was then fired and replaced by a News Corp. executive, David Boylan, who told the two journalists, 'We paid $3 billion for these television stations. We'll decide what the news is. The news is what we say it is' (Wilson 1998: 20).

After refusing a cash settlement that would have silenced them on the issue, and rewriting the story over eighty times, both journalists were fired in December 1997. Wilson notes that press reports have been spiked in the past, but this case set another precedent in the ongoing decline of news integrity. 'What is so unusual and egregious about our case is that this is the first time I know of that a newspaper or broadcaster has opted to distort and mold the story into a shape that the potential litigant and advertiser—in this case Monsanto—would like' (Boothroyd 1999: 23). Wilson believes the incident 'should raise concerns not only about the rapidly decreasing number of companies that control our media but also about the true character and motivation of those who seek to use the public airwaves to enhance their corporate bottom lines' (Wilson 1998: 20).

---

[1] We learned that routine tests for drug residue in milk don't screen for a wide variety of antibiotics. We confirmed that two Canadian government regulators have charged that Monsanto offered a $1–2 million bribe in exchange for approval of the drug without further testing. We documented a revolving door between Monsanto and the FDA. We followed the money trail to the University of Florida, where Monsanto sent millions in gifts and research grants; FDA approval was granted. Meanwhile, we found farmers who said the company wasn't properly reporting the drug's adverse effects on animals, a charge Monsanto eventually acknowledged (Wilson 1998: 20).

Let's return to one of the main points offered by Mr Jollymore, that church and state remain separate because the perception of independence is paramount for continued profits. The motivation to increase audience share through investigative independence was obvious at Fox 13 when they hired Akre and Wilson. The station aired spots that featured the two journalists walking down a smoke-filled alley as a baritone announcer promised the team would never take no for an answer. They would find the truth and tell it (Akre and Wilson 1999: 153). They were described as 'the Dream Team of investigative reporting', and promised total independence, no matter where a story led.

Far from being a story involving one station, this case involved the highest levels of management at News Corporation. The corporate willingness to suppress information is particularly disturbing considering the company's vast empire in the US and abroad. Celebrating his recent naturalization to US citizenship, Murdoch went on a media buying spree. He now owns twenty-two major US television stations, reaching more than half of all American TV viewers. His global media holdings include major newspapers in the US, Britain and Australia, HarperCollins book publisher, 20th Century–Fox films, and Star satellite TV in Asia with a reach into 40 million households in China as well (Boothroyd 1999).

With such media empires, editorial independence has proven to be too costly and other strategies for profits have come to supplant news autonomy.

Marketing the news

What many news analysts have begun to realize is that the relentless push for increased profits by megacorporation owners has been systematically subjugating the integrity of journalism to the pursuit of profits. Media companies have long felt the responsibility to make a profit, but more intense economic pressures have dramatically affected news judgements. Award-winning editor Geneva Overholser of the *Des Moines Register* described the process this way: 'As we sweat out the end of the ever increasing quarterly earnings, as we necessarily attend to the needs and wishes of our shareholders and our advertisers, are we worrying enough about . . . our employees, our readers, and our communities? I'll answer that: no way' (Hickey 1998: 31). Walter Cronkite is an outspoken critic of TV's new 'corporate chieftains' in control of news because they show little understanding of the 'responsibilities of being news disseminators' (Hickey 1998: 30). They have impossible expectations that news should return the same profits as entertainment. In the pursuit of profits they even close down news bureaux, as ABC did in San Francisco in April 1998, after the Disney company told the news division to cut costs by up to $50 million.

Stockholders in publicly held newspaper chains expect short-term profits similar to those of other enterprises. John Soliski, director of the University of Iowa's School of Journalism, notes that in publicly traded companies 'a huge percentage of their stock is owned by institutions—mutual funds, retirement funds, insurance companies—which care little about the quality of the journalism of the companies they invest in (Hickey 1998: 30).

The mid-1990s saw the demoralization and even resignations of a number of journalists and newspaper editors who refused to cripple their news operations in the quest for profits. James Naughton, editor of the *Philadelphia Inquirer*, resigned because of 'unrelenting pressures' on the newsroom (Hickey 1998: 31). Business-minded managers are replacing veteran journalists. In 1997 the *Los Angeles Times* appointed a senior vice-president for marketing as the general manager for news (Peterson 1997). Mark H. Willes had been a vice-chairman at General Mills and quickly acquired the nickname 'Captain Crunch and the Cereal Killers' because of the cuts he made in the news budget. In addition, he declared he would 'take a bazooka' to the sacred wall that separates editorial judgement and practices from the advertising and marketing departments. Instead, the *LA Times* would practise 'entrepreneurial creativity'. His hand-picked successor, Kathryn M. Downing, continued such 'creativity'. The 10 October 1999 edition of the *Times*'s Sunday magazine was a 164-page single-issue publication about the opening of the Staples Center sports arena. The *Times* is one of the 'founding partners' of the arena, and the special issue was a joint profit-sharing venture between the *Times* and the Staples Center (Barringer 1999a). The content of the magazine blurred the distinction between editorial copy, written by journalists, and advertising.

Two high-ranking *Times* editors criticized advertising influence in the news, and also revealed that a daily editorial feature entitled 'Stories that Shaped the Century' had its genesis in the advertising department (Barringer 1999b). A petition signed by three hundred members of the editorial staff asserted that the paper's financial dealings with the Staples Center compromised its integrity and editorial heritage. They demanded that the wall between advertising and news be rebuilt.

Don Hewitt, whose career at CBS spans nearly fifty years, attributes the decline in broadcast news to the blurring of the boundaries between entertainment and news reporting, and says that the line between them is 'crossed and crisscrossed repeatedly' (Hewitt 1998: 4). He singled out news magazines for particular criticism. 'Sad to say, but soap operas have moved upstairs and run at night under the guise of "newsmagazines." The measure of how they are doing is what kind of promotable nonsense they can come up with to draw people away from the sitcom that's opposite them on another channel' (Hewitt 1998: 3).

Long-time ABC newsman Ted Koppel (1998: 23) defined the threat to American journalism this way: 'our enemies are declining advertising revenues, the rising cost of newsprint, lower ratings, diversification and the vertical integration of communications empires.' He lamented the fading lines between television news and entertainment and noted that what 'threatens us as American journalism, is the trivialization of our industry'. (Koppel 1998: 23). This point is borne out by a massive survey of the content of broadcast news, newspapers, and magazines which found that scandal, gossip and celebrity pseudo-news increased from 15 per cent in 1977 to an astonishing 43 per cent of the total by 1997 (Hickey 1998: 33). An example of the type of 'news' produced in such an environment is the Clinton–Lewinsky scandal. It was cheap and therefore profitable, especially as it wore on. Like the blockbuster film supernarrative, the story could be spread over a variety of news outlets, ad infinitum, at little or no extra cost.

Economic incentives are offered to the new business-minded managers, as stock options become part of benefit packages. Cost-cutting and layoffs produce the quarterly returns that enrich those responsible for the cutbacks, making the task a little easier. As megacorporations demand higher rates of short term profit, money is not reinvested into training and improving the quality of news.

The respected *Columbia Journalism Review* summarizes the problem this way:

as editors collude ever more willingly with marketers, promotion 'experts' and advertisers, thus ceding a portion of their sacred editorial trust; as editors shrink from tough coverage of major advertisers lest they jeopardize ad revenue; as news holes grow smaller in column inches to cosmeticize the bottom line; as news executives cut muscle and sinew from budgets to satisfy their corporate overseers' demands for higher profit margins each year; as top managers fail to reinvest profits in staff training, investigative reports, salaries, plant, and equipment—then the broadly-felt consequences of those factors and many others, collectively, is a diminished and deracinated journalism of a sort that hasn't been seen in this country until now and which, if it persists, will be a fatal erosion of the ancient bond between journalists and the public (Hickey 1998: 29).

Foreign coverage

In an era of globalization, US coverage of the world outside its own borders has shrunk dramatically. In 1997 *Time* magazine published one cover story on international news, down from eleven covers in 1987. The overall trend from 1985 to 1995 in *Time* was a decline in foreign news from 24 per cent to 14 per cent, and in *Newsweek* from 22 per cent to 12 per cent (Hickey 1998). TV news follows the same trend. In the 1970s, 45 per cent of airtime was devoted to international coverage. By 1995 that percentage was down to 13.5 (Hickey 1998). Foreign correspondents and international news bureaux are expensive, and megamedia bottom-line journalism simply does without. As a former editor of the *New York Times* noted, the loss of foreign news is 'not so much a lack of the public's interest as it is a concentration of ownership that is profit-driven and a lack of inclination to meet responsibilities, except that to the bottom line' (Hickey 1998: 32).

Most disturbing is the habitual suppression of an entire body of information deemed unacceptable to corporate business interests. The responsibility of journalism and the public's right to know have been casualties of the corporate conglomeration of the media. Will a conglomerate such as Disney allow ABC news to report the conditions under which Teletubbies toys are made? How many investigative stories will be seen about Chinese workers toiling 16 hours a day, up to 112 hours a week, with an average wage of 13 cents an hour, to make the merchandise tied to the programme offered in Disney's 590 retail outlets? And with the interlocking directorships between Time Warner and Chevron Corp., it is no wonder that Chevron's role in the destruction of Nigerian wetlands made the censored news list for 1999. 'For decades, the people of the Niger Delta have been protesting the destruction of their wetlands. Discharges into the creeks and waterways have left the region a dead land, resulting in the Niger Delta becoming one of the most heavily polluted regions in the world' (Phillips 1999: 57).

From news about faulty and unhealthy products to the human and environmental consequences of corporate practices, from magazine feature stories to broadcast news programmes, information essential to a democratic society is becoming harder to find on the news agendas of the megacorporate media. Even though corporate media giants deny that consolidation of the industry influences news content, media mergers have created megacorporations whose business interests coincide with those of the rest of the corporate world. 'As the notion of journalistic autonomy from owners and advertisers weakens, the journalistic product will increasingly reflect the interests of the wealthy few that own and advertise in the news media' (McChesney 1998: 104). With such corporate bias in the news agenda, the need to present the appearance of authenticity and to assert legitimacy can account for the examples of independence that have become exceptions to the rule. But those exceptions must be nurtured and celebrated as ideals that must be reinvigorated.

Making the Internet fit for consumption

As the twentieth century comes to an end and media transformations are tracked and the trajectory of democracy is assessed, discussions and forums considering freedom, information, and the media invariably point to the Internet as the cyberspace for democracy for the new millennium. Unfortunately, since 1997 the Internet has taken giant leaps towards becoming the quintessential commercial medium of the next century. Stock prices for high-tech and Internet companies skyrocketed at the beginning of 1999, as investors looked to the Internet for the next big windfall, buoyed no doubt by reports that one-quarter of American households were online, and that two-thirds of those had been connected over the previous two years. The 1998 Christmas shopping season on the Internet only provided more fuel in the rush to commercialization.

With 15 million members, America Online (AOL) is the predominant gateway to cyberspace. In less than a decade, from 1991 to 1998, AOL captured 42.6 per cent of market share, with more members than the next fifteen Internet service providers combined. While people go online primarily for e-mail, to browse web sites and chat, online shopping is seen as the wave of the future. AOL seeks to 'drive the traffic' already on the Net onto a newly built e-commerce superhighway. At a frantic pace, AOL has been at the forefront of the commercialization of the Internet, developing e-commerce, seeking to provide the portal and the gateway to a brave new world of interactive consumption.

AOL's promotional material describes it as 'the world's leading provider of branded interactive services'. The term 'interactive', once evoked a range of practices by which media audiences, through new technologies, would be transformed into active participants, able to 'talk back' to the media. Once they were relegated to passive consumption, 'interactive' signified a coming utopia where readers of electronic texts of all sorts would participate in any number of ways, from voting, to playing, to registering their opinions, to resolving fictional narratives according to their own creative design. But in the language that speaks of 'helping consumers benefit from the enormous power of the Internet', interactive now means 'shop'.

In a letter posted online to members, Steve Case (1998), chairman and chief executive of America Online, announced AOL's merger with Netscape. Case was impressed with 'how quickly Netscape has transformed its business—shifting its focus away from browsers and platforms and toward high-growth portal and e-commerce opportunities'. The merger would help broaden their global audience at home and at work. The same day it acquired Netscape, AOL formed a strategic alliance with Sun Microsystems, 'to accelerate the growth of enterprise-class e-commerce'. The three-year development and marketing alliance would 'help companies and internet providers rapidly enter the e-commerce market and scale their e-commerce operations by making it easier and faster for companies to set up shop online'. Combining the strengths of Sun with AOL and its brands, would, in their words 'lead our customers into the electronic commerce marketplace of the future'. All this futuristic jargon describes little more than turning the Internet into the cybermall of America, through the development and application of business software. E-commerce is technology designed for online marketing, orders, billing, and payments. AOL will help provide companies with such software, and their corporate mergers will direct members onto the sites of their newly aligned corporate partners. Thus, AOL's corporate strategies mirror the merger/monopolization craze of the rest of the media industries, offering essentially a single dominant set of hardware, software, browsers, portals, and services.

Just as programming provided the audiences for television, e-mail, chat rooms and information services have connected people to the Internet. As people began to watch TV to be entertained and informed about current events, they were delivered to advertisers, allowing broadcasters to profit from advertising revenue. Now AOL members go online to communicate with friends, family, business associates (parents even talk to their children on e-mail), and just as TV audiences were sold to advertisers, Internet subscribers can now be delivered to online businesses, sold to AOL's e-commerce associates. What is heralded as the 'power of the Internet' a new wave of the future, is a repeat of broadcasting's commercial past. As members of the public seek to benefit from communication technologies, they are transformed into market shares.

You've Got Mail

America Online has embraced mergermania and the cultural productions that accompany it. This attitude is nowhere better communicated than in the film *You've Got Mail*. Billed as a quaint remake of *The Shop around the Corner*, with an Internet twist, the movie is much more a contemporary ode to monopolies, mergers, synergy and programming environments. The film opens with Manhattan pictured in the graphic style of a computer program, the city space rendered in the language of cyberspace. But that space is grounded to the geography of AOL. The menu and graphic design of AOL are featured throughout the movie during the chats between Meg Ryan and Tom Hanks. The film is very much a vehicle for the promotion of AOL and, in no small way, this commercial imperative affects its content.

As AOL completes one business merger after another in an attempt to transform the Internet to a tightly diversified marketing device, it comes as no surprise that it should cross-market a film that celebrates that process. *You've Got Mail* is a super-narrative designed for business synergy, this time over the Internet, whose content extols corporate centralization and monopolistic practices. On the surface, the film seems to venerate small businesses in the person of Kathleen, played by Meg Ryan, the creative, dedicated proprietor of a small children's bookstore. But, ironically, both main characters prefer to buy their coffee at Starbucks, instead of at a small boutique coffee house. In fact, the Starbucks chain is featured as a central cultural site.

It is primarily the acquiescence in monopolization and the corresponding loss of entrepreneurial enterprise that defines the movie's dominant signification. While it is clear that Kathleen's little book shop being put out of business is an injustice, the film's resolutions help both characters and viewers become accustomed to 'tight diversification' and business centralization. Kathleen's future will be rosy, as a children's book writer or editor. In addition, while the business practices of Joe Fox, the young book mogul played by Hanks, put Kathleen out of business, his romantic allure also saves her.

The promotion of the retail chains and business monopolization, be they bookstore chains representing Barnes and Noble or coffee shops, mirrors the centralization of Corporate America and the marketing priorities that drive it, the structures AOL is rapidly emulating. Towards the end of the movie, the stress of closing the shop has caused Kathleen to come down with the flu, and Fox arrives with a bouquet of daisies. Shortly after the movie's release, as Valentine's Day approached, AOL's home page featured the *You've Got Mail* Bouquet, and with a click of the mouse subscribers were sent to 1–800 flowers. Thus are merchandising and movie tie-ins fully incorporated into Internet consumer culture as the Internet becomes the primary marketing device of the twenty-first century.

Recreating the Internet in the image of existing industry structures, complete with mergers, synergy, and supernarratives, all fuelled by the mechanics of marketing, will serve to close down information, just as in the mainstream media. The new medium, in following the commercial imperative of the old, is replicating each of the steps that favour corporate profits over a democratic domain of free-flowing information. For example, AOL closed down the Irish Heritage discussion group for seventeen days, and wiped clean the discussion archives so that no trace of the contended discourse remains (Harmon 1999: A20). This action was only the most dramatic in a series of practices designed to circumvent freedom of speech in cyberspace. AOL deletes individual message-board postings, assigns 'demerit' marks to subscribers who are 'offensive', and bars individuals from logging on and accessing their e-mail. Some subscribers are forced to operate under 'mutual non-harassment notices' whereby they agree never to chat with each other online. AOL says it looks for the 'tone' of discourse, such as threatening, harassing, profane, or vulgar speech. But such judgements are inherently insidious. One couple participating in an abortion debate was cited by AOL for posting the phrase 'If you can't stand the heat get out of the kitchen' (Harmon 1999: A20). Members are cited when others complain to AOL. One woman taking part in a Women in Action discussion board had her account closed when she and others were 'picked as targets for complaints by those who [disagreed] with their liberal views' (Harmon 1999: A20).

The Telecommunication Act of 1996 designated Internet providers common carriers, making them immune from legal prosecution for content. As a common carrier, like a telephone line, AOL provides the technology for carrying information, and is not responsible for information content itself. Its censorious practices, it claims, are motivated by a desire to provide a 'family-oriented' service, and make the Internet a safe place for subscribers. But such claims frequently belie business motivations. Controversy, especially political contentions, is routinely considered to be antithetical to commercial media environments.

As we have seen with *You've Got Mail*, romantic comedy extolling business centralization is content fit for consumption. But, as Andrew Shapiro points out, 'We've moved distressingly close to the model that the Internet was supposed to replace, which is a couple of big companies having a disproportionate amount of control over the information market. A good argument can be made that AOL needs to take on more responsibility for protecting free speech' (Harmon 1999: A20). At AOL corporate dominance and commercial pressures have created a new institution with incredible social and political power, but one that is immune from first amendment requirements.

Bots 'reassessed'

Studies show that a key attraction for people who make purchases on the Internet is the availability of information about product options and comparative pricing. To date most portal sites have featured 'bots', or 'shopping agents', that search the Net for the lowest price on a particular item. But as retailers pay millions of dollars for portal real estate, they will not sit idly by as consumers are allowed to make choices based on price. Portals are 're-evaluating their retail strategies and the way they balance the needs of consumers with those of their retail/advertising partners' (Riedman 1999: 28). As one Net marketing director noted, 'it trains the customer to think that pricing is foremost [sic] important, not value and brand' (Riedman 1999: 28). Excite, the company that owns NetBot is 'improving' its Product Finder so that a search will also bring *relevant advertising*. As Lycos continues to develop its e-commerce software, it will not be 'deeply integrating the bot into the buying process. We don't think that's a good proposition for us or our merchant partners' (Riedman 1999: 28). The profoundly anti-competitive nature of corporate media, and now new media, seems to prove once again that marketing and promotions are anathema to information.

Some critics have pointed out that anti-competitive practices have led to cartel-like tendencies of the largest US media firms. Increasingly, media giants are entering into 'equity joint ventures' with their 'competitors', whereby two or more media giants share the ownership between them. Industry claims that centralization and business mergers are necessary to compete in the global marketplace, and that only such business success can offer consumers more choice and lower rates, do not withstand scrutiny. Corporate monopolies are formed to stifle competition, not to encourage it. Take the 1996 Telecommunication Act, for example. The cable industry was deregulated because, it was argued, that would increase competition. Phone companies would compete with cable companies, providing consumers with alternatives to cable and Internet services. The result would be a reduction of rates. In fact the opposite occurred. In the three years 1996–9, cable rates rose by 20 per cent. The cap on rates established then was lifted, and it is predicted that cable rates will increase dramatically. What the law did allow was increased monopolization of the entire telecommunications industry, and the acceleration of a unified media voice. As word of the merger between AOL and Time Warner circulates, the swallowing of a huge market share with convergent technology does not bode well for a technologically or economically diverse digital environment for the future. The AOL/Time Warner service will deliver Internet and television and acquire a huge market share. Only e-commerce businesses willing to pay for Internet real estate will be included, closing down the last technological information frontier.

Let's return to the HBO TV advertisement we started with that features cute chimpanzees mimicking the dramatic dialogue of American movies. The charming commercial and its production illustrate a now monolithic discourse in which science, nature, information, and human activity are marshalled and commodified under the rubric of entertainment, employed with the purpose of creating the ultimate sales pitch. We know little about the global corporate behaviours that now endanger primate habitats, and precious little information critical of corporate practices is available outside the endangered space of the Internet. But images of the chimps, subsumed under the aegis of media marketing, are used to promote corporate monopolies that control information. In a cynical bid to create profits out of curiosity, imagination and science, the megamedia industry hopes that the public can be subdued, enjoined to shut up and shop, or, like the chimps in the HBO ad, persuaded to mimic mindlessly the media fare acceptable to corporate owners.

We hope to demonstrate that the end of media history will be characterized by the triumph of media commercialism. We offer this book to help establish the parameters of that process, and as a critical unmasking that seeks to illuminate the real threats to democracy. We offer analysis from a variety of perspectives and a discussion of possible pathways to take in hopes of arresting such a process.

References

Akre, B., and Wilson, S. (1999). 'How Fox TV Censored Their Own Reporters', in P. Phillips and Project Censored (eds.), *Censored 1999: The News that Didn't Make the News.* New York: Seven Stories Press.

Andersen, R. (1995). *Consumer Culture and TV Programming.* Boulder, CO: Westview Press.

Bagdikian, B. (1997). *The Media Monopoly* (5th edn). Boston, MA: Beacon Press.

Barnouw, E. (1975). *Tube of Plenty.* New York: Oxford University Press.

Barnouw, E., Aufderheide, P., Cohen, R. M., Frank, T., Gitlin, T., Lieberman, D., Miller, M. C., Roberts, G., and Schatz, T. (1997). *Conglomerates and the Media.* New York: The New Press.

Barringer, F. (1999*a*). 'Day of Contrition at The Los Angeles Times', *New York Times,* 29 October: C2.

—— (1999*b*). 'After a News–Ad Clash, A "Wall" May Go Up Again at The Los Angeles Times', *New York Times,* 1 November: C19.

Bart, P. (1999). *The Gross: The Hits, the Flops–The Summer that Ate Hollywood.* New York: St Martin's Press.

Boothroyd, J. (1999). 'The Sacking of Two Distinguished Journalists'. *Adbusters* 24 winter: 22–3.

ElHassan, L. (1998). *The Commercial Success of the Rosie O'Donnell Show and its Challenge to Modern Women.* Unpublished manuscript, Fordham University, Department of Communication and Media Studies, Bronx, NY.

Engelhardt, T. (1986). 'The Shortcake Strategy', in T. Gitlin (ed.), *Watching Television.* New York: Pantheon, 68–110.

Fuller, L. (1997). 'We Can't Duck the Issue: Imbedded Advertising in the Motion Pictures', in K. Frith (ed.), *Undressing the Ad: Reading Culture in Advertising.* New York: Peter Lang, 109–29.

Glaser, M. (1997). 'Censorious Advertising'. *The Nation,* 22 September: 7.

Harmon, A. (1999). 'Worries about Big Brother at America Online'. *New York Times,* 31 January: A1, 20.

Hazen, D., and Winokur, J. (1997). *We the Media: A Citizen's Guide to Fighting for Media Democracy.* New York: The New Press.

Hentoff, N. (1998). Swoosh! goes CBS's integrity. *The Village Voice,* 3 March: 22.

Herman, E. S., and McChesney, R. (1997). *The Global Media: The New Missionaries of Global Capitalism.* New York: Cassell.

Hewitt D. (1998). 'Filling Time with Second-rate Newsmagazines'. The 21st Annual Frank E. Gannett Lecture, Media Studies Center, New York City, 10 December.

Hickey, N. (1998). 'Money Lust: How Pressure for Profit is Perverting Journalism'. *Columbia Journalism Review,* July/August: 28–36.

Jacobson, M., and Mazur, L. (1995). *Marketing Madness: A Survival Guide for a Consumer Society.* Boulder, CO: Westview Press.

Jaquet, J. (1998). 'Taking Back the People's Air'. *The Nation,* 8 June: 13–16.

—— (1999). 'Convergence: Necessary, Evil or Both'. Symposium series on First Amendment and the media, Fordham University, NY, 9 February.

Jollymore, N. (1999). 'Convergence: Necessary, Evil or Both'. Symposium series on First Amendment and the media, Fordham University, NY, 9 February.

Kent, A. (1998). 'Bringing Down the Barriers'. *The Nation,* 8 June: 29.

Koppel, T. (1997). 'Journalism Under Fire'. *The Nation,* 24 November: 23–4.

McAllister, M. (1996). *The Commercialization of American Culture: New Advertising, Control and Democracy.* Thousand Oaks, CA: Sage Publications.

McChesney, R. (1998). 'This Communication Revolution is Brought to You by U.S. Media at the Dawn of the 21st Century', in P. Philips (ed.), *Censored 98: The News that Didn't Make the News*. New York: Seven Stories Press, 95–108.

Miller, M. C. (1990). 'Advertising: End of Story', in M. C. Miller (ed.), *Seeing Through Movies*. New York: Pantheon Books, 186–246.

Nicholson, D. (1998). 'The Diesel Jeans Workwear Advertising Campaign and the Commodification of Resistance', in K. Frith (ed.), *Undressing the Ad: Reading Culture in Advertising*. New York: Peter Lang, 175–96.

Patat, K. (1999). *Dawson's up a Creek*. Unpublished manuscript, Fordham University, Department of Communication and Media Studies, Bronx, NY.

Peterson, I. (1997). 'At Los Angeles Times, a Debate on News–Ad Interaction'. *New York Times*, 17 November: D1, 11.

Phillips, P. (1998). *Censored 98: The News that Didn't Make the News*. New York: Seven Stories Press.

Phillips, P. (1999). *Censored 99: The News that Didn't Make the News*. New York: Seven Stories Press.

Riedman, P. (1999). 'Portals Rethink Retail Strategies, Shopping Agents'. *Advertising Age*, 28 February: 32.

Shapiro, A. (1998). 'Aol.mergergame.com'. *The Nation*, 21 December: 7.

Schatz, T. (1997). 'The Return of the Hollywood Studio System', in. E. Barnouw (ed.), *Conglomerates and the Media*. New York: The New Press, 73–106.

Schwartzman, A. D. (1999). 'Ganging up on the FCC'. *The Nation*, 1 February: 6–7.

Solomon, N. (1999). 'Down the Media Rabbit Hole in 1999'. *Mediabeat*, online column, 14 January.

Wilson, S. (1998). 'Fox in the Cow Barn'. *The Nation*, 8 June: 20.

Part I

Human Need and the Commercial Imperative

Introduction

CRITICS of consumer culture often lament the misdirected desire for manufactured products, those things that seem to be the motivating force behind consumption. They fault the apparently irrepressible impulse toward acquisition. Such materialism is condemned as the triumph of greed and envy, and signals the decline of social values and the ascendancy of a culture based on superficial accumulation and waste. It is most certainly a culture based on waste, for the objects of consumer culture move in and out of our lives with such speed that landfills can no longer absorb the unwanted by-products of purchasing. We are running out of room for the packaging so quickly discarded after it has served its purpose of coating the product with an irresistible sheen, and for the product itself, which is discarded to make room for a newer, improved version of itself. But if the point is simply materialism, and the inherent human desire for things, how can we so easily dump our prized possessions so unceremoniously? Why do we buy things we cannot do without and never use? And why do those who have so much more spending power than the rest not consider themselves so much more 'happy'? If buying were truly the be-all and end-all of existence, these contradictions would not exist. While everyone needs to attain a certain standard of living, and a reasonable level is not met by most of the world's population, some in the highly developed countries seem to have it all, yet they still live with unhappiness and discontent. These contradictions force us to re-evaluate our culture of consumption, using a different set of criteria, one which takes into account the symbolic media environment that surrounds the objects which come to define our desires.

That symbolic culture is the world created by advertising and marketing, a world which now dominates the media. It is the wildly escapist, stunningly visual, profoundly compelling world of promotion that ties the products we buy to the reasons why we buy them. They offer everything from sexual gratification to power and control, from fulfilling personal relationships to pleasure and fantasy. These are the things that we want, and marketers have created pathways of association that tie consumer goods to the promise of contentment and well-being. Indeed, often the products themselves are not featured in ads because as vehicles for meaning they are not necessary: brand names suffice. Products become the signs of the psychocultural referents, and in doing so they evoke the desires that motivate spending. Some argue that because products can never really provide fulfilment, the promises they make are always false, the practice is always frustrating. Others note that products do come to occupy powerful psychocultural positions—they give us confidence, provide us with pleasure and offer us social status. But if those emotional states represent our desires, is it necessary to find them through consumption, a practice with severe environmental and economic consequences? Such powerful messages raise questions about the ability of consumer culture to offer genuine gratification, and also raise profound moral and ethical questions. How should we think of global practices which exploit people in underdeveloped labour markets to supply consumers in wealthy countries?

Advertising critic Sut Jhally addresses these and related issues as he explores the symbolic geography of consumer culture in 'Advertising at the Edge of the Apocalypse'. He reveals the connections between the material world and the social forces which drive it, pointing out the consequences of a set of practices once thought to be the very essence of material well-being. The close of the twentieth century offers a moment of contemplation, the reassessment of the nature of human pleasure and symbolic culture, and an understanding of the necessity to preserve the social and environmental worlds that sustain it.

Media theorist Marshall McLuhan was one of the first scholars to provide serious analysis of and commentary on advertising, notably in his 1951 book, *The Mechanical Bride.* In 'American Advertising', an article first published in 1947, he argues that advertising needs to be taken seriously, as a form of culture, a programme of education, and a mode of political control and social engineering. Critics holding different views can find common ground in his conclusion concerning advertising's threat to democracy.

Technology critic Neil Postman focuses on the consequences of commercialism in television broadcasting in 'The Social Effect of Commercial Television'. When the media are commercial, market relations come to exert enormous influence on content. Programming must provide an environment that attracts audiences for the display of products. Commercial imperatives shape the cultural expression of the mass media, as TV shows, magazine articles, and films are sold to advertisers on that basis. The stars, their surroundings, and their words must compel viewers to purchase the products they endorse as well as those boosted during commercial breaks. But, as Postman points out, there are also social consequences to the commercial media, literacy rates, values, and human well-being, among other things.

Chapter 1

Advertising at the Edge of the Apocalypse

Sut Jhally

I WISH to make a simple claim: twentieth-century advertising is the most power-ful and sustained system of propaganda in human history, and its cumulative cultural effects, unless quickly checked, will be responsible for destroying the world as we know it.[1] As it achieves this it will be responsible for the deaths of hundreds of thousands of non-western peoples and will prevent the peoples of the world from achieving true happiness. Simply stated, our survival as a species is dependent upon minimizing the threat from advertising and the commercial culture that has spawned it. I am stating my claims boldly at the outset so there can be no doubt as to what is at stake in our debates about the media and culture as we enter the new millennium.

Colonizing culture

Karl Marx, the pre-eminent analyst of nineteenth-century industrial capitalism, wrote in 1867, in the opening lines of *Capital* that 'The wealth of societies in which the capitalist mode of production prevails appears as an "immense collection of commodities"' (Marx 1976: 125). In seeking initially to distinguish his object of analysis from preceding societies, Marx referred to the way the society showed itself on a surface level and highlighted a quantitative dimension—the number of objects that humans interacted with in everyday life.

Indeed, no other society in history has been able to match the immense product-ive output of industrial capitalism. This feature colours the way in which the society presents itself—the way it *appears*. Objects are everywhere in capitalism. In this sense, capitalism is truly a revolutionary society, dramatically altering the very landscape of social life, in a way no other form of social organization had been able to achieve in such a short period of time. (In *The Communist Manifesto* Marx and Engels coined the famous phrase 'all that is solid melts into air' to highlight capital-ism's unique dynamism.) It was this that struck Marx as distinctive as he observed nineteenth-century London. The starting point of his own critique, therefore, is not what he believes is the dominating agent of the society, capital, nor is it what he

---

[1] Some of the ideas in this chapter have been presented before, in 'Commercial Culture, Collective Values, and the Future' (Jhally 1993) and the videotape *Advertising and the End of the World* (Media Education Foundation, Northampton, MA, 1998).

believes creates the value and wealth, labour—instead it is the commodity. From this surface appearance Marx then proceeded to peel away the outer skin of the society and to penetrate to the underlying essential structure that lay in the 'hidden abode' of production.

It is not enough of course only to produce the 'immense collection of commodities'—they must also be sold, so that further investment in production is feasible. Once produced, commodities must go through the circuit of distribution, exchange and consumption, so that profit can be returned to the owners of capital and value can be 'realized' again in money form. If the circuit were not completed the system would collapse into stagnation and depression. Capitalism therefore has to ensure the sale of commodities on pain of death. In that sense the problem of capitalism is not mass production (which has been solved) but is instead the problem of consumption. That is why from the early years of this century it is more accurate to use the label 'the consumer culture' to describe the Western industrial market societies.

So central is consumption to its survival and growth that at the end of the nineteenth century industrial capitalism invented a unique new institution—the advertising industry—to ensure that the 'immense accumulation of commodities' were converted back into money form. The function of this new industry was to recruit the best creative talent of the society and to create a culture in which desire and identity would be fused with commodities—to make the dead world of things come alive with human and social possibilities (what Marx prophetically called the 'fetishism of commodities'). And indeed there has never been a propaganda effort to match the effort of advertising in the twentieth century. More thought, effort, creativity, time, and attention to detail have gone into the selling of the immense collection of commodities than into any other campaign in human history to change public consciousness. One indication of this is simple: the amount of money that has been exponentially expended on this effort. Today, in the United States alone, over $175 billion a year is spent to sell us things. This concentration of effort is unprecedented.

It should not be surprising that something this central and with so much being expended on it should become an important presence in social life. Indeed, commercial interests intent on maximizing the consumption of the immense collection of commodities have colonized more and more of the spaces of our culture. For instance, almost the entire media system (television, radio, and print) has been developed as a delivery system for marketers—its prime function is to produce audiences for sale to advertisers. Both the advertisements it carries and the editorial matter that acts as a support for it celebrate the consumer society. The movie system, at one time outside the direct influence of the broader marketing system, is now fully integrated into it through the strategies of licensing, tie-ins, and product placement. The prime function of many Hollywood films today is to aid the selling of the immense collection of commodities. As public funds are drained from the non-commercial cultural sector, art galleries, museums, and symphony orchestras bid for corporate sponsorship. Even those institutions thought to be outside the market are being sucked in. High schools now sell the sides of their buses, the spaces of their hallways, and the classroom time of their students to hawkers of candy bars, soft drinks, and jeans. In New York City, sponsors are being sought for public playgrounds. In the contemporary world everything is sponsored by someone. The latest plans of Space Marketing Inc. call for rockets to deliver mile-wide mylar billboards to compete with the sun and the moon for the attention of the earth's population.

With advertising messages on everything from fruit on supermarket shelves to urinals, and literally to the space beneath our feet (Bamboo lingerie conducted a spray-paint pavement campaign in Manhattan telling consumers that 'from here it looks like you could use some new underwear'), it should not be surprising that many commentators now identify the realm of culture as simply an adjunct to the system of production and consumption.

Indeed, so overwhelming has the commercial colonization of our culture become that it has created its own problems for marketers, who now worry about how to ensure that their individual message stands out from the 'clutter' and 'noise' of this busy environment. In that sense the main competition for marketers is not simply other brands in their product type, but all the other advertisers competing for the attention of an increasingly cynical audience which is doing all it can to avoid ads. In a strange paradox, as advertising takes over more and more space in culture, the job of the individual advertisers becomes much more difficult. Therefore even greater care and resources are poured into the creation of commercial messages— much greater care than is given to the surrounding editorial matter designed to capture the attention of the audience. Indeed, if we wanted to compare national television commercials to something equivalent, it would be the biggest-budget movie blockbusters. Second by second, it costs more to produce the average network ad than to produce a movie like *Jurassic Park*.

The twin results of these developments are that advertising is everywhere and huge amounts of money and creativity are expended upon it.

If Marx were writing today, I believe that he would be struck not only by the presence of even more objects, but also by the ever-present 'discourse through and about objects' that permeates the spaces of our public and private domains (see Leiss, Kline, and Jhally 1990: 1). This commercial discourse is the ground on which we live, the space in which we learn to think, the lens through which we come to understand the world that surrounds us. In seeking to understand where we are headed as a society, an adequate analysis of this commercial environment is essential.

Seeking this understanding will involve clarifying what we mean by the power and effectiveness of ads, and of being able to pose the right question. For too long debate has been concentrated around the issue of whether ad campaigns create demand for a particular product. If you are Pepsi-Cola, or Ford, or Anheuser Busch, that may be the right question for your interests. But if you are interested in the social power of advertising—the impact of advertising on society—that is the wrong question.

The right question would ask about the cultural role of advertising, not its marketing role. Culture is the place and space where a society tells stories about itself, where values are articulated and expressed, where notions of good and evil, of morality and immorality, are defined. In Western, industrialized culture it is the stories of advertising that dominate the spaces that mediate this function. If human beings are essentially a storytelling species, then to study advertising is to examine the central storytelling mechanism of our society. The correct question to ask from this perspective is not whether particular ads sell the products they are hawking, but what are the consistent stories that advertising spins as a whole about what is important in the world, about how to behave, about what is good and bad. Indeed, it is to ask what values advertising consistently pushes.

Happiness

Every society has to tell a story about happiness, about how individuals can satisfy themselves and feel both subjectively and objectively good. The cultural system of advertising gives a very specific answer to that question for our society: the way to happiness and satisfaction is through the consumption of objects through the marketplace. Commodities will make us happy (Leiss 1976: 4). In one very import-ant sense, that is the consistent and explicit message of every single message within the system of market communication.

Neither the fact of advertising's colonization of the horizons of imagination nor the pushing of a story about the centrality of goods to human satisfaction should surprise us. The immense collection of goods has to be consumed (and even more goods produced) and the story that is used to ensure this function is to equate goods with happiness. Insiders in the system have recognized this obvious fact for many years. Retail analyst Victor Liebow said, just after the Second World War

Our enormously productive economy . . . demands that we make consumption our way of life, that we convert the buying and the selling of goods into rituals, that we seek our spiritual satisfaction, our ego satisfaction in commodities . . . We need things consumed, burned up, worn out, replaced, and discarded at an ever increasing rate. [Durning 1991: 153].

So economic growth is justified not simply on the basis that it will provide employment (after all, a host of alternative non-productive activities could also provide that) but because it will give us access to more things that will make us happy. This rationale for the existing system of ever-increasing production is told by advertising in the most compelling form possible. In fact it is this story, that human satisfaction is intimately connected to the provisions of the market, to economic growth, that is the major motivating force for social change as we start the twenty-first century.

The social upheavals of Eastern Europe were pushed by this vision. As Gloria Steinhem described the East German transformation: 'First we have a revolution, then we go shopping' (Ehrenreich 1990: 46). The attractions of this vision in the Third World are not difficult to discern. When your reality is empty stomachs and empty shelves, no wonder the marketplace appears the panacea for your problems. When your reality is hunger and despair, it should not be surprising that the seductive images of desire and abundance emanating from the advertising system are so influential in thinking about social and economic policy. Indeed not only happiness but political freedom itself are made possible by access to the immense collection of commodities. These are very powerful stories which equate happiness and freedom with consumption—and advertising is the main propaganda arm of this view.

The question that we need to pose at this stage (and that is almost never asked) is 'Is it true?' Does happiness come from material things? Do we get happier as a society as we get richer, as our standard of living increases, as we have more access to the immense collection of objects? Obviously these are complex issues, but the general answer to these questions is 'no' (see Leiss, Kline, and Jhally 1990, Chapter 10 for a fuller discussion of these issues).

In a series of surveys (labelled 'the happiness surveys') conducted in the United States starting in 1945, researchers sought to examine the link between material wealth and subjective happiness, and concluded that, when examined cross-culturally as well as historically in one society, there is a very weak correlation. Why should this be so?

When we examine this process more closely the conclusions are less surprising than our intuitive perspective might suggest. In 'quality of life surveys', people are asked about the kinds of things that are important to them—about what would constitute a good quality of life. The findings of this line of research indicate that if the elements of satisfaction are divided into social values (love, family, friends) and material values (economic security and success), the former outranks the latter in terms of importance. What people say they really want out of life is: autonomy and control of life; good self-esteem; warm family relationships; tension-free leisure time; close and intimate friends; and romance and love. This is not to say that material values are not important. They form a necessary component of a good quality of life. But above a certain level of poverty and comfort, material things stop giving us the kind of satisfaction that the magical world of advertising insists they can deliver.

These conclusions point to one of the great ironies of the market system. The market is good at providing those things that can be bought and sold and it pushes us—via advertising—in that direction. But the real sources of happiness—social relationships—are outside the capability of the marketplace to provide. The marketplace cannot provide love, it cannot provide real friendships, it cannot provide sociability. It can provide material things and services—but they are not what make us happy.

The advertising industry has known this since at least the 1920s and in fact has stopped trying to sell us things based on their material qualities alone. If we examine the advertising of the end of the nineteenth century and the first years of the twentieth, we see that advertising talked a lot about the properties of commodities—what they did, how well they did it, etc. But starting in the 1920s advertising shifted to talking about the relationship of objects to the social life of people. It started to connect commodities (the things they had to sell) with the powerful images of a deeply desired social life that people said they wanted.

No wonder, then, that advertising is so attractive to us, so powerful, so seductive. What it offers us is images of the real sources of human happiness—family life, romance and love, sexuality and pleasure, friendship and sociability, leisure and relaxation, independence and control of life. That is why advertising is so powerful, that is what is real about it. The cruel illusion of advertising, however, is the way that it links those qualities to a place that by definition cannot provide it—the market and the immense collection of commodities. The falsity of advertising is not in the appeals it makes (which are very real) but in the answers it provides. We want love and friendship and sexuality—and advertising points the way to them through objects.

To reject or criticize advertising as false and manipulative misses the point. Ad executive Jerry Goodis puts it this way: 'Advertising doesn't mirror how people are acting but how they are dreaming' (quoted in Jhally 1990: 129). It taps into our real emotions and repackages them back to us connected to the world of things. What advertising really reflects in that sense is the dreamlife of the culture. Even saying this, however, simplifies a deeper process because advertisers do more than mirror our dreamlife—they help to create it. They translate our desires (for love, for family, for friendship, for adventure, for sex) into our dreams. Advertising is like a fantasy factory, taking our desire for human social contact and reconceiving it, reconceptualizing it, connecting it with the world of commodities, and then translating it into a form that can be communicated.

The great irony is that as advertising does this it draws us further away from what really has the capacity to satisfy us (meaningful human contact and relationships) to what does not (material things). In that sense advertising reduces our capacity to become happy, by pushing us, cajoling us, to carry on in the direction of things. If we really wanted to create a world that reflected our desires, the consumer culture would not be it. It would look very different—a society that stressed and built the institutions that would foster social relationships rather than endless material accumulation.

Advertising's role in channelling us in these fruitless directions is profound. In one sense, its function is analogous to that of the drugs-pusher on the street corner. As we try to break our addiction to things it is there, constantly offering us another 'hit'. By persistently pushing the idea of the good life being connected to products, and by colonizing every nook and cranny of the culture where alternative ideas could be raised, advertising is an important part of the creation of what Tibor Scitovsky (1976) calls 'the joyless economy'. The great political challenge that emerges from this analysis is how to connect our real desires to a truly human world, rather than to the dead world of the 'immense collection of commodities'.

'There is No Such Thing as "Society" '

A culture dominated by commercial messages that tell individuals the way to happiness is through consuming objects bought in the marketplace gives a very particular answer to the question 'What is society?'—what is it that binds us together in a collective way, what concerns or interests do we share? In fact, Margaret Thatcher, the former Conservative British prime minister, gave the most succinct answer to this question from the viewpoint of the market. In perhaps her most (in)famous quote she announced: 'There is no such thing as "society". There are just individuals and their families.' According to Mrs Thatcher, there is nothing solid we can call society, no group values, no collective interests; society is just a bunch of individuals acting on their own.

Indeed this is precisely how advertising talks to us. It addresses us not as members of society talking about collective issues, but as individuals. It talks about our individual needs and desires. It does not talk about those things we have to negotiate collectively, such as poverty, healthcare, housing and the homeless, the environment, and so on.

The market appeals to the worst in us (greed, selfishness) and discourages what is best about us (compassion, caring, and generosity).

Again, this should not surprise us. In those societies where the marketplace dominates, what will be stressed is what the marketplace can deliver—and advertising is the main voice of the marketplace—so discussions of collective issues are pushed to the margins of the culture. They are not there in the centre of the main system of communication that exists in the society. It is no accident that politically the market vision associated with neo-conservatives has come to dominate at exactly that time when advertising has been pushing the same values into every available space in the culture. The widespread disillusionment with 'government' (and hence with thinking about issues in a collective manner) has found extremely fertile ground in the fields of commercial culture.

Unfortunately, we are now in a situation, both globally and domestically, where solutions to pressing nuclear and environmental problems will have to be collective. The marketplace cannot deal with the problems that face us at the turn of the millennium. For example, it cannot deal with the threat of nuclear extermination, which is still with us in the post-Cold War age. It cannot deal with global warming, the erosion of the ozone layer, or the depletion of our non-renewable resources. The effects of the way we do 'business' are no longer localized, they are now global, and we will have to have international and collective ways of dealing with them. Individual action will not be enough. As the environmentalist slogan puts it, 'We *all* live downstream now'.

Domestically, how do we find a way to tackle issues such as the nightmares of our inner cities, the ravages of poverty, the neglect of healthcare for the most vulnerable section of the population? How can we find a way to talk realistically and passionately of such problems within a culture where the central message is 'Don't worry. Be happy.' As Barbara Ehrenreich (1990: 47) says:

Television commercials offer solutions to hundreds of problems we didn't even know we had—from 'morning mouth' to shampoo build-up—but nowhere in the consumer culture do we find anyone offering us such mundane necessities as affordable health insurance, childcare, housing, or higher education. The flip side of the consumer spectacle . . . is the starved and impoverished public sector. We have Teenage Mutant Ninja Turtles, but no way to feed and educate the one-fifth of American children who are growing up in poverty. We have dozens of varieties of breakfast cereal, and no help for the hungry.

In that sense, advertising systematically relegates discussion of key societal issues to the peripheries of the culture and talks in powerful ways instead of individual desire, fantasy, pleasure, and comfort.

Partly this is because of advertising's monopolization of cultural life. There is no space left for different types of discussion, no space at the centre of society where alternative values could be expressed. But it is also connected to the failure of those who care about collective issues to create alternative visions that can compete with the commercial vision. The major alternative offered to date has been a grey and dismal stateism. This occurred not only in Western societies but also in the former so called 'socialist' societies of Eastern Europe. These repressive societies never found a way to connect to people in any pleasurable way, relegating issues of pleasure and individual expression to the non-essential and distracting aspects of social life. This indeed was the core of the failure of communism in Eastern Europe. As Ehrenreich (1990: 47) reminds us, not only was it unable to deliver the material goods, but it was unable to create a fully human 'ideological retort to the powerful seductive messages of the capitalist consumer culture.' The problems are no less severe domestically.

Everything enticing and appealing is located in the (thoroughly private) consumer spectacle. In contrast, the public sector looms as a realm devoid of erotic promise—the home of the IRS [Internal Revenue Service], the DMV [Department of Motor Vehicles], and other irritating, intrusive bureaucracies. Thus, though everyone wants national health insurance, and parental leave, few are moved to wage political struggles for them. 'Necessity' is not enough; we may have to find a way to glamorize the possibility of an activist public sector, and to glamorize the possibility of public activism [Ehrenreich 1990: 47].

The imperative task for those who want to stress a different set of values is to make the struggle for social change fun and sexy. By that I do not mean that we have to use images of sexuality, but that we have to find a way of thinking about the struggle against poverty, against homelessness, for healthcare and childcare, to protect the environment, in terms of pleasure and fun and happiness.

To make this glamorization of collective issues possible will require that the present commercial monopoly of the channels of communication be broken in favour of more democratic access whereby difficult discussion of important and relevant issues may be possible. While the situation may appear hopeless, we should remind ourselves of how important capitalism deems its monopoly of the imagination to be. The campaigns of successive United States governments against the Cuban revolution, and the obsession of our national security state with the Sandinista revolution in Nicaragua in the 1980s, demonstrates the importance that capitalism places on smashing the alternative model. Even as the United States government continues to support the most vicious, barbarous, brutal, and murderous regimes around the world, it takes explicit aim at those governments that have tried to redistribute wealth to the most needy—who have prioritized collective values over the values of selfishness and greed. The monopoly of the vision is vital, and capitalism knows it.

The end of the world as we know it

The consumer vision that is pushed by advertising and which is conquering the world is based fundamentally, as I have argued, on a notion of economic growth. Growth requires resources (both raw materials and energy) and there is a broad consensus among environmental scholars that the Earth cannot sustain past levels of expansion based upon resource-intensive modes of economic activity, especially as more and more nations struggle to join the feeding trough.

The environmental crisis is complex and multi-layered, cutting across both production and consumption issues. For instance, just in terms of resource depletion, we know that we are rapidly exhausting what the Earth can offer and that, if present growth and consumption trends continue unchecked, the limits to growth on the planet will be reached some time within the next century. Industrial production uses up resources and energy at a rate that has never before even been imagined. Since 1950 the world's population has used up more of the Earth's resources than all the generations that came before (Durning 1991: 157). In fifty years we have matched the use of thousands of years. The West, especially the USA, has used most of these resources, and so has a special responsibility for the approaching crisis. In another hundred years we will have exhausted the planet.

But even more than that, we will have done irreparable damage to the environment on which we depend for everything. As environmental activist Barry Commoner (1971: 16–17) says:

The environment makes up a huge, enormously complex living machine that forms a thin dynamic layer on the earth's surface, and every human activity depends on the integrity and proper functioning of this machine ... This machine is our biological capital, the basic apparatus on which our total productivity depends. If we destroy it, our most advanced technology will become useless and any economic and political system that depends on it will flounder. The environmental crisis is a signal of the approaching catastrophe.

The clearest indication that the way we produce is affecting the eco-sphere of the planet is the depletion of the ozone layer. It has dramatically increased the amount of ultraviolet radiation, which is damaging or lethal to many life forms. In 1985 scientists discovered, in the ozone layer over the South Pole, a hole the size of the USA, illustrating how the activities of humans are changing the very make-up of the Earth. In his book *The End of Nature* Bill McKibben (1989: 45) reminds us that 'we have done this ourselves . . . . by driving our cars, building our factories, cutting down our forests, turning on air conditioners'. He writes that the history of the world is full of the most incredible events that changed the way we lived, but they are all dwarfed by what we have accomplished in the last fifty years.

Man's efforts, even at their mightiest, were tiny compared with the size of the planet—the Roman Empire meant nothing to the Arctic or the Amazon. But now, the way of life of one part of the world in one half-century is altering every inch and every hour of the globe [McKibben 1989: 46].

The situation is so bad that the scientific community is desperately trying to get the rest of us to wake up to the danger. The Union of Concerned Scientists (representing 1,700 of the world's leading scientists, including a majority of Nobel laureates in the sciences) recently issued this appeal:

Human beings and the natural world are on a collision course. Human activities inflict harsh and irreversible damage on the environment and on critical resources. If not checked, many of our current practices put at serious risk the future that we wish for human society and the plant and animal kingdoms, and may so alter the living world that it will be unable to sustain life in the manner we know. Fundamental changes are urgent if we are to avoid the collision our present course will bring.

It is important to avoid predictions of immediate catastrophe. We have already done a lot of damage but the real environmental crisis will not hit until some time in the middle of the next century. However, to avoid that catastrophe we have to take action *now*. We have to put in place the steps that will save us in seventy years' time.

The metaphor that best describes the task before us is an oil tanker heading for a crash on the shore. Because of its momentum and size, to avoid crashing the tanker has to start turning well before it reaches the coast, anticipating its own momentum. If it starts turning too late, it will smash into the coast. That is where the consumer society is right now. We have to make fundamental changes in the way we organize ourselves, in what we stress in our economy, if we want to avoid the catastrophe in seventy years' time. We have to take action *now*.

In that sense the present generation has a unique responsibility in human history. It is literally up to us to save the world, to make the changes we need to make. If we do not, we will revert to barbarism and savagery towards each other. We have to make short-term sacifices. We have to give up our non-essential appliances. In particular, we have to rethink our relationship with the car. We have to make *real* changes—not just recycling but fundamental changes in how we live and produce. And we cannot do this individually, we have to do it collectively. We have to find the political will to do this—and we may even be dead when its real effects will be felt. The vital issue is: how do we identify with that generation in the next century? As the political philosopher Robert Heilbroner (1980: 134–5) says:

A crucial problem for the world of the future will be a concern for generations to come. Where will such concern arise? ... Contemporary industrial man, his appetite for the present whetted by the values of a high-consumption society and his attitude toward the future influenced by the prevailing canons of self-concern, has but a limited motivation to form such bonds. There are many who would sacrifice much for their children; fewer would do so for their grandchildren.

Forming such bonds will be made even more difficult within our current context, which stresses individual (not social) needs and the immediate (not the long-term) situation. The advertising system will form the ground on which we think about the future of the human race, and there is nothing there that gives us any hope for the development of such a perspective. The time-frame of advertising is very short-term. It does not encourage us to think beyond the immediacy of present sensuous experience. Indeed, it may well be that as the advertising environment gets more and more crowded, with more and more of what advertisers label 'noise' threatening to drown out individual messages, the appeal will be made to levels of experience that cut through clutter, appealing immediately and deeply to very emotional states. Striking emotional imagery that grabs the 'gut' instantly leaves no room for thinking about anything. Sexual imagery, especially in the age of AIDS when sex is being connected to death, will need to become even more powerful and immediate, to overcome any possible negative associations—indeed to remove us from the world of connotation and meaning construed cognitively. The value of a collective social future is one that does not, and will not, find expression within our commercially dominated culture. Indeed the prevailing values provide no incentive to develop bonds with future generations and there is a real sense of nihilism and despair about the future, and a closing of ranks against the outside.

Imagining a different future

Over a hundred years ago, Marx observed that there were two directions that capitalism could take: towards a democratic 'socialism' or towards a brutal 'barbarism'. Both long-term and recent evidence seems to indicate that the latter is where we are headed, unless alternative values quickly come to the fore.

Many people thought that the environmental crisis would be the linchpin for the lessening of international tensions as we recognized our interdependence and our collective security and future. But as the Gulf war made clear, the New World Order will be based upon a struggle for scarce resources. Before the propaganda rationale shifted to the 'struggle for freedom and democracy', George Bush reminded the American people that troops were being dispatched to the Gulf to protect the resources that make possible 'our way of life'. An automobile culture and commodity-based culture such as the USA's is reliant upon sources of cheap oil. And if the cost of that is 100,000 dead Iraqis, well, so be it. In such a scenario the peoples of the Third World will be seen as enemies who are making unreasonable claims on 'our' resources. The future and the Third World can wait. In the West, commercially dominated cultural discourse reminds us powerfully every day, we need *ours* and we need it *now*. In that sense the Gulf war was a preview of what is to come. As the world runs out of resources, the most powerful military alliances will use their might to ensure access.

The destructive aspects of capitalism (its short-term nature, its denial of collective values, its stress on the material life), are starting to be recognized by some people who have made their fortunes through the market. The billionaire-turned-philanthropist George Soros (1997) talks about what he calls 'the capitalist threat'— and, culturally speaking, advertising is the main voice of that threat. To the extent that it pushes us towards material things for satisfaction and away from the construction of social relationships, it pushes us down the road to increased economic production that is driving the coming environmental catastrophe. To the extent that it talks about our individual and private needs, it pushes discussion about collective issues to the margins. To the extent that it talks about the present only, it makes thinking about the future difficult. To the extent that it does all these things, advertising becomes one of the major obstacles to our survival as a species.

Getting out of this situation, coming up with new ways to look at the world, will require enormous work, and one response may be just to enjoy the end of the world—one last great fling, the party to end all parties. The alternative response, to change the situation, to work for humane, collective, long-term values, will require an effort of the most immense kind.

And there is evidence to be hopeful about the results of such an attempt. It is important to stress that creating and maintaining the present structure of the consumer culture takes enormous work and effort. The reason consumer ways of looking at the world predominate is because billions of dollars are spent on it every single day. The consumer culture is not simply erected and then forgotten. It has to be held in place by the activities of the ad industry, and increasingly the activities of the public relations industry. Capitalism has to try really hard to convince us about the value of the commercial vision. In some senses consumer capitalism is a house of cards, held together in a fragile way by immense effort, and it could just as easily melt away as hold together. It will depend if there are viable alternatives that will motivate people to believe in a different future, if there are other ideas as pleasurable, as powerful, as fun, as passionate, with which people can identify.

I am reminded here of the work of Antonio Gramsci, who coined the famous phrase 'pessimism of the intellect, optimism of the will' (quoted in Morley and Chen 1996: 267). 'Pessimism of the intellect' means recognizing the reality of our present circumstances, analysing the vast forces arrayed against us, but insisting on the possibilities and the moral desirability of social change—that is 'the optimism of the will', believing in human values that will inspire us to struggle for our survival.

I do not want to be too Pollyanna-ish about the possibilities of social change. It is not just collective values that need to be struggled for, but collective values that recognize individual rights and individual creativity. Many repressive collective movements already exist—from Christian fundamentalists in the USA to the Islamic zealots of the Taliban in Afghanistan. The task is not easy. It means balancing and integrating different views of the world. As Ehrenreich (1990: 47) writes:

Can we envision a society which values—not 'collectivity' with its dreary implications of conformity—but what I can only think to call *conviviality*, which could, potentially, be built right into the social infrastructure with opportunities, at all levels for rewarding, democratic participation? Can we envision a society that does not dismiss individualism, but truly values individual creative expression—including dissidence, debate, nonconformity, artistic experimentation, and in the larger sense, adventure . . . the project remains what it has always been: to replace the consumer culture with a genuinely *human* culture.

The stakes are simply too high for us not to deal with the real and pressing problems that face us as a species—finding a progressive and humane collective solution to the global crisis and ensuring for our children and future generations a world fit for truly human habitation.

References

Commoner, B. (1971). *The Closing Circle: Nature, Man and Technology.* New York: Knopf.

Durning, A. (1991). 'Asking How Much is Enough', in L. Brown *et al.* (eds.), *State of the World 1991.* New York: Norton pp. 153, 169.

Ehrenreich, B. (1990). 'Laden with Lard'. *ZETA*, July/August: 46–7.

Heilbroner, R. (1980). *An Inquiry into the Human Prospect: Updated and Reconsidered for the 1980s.* New York: Norton.

Jhally, S. (1990). *The Codes of Advertising.* New York: Routledge.

—— (1993). 'Commercial Culture, Collective Values, and the Future'. *Texas Law Review*, 71/4: 805–14.

Leiss, W. (1976). *The Limits to Satisfaction.* London: Marion Boyars.

Leiss, W., Kline, S., and Jhally, S. (1990). *Social Communication in Advertising* (2nd edn). New York: Routledge.

Marx, K. (1976). *Capital, vol. 1* (trans. B. Brewster). London: Penguin.

McKibben, B. (1989). *The End of Nature.* New York: Random House.

Morley, D., and Chen, K.-H. (eds.) (1996). *Stuart Hall: Critical Dialogues in Cultural Studies.* London: Routledge.

Scitovsky, T. (1976). *The Joyless Economy.* New York: Oxford University Press.

Soros, G. (1997). 'The Capitalist Threat'. *Atlantic Monthly*, February.

Chapter 2

American Advertising

Marshall McLuhan

A FEW months ago an American army officer wrote for *Printer's Ink* from Italy. He noted with misgiving that Italians could tell you the names of cabinet ministers but not the names of commodities preferred by Italian celebrities. Furthermore, the wall space of Italian cities was given over to political rather than commercial slogans. Finally, he predicted that there was small hope that Italians would ever achieve any sort of domestic prosperity or calm until they began to worry about the rival claims of cornflakes or cigarettes rather than the capacities of public men. In fact, he went so far as to say that democratic freedom very largely consists in ignoring politics and worrying about the means of defeating underarm odour, scaly scalp, hairy legs, dull complexion, unruly hair, borderline anaemia, athlete's foot, and sluggish bowels, not to mention ferro-nutritional deficiency of the blood, wash-day blues, saggy breasts, receding gums, shiny pants, greying hair, and excess weight. Here we are perhaps in the presence of an excluded middle rather than a non sequitur, because American advertising has developed into a jungle of folklore beside which the tales from the Schwartzwald belong with Winnie the Pooh.

It is, therefore, quite possible that there is a core of political reality and even health in the wildly proliferating forms of American advertising. The hyper-aesthesia of the ad-men's rhetoric has knocked the public into a kind of groggy, slap-happy condition in which perhaps are cushioned a good many of the brutal shocks felt more keenly by the realistic European. Viewed merely as an interim strategy for maintaining hope, tolerance, and good humour in an irrational world, this orgy of irrationalism may not be without its cathartic function. At any rate, the multibillion-dollar, nationwide educational programmes of the ad-men (dwarfing the outlay on formal education) provide a world of symbols, witticism, and behaviour patterns which may or may not be a fatal solvent for the basic political traditions of America, but which certainly do comprise a common experience and a common language for a country whose sectional differences and technological specialities might easily develop into anarchy. The comedian at the microphone or the professor in the classroom can always be sure of an effective gibe or illustration based on the ads. And both community and communication, in so far as they are managed at all at the popular level, are in the same debt. Moreover, by various means, the whole technique and hallucination of Hollywood has been assimilated to the ads via pictorial glamour, so that the two are inseparable. They constitute one world.

Marshall McLuhan, 'American Advertising' from *Horizon*, October 1947, by permission of the McLuhan Estate.

It is just as well to preface a glance at American ads with a consideration of the imponderables, because the ads themselves are deceptively easy to assess. A similar abeyance of judgement about the social effects of the sadism purveyed, for example, by thriller and detective literature is indicated. For the extent to which armchair sadism, so fostered, acts as a preservative of good humour in a lethal and chaotic world it is impossible to say. But anybody can check for himself the fact that persons with a penchant for strong-arm political methods are not given to this form of fantasy life. It is, of course, true that the thriller and sleuth fans, from Poe to Ellery Queen, are the willing victims of a psychological trick. By identifying their mental processes with those of the manhunter, the readers achieve a sort of megalomaniac thrill. At the same time they enjoy the illusion of sharing in the scientific techniques of the society which permits them almost no other kind of congenial adjustment or direct participation. 'Happiness', said Swift, 'is the possession of being perpetually well-deceived.' And in a merely political regard we cannot any longer dispense with any source of happiness which will win us a bit of time while we consult the means of survival.

The intellectual claims to perceive and enjoy an order and symmetry in the world and in his own life denied to other men. He arms himself today against the impact of the stereotypes of commercialized culture by keenness of recognition and analysis and engages in a perpetual guerrilla activity. He is a sort of noble savage freelancing amidst a zombie horde. The dangers attending this mode of existence are obvious. Should he find his energies suddenly depleted or his patience exasperated, he may be tempted to revive them by adopting some lethal myth-mechanism. And at all times he finds it hard to remember the common human nature which persists intact beneath all the modes of mental hysteria rampant from Machiavelli and Calvin until our own day. Yet it is only in the degree to which he is motivated by the benevolence imposed by the perception of the rational form rather than the psychological condition of all men, that he is justified or that he is tolerable. Benda was right. When the intellectual sells out to any brand of social or political neurosis, when fear or loneliness beckon him into some party, he is worse than useless. *Corruptio optimi pessima.*

American 'market research', which has developed very rapidly in the past ten years, has a strong totalitarian squint—that of the social engineer. Two recent items will illustrate this. *Time* magazine for 22 July 1946 described a new gadget:

The finished—but still uncut—picture [movie] is given the works with an electrical contraption called the Hopkins Televoting System. Each member of ARI's [Audience Research Inc.] hand-picked, cross-section audience sits in a wired section of a preview theater. With his eyes on the screen, he clutches a gadget that resembles a flashlight. On the gadget's round face is an indicator that can easily be turned with the fingers. A turn to the right means 'Like', further right 'Like Very Much'. A left twist registers as 'Dull' or 'Very Dull'. The emotional reactions of ARI's watchers flow into a central machine which combines them all into one big wavy line. This chart, picturing the audience's peaks of ecstasy and valleys of apathy, shows the manufacturer where to trim out dull spots in his picture. It is known as Preview Profile.

Moviemakers used to throw good advertising money after bad to promote an expensive flop. ARI advises just the opposite. If the Preview Profile looks bad, the ad budget might just as well be slashed. If the preview pans out better than expected, the picture is given special treatment and bigger ballyhoo.

Criteria of cinema art aside, this kind of action for direct social control is politics. It aims not only at providing more and more sensation, but at the exploitation of all emotional sets and preferences as just so much raw material to be worked up by centralized control for purposes of superprofits. Clearly the manipulators of such controls are irresponsible and will probably so continue as long as the flow of merchandise and profits remains unchecked.

Meantime, these appetites for private power are inventing the means of possible political power for the future. And even these private activities are obviously polit-ical, indirectly. Perhaps, however, the relevant observation here is simply that appe-tite is essentially insatiable, and where it operates as the criterion of both action and enjoyment (that is, everywhere in the Western world since the sixteenth century) it will infallibly discover congenial agencies (mechanical and political) of expression. Almost any political steps taken to curb the ARI type of mind would inevitably transfer this private anarchy into a public tyranny, because that 'mind' is not an exceptional one—it is universal. Actually, the ARI type of activity provides our world with a spectacular externalized paradigm of its own inner drives. Creative political activity today, therefore, consists in rational contemplation of these para-digms. Carried out as an educational programme directed towards self-knowledge and self-criticism, the study of these sprightly fantasies of unrestricted appetitive life would constitute precisely that step toward moral and intellectual regeneration which we have always known must precede any sort of genuine improvement. To contemplate the products of our own appetites rather than to anathematize the people who are keen enough to exploit them—that is surely no programme which must await the setting up of committees or social machinery. It is the only form of adult education which could be called realistic and it is instantaneously practicable. That the highbrows have been content merely to cock a snook at the fauna and flora of popular commercial culture is sufficient testimony to the superficiality with which they have envisaged the nature of politics.

In this respect, the American is in a much happier position than the Englishman whose advertisements are such half-hearted and apologetic attempts to externalize his hopes and fears and appetites. American advertising is Cartesian. The English is Baconian. The American responds to showmanship, clarity of layout, and distinct-ness of formulation. The Englishman, to judge by his ads (and I have some scores by me, collected in England over a period of three years), in his timid concern for demure good form falls into the empirical bog of self-defensive puns, archness, and snob-appeal. The American ad-men put on a decisively superior show and provide the analyst with a much greater variety of lively game. But to establish a national pre-eminence in this province is not to make more general claims. The second item illustrating the totalitarian techniques of American market research occurs in a paper called 'New Facts about Radio Research', by Arthur C. Nielsen, president of the A. C. Nielsen Company, 'the world's largest marketing research organization'. The paper appeared in 1946. It begins:

A. C. Nielsen Company, founded in 1923, provides an example of outstanding success based on long, unswerving and intelligent devotion to a difficult but worthy task. Educated in various branches of engineering and science, and accustomed to dealing with tangible facts, the early leaders of this company were convinced that some means could be found to substitute facts for much of the guesswork then used in guiding corporate marketing operations.

Despite the commercial failure of all methods developed during the first ten years of operation, despite staggering operating losses which twice brought them to the brink of disaster, this group of pioneers persevered—because the great importance of the goal was very clear, and because some of the experiments seemed to show promise.

The tone of austere scientific dedication to a noble task is not phoney in any simple sense. The language of 'human service' is rooted in the respectable neurotic formula of Adam Smith—public good through private greed—a face-saving device which developed a complex face of its own in the nineteenth century. In other words, the kind of self-deception in the language of 'public service' is no longer private, but is vertically and horizontally effective, in the English-speaking world at least. The Rousseauistic formula to get the good society by liquidating 'civilization', and the Marxian formula to get the classless society by liquidating the 'middle class', are psychologically analogous—massive mechanisms of evasion and irresponsibility.

Well, the Nielsen Company have now lifted the problem of estimating audience character from the level of conjecture to that of certitude. The advertiser sponsoring any given programme wants to know precisely:

(1) Average duration of listening; i.e., 'holding power' of the programme.
(2) Variations in audience size at each minute during the broadcast—to permit detection of programme elements which cause audience gains or losses, to locate commercials at moments when the audience is high, etc.
(3) Whether the programme reaches homes that *already* use the product, or homes that offer opportunities for conversion of new users.

For this purpose the Nielsen Audimeter has been devised, 'the graphic recording instrument installed in a radio receiver in a scientifically selected radio home. By recording every twist of the dial, every minute of the day or night, the Audimeter obtains precious radio data not available through any other means.' The Audimeter's data are then tabulated by 'The Nielsen Decoder', which is only 'one of the many mechanized operations which are producing high values for NIELSEN RADIO INDEX clients'. And the installation of audimeters is determined 'with utmost care to insure precise proportioning in accordance with a long list of marketing characteristics, including: 1, City size; 2, Family size; 3, Number of rooms; 4, Education; 5, Occupation; 6, Income; 7, Type of dwelling; 8, Number of radio receivers. The characteristics of each NRI home are rechecked monthly, and replacement homes are chosen in a manner which keeps the sample accurately balanced at all times.' Moreover, 'relations with NRI homes are maintained on such a sound basis that home turnover is limited largely to unavoidable and normal occurrences (e.g., deaths, divorces, fires, removals)'.

The direction, as well as the appetitive drive, in this sort of research (the Gallup polls of public opinion are a more obvious but less impressive instance of the same thing) is to be noted in a recent book on *Reaching Juvenile Markets*. Like most American texts on advertising, it was written by a professional psychologist—in this case a child-psychologist. The book points to the enormous proportion of American income which is expended by and for children and analyses a variety of means for bringing child-pressure on the parents to increase and to control such expenditures. Children are more snobbish than adults, more concerned to conform to the tastes of the community in the use of well-known commercial brands, and so on. The schools offer a means for the subtle subsidization of various products. Special Lone Ranger and Superman radio features for children can do much, but the potentialities of this market are only beginning to be appreciated, etc.

A more common type of advertising manual, however, is that represented by *Psychology in Advertising* by A. T. Poffenberger, Ph.D., Sc.D., professor of psychology at Columbia University. This sort of book makes available to the copywriter the results of psychiatric research: 'The psychoanalysts have made popular the conception of a kind of behavior which is a sort of compromise between the behavior growing out of desire and thinking behavior' (p. 15). To exploit the irrational and, at all times, to avoid the pitfalls of rational 'sales resistance' aroused by the inept ad is the first law of advertising dynamics. Forty-four kinds of 'attention-getting power' are graded (p. 90) in accordance with their statistically tested potency in an average community. At the top of the list are: Appetite–hunger 9.2; Love of offspring 9.1; Health 9.0; Sex attraction 8.9. And at the end of the list: Amusement 5.8; Shyness 4.2; Teasing 2.6. 'Announcing the birth of a Petunia', said an ad in which a man and woman were bent over a flowerpot: 'It takes emotion to move merchandise. *Better Homes and Gardens* [a magazine] is perpetual emotion.'

Recently, with much public irritation being expressed at the blatancy, duration, and frequency of radio commercials, careful tests have been made to determine the effect on the market. The result has been the discovery that irritation has great 'attention-getting power' and that those irritated in this respect are reliable customers. Nausea has, therefore, become a new principle of commercial dynamics as of aesthetics. It is likely, however, not to supplant but to reinforce the more familiar techniques, the most important of which is noted many times by Professor Poffenberger: 'An appeal through the visual representation of motion will almost invariably find the nerve paths for that motion open, and is thus bound to get the attention of the reader and to induce in him some form of action' (p. 297). It is in their imaginative grasp of this dramatic principle that the American ad-men are first and the rest nowhere.

'Have you the courage to look ready for Romance: Want to look like a dream walking? . . . Well, you can, so easily! *Just by changing your powder shade!* . . . A delightful "come hither" look that's so young and feminine—so very inviting!' (A bride in wedding dress is joyfully whispering this to a thoughtful lady.)

A rugged and determined man with a cigar glints at the reader of a full-page ad of a clothing shop: 'I'm TOUGH. Panty-waist stuff burns me. Work ten hours a day. Been at it since I was a kid. Gang at the plant call me "Chief". Own the place, now. Sure I've made money. Not a million—but enough to buy steak . . . And good clothes. Been getting my duds at Bond's ever since I shed knee pants . . . No big promises. No arty labels dangling high-hat prices. Just good clothes with plenty of guts.'

Obviously the dramatic ad is a maker of 'patterns of living' as much as the speech and gestures of movie idols. The peculiar idiom of a dead-end kid or a psychological freak may thus be sent up to the firing line of a nationwide advertising campaign to provide temporary emotional strategies for millions of adolescents. A wishful but futile gent beside a self-possessed girl on a love-seat: '"I love you!" said Pete. "I like you, too!" said Ann. "Tell me more," said Pete. "You look so nice, especially around the neck." "Ah," said Pete. "That is my Arrow Collar." . . . P.S. Tough, Pete. But remember—where there's an Arrow, can a girl be far behind?' The ads help old and young to 'get hep'.

An extremely popular technique is the dramatic sequence presented in four or five separate scenes. Tommy comes home from school with a black eye and is questioned by his lovely young mother. He reluctantly tells her that the kids have been taunting him about how his father is going out with other women. He has had to defend his mother's sex appeal. Mortified, she hastens to get the appropriate toothpaste. Next morning, Mom, radiant in panties and bra, brushing her teeth in the bathroom, tells Tommy, 'It works.' Later, Tommy and his friends peek round the corner into the living room where Dad is waltzing Mom around to radio music. 'Gee,' says one of the kids, 'looks like he's going to haul off and, kiss her.' 'Yep,' says Tommy, 'you can't say my Dad hangs around with other girls now.' This sort of ad appears in the Sunday Comic Section. Reaching the Juvenile Market.

'Success story of a man in a high position.' Picture of blithesome business man seated aloft in the petals of a huge daffodil: 'Sitting pretty? You bet . . . this fellow knows how to win and influence customers! He keeps track of their important business events and honors each occasion by sending wonderful fresh flowers by Wire.' The wit of the pictorial feature includes an allusion to Jack's beanstalk.

A nearly nude debutante with zestful abandon applying perfume and sparkling at the reader: 'I'm using "Unconditional Surrender" since he got 6NX Appeal!' 'How can you get 6NX Appeal? . . . by using the only blades created by the scientific, secret 6NX process . . . . "Single" men can reach for a star, too!' This is typical of the indirect approach to the American male. Psychological tests prove that he is shy of direct efforts to interest him in glamorizing himself. As social catalysts the ads help also to overcome boy–girl shyness. The girl spots 6NX or some other approved mark of compliance with nationally accredited goods. The boy smells 'Unconditional Surrender', and the first thing you know they're able to converse. College courses in 'charm' and 'gallantry' may soon be unnecessary.

A beautiful girl seated by the telephone while Mom, troubled, hovers in doorway. 'Borderline Anaemia deprives a girl of glamor . . . and dates! Medical science says: Thousands who have pale faces—whose strength is at low ebb—may have a blood deficiency. So many girls are "too tired" to keep up with the crowd—watch romance pass them by because they haven't the energy to make them attractive!'

These ads console and encourage the forlorn by picturing the solitude and neglect suffered by the most ravishing chicks. They analyse the causes of every type of human failure and indicate the scientifically certified formula for 'instantaneous or money-back results'. The fault is not in our stars but in our jars that we are underlings. They display the most ordinary persons surrounded by luxury and old-world charm, suggesting that 'a prince and a castle are given away free with every package'. The most trashy types of food, crockery, or furniture are exhibited in palatial circumstances. And this 'law of association' leads the larger business monopolies to sponsor 'the arts' by presenting their product always in conjunction with some aroma of the old masters of paint, pen, or music. But just how far these billionaire campaigns of systematic sophistry and hallucination contribute to worsening any given state of affairs would be hard to say. Because there is really nothing in these richly efflorescent ads which has not been deeply wished by the population for a long time. They aren't so much phenomena of a Machiavellian tyranny as the poor man's orchids—both a compensation and a promise for beauty denied. Now, moreover, that the luxuriant and prurient chaos of human passions is thrust forward and gyrated in this way for our daily contemplation, there is the increasing possibility of the recovery of rational detachment. The authors of the Declaration of Independence and the American Constitution were not obsessed with some compulsive psychological strategy for disguising their own irrational wishes or intentions like a Rousseau or a Nietzsche. And their wisdom is far from extinct in the USA. So that, should the energy which activates the ad-men (and the industrial stalks on which they are the passion-flowers) be transferred to the world of political speculation and creation, America could still fulfil many of its broken utopian promises, because its Jeffersonian tradition is still intact, and likewise its psychological vigour. The two things aren't flowing in the same channels, however, and that is precisely the thing which could be brought about by a frank educational programme based on the curriculum provided by the ad-men.

Chapter 3

The Social Effects of Commercial Television

Neil Postman

E VERY age has its own special forms of imperialism. And so does each con-
queror. In the eighteenth and nineteenth centuries, when the British mastered
the art, their method of invasion was to send their navy, then their army, then their
administrators, and finally their educational system. The Americans now do it
differently. We send our television shows. The method has much to recommend it.
Neither armies nor navies clash by night; the invasion occurs without loss of life
and without much resistance. It is also both pleasurable and quick. In a few years,
we shall be able to boast that the sun never sets on an American television
show. The Russians have not yet figured out what is happening. When Khrushchev
said of the West (but mostly thinking of America), 'We will bury you,' he spoke as a
pre-electronic man, thinking in terms of nineteenth-century *realpolitik*. Had he
been a more careful student of Marx, he would have remembered that political
consciousness is borne on the wings of technology. He might then have grasped
that electromagnetic waves penetrate more deeply than armies. Perhaps Gorbachev
understands. But if the Russians keep relying on nineteenth-century forms of
imperialism while continuing to make terrible television shows, they may find
themselves turning into a Third World country.

One would think, of course, that Europeans would be fully aware of what is
happening. And many are. Those who are not are probably confounded by the fact
that the American method of imperialism is more subtle than it might seem. I said
that what we do is send our television programmes. Not exactly. What we really
send is our idea of television. To understand what is meant by the idea of television,
one must allow a distinction between a technology and a medium. A technology is
to a medium what the brain is to the mind. Like the brain, a technology is a physical
apparatus. Like the mind, a medium is a use to which a physical apparatus is put.
Television is essentially the same technology in America and in Europe. But for
forty years it has been two different media, used in different ways, for different
purposes, based on different suppositions.

The following essay bears on that point and the issues that arise from it. It
originated as a lecture given in Austria to the Club of Vienna, a group of conservative business people and academics.

Neil Postman, 'The Social Effects of Commercial Television' from Neil Postman, *Conscientious Objections: Stirring up Trouble about Language, Technology, and Education* (New York: Knopf 1988), as 'The
Conservative Outlook'. Reproduced by permission of the author.

As a visitor in your country—indeed, as one who does not even know your language well enough to use it in these circumstances—I feel obliged to add something to the introduction I have been given. You are entitled to know at the start from what cultural and political perspectives I see the world, since everything I will have to say here reflects a point of view quite likely different from your own. I am what may be called a conservative. This word, of course, is ambiguous, and you may have a different meaning for it from my own. Perhaps it will help us to understand each other if I say that from my point of view, Ronald Reagan is a radical. It is true enough that he continually speaks of the importance of preserving such traditional institutions and beliefs as the family, childhood, the work ethic, self-denial, and religious piety. But in fact President Reagan does not care one way or another whether any of this is preserved. I do not say that he is against preserving tradition; I say only that this is not where his interests lie. You cannot have failed to notice that he is mostly concerned to preserve a free-market economy, to encourage the development of what is new, and to keep America technologically progressive. He is what may be called a free-market extremist. All of which is to say he is devoted to capitalism. A capitalist cannot afford the pleasures of conservatism, and of necessity regards tradition as an obstacle to be overcome. How the idea originated that capitalists are conservative is something of a mystery to me. Perhaps it is explained by nothing more sinister than that capitalists are inclined to wear dark suits and matching ties.

In any case, it is fairly easy to document that capitalists have been a force for radical social change since the eighteenth century, especially in the United States. This is a fact that Alexis de Tocqueville noticed when he studied American institutions in the early nineteenth century. 'The American lives', he wrote, 'in a land of wonders; everything around him is in constant movement, and every movement seems an advance. Consequently, in his mind the idea of newness is closely linked with that of improvement. Nowhere does he see any limit placed by nature to human endeavour; in his eyes something that does not exist is just something that has not been tried.'

This is the credo of capitalists the world over, and, I might add, is the source of much of the energy and ingenuity that have characterized American culture for almost two hundred years. No people have been more entranced by newness—and particularly technological newness—than Americans. That is why our most important radicals have always been capitalists, especially capitalists who have exploited the possibilities of new technologies. The names that come to mind are Samuel Morse, Alexander Graham Bell, Thomas Edison, Henry Ford, William Randolph Hearst, Samuel Goldwyn, Henry Luce, Alan Dumont, and Walt Disney, among many others. These capitalist radicals, inflamed by their fascination for new technologies, created the twentieth century. If you are happy about the twentieth century, you have them to thank for it.

But, as we all know, in every virtue there lurks a contrapuntal vice. I believe Tocqueville had this in mind in the passage I quoted. He meant to praise our ambition and vitality but at the same time to condemn our naivety and rashness. He meant, in particular, to say that a culture which exalts the new for its own sake, which encourages the radical inclination to exploit what is new and is therefore indifferent to the destruction of the old, that such a culture runs a serious risk of becoming trivial and dangerous, especially dangerous to itself.

This is exactly what is happening in the United States in the latter part of the twentieth century. In today's America, the idea of newness not only is linked to the idea of improvement but is the definition of improvement. If anyone should raise the question 'What improves the human spirit?' or even the more mundane question 'What improves the quality of life?' Americans are apt to offer a simple formulation: that which is new is better; that which is newest is best.

The cure for such a stupid philosophy is conservatism. My version, not President Reagan's. A true conservative, like myself, knows that technology always fosters radical social change. A true conservative also knows that it is useless to pretend that technology will not have its way with a culture. But a conservative recognizes a difference between rape and seduction. The rapist cares nothing for his victim. The seducer must accommodate himself to the will and temperament of the object of his desires. Indeed, he does not want a victim so much as an accomplice. What I am saying is that technology can rape a culture or be forced to seduce it. The aim of a genuine conservative in a technological age is to control the fury of technology, to make it behave itself, to insist that it accommodate itself to the will and temperament of a people. It is his best hope that through his efforts a modicum of charm may accompany the union of technology and culture.

The United States is the most radical society in the world. It is in the process of conducting a vast, uncontrolled social experiment which poses the question 'Can a society preserve any of its traditional virtues by submitting all its institutions to the sovereignty of technology?' Those of us who live in America and who are inclined to say 'No' are therefore well placed to offer warnings to our European cousins—who are themselves wondering whether or not to participate fully in such an experiment.

In order to give focus to my advice, I shall confine myself to the technology of television, which, at the moment, poses the most serious threat to traditional patterns of life in all industrialized nations, including Austria. And I hope you will forgive me if I begin by quoting Karl Marx. Marx once wrote, 'There is a spectre haunting Europe.' The spectre he had in mind was the rising up of the proletariat. The spectre I have in mind is commercial television. Everywhere one looks in Europe—West Germany, Sweden, France, Holland, Switzerland, Denmark—the ghostly form of commercial television is making its presence felt. That it threatens the foundations of each West European nation ought to be obvious, but, one fears, the possibility has not been sufficiently discussed.

In Paris alone there are seven advertiser-supported television stations, and now an eighth one has been installed in three Paris Métro stations. It consists of 150 closed-circuit units, each unit carrying thirty minutes of programming: four minutes of news about the Métro, sixteen minutes' worth of programmes, and ten minutes of advertising. The ads cost $7,500 per week for each thirty-second spot. In the understatement of the year, the marketing director of the Métro said, 'It's a way of changing the ambience of the subway station.' Of course, this man has confused cause and effect. If the French require television entertainment when they go from one end of town to the other, then we may say that it is not the ambience of the Métro that has changed but the ambience of French culture. We may take 'ambience' to mean, here, the psychic habits of the people.

In Britain, which has three commercial television stations, extended political commercials have already appeared. In one such commercial, a star of *Monty Python's Flying Circus*, John Cleese, did a fifteen-minute comedy routine, the purpose of which was to solicit support for a new political party. British advertising agencies believe this mixing of comedy and politics is the wave of the future. You get support for a party by having a party.

In Denmark, which has consistently opposed commercial television, plans have now been completed to allow advertising on the second national television channel, which begins broadcasting in 1988. As is presently the case in Austria, advertising for tobacco and alcohol will be prohibited. Also banned are ads for medicine, banks, political parties, and religious organizations, as well as commercials aimed specifically at young people. The Danes are usually a realistic and clear-headed people. But does anyone believe that the spectre of commercial television will be appeased by such compromises? Perhaps. And perhaps it will be appeased in Austria as well. But if it is not, you can lose very quickly much that you love and admire about your country. What I should like to do, then, is to frighten you by making a series of prophecies about what will occur if Austria allows its television technology to become a free-market commodity. These prophecies are largely based on the experiences of my country, which is the only nation, at present, where commercial interests dominate television.

By way of preface, I want to make two points. The first is that, in principle, a conservative is not obliged to be opposed to state-controlled broadcasting. One of the best-known American conservatives of this century, Herbert Hoover, our thirty-first president, was appalled at the prospect of opening up broadcasting to commercial interests. In 1923, when he was secretary of commerce, he expressed in the most emphatic terms his hope that radio, which he viewed as an instrument of public education, would be kept free of the marketplace. There can be no doubting that, were he to see American television today, he would deplore the fact that his advice was ignored. While conservatives are rightly suspicious of state authority, and therefore of state-controlled television, they need not be so foolish as to suppose that the state is the only antagonist of freedom of choice, or necessarily the worst.

Which leads me to my second point. If one asks 'Does a state-controlled television system limit freedom of expression and choice?' the answer is, obviously, 'Yes, it does.' But it is extremely naive to believe that a free-market television system does not also limit freedom. In the United States, where television is controlled by advertising revenues, its principal function is, naturally enough, to deliver audiences to advertisers. The more popular a programme is, the more money it can charge an advertiser for commercials. In 1984, when *The Cosby Show* got under way, the cost for thirty seconds of advertising time on that programme was $50,000. In 1985, when *The Cosby Show* is number one in the ratings, the cost is $300,000 for thirty seconds. What is popular pays and therefore stays; what is in arrears disappears. American television limits freedom of expression and choice because its only criterion of merit and significance is popularity. And this, in turn, means that almost anything that is difficult, or serious, or goes against the grain of popular prejudices will not be seen.

What will happen if commercial television takes hold in a serious way in Austria? By serious commercial television, I mean a system that is largely supported by advertising revenues, and that has a minimum of government regulations about what can be broadcast and when. Should anything like this come to Austria, here's what I predict.

First, commercial television will increase pressure to extend the number of hours of broadcasting each day. There is simply too much money at stake to allow any part of the day to go unused. Where there is one fully functioning commercial channel, there will be pressure for others to emerge. When there are two or more, the channels will compete with each other for the audience's attention, and for advertising money. This will lead to an increase in American-style television programmes—fast-paced, visually dynamic programmes with an emphasis on interesting images rather than serious content. This means an increase in comedy, car chases, violence, and sexually oriented material.

To hold their audiences, state-controlled channels will be forced to compete with commercial-style programming, and will also become similar to American television. This is exactly what has happened to the BBC in England and the Public Broadcasting System in America.

As audiences come to expect fast-paced, visually exciting programmes, they will begin to find issue-oriented public-affairs and news programmes dull. To compete with entertainment, news and public-affairs programmes will become more visual and more personality-oriented. As a result, there will be a decline in the public's capacity to understand and discuss events and issues in a serious way.

Of course, television advertising will draw advertisers away from newspapers and magazines. Some newspapers and magazines will go out of business; others will change their format and style to compete with television for audiences, and to match the style of thought promoted by television. They will become more picture-oriented and will feature dramatic headlines, celebrities, and sensational stories. Of course, there will be less substantive and complex writing. For some idea of what I mean, I suggest you look at America's newest, most successful national newspaper, *USA Today*; you ought also to take note of the fact that one of America's oldest and most distinguished literary magazines, *Harper's*, has found it necessary to reduce substantially the length of its articles and stories in order to accommodate the reduced attention span of its readers.

The uses of books will also change. I suspect there will be an erosion of the concept of the common reader, the type of person who gets most of his or her literary experience and information from novels and general non-fiction books. There will almost certainly be an increase in both illiteracy and aliteracy (an aliterate being a person who can read but doesn't). It has been estimated that in the United States there are now 60 million illiterates, and according to a report from our librarian of Congress, there may be an equal number of aliterates. In any case, a general impatience with books will develop, especially with books in which language is used with subtlety to express complex ideas. Most likely there will be a decline in readers' analytical and critical skills. According to the results of standardized tests given in schools, this has been happening in the United States for the past twenty-five years. I suspect concern for history will also decline, to be replaced by a consuming interest in the present.

The effect on political life will be devastating. There will be less emphasis on issues, substance, and ideology, an increase in the importance of image and style. Politicians will have greater concern for moment-to-moment shifts in public opinion, less concern for long-range policies. Unless the use of television for political campaigns is strictly prohibited, elections may be decided by which party spends more on television and media consultants. Even if political commercials are prohibited, politicians will appear on entertainment programmes and will almost certainly be asked to endorse non-political products such as cars, beer, and breakfast foods. The line between political life and entertainment will blur, and movie stars may be taken seriously as political candidates.

Once the population becomes accustomed to spending much of its time watching television—in the United States, the average household has the television on about eight hours a day—there will be a decrease in activities outside the home: fewer and smaller gatherings in parks, beer halls, concert halls, and other public places. As street life decreases, there may well be an increase in street crime.

Young people will, of course, become disaffected from school and reading. Children's games are likely to disappear. In fact, it will become important to keep children watching television because they will be a major consumer group. In the United States, children watch 5,000 hours of television before they enter kindergarten and 16,000 hours by high school's end. Commercial television does not dislike children; it simply cannot afford the idea of childhood. Consumerhood takes precedence.

Naturally, family life will be significantly changed. There will be less interaction among family members, certainly less talk between parents and children. Such talk as there is will be noticeably different from what you are now accustomed to. The young will speak of matters that once were confined to adults. Commercial television is a medium that does not segregate its audience, and therefore all segments of the population share the same symbolic world. You may find that in the end the line between adulthood and childhood has been erased entirely.

Since Austria already has some television commercials, you have seen how commercials stress the values of youth, how they stress consumption, the immediate gratification of desires, the love of the new, a contempt for what is old. Television screens saturated with commercials promote the utopian and childish idea that all problems have fast, simple, and technological solutions. You must banish from your mind the naive but commonplace notion that commercials are about products. They are about products in the same sense that the story of Jonah is about the anatomy of whales. Which is to say, they aren't. They are about values and myths and fantasies. One might even say they form a body of religious literature, a montage of voluminous, visualized sacred texts that provide people with images and stories around which to organize their lives. To give you some idea of exactly how voluminous, I should tell you that the average American will have seen approximately 1 million television commercials, at the rate of a thousand per week, by the age of twenty. By the age of sixty-five, the average American will have seen more than 2 million television commercials. Commercial television adds to the Decalogue several impious commandments, among them that thou shalt have no other gods than consumption, thou shalt despise what is old, thou shalt seek to amuse thyself continuously, and thou shalt avoid complexity like the ten plagues that afflicted Egypt.

Perhaps you are thinking that I exaggerate the social and psychic results of the commercialization of television and that, in any case, what has happened in the United States could not happen in Austria. If you are, you overestimate the power of tradition and underestimate the power of technology. To enliven your sense of the forces unleashed by technological change, you need only remind yourself of what the automobile has brought to Austria. Has it not changed the nature of your cities, created the suburbs, poisoned your air and forests, restructured your economy? You must not mislead yourselves by what you know about Austrian culture as of 1987. Austria is still living in the age of Gutenberg. Commercial television attacks such backwardness with astonishing ferocity. For example, at the present time, less than 20 per cent of the Austrian population watches television in the evening. A commercial television system will find this situation intolerable. In the United States, about 75 per cent of the adult population watches television during evening hours, and broadcasters find even those numbers unsatisfactory. In Austria, such commercials as you have are bunched together so that they do not interfere with the continuity of programmes. Such a situation makes no sense in a commercial system. The whole idea is precisely to interrupt the continuity of programmes so that one's thoughts cannot stray too far from considerations of consumership. Indeed, the aim is to obliterate the distinction between a programme and a commercial. In Austria, you do not have many advertising agencies, and those you have are small and without great influence. In America, our advertising agencies are among the largest and most powerful corporations in the world. The merger of Doyle, Dane, Bernbach with BBD&O and Needham Harper will provide the new company with the possibility of $5.5 billion in billings each year, and possibly $500 million per year for American network television alone. This is serious money and these are serious radicals. They cannot afford to permit a culture to retain old ideas about work or religion or politics or childhood. And it will not be long before they and their kind show up in Austria.

If, like me, you claim allegiance to an authentic conservative philosophy, one that seeks to preserve that which nourishes the spirit, you would be wise to approach all proposals for a free-market television system with extreme caution. Indeed, I will go further than that: it is either hypocrisy or ignorance to argue that the transformation of Austria or any other country from a print-based culture to a television-based culture can leave that country's traditions intact. Conservatives know this is nonsense, and so they worry. Radicals also know this is nonsense. But they don't care.

Part II

Conglomeration, Synergy, and Global Media

Introduction

NOTHING could be further from the philosophy of the contemporary media industries than the adage 'Small is beautiful'. It is uncontrolled growth through conglomeration that is the driving force in the media marketplace. Size brings with it power and control, in an attempt to reduce the uncertainty inherent in the free market. Synergy, a term coined by Buckminster Fuller to refer to the tendency of the whole to become greater than the sum of its parts, has become the buzzword of media gigantism as it is used to refer to the ability of media megacorporations to launch coordinated marketing and promotional campaigns (for example, motion picture, novelization, soundtrack album, comic book, T-shirts, toys, etc.). Size and synergy transcend national boundaries, so that multinational corporations yield global media which not only continue the pattern of growth and acquisition but also free the conglomerates from significant regulation or accountability.

The issue of ownership has become a central concern to media scholars, as fewer and fewer corporate conglomerates take control over the entertainment, information, and cultural industries. Along with Herbert I. Schiller, Ben Bagdikian, and others, researcher Robert W. McChesney has documented the steady push toward conglomeration and economic centralization of the global media over the last twenty years. Given the size and dynamics of media multinationals in this era of late capitalism, cataloguing the major corporations and their extensive holdings is no easy task, but in 'The Global Media Giants', McChesney provides a thorough accounting. In this 'Age of Behemoths', profit and efficiency impede any consideration of the ethical implications of conglomeration, but author Anthony Smith is able to address the issues and concerns of media globalization. In doing so, he outlines the major ethical questions raised by an environment where so few own the industries responsible for creating and maintaining local and national cultures, and providing information essential to democratic structures.

An important consequence of corporate consolidation and ownership has been the prioritizing of profit. In 'Sold American: US News Consultants and News Issues Abroad', Craig Allen, himself a former public relations professional, documents how news content changes as commercial media owners seek to make their operations more profitable. His extensive research in four countries, Great Britain, Germany, Greece and the Czech Republic, demonstrates how news is transformed by commercial pressures.

Media scholar Matthew P. McAllister explores the promotional activities of the media conglomerates, tracing the growth in entertainment marketing including television advertising and the increasing marketing frenzy that surrounds blockbuster films. This powerfully unified promotion of megahits by megacorporations precludes the continuing development of independent and alternative film, documentary and video forms. In addition, he argues in 'From Flick to Flack: The Increased Emphasis on Marketing by Media Entertainment Corporations' that economic synergy is blurring the boundary between advertising and media content, compromising our ability to choose and evaluate in this new promotional media environment.

Chapter 4

The Global Media Giants

Robert W. McChesney

A SPECTRE now haunts the world: a global commercial media system domin-ated by a small number of superpowerful, mostly USA-based transnational media corporations. It is a system that works to advance the cause of the global market and promote commercial values, while denigrating journalism and culture not conducive to the immediate bottom line or long-term corporate interests. It is a disaster for anything but the most superficial notion of democracy—a democracy where, to paraphrase John Jay's maxim, those who own the world ought to govern it.

The global commercial system is a very recent development. Until the 1980s, media systems were generally national in scope. While there have been imports of books, films, music, and TV shows for decades, the basic broadcasting systems and newspaper industries were domestically owned and regulated. Beginning in the 1980s, pressure from the IMF, World Bank and US government to deregulate and privatize media and communication systems coincided with new satellite and digital technologies, resulting in the rise of transnational media giants.

How quickly has the global media system emerged? The two largest media firms in the world, Time Warner and Disney, generated around 15 per cent of their income outside of the United States in 1990. By 1997, that figure was in the 30–35 per cent range. Both firms expect to do a majority of their business abroad at some point in the next decade.

The global media system is now dominated by a first tier of nine giant firms. The five largest are Time Warner (1997 sales: $24 billion), Disney ($22 billion), Bertels-mann ($15 billion), Viacom ($13 billion), and Rupert Murdoch's News Corporation ($11 billion). Besides needing global scope to compete, global media giants have two rules of thumb. First, get bigger so you dominate markets and your competition can't buy you out. Firms like Disney and Time Warner have almost tripled in size this decade. Second, have interests in numerous media industries, such as film production, book-publishing, music, TV channels and networks, retail stores, amusement parks, magazines, newspapers, and the like. The profit whole for the global media giant can be vastly greater than the sum of the media parts. A film, for example, should also generate a soundtrack, a book, and merchandise, and possibly spin-off TV shows, CD-ROMs, video games, and amusement-park rides. Firms that do not have conglomerated media holdings simply cannot compete in this market.

Robert W. McChesney, 'The Global Media Giants' from *Extra!*, 10/6, November–December 1997, by permission of the publisher.

The first tier is rounded out by TCI, the largest US cable company, which also has US and global media holdings in scores of ventures too numerous to mention. The other three first-tier global media firms are all part of much larger industrial corporate powerhouses: General Electric (1997 sales: $80 billion), owner of NBC; Sony (1997 sales: $48 billion), owner of Columbia and TriStar Pictures and major recording interests; and Seagram (1997 sales: $14 billion), owner of Universal film and music interests. The media holdings of these four firms do between $6 billion and $9 billion in business per year. While they are not as diverse as the media holdings of the first five global media giants, these four firms have global distribution and production in the areas where they compete. And firms like Sony and GE have the resources to make deals to get a lot bigger very quickly if they so desire.

Behind these firms is a second tier of some three or four dozen that each do between $1 billion and $8 billion per year in media-related business. They tend to have national or regional strongholds or to specialize in global niche markets. About half of them come from North America, including the likes of Westinghouse (CBS), the New York Times Co., Hearst, Comcast and Gannett. Most of the rest come from Europe, with a handful based in East Asia and Latin America.

In short, the overwhelming majority (in revenue terms) of the world's film production, TV-show production, cable-channel ownership, cable- and satellite-system ownership, book-publishing, magazine-publishing and music production is provided by these fifty or so firms, and the first nine firms thoroughly dominate many of these sectors. By any standard of democracy, such a concentration of media power is troubling, if not unacceptable. But that hardly explains how concentrated and uncompetitive this global media power actually is. In addition, these firms are all actively engaged in equity joint ventures whereby they share ownership of concerns with their 'competitors' so as to reduce competition and risk. Each of the nine first-tier media giants, for example, has joint ventures with, on average, two-thirds of the other eight. And the second tier is every bit as aggressive about making joint ventures.

We are the world

In some ways, the emerging global commercial media system is not an entirely negative proposition. It occasionally promotes anti-racist, anti-sexist, or anti-authoritarian messages that may be welcome in some of the more repressive corners of the world. But on balance the system has minimal interest in journalism or public affairs except for that which serves the business and upper-middle classes, and it privileges just a few lucrative genres that it can do quite well—like sports, light entertainment and action movies—over other fare. Even at its best the entire system is saturated by a hyper-commercialism, a veritable commercial carpetbombing of every aspect of human life. As the chief executive of Westinghouse put it (*Advertising Age*, 3 February 1997), 'We are here to serve advertisers. That is our *raison d'être.*'

Some once posited that the rise of the Internet would eliminate the monopoly power of the global media giants. Such talk has declined recently as the largest media, telecommunications and computer firms have done everything within their immense powers to colonize the Internet, or at least neutralize its threat. The global media cartel may be evolving into a global communications cartel.

But the global media and communications system is still in flux. While we are probably not too far from crystallization, there will probably be considerable merger and joint-venture activity in the coming years. Indeed, by the time you read this, there may already be some shifts in who owns what or whom.

What is tragic is that this process of global media concentration has taken place with little public debate, especially in the US, despite the clear implications for politics and culture. After the Second World War, the Allies restricted media concentration in occupied Germany and Japan because they noted that such concentration promoted anti-democratic, even fascist, political cultures. It may be time for the United States and everyone else to take a dose of that medicine. But for that to happen will require concerted effort to educate and organize people around media issues. That is the task before us.[1]

Time Warner: $25 billion (1997 sales)

Time Warner, the largest media corporation in the world, was formed in 1989 through the merger of Time Inc. and Warner Communications. In 1992, Time Warner split off its entertainment group, and sold 25 per cent of it to US West, and 5.6 per cent of it to each of the Japanese conglomerates Itochu and Toshiba. It regained from Disney its position as the world's largest media firm with the 1996 acquisition of Turner Broadcasting.

Time Warner is moving toward being a fully global company, with over two hundred subsidiaries worldwide. In 1996, approximately two-thirds of Time Warner's income came from the United States, but that figure is expected to drop to three-fifths by 2000 and eventually to less than half. Time Warner expects globalization to provide growth tonic; it projects that its annual sales growth rate of 14 per cent in the middle 1990s will climb to over 20 per cent by the end of the decade.

Music accounts for just over 20 per cent of Time Warner's business, as does the news division of magazine and book publishing and cable television news. Its US cable systems account for over 10 per cent of income, and the remainder is accounted for largely by extensive entertainment film, video and television holdings. Time Warner is a major force in virtually every medium and on every continent.

Time Warner has zeroed in on global television as the most lucrative area for growth. Unlike News Corporation, however, Time Warner has devoted itself to producing programming and channels rather than developing entire satellite systems. Time Warner is also one of the largest cinema owners in the world, with approximately 1,000 screens outside the United States and further expansion projected.

---

[1] This chapter and the corporate profiles are based on Herman and McChesney (1997).

The Time Warner strategy is to merge the former Turner global channels CNN and TNT/Cartoon Channel with their HBO International and recently launched Warner channels to make a four-pronged assault on the global market. HBO International has already established itself as the leading subscription TV channel in the world; it has a family of pay channels and is available in over thirty-five countries. In 1996, HBO president Jeffrey Bewkes stated that global expansion is HBO's 'manifest destiny'.

CNN International, a subsidiary of CNN, is also established as the premier global television news channel, beamed via ten satellites to over two hundred nations and 90 million subscribers by 1994, a 27 per cent increase over 1993. The long-term goal for CNN International is to operate (or participate in joint ventures to establish) CNN channels in French, Japanese, Hindi, Arabic, and perhaps one or two other regional languages. CNN launched a Spanish-language service for Latin America in 1997, based in Atlanta. CNN International will also draw on the Time Warner journalism resources as it faces new challenges from news channels launched by News Corporation and NBC–Microsoft.

Before their 1996 merger, Turner and Time Warner were both global television powers with the TNT/Cartoon Network and Warner channels, drawing upon their respective large libraries of cartoons and motion pictures. Now these channels will be redeployed to utilize each other's resources better, with plans being drawn up to develop several more global cable channels to take advantage of the world's largest film, television, and cartoon libraries.

Time Warner selected holdings

(1) majority interest in WB, a US television network launched in 1995 to provide a distribution platform for Time Warner films and programmes. It is carried on the Tribune Company's sixteen US television stations, which reach 25 per cent of US TV households;

(2) significant interests in non-US broadcasting joint ventures;

(3) the largest cable system in the United States, controlling twenty-two of the hundred largest markets;

(4) several US and global cable television channels, including CNN, Headline News, CNNfn, TBS, TNT, Turner Classic Movies, the Cartoon Network and CNN–SI (a cross-production with Sports Illustrated);

(5) partial ownership of the cable channel Comedy Central and a controlling stake in Court TV;

(6) HBO and Cinemax pay cable channels;

(7) minority stake in PrimeStar, US satellite television service;

(8) Warner Brothers and New Line Cinema film studios;

(9) more than 1,000 movie screens outside the United States;

(10) a library of over 6,000 films, 25,000 television programmes, books, music and thousands of cartoons;

(11) Twenty-four magazines, including *Time, People* and *Sports Illustrated*;

(12) 50 per cent of DC Comics, publisher of *Superman, Batman* and sixty other titles;

(13) the second largest book-publishing business in the world, including Time–Life Books (42 per cent of sales outside the United States) and the Book-of-the-Month Club;

(14) Warner Music Group, one of the largest global music businesses with nearly 60 per cent of revenues from outside the United States;

(15) Six Flags theme-park chain;

(16) the Atlanta Hawks and Atlanta Braves professional sports teams;

(17) retail stores, including over 150 Warner Bros. stores and Turner Retail Group;

(18) minority interests in toy companies Atari and Hasbro.

Disney: $24 billion (1997 sales)

Disney is the closest challenger to Time Warner for the status of world's largest media firm. In the early 1990s, Disney successfully shifted its emphasis from its theme parks and resorts to its film and television divisions. In 1995, it made the move from being a dominant global content producer to being a fully integrated media giant with the purchase of Capital Cities/ABC for $19 billion, one of the biggest acquisitions in business history.

Disney now generates 31 per cent of its income from broadcasting, 23 per cent from theme parks, and the balance from 'creative content', meaning films, publishing and merchandising. The ABC deal provided Disney, already regarded as the industry leader at using cross-selling and cross-promotion to maximize revenues, with a US broadcasting network and widespread global media holdings to incorporate into its activities.

Consequently, according to *Advertising Age* (7 August 1995), Disney 'is uniquely positioned to fulfill virtually any marketing option, on any scale, almost anywhere in the world'. It has already included the new Capital Cities/ABC brands in its exclusive global marketing deals with McDonald's and Mattel toymakers. Although Disney has traditionally preferred to operate on its own, chief executive Michael Eisner has announced plans to expand aggressively overseas through joint ventures with local firms or other global players, or through further acquisitions. Disney's stated goal is to expand its non-US share of revenues from 23 per cent in 1995 to 50 per cent by 2000.

Historically, Disney has been strong in entertainment and animation, two areas that do well in the global market. In 1996 it reorganized, putting all its global television activities into a single division, Disney/ABC International Television. Its first order of business is to expand the children- and family-oriented Disney Channel into a global force, capitalizing upon the enormous Disney resources. Disney is also developing an advertising-supported children's channel to complement the subscription Disney Channel.

For the most part, Disney's success has been restricted to English-language channels in North America, Britain, and Australia. Its absence has permitted the children's channels of News Corporation, Time Warner, and especially Viacom to dominate the lucrative global market. Disney launched a Chinese-language channel based in Taiwan in 1995, and plans to launch channels in France, Italy, Germany, and the Middle East. 'The Disney Channel should be the killer children's service throughout the world,' Disney's executive in charge of international television states.

With the purchase of ABC's ESPN, the television sports network, Disney owns the unquestioned global leader. ESPN has three US cable channels, a radio network with 420 affiliates, and the ESPN SportsZone website, one of the most heavily used locales on the Internet. One Disney executive notes that with ESPN and the family-oriented Disney Channel, Disney has 'two horses to ride in foreign markets, not just one'.

ESPN International dominates televised sport, broadcasting 24 hours a day in 21 languages to over 165 countries. It reaches the one desirable audience that had eluded Disney in the past: young, single, middle-class men. 'Our plan is to think globally but to customize locally,' states the senior vice-president of ESPN International. In Latin America the emphasis is on soccer, in Asia it is table tennis, and in India ESPN provided over 1,000 hours of cricket in 1995.

Disney plans to exploit the 'synergies' of ESPN much as it has exploited its cartoon characters. 'We know that when we lay Mickey Mouse or Goofy on top of products, we get pretty creative stuff,' says Eisner. 'ESPN has the potential to be that kind of brand.' Disney's plans call for a chain of ESPN theme sports bars, ESPN product-merchandising, and possibly a chain of ESPN entertainment centres based on the Club ESPN at Walt Disney World. ESPN has released five music CDs, two of which have sold over 500,000 copies. In late 1996, Disney began negotiations with Hearst and Petersen Publishing to produce ESPN *Sports Weekly* magazine, to be a 'branded competitor to *Sports Illustrated*'.

Disney selected holdings

(1) the US ABC television and radio networks;
(2) ten US television stations and 21 US radio stations;
(3) US and global cable television channels Disney Channel, ESPN, ESPN2 and ESPNews; holdings in Lifetime, A & E and History channels;
(4) Americast, interactive TV joint venture with several telephone companies;
(5) several major film, video and television production studios including Disney, Miramax, and Buena Vista;
(6) magazine- and newspaper-publishing, through its subsidiaries, Fairchild Publications and Chilton Publications;
(7) book-publishing, including Hyperion Books and Chilton Publications;
(8) several music labels, including Hollywood Records, Mammoth Records and Walt Disney Records;
(9) theme parks and resorts, including Disneyland, Disney World, and stakes in major theme parks in France and Japan;
(10) Disney Cruise Line
(11) DisneyQuest, a chain of high-tech arcade-like game stores;
(12) controlling interests in the Anaheim Mighty Ducks ice-hockey team and major-league baseball's Anaheim Angels;
(13) consumer products, sold in more than 550 Disney retail stores worldwide.

Bertelsmann: $15 billion (1996 sales)

Bertelsmann is the one European firm in the first tier of media giants. Its empire was built on global networks of book and music clubs. Music and television provide 31 per cent of its income, book-publishing 33 per cent, magazines and newspapers 20 per cent, and a global printing business accounts for the remainder. In 1994 its income sources were Germany (36 per cent), the rest of Europe (32 per cent), the United States (24 per cent) and the rest of the world (8 per cent).

Bertelsmann's stated goal is to evolve 'from a media enterprise with international activities into a truly global communications group'. The company's strengths in global expansion are its global distribution network for music, its global book and music clubs, and its facility with languages other than English. It is working to strengthen its music holdings to become the world leader, through a possible buy-out of or merger with EMI and through establishing joint ventures with local music companies in emerging markets. Bertelsmann is considered to be the best-placed contender of all the media giants to exploit the Eastern European markets.

Bertelsmann has two severe competitive disadvantages in the global media sweepstakes. It has no significant film or television production studios or film library, and it has minimal involvement in global television, where much of the growth is taking place.

The company began to address this problem in 1996 by merging its television interests (Ufa) into a joint venture with Compagnie Luxembourgeoise de Télédiffusion (CLT), a Luxembourg-based European commercial broadcasting power. According to a Bertelsmann executive, the CLT deal was 'a strategic step to become a major media player, especially in light of the recent European and American mergers'.

Bertelsmann selected holdings
  (1) German television channels RTL, RTL2, SuperRTL and Vox;
  (2) part ownership of Premiere, Germany's largest pay-TV channel;
  (3) stakes in British, French and Dutch TV channels;
  (4) 50 per cent stake in CLT–Ufa, which owns nineteen European TV channels and twenty-three European radio stations;
  (5) eighteen European radio stations;
  (6) newspaper- and magazine-publishing, including more than 100 magazines;
  (7) book-publishing, with some forty publishing houses, concentrating on German-, French-, and English-language (Transworld) titles;
  (8) major recording studios Arista and RCA;
  (9) leading book and record clubs in the world.

Viacom: $13 billion (1997 sales)

Chief executive Sumner Redstone, who controls 39 per cent of Viacom's stock, orchestrated the deals that led to the acquisitions of Paramount and Blockbuster in 1994, thereby promoting the firm from $2 billion in 1993 sales to the front rank.

Viacom generates 33 per cent of its income from its film studios, 33 per cent from its music, video rentals and theme parks, 18 per cent from broadcasting, and 14 per cent from publishing. Redstone's strategy is for Viacom to become the world's 'premier software-driven growth company'.

Viacom's growth strategy is twofold. First, it is implementing an aggressive policy of using company-wide cross-promotions to improve sales. It proved invaluable that MTV constantly plugged the film *Clueless* in 1995, and the same strategy was applied to the Paramount television series based on the movie. Simon & Schuster has established a Nickelodeon book imprint and a *Beavis and Butthead* book series based on the MTV characters. Viacom also plans to establish a comic-book imprint based upon Paramount characters, it is considering creating a record label to exploit its MTV brand name, and it plans to open a chain of retail stores to capitalize upon its 'brands' à la Disney and Time Warner. In 1997 Paramount began producing three Nickelodeon and three MTV movies annually. 'We're just now beginning to realize the benefits of the Paramount and Blockbuster mergers,' Redstone said in 1996.

Second, Viacom has targeted global growth, with a stated goal of earning 40 per cent of its revenues outside of the United States by 2000. As one Wall Street analyst put it, Redstone wants Viacom 'playing in the same international league' with News Corporation and Time Warner. Between 1992 and 1996 Viacom invested between $750 million and $1 billion in international expansion. 'We're not taking our foot off the accelerator,' one Viacom executive states.

Viacom's two main weapons are Nickelodeon and MTV. Nickelodeon has been a global powerhouse, expanding to every continent but Antarctica in 1996 and 1997 and offering programming in several languages. It is already a world leader in children's television, reaching 90 million TV households in 70 countries other than the United States—where it can be seen in 68 million households and completely dominates children's television.

MTV is the pre-eminent global music television channel, available in 250 million homes worldwide and in scores of nations. In 1996 Viacom announced plans to 'significantly expand' its global operations. MTV has used new digital technologies to make it possible to customize programming inexpensively for different regions and nations around the world.

Viacom selected holdings
   (1) thirteen US television stations;
   (2) a 50 per cent interest in the US UPN television network with Chris-Craft Industries;
   (3) US and global cable television networks, including MTV, M2, VHI, Nickelodeon, Showtime, TVLand and Paramount Networks;
   (4) a 50 per cent interest in Comedy Central channel (with Time Warner);
   (5) film, video and television production, including Paramount Pictures;
   (6) 50 per cent stake in United Cinemas International, one of the world's three largest theatre companies;
   (7) Blockbuster Video and Music stores, the world's largest video-rental stores;
   (8) book-publishing, including Simon & Schuster.
   (9) five theme parks.

News Corporation: $10 billion (1996 sales)

The News Corporation is often identified with its head, Rupert Murdoch, whose family controls some 30 per cent of its stock. Murdoch's goal is for News Corporation to own multiple forms of programming—news, sports, films, and children's shows—and beam them via satellite or TV stations to homes in the United States, Europe, Asia, and South America. Viacom chief executive Sumner Redstone says of Murdoch that 'he basically wants to conquer the world'.

And he seems to be doing it. Redstone, Disney's Michael Eisner, and Time Warner's Gerald Levin have each commented that Murdoch is the media executive they most respect and fear, and the one whose moves they study. TCI's John Malone states that global media vertical integration is all about trying to catch Rupert. Time Warner executive Ted Turner views Murdoch in a more sinister fashion, having likened him to Adolf Hitler.

After establishing News Corporation in his native Australia, Murdoch entered the British market in the 1960s and by the 1980s had become a dominant force in the US market. News Corporation went heavily into debt to subsidize its purchase of Twentieth Century–Fox and the formation of the Fox television network in the 1980s; by the mid-1990s News Corporation had eliminated much of that debt.

News Corporation operates in nine different media on six continents. Its 1995 revenues were divided relatively evenly among filmed entertainment (26 per cent), newspapers (24 per cent), television (21 per cent), magazines (14 per cent) and book-publishing (12 per cent). News Corporation has been masterful in utilizing its various properties for cross-promotional purposes, and at using its media power to curry influence with public officials worldwide. 'Murdoch seems to have Washington in his back pocket,' observed one industry analyst after News Corporation received another favorable ruling (*New York Times*, 26 July 1996). The only media sector in which News Corporation lacks a major presence is music, but it has a half-interest in the Channel V music television channel in Asia.

Although News Corporation earned 70 per cent of its 1995 income in the United States, its plan for global expansion looks to Continental Europe, Asia, where it owns Star satellite TV, and Latin America, areas where growth is expected to be greatest for commercial media. Until around 2005, Murdoch expects the surest profits in the developed world, especially Europe and Japan. News Corporation is putting most of its eggs in the basket of television, specifically digital satellite television. It plans to draw on its experience in establishing the most profitable satellite television system in the world, the booming British Sky Broadcasting (BSkyB). It can also use its US Fox television network to provide programming for its nascent satellite ventures. The corporation is spending billions of dollars to establish these systems around the world; although the risk is considerable, if only a few of them establish monopoly or duopoly positions the entire project should prove lucrative.

News Corporation selected holdings

(1) The US Fox broadcasting network;

(2) Twenty-two US television stations, the largest US station group, covering over 40 per cent of TV households;

(3) Fox News Channel;

(4) Fifty per cent stake (with TCI's Liberty Media) in several US and global cable networks, including fx, fxM and Fox Sports Net;

(5) Fifty per cent stake in Fox Kids Worldwide, production studio and owner of US cable Family Channel;

(6) Ownership or major interests in satellite services reaching Europe, the US, Asia, and Latin America, often under the Sky Broadcasting brand;

(7) Twentieth Century–Fox, a major film, television, and video production centre, which has a library of over 2,000 films to exploit;

(8) Over 130 newspapers (primarily in Australia, Britain, and the United States, including *The Times* and the *New York Post*), making it one of the three largest newspaper groups in the world;

(9) Twenty-five magazines, most notably *TV Guide*;

(10) Book-publishing interests, including HarperCollins;

(11) Los Angeles Dodgers baseball team.

Sony: $9 billion (1997 sales, media only)

Sony's media holdings are concentrated in music (the former CBS records) and film and television production (the former Columbia Pictures), each of which it purchased in 1989. Music accounts for about 60 per cent of Sony's media income and film and television production account for the rest. Sony is a dominant entertainment producer, and its media sales are expected to surpass $9 billion in 1997. It also has major holdings in cinemas in a joint venture with Seagram. As Sony's media activities seem divorced from its other extensive activities—it expects $50 billion in company-wide sales in 1997—there is ongoing speculation that it will sell its valuable production studios to vertically integrated chains that can better exploit them.

Sony was foiled in its initial attempt to find synergies between hardware and software, but it anticipates that digital communication will provide the basis for new synergies. It hopes to capitalize upon its vast copyrighted library of films, music and TV programmes to leap to the front of the digital video-disc market, where it is poised to be one of the two global leaders with Matsushita. Sony also enjoys a 25 per cent share of the multibillion-dollar video-games industry; with the shift to digital formats these games can now be converted into channels in digital television systems.

TCI (AT&T): $7 billion (1996 sales)

TCI (Tele-Communications Inc.) is smaller than the other firms in the first tier, but its unique position in the media industry has made it a central player in the global media system. TCI's foundation is its dominant position as the second biggest US cable television system-provider. Chief executive John Malone, who has effective controlling interest over TCI, has been able to use the steady cash influx from the lucrative semi-monopolistic cable business to build an empire.

Malone understands the importance of the US cable base to the bankrolling of TCI's expansion; in 1995 and 1996 he bought several smaller cable systems to consolidate TCI's hold on the US cable market. TCI faces a direct and potentially very damaging challenge to its US market share from digital satellite broadcasting. It is responding by converting its cable systems to digital format so as to increase channel capacity to 200, and is also using its satellite spin-off to position itself in the rival satellite business and retain some of the 15 to 20 million Americans expected to switch from cable broadcasting to satellite broadcasting by 2000. In addition to owning two satellites valued at $600 million, TCI holds a 21 per cent stake in Primestar, a US satellite television joint venture with the other leading US cable companies, News Corporation and General Electric, which already had 1.2 million subscribers in 1996.

TCI has used its control of cable systems to acquire equity stakes in many of the cable channels that need to be carried over TCI to be viable. It has significant interests in Discovery, QVC, Fox Sports Net, Court TV, E!, Home Shopping Network and Black Entertainment TV, among others. In 1996, it negotiated the right to purchase a 20 per cent stake in News Corporation's new Fox News Channel in return for access to TCI systems. Through its subsidiary Liberty Media, TCI has interests in 91 US programme services.

Nor does TCI restrict its investments to cable channels and content producers. It has a 10 per cent stake in Time Warner as well as a 20 per cent stake in Silver King Communications, where former Fox network-builder Barry Diller is putting together another US television network.

TCI has applied its expansionist strategy to the global as well as domestic media market. On the one hand, it develops its core cable business and has become the global leader in cable systems, with strong units in Britain, Japan, and Chile. Merrill Lynch estimates that TCI International's cable base outside the United States will increase from 3 million subscribers in 1995 to 10 million in 1999.

On the other hand, TCI uses its cable resources to invest across all global media and to engage in numerous non-cable ventures. 'When you are the largest cable operator in the world,' a TCI executive states, 'people find a way to do business with you.' It also has thirty media deals outside the United States, including a venture with Sega Enterprises to launch computer-game channels, a joint venture with News Corporation for a global sports channel, and a 10 per cent stake in Sky Latin America.

Universal (Seagram): $7 billion (1997 sales)

Effectively controlled by the Bronfman family, the global beverage firm Seagram purchased Universal (then MCA) from Matsushita for $5.7 billion in 1995. Matsushita was unable to make a success of MCA and had refused to go along with MCA executives who wanted to acquire CBS in the 1990s. Universal is expected to account for approximately half of Seagram's $14 billion in sales in 1997.

Over half Universal's income is generated by Universal Studios' production of films and television programmes. Universal is also a major music producer and book publisher and operates several theme parks. As many of the broadcast networks and channels vertically integrate with production companies, Universal has fewer options for sales and is less secure in its future. It owns the cable USA Network and the Sci-Fi Network, buying out its uneasy partner Viacom.

NBC (GE): $5 billion (1996 sales)

General Electric is one of the leading electronics and manufacturing firms in the world with nearly $80 billion in sales in 1996. Its operations have become increasingly global, with non-US revenues increasing from 20 per cent of the total in 1985 to 38 per cent in 1995, and an expected 50 per cent in 2000. Although NBC currently constitutes only a small portion of GE's total activity, after years of rapid growth it is considered the core of GE's strategy for long-term global growth.

NBC owns US television and radio networks and eleven television stations. It has been aggressive in expanding into cable, where it now owns several channels outright, like CNBC, as well as shares in some 20 others, including the A&E network. The most dramatic expression of GE's media-centred strategy is its 1996 alliance and joint investment with Microsoft to produce the cable news channel MSNBC, along with a complementary on-line service. From this initial $500 million investment, NBC and Microsoft plan to expand MSNBC quickly into a global news channel, followed perhaps by a global entertainment and sports channel. They are also developing a series of TV channels in Europe aimed at computer users.

References

Herman, E. S., and McChesney, R. W. (1997). *The Global Media: The Missionaries of Corporate Capitalism.* London: Cassell Academic.

Chapter 5

Global Ethics in the Age of Behemoths

Anthony Smith

L ET me begin by complaining about the difficulty of the task. It is to shed light upon a process of change, still in its early stages, that is occurring worldwide— with explosive implications for industry and culture. It is also to try to pinpoint the social and moral consequences of this transformation—which has not inaptly acquired the name 'globalization'—in societies that are, in any case, hard to compare.

By globalization of mass-media firms I mean the concentration into large international companies of previously more locally owned information and entertainment businesses. In one sense, a form of concentration has been under way, at national levels, for a century—especially in the newspaper and magazine industries. Even in the nineteenth century, the number of news agencies around the world began to shrink into a tiny group, dominated by French, German, British, and American firms that divided the world according to the spheres of influence of their respective governments. This process aroused concern that governments were trying to influence the shaping of news values—even deliberately manipulating the information that circulated the globe.

The concern aroused by concentration of the media today is more intractable, but probably similarly irreversible. We are seeing an extension of three familiar processes onto an international plane: chain ownership of newspapers, cross-ownership between media, and acquisition of media by ordinary industrial concerns. This means that even the modest rules and procedures adopted to regulate at the national level can no longer easily be applied.

Governments, on the whole, do not like major newspapers passing into foreign hands—even those governments that espouse the cause of free enterprise. Australia, for example, foiled an attempt by Robert Maxwell to purchase an Australian paper; but the (originally) Australian Rupert Murdoch enjoys unchallenged ownership of newspapers in Britain, the United States, the Far East, and elsewhere.

Today, we are seeing in many countries—including some in Central Europe— information media that are crucial to political and social life passing into the influence or control of people who are not resident in those societies. We are seeing whole sections of the entertainment industry—traditionally part of national, city,

Anthony Smith, 'Global Ethics in the Age of Behemoths' from Anthony Smith, *The Age of Behemoths: The Globalization of Mass Media Firms* (New York: Priority Press, 1991), by permission of the Twentieth Century Fund.

local, regional, or ethnic life and manners—pass into the hands of managements whose outlook is exclusively global.

Perhaps this is just one aspect of the gradual ending of the nationalist phase in world history. Perhaps ownership is irrelevant to a company's ability to respond to the cultural needs of specific audiences. Perhaps our very concern emerges from a nostalgic, sentimentalized, and patronizing view of popular culture.

What is particularly fascinating and, to some, very surprising about the present phase of corporate change is that it is occurring precisely at a moment in techno-logical history when it has become extremely cheap, and in practical organizational terms easier than for several decades, for new firms to enter the media market. It costs very little to start a new radio station, for example, and much less than in the 1960s to start a local television station. Once the necessary licence or franchise is obtained, the raw materials—films and programmes—are plentifully available in an international marketplace. Further, publishing was transformed in the 1980s by the arrival of desktop computers. Bookstores have grown in number throughout the developed world, so that it should today be much easier for authors to find their readers and vice versa. The same techniques in computerization and digitization are transforming video production and sound-recording; through cable it is becoming annually easier, in theory, to purchase whole television channels offering specialist services, and it is relatively cheap to distribute such material to audiences within a city or a region.

Therefore, we ought to be witnessing at the end of the twentieth century a transformation of media industries into hundreds and hundreds of small com-panies. That, anyway, is what was predicted at the start of the computer revolution. We are supposed to be living at the end of 'mass' society. This is the age of media individualism, infinite free choice, consumer sovereignty. Deregulation, espoused by politicians in country after country, should be guaranteeing this great opening of the information and entertainment market.

To some extent, the proliferation is taking place. While new media giants are gobbling up the smaller giants everywhere from Buenos Aires and Hollywood to Paris and Tokyo, armies of small-scale entrepreneurs are also establishing them-selves. Still, these are all highly vulnerable, and everywhere the talk is of rationaliza-tion and takeover—of new small independents taking over tiny ones or all of them having to take shelter together in the bosom of a Behemoth.

The present development, then, is a dual one. On the one hand, a process of homogenization (of the kind that Hollywood has already made familiar), and, on the other, a paradoxical determination by governments to encourage new competi-tive enterprises. We see the two working simultaneously in the same societies. In France, the talk is not only of media giants such as Hersant and Berlusconi, but also of the Télétel service which makes vast quantities of information easily available electronically to everyone, of scores of new radio stations, of a whole new gener-ation of viable artisanal film-makers. But the really powerful outlets for creative work in print and the moving image seem all to be slipping into the capacious hands of a group of giant international companies.

In Britain, Channel Four, for example, conjured three or four hundred small production companies into existence in the 1980s. But at the start of the 1990s, these producers still had only a tiny number of potential patrons and buyers for their wares. The new cable and satellite channels were commissioning very little new work, the BBC had barely started to honour its commitment to buy a quarter of its programmes from the independent sector, and Channel Four itself began competing for sales of advertising time and was drawn into the competition for audiences and cheap production. There thus exists in Britain, as elsewhere, a large number of small media businesses, but their lives have been made no easier as a result of all the labour deregulation of recent times. The potential buyers of their work have increased, but they are more intensely locked in competition than in the past and have little to spend on experiment and innovation.

Independents do not make cheap programmes. Cheap programmes are acquired from international salesmen, selling off the rights to old programmes that have amortized their costs in their originating societies. Or they are acquired by participating in new international co-productions, turned out and packaged in a dozen languages. The pressure to rationalize the costs of software jeopardizes the quality of television that is internationally available. Of course, there are other pressures upon major national networks that force them to produce more expensive and often extremely good programmes.

The television world has dissolved from a world of patronage into a series of marketplaces. The American networks are still—despite the growing success of their chief rival, cable—the most lucrative markets into which to sell television material, but they are almost completely locked into a tiny number of competing suppliers. It is almost unheard of for an independent in, say, Kansas City—whatever the skill, however powerful the message—to sell a programme to CBS. For an independent in Stockholm, let alone Sri Lanka, to write to NBC is like corresponding with Father Christmas. Either the major buyers of material are, as in Western Europe, locked into inexorable and inaccessibly vast state organizations or else they are the hyperactive programme schedulers and packagers employed by eight or ten mega-institutions whose main interest lies in increasing audience share. And, in any case, deregulation has now reached the US networks, which are to be allowed again to go directly into production for themselves.

The problems posed by globalization, however, go much deeper than whether professional opportunities are being opened up or closed down. The process raises ethnic and political concerns. The new ubiquity—via satellite and cable—of television channels originating in America, Britain, and France seems inevitably to damage the aspirations of smaller nations and the ethnic audiences within them. True, there remains the opportunity for programmes in Welsh or Flemish to appear, and possibly to be translated for wider audiences, but as a higher proportion of the total television available is coming from the dominant television nations, there is a decreasing chance of those Welsh and Flemish programmes reaching a majority of the Welsh- or Flemish-speaking people for whom they were intended. It is easier than ever to provide for micro-audiences of many varieties, but those audiences are now subjected to the more powerful materials of larger nations.

Of course, there remains the possibility that entrepreneurs within minority audiences will find ways of making commercial channels work effectively even within the compass of a small ethnic or national community. That was the promise always embedded in the new technology. But, beyond a few vaunted experiments, this promise has yet to be realized. It was government action, in response to intense political pressure, that brought Welsh and Breton and Inuit television channels into existence; no one really believes that the market would ever have created them. Politics, not markets, still seems to be the only effective saviour of minority cultures. But there are many technological, regulatory, and industrial changes still to come, their results unforeseeable.

In Western Europe, there has been a decade-long search for a cultural counterpart to the advancing trans-European political movement. A rash of satellite plans was announced—both public and private—many of them, intentionally or accidentally, 'transnational' in character. Now in Europe, that term may refer to a medium that circulates or transmits across Germany, Austria, and Switzerland, say, intended for the German-speakers in those nations. Or it may, like Télé Luxembourg, emanate from a small territory in all the major languages of Europe, intended to compete with the indigenous television programming of a number of countries.

The European Community began to develop its own cultural policy in the 1980s and published an important Green Paper, *Television Without Frontiers*, intended to open up an opportunity for the members' national programmes to circulate throughout the Community. It envisaged 'the step-by-step establishment of a common market for broadcasters and audiences and hence moves to secure the free flow of information, ideas, opinions and cultural activities within the Community'. The plan was designed to promote a shift toward commercial, rather than public-service, European television.

But it also meant the creation of a trade barrier to American entertainment imports—the creation of 'quotas' in the name of national cultural 'preservation'. To the powerful lobbyists in the Motion Picture Association of America, the European Community's talk of quotas was a blow to legitimate commercial interests. To the Europeans, the Association just wanted to grab their vast new market, which might mitigate Hollywood's uncontrollable costs spiral, while turning Europe's 350 million viewers into cultural vassals of America.

The ensuing debate has been long and fierce; the outcome is still uncertain. An official of Irish broadcasting suggested that a new Green Paper be commissioned, under the title *Television: Europe—Its Peoples and Their Cultures* (Programmes 1986: 22). That summed up a widely shared fear that transnationalism in all its forms—even when issuing from the European Community's office in Brussels—is inimical to the whole tradition of nationally based broadcasting to national audiences. The opposition was not national*ist* in character. It was based, as is much of the fear of globalization (public and private), on the belief that the world is losing the logic of indigenousness and therefore a kind of authenticity; whereas we hoped that the new media of the postwar era would act as means of reconciliation, they were turning into instruments of homogenization; and whereas we saw technology as part of a long process of modernization, it would, in the form in which it actually arrived, deprive us of a home while pretending to give us a larger one.

Of course, such thoughts do not produce evidence in audience figures. The reverse is the case. The marketplace gives expression, almost unanswerably, to the needs of consumers. But perhaps we exist also as citizens and hold preferences that our behaviour as consumers does not reveal. These find expression at times in the political sphere. The fact that we cheerfully used to buy ozone-unfriendly hair-sprays does not mean that we were freely deciding we wanted a polluted atmos-phere. The products available did not allow us to articulate a more collectively beneficial choice.

This conundrum is an old one, and one can duck and weave around it. The point is that the institutional changes accompanying the new media are raising long-term and familiar cultural/political issues; these may be resolved before any real choice is made by people or nations.

What lay, half forgotten, behind the cultural decision-making was the industrial changes that government decisions, made simultaneously across much of the world, had brought about; the deregulation of the electronics and communications industries. This process acted as a booster fuel to the regrouping and globalization of industries dealing in telecommunications goods and services, in computers and robotics, in private branch exchanges (PBXs), audio equipment, television receivers, all the basic materials of the information industries.

The information revolution of the 1980s was a continuation of the automation revolution that had progressively replaced people with technology in previous dec-ades. In its wake, whole new industries came into existence to supply the new equipment that transformed industrial processes. As automation progressed, it became apparent that there was one sector within industry that remained, as it were, unreconstructed, untouched by the processes of automation; that was the vast information sector.

Information used by industry constitutes a large and increasing proportion of the total value of manufactured goods. It is used and processed not only by the bureaucracy of industry—from accounting and record-keeping to research and advertising, distribution, management, and secretarial services—but by all the out-side researchers and consultants, designers and professionals, employed by indus-try. All these remained stubbornly in the pre-automatic mode.

The computer industry created the tools for a vast transformation of this whole sector and achieved, in respect of the information quotient within the production process, the same kind of economies that automation at the shop-floor level had already achieved. The information revolution is thought of sometimes as a new industrial revolution. In its wake, class, gender, and professional identity, all our ideas and attitudes, have undergone a series of important shifts.

The French call the process 'informatisation'—the means by which all of manu-facturing, distribution, research, and administration are transformed into com-puterized, digitized systems. All the goods involved in this gigantic re-tooling of the swollen information sectors of Western societies share certain characteristics: they require huge investment, item by item, in research and development; the complexity of their ingredient elements (computer chips in particular) grows appreciably year by year; the price of electronic components falls rapidly annually. The result is that the firms engaged in this work are subject to the constant temptation to merge into ever-larger entities. Their markets are always potentially larger if they can achieve the next range of economies of scale, if they can muster larger quantities of research money, if they can benefit from the next level of price reductions (for a detailed exposition of this argument, see Palmer and Tunstall 1990).

Further, the market created by the latest technical innovation is always larger; the capital required to fill the gap always more than for the last development. The establishment of the video disc is a larger enterprise than the establishment of VHS; high-definition television (HDTV) is potentially a bigger project still. A similar pattern applies to the new PBXs, to the satellite industry. And, always, the information content of the finished goods grows greater; each generation of equipment encodes a higher degree of expert knowledge—built into chips and software—than the previous one. It is cheaper to acquire and lock in the software—whether it is entertainment for a new form of video disc or cable, or chips for a new PC—than to add a new dimension to the hardware. Increasingly, the distinction between the two is eroding.

In the United States, deregulation became almost an article of political faith. The goal of the deregulators was, as a recent study points out, to ensure that prices move toward costs. Because the marginal cost of serving a customer—whether with a chip or a telephone connection—is small or nil, companies charge widely differing prices for identical goods. Intelsat, for example, charges a customer ten times the actual cost of providing a transatlantic connection. The cost of an old television programme sold to a television channel, or of a classic orchestral performance transferred to CD, has nothing to do with the cost of supplying the software (which is almost nil), but a great deal to do with the ways in which the item is promoted to movie and CD purchasers.

Changes have swept into all information businesses including the old ones, such as newspapers and magazines. The goal is control of software with a recognized and economically viable market. Technology is not the important boundary line. So long as there is a market, it does not matter whether a particular form of information is tied to a newspaper or to radio or television, or is disseminated by satellite. The computer can always render a suitable cost reduction, make the unviable viable. Right across the industries of information—whether based on text or image, on paper or the cathode-ray tube—contemporary economics have come to prevail, and politicians and regulators see it as their duty to help, through deregulatory measures, to serve the consumer by forcing margins down. Thus, deregulation and computerization have become the parents of globalization.

The result is that all the companies concerned are driven toward self-protective merger, scale economy, constant reorganization, and a search for the ultimate in rationalized markets. Such has been the central energy of globalization. Few really quarrel with the legal, institutional, and political motivations. No one calculated, however, the moral consequences. It is possible that some will conclude that there aren't any—that information goods are fundamentally the same as others and that we all benefit from the results (whatever they may be) of the enforced efficiencies of deregulation and a more competitive economy.

Globalization is one of those phenomena of the twentieth century in which cultural and political decisions are made in ways that outmanoeuvre the democratic process. Many ecological issues were identified similarly late in their evolution; media globalization is still early in its history. The energy behind the process emerges from a democratically made decision—that of deregulation (in electronics and communications)—but it is an unforeseen consequence of this policy and it raises a range of questions that are of rather more moment, perhaps, than the originating intention.

The purpose of what follows is not to establish any final judgement—the processes are too inexorable and still too incomplete for that—but to suggest the issues at work and some of the possible lines of future thought and research.

Regulation in a changing media environment

The method by which newspapers are manufactured and distributed has always had profound implications for what might be called the moral condition of journalism. Newspapers (and other media, including the twentieth-century arrivals of radio, cinema, and television) have always had to balance their commercial and intellectual roles against the overlapping and conflicting needs of readers and advertisers, proprietors and editors, sources and governments. The essential requirement of freedom has always been available only on qualified terms, never absolutely; the level of press freedom at any moment is greatly dependent not only upon constitutional and legal arrangements and the state of mind of prevailing governments but also on the way that the medium as an enterprise is being managed. Moreover, freedom from constraint by government is but one of the necessary ingredients of an effective media system: those responsible for content require an overall environment that encourages the good qualities and discourages the bad.

In the 1950s and 1960s, journalists and academics were concerned with audience effects and agenda-setting, with the training and outlook of journalists and creative workers within the media, and above all with media content. Today, in the era of privatization and the worldwide scramble for the acquisition and control of media industries, there is heightened interest in the way media enterprises operate, in their growing interlinkages, and in the commercial judgements that underlie them.

We are all aware that the battles between the great media empires formed in the past few decades will be decisive in shaping the general culture of societies. We do not know precisely how. But we sense that we need during the coming years to understand more clearly the way in which a new small group of industrial giants, now controlling vast areas of the information and entertainment media, exert their impact on the way national and world culture is evolving. Even more urgently we have to inquire whether individual societies can usefully seek to limit or channel the process of global amalgamations in the interest of maintaining fundamental freedoms.

It was not the printing press in itself that inaugurated the past several centuries of debate and tension over press freedom. Governments (and other institutions) have always seen the media as potential rival sources of authority. They have concerned themselves with the nature of the material (pamphlets, books, liturgies, newspapers, the novel) that emerged from the press and from other information and entertainment technologies. When a single text was produced, it raised questions about the rights and privileges entailed. Achievement of periodic publication in the early seventeenth century intensified all the juridical, confessional, and political matters at issue. Regular weekly, monthly, and, even more particularly, daily publication created a form of personality within the source itself. Regular anticipated flow of material from the same source more intensely aroused questions of moral and legal rights and obligations.

The regulatory systems developed to govern modern communication devices derive from the bureaucracy for licensing that was created to cope with the newspaper. In the electronic systems that today deliver endlessly updated information, we have the ultimate extension or culmination of periodicity—for in electronic mode the information source is permanently present. We have learned since the arrival of radio and television what had already been suspected in the late nineteenth century: information media shape the realities of a society; they interact with the processes of government and provide the terms of the relationship between governors and governed—even, perhaps especially, in totalitarian societies. Social scientists have worked on a dozen different formulae for describing and evaluating this phenomenon. We now understand rather well how the media amplify, sustain, distort, shape, predetermine, the realities of the world in which we live as citizens. It is the permanence of the presence of the flows of information that turns the media into a determinant of reality. Their role is greater than any truth or falsehood that they offer; it emerges from their inevitability.

Regulatory systems evolved to police, select, control, or otherwise demarcate the boundaries between media; to prevent concentrations of what was deemed excessive power; to calculate the consequences of media operations in order to counteract them; to make certain that those in control of specific media command the trust of government; to guarantee forms of economic competition sufficient to prevent the evolution of monopolies. It is this regulatory paraphernalia that has largely drawn the map of the media world we know today. In the United States, for example, the doctrine of localness governing the franchising of broadcast outlets, and the legal limits on the number of local stations in a network, added to the controls on cross-ownership of media and other doctrines governing monopoly, fairness, and business practices, have between them created the American broadcasting system as we know it. It is the changing of the regulatory systems now taking place in many countries and the consequent changes in the institutions and practices to which they give rise (allied to a gigantic transformation in the technologies at work) that are today bringing about a reworking of all the boundaries on the world's media map.

Each technological transformation has been fitted with its own appropriate organizational devices—what one might call its 'enterprise formation'. The characteristic form of the newspaper of the eighteenth century was a printing-house that took in jobbing work and added books and periodical publications as a way to use its capacity to the full (which was determined by the working practices of a highly organized workforce divided into minute craft specialties). The newspaper of the nineteenth century required far more working capital to operate, with its growing teams of correspondents attached to the new technologies of the telegraph, and began progressively to detach itself from the general printing business. It became more technology-specific. Newspaper owners remained close to the world of political patronage, their independence being secure only when their readership was sufficient to cover their increasing costs. The twentieth-century newspaper has required still larger quantities of capital; but it has found itself, through its dependence on advertising, deeply implicated in the general market economy.

Since the First World War, the newspaper has ceased to be dependent on the economics of the political world, earning its income from its citizen readers, and becoming more wholeheartedly an instrument of advertising, its revenue deriving decreasingly from the cash directly paid by its readers. The newspaper and the magazine (broadcasting, too, in some societies) quickly became engines of the twentieth-century consumer economy, their information fuelling the growth of tastes and fashions, their internal economics greatly influenced by the cycles of trade. 'The real problem is that the readers of a newspaper,' wrote Walter Lippmann in 1922, commenting on the new tension with which the newspaper editor had to live, 'unaccustomed to paying the cost of newsgathering, can be capitalized only by turning them into circulation that can be sold to manufacturers and merchants. And those whom it is most important to capitalize are those who have the most money to spend' (Lippmann 1922: 324).

Since the 1920s, we have seen the growth of group ownership of newspapers, and the reduction of competition among daily newspapers within given markets; some countries—notably Japan and many within Western Europe—have seen intensified competition between national newspapers, with a consequent decline in the importance of city-based papers. Since the early years of the century there have been repeated expressions of fear about the loss of an essential disinterestedness in journalism as a result of the growth of newspaper combines, and there have been many fitful attempts to stop newspaper proprietors gobbling one another up. But the process has seemed relentless, except where governments have provided financial subsidy and/or vigorous regulation.

The new economic system establishing itself in media industries throughout the world emphasizes the ownership of information itself rather than of the mechanically produced forms that information takes. Narrative fiction, for example, plays a part in publishing, in magazines, in cinema and television, and the same work can find a place in all these media in a world market. Publishers want to be in a position to exploit a work of talent across the whole media landscape; they have come to fear the consequences of being excluded from an audience if they do not have a finger in every kind of media pie. Furthermore, it is becoming easier in technological terms to become involved in a wider range of media. Transnational media empires are thus coming into being to exploit new opportunities and as a protection against possible losses of opportunity. Newspapers, film businesses, radio, television, and publishing are passing into the same institutional hands.

In many of the countries involved such linkages were thought, in the past, to be a danger to society, and in some cases the law sought to prevent them. To turn back the present tide altogether would be to stand in the path of the inevitable and commercially necessary. Audiences appear to want the new diversities of information that are the counterpart of the new concentrations in media ownership. A viewer can choose to see a film on video, on cable or satellite, or (later) on conventional television, or can read the book instead, possibly published by the same company. The new enabling technologies are arriving as a result of other, wider changes in telephony, in electronics, in the exploitation of space. National legal systems are powerless to prevent the arrival of alien television channels from unregulated satellites, and in any case markets are no longer containable inside the inherited national forms. It is impossible to regulate the media and information industries in one way and the markets for apples in another.

Behind this new drive to link print and electronic media there lies an important change in thinking about the very nature of communication through wires and through air and space. All broadcasting depends upon the deployment of the natural resource of the electromagnetic spectrum, which, until the recent past, was believed to be by its nature an essentially unsaleable commodity—more nebulous than land but equally pertaining to sovereignty, distributable by government patronage alone, not really a commercially manageable resource.

The frequency spectrum has evolved in our political thinking as if it were a constant, unrenewable, and scarce resource. In scientific reality it is none of these, for technology has found seemingly infinite ways to extend the usable areas of the spectrum and to make more and more productive use of it. The scarcity was the result of the regulatory system. Newer techniques for managing the spectrum, both nationally and internationally, in addition to new digitized techniques of the communications media, are making it possible to think of the spectrum today almost as an infinite resource. The market forces operators to use it more carefully and thriftily, and with greater benefit to society (if you accept the diversity of information services and the multiplicity of channels as benefits).

Moreover, the development of telephony through optic and other cables means that a communication may pass through a variety of technologies in the course of the same transaction. A single telephone call can pass via satellite, microwave, optic fibre, coaxial cable; but so may the signal of a radio station or a point-to-point radio message. This phenomenon cancels out, in effect, the validity of boundaries between different kinds of information service-dividing lines that have appeared to exist in nature between mass and private communication, between sound- and vision-based media, between text and video, between emulsion-based images and electronic ones, and even the boundary between book and screen.

This has, in turn, invalidated the constraints that formerly seemed to justify, even necessitate, the old familiar forms of regulation. Now they appear increasingly to be restrictive or counter-productive of cultural and commercial benefit.

A new era of regulation has thus dawned, under the banner of deregulation, which is actually a means for altering the ways in which communication enterprises operate. It is a new kind of regulation—a public policy that drives forward the process of industrial and technical change. But, as we have seen, this change is also producing consequences that tend to conflict with other socially desirable objectives—among them the maintenance of diverse sources of ownership of the companies that produce our information and entertainment.

The social implications of media monopoly

So great are the institutional and corporate changes that flow from these funda-mental shifts in technology, and in its governance, that it is difficult as yet to discern the long-term social implications.

In respect of newspapers, we are used to a system that involves both mutual competition and competition with radio and television. We are used to cinema and television existing in a state of mutual tension, but also in joint competition with video. We think of newspapers, magazines, and book-publishing as completely different businesses. We think of the newspaper as a lightly or entirely unregulated medium, but of television as highly regulated, with obligations in terms of impartiality and balance, with prohibitions on material that might scare or offend—justified in our minds because of the medium's (supposedly) powerful political presence, its highly persuasive nature.

But we are moving into an era in which the distinction between the corporations and institutions that own and manage these different media entities is becoming impossible to draw. The processes of the new technologies and the pressures gener-ated in the new regulatory environment are beginning to suggest to managers of these enterprises that survival and further growth depend upon mergers and alli-ances across the divides that were so carefully contrived in the past.

That which nations are powerless to prevent does not, of course, automatically become desirable; but it does become necessary to ask again what the former constraints were intended to protect or secure, and to ask whether society might achieve the same objectives by other and less prohibitive means.

It has always been the task of the press and broadcasting to act as conduits for the flow of information and debate. Democratic societies could not exist in the absence of such a facility. But the media consist of enterprises that function within a market economy (within the Western group of countries) and markets are always prone to the arrival of concentrations of ownership or control and to the amalgamating of competing forces for mutual protection. In the new climate, there are clearly new advantages and opportunities for companies that combine in various parts of the information sector.

Moreover, there is an inevitable tension between the dual roles of media institu-tions in the private sector, as instruments of society and as profit-seeking busi-nesses. Those that operate in the public sectors of market-oriented societies are also subject to some of the same corporate temptations. In democracies, citizens should be exposed—not just in theory but in daily practice—to a multiplicity of information sources. This essential pluralism is jeopardized by the tendency towards amalgamation among previously competing organizations. While the sheer dynamic of an unconstrained market, it may be argued, creates new compensating pluralizing chances, it is increasingly possible for people not to be subject to competing views and outlooks. In the new culture of diversity, the individual has to choose his or her sources of influence rather than to chance upon them willy-nilly. In a one-channel society all of the audience is obliged—almost—to hear opposing views expressed; in a multi-channel society, in which providers of information are not even obliged to reflect the main debates of the day, it is easy to avoid the conflict of ideas.

There has been very little research into such intellectual consequences of media monopoly. In a modern society, with many sources of potential influence playing upon opinion, we do not yet know whether a decline in competition between, say, newspapers really makes any difference. In 1989, the Broadcasting Research Unit based in London conducted a survey of opinions on a range of topics held by readers of three British national daily newspapers (*The Times*, the *Sun*, and *Today*), which are all owned by News Corporation. The opinions of this group of readers were compared with those of readers of other journals. While the three daily titles are designed to appeal to quite different social groups (*The Times* is a 'quality' paper, the *Sun* a 'popular' paper, and *Today* seeks a middle-income readership), all three have consistently taken a broadly similar editorial line on a number of issues affecting the future of the media.

All these papers have supported the abolition of the licence fee by which the BBC is funded; they have argued that the BBC should be obliged to take advertising; and they have celebrated in banner headlines the launching of the first satellite channels available in Britain. It should be noted that if the BBC were adequately funded, a large portion of the British audience might be watching it, rather than Sky TV, the new satellite system that belongs to Rupert Murdoch, proprietor of News Corporation. The editor of one of the papers agreed that its intention was 'to destabilise the set-up' of British television. And a Broadcasting Research Unit survey indicates that readers of the News Corporation dailies are markedly more likely to be 'critical of terrestrial television; to welcome new channels; and to oppose the licence fee' ('You Can Have Anything They Want', 1989). This opinion profile is not consistent with the political leanings or demographic profile of these readers.

The question is: should a media enterprise use the influence of one of its parts (and that inflated by multiple-title ownership) to pursue the interests of another? Readers, it may be argued, know what they are reading and ought to be able to discount legitimately advanced arguments that they suspect of being tendentious. But can they? Do they? The argument that they may make a free choice is, perhaps, no longer sufficient in the era of information abundance. A democratic society surely needs all or most of its citizens to have been exposed to contradictory opinions. Is it enough for those differences and contradictions to be merely somewhere available? That is the heart of the problem of 'globalization' in so far as it effects the workings of a democratic society.

In the West, where information industries are dominated to a great extent by public-sector bodies, the issue used to lie concealed or perhaps just ignored. We are now living in what is really the aftermath of mass society; the new media environment is one in which it is decreasingly likely that whole populations will be subject to the same shared flows of information, and can participate in a common pool of knowledge and allusion. But behind the diversities there are new homogeneities in information and entertainment. To see all the implications, one has to look also at the circumstances that are bringing into existence new media empires and a new generation of media moguls.

References

Lippmann, W. (1922). *Public Opinion*. New York: Harcourt, Brace.

Palmer, M. and Tunstall, J. (1990). *Liberating Communications: Policy-making in France and Britain*. Oxford: Basil Blackwell.

'Programmes, Administration, Law'. (1986). *EBU Review* 37/1: 22.

'You Can Have Anything They Want'. (1989). *The Guardian*, 12 June: 6.

Chapter 6

Sold American: US News Consultants and News Issues Abroad

Craig Allen

A DEFINING moment in media criticism occurred in the mid-1970s, when a commercial function called news consultancy took root in TV news. It was the era of Woodward, Bernstein, and Walter Cronkite, when the image of news as sacrosanct and above reproach had reached a peak. Although observers had long accepted the inevitability of some commercial values in news, they had retained their belief that as long as journalists stayed focused on journalism commercialism would be contained. Then news consultancy hit, and it was as if a commercial engine had broken through the newsroom door. Ron Powers's 1977 *The Newscasters* became a standard work in news literature for its scathing commentary exposing the consultants' behind-the-scenes manipulations. Cronkite himself and scores of others blamed news consultants for galvanizing an evangel of high ratings, teaching journalists how to achieve them, sensationalizing the day's events, and transforming news presentations into half-hour advertisements—issues which have not gone away.

And neither have the news consultants, who, from the 1990s, were on the cusp of yet another defining controversy. After unbridled growth and commercial reward in the United States, American news consultants are entering the newsrooms of other countries. As foreign governments privatize their broadcast media, news consultants have been among the chief beneficiaries, their expertise in demand throughout Europe, many parts of Latin America, and all round the Asian Pacific Rim. At present American news consultants are partnered with about sixty-five overseas media in twenty-five countries. The same consultants who changed the news in Bangor and Boise are at it again, in some of the world's most prestigious news domains.

Here I examine the consultancy phenomenon, including this latest development, not so much as another exposé but as a tool that can bring critical perspective to the journalism–commercialism relationship. First, I identify the consultants and establish their overseas activities as an extension of their experiences at home, the effects then illustrated in four European countries where commercial values as imported by the Americans are vividly displayed. Finally, interviews with those involved reveal a pattern decades old in the United States, in which commercialism shifts priorities from journalism to the bottom line. Consultants arrive and implant an audience-fitted formula, the news never the same again.

All of this leaves scholars a bounty of questions. Already maligned for invading American newsrooms, are consultants perpetrating something worse abroad? Are American-style newscasts something the rest of the world really wants, or do they result from the power consultants are known to exert behind the scenes? What will be the fate of non-commercial 'public' media, a symbol of quality news in many countries but which now face an 'American' siege? Yet, on the other side of the coin, should the global expansion of news consultants serve as a wake-up call to the many critics who have striven to belittle them? Is what bothers critics not so much news consultants as the deeper realities of privately controlled media? Given the spread of this system around the world, can the analysis of news, warts and all, rise to a practical and global level, or will it remain confined to armchair domestic debates?

News consultants in the United States

One thing is certain: news consultancy has been and always will be an elusive subject. News consultants maintain confidential relationships with the media who hire them. Sworn to proprietary secrecy, news consultants do not speak in public and are rarely seen in the media, nor do any of their names appear in the credits of the hundreds of newscasts on which they advise. Their obscurity raises two opening questions: just who are the consultants and why do they matter?

Essentially, consultants are applied researchers whose main activities are driven by ongoing studies of those who use the media. The popular view that consultants engage in research as a sideline, and limit it to an occasional focus group or a yes–no opinion poll, is a myth. Research is their core function, and it is no less systematic, sophisticated, and voluminous than that long associated with the consumer-products sector or other phases of commercial enterprise. While it is logical to think of consultants strictly as advisers, researchers greatly outnumber the advising staff at the major firms. Moreover, the vast majority of those who manage the news media say they hire consultants mainly to open a research dialogue with the audience. They pay big money to do so. Single projects can cost upwards of $50,000. In a nutshell, news consultants are important in journalism, their proliferation a right-angle turn in that field, because they have given the audience a voice in the news process which previously, was intensely coveted as the sole domain of journalists.

Today, news consultancy flourishes, its impact visible in warm-and-fuzzy and action-oriented local TV newscasts and in newspapers that look like *USA Today*. Research-consulting has grown into a $100 million industry, the number of con-sulted media, in the dozens just a few years ago, having swollen to nearly 1,000. Around 350 of these contracts are owned by Frank N. Magid Associates of Marion, Iowa, Audience Research & Development (AR&D) of Dallas, and McHugh & Hoffman of Detroit, the oldest and largest of about ten US-based firms. Each started in the 1960s and 1970s by selling research to local television stations before grad-ually expanding into other news media. Still catering mainly to local TV stations and formerly resisted by national news media, the consultants made significant inroads when without fanfare or notoriety the worldwide Cable News Network signed AR&D in 1996.

Their basic function has changed little over the years, and, indeed, the same consulting regimen perfected in the US is that which today moves abroad. News consultants typically sign clients to multi-year contracts for a combination of advising and research. Field data lead to recommendations aimed at helping client newsrooms maximize their share of the audience and, in turn, profitability. By asking viewers to rate the appeal of newscasters and news content, for example, consultants can fit news presentations to the largest audience sector, usually a middle-class and largely working-class group. News consultants do not limit advising to written reports but also exert a physical presence inside newsrooms. They counsel newsworkers during periodic seminars, clinics, critiquing sessions, and one-on-one interactions (Magid 1996). Both Magid and AR&D operate talent schools, where selected newsworkers gather for specialized instruction (Bock 1986: 62–71). No client is obligated to follow the recommendations, although compliance usually occurs because of the high fees that are paid. News consultants are in greatest demand where two or more news media vie for the same audience, this situation the pretext for the arrival of consultants at CNN, which in 1996, after monopolizing the 24-hour cable news market, suddenly faced competition from Fox and MSNBC.

The consultants have contributed as much to news criticism as to the news process itself. For years television critics had been concerned with vapid entertainment fare, the so-called 'vast wasteland,' and had regaled the nightly news as a hallmark of achievement. This laudatory attitude changed practically overnight in the 1970s, when whiz-bang local newscasts known as 'Action' and 'Eyewitness News' first appeared and the consultants' role in them became publicly known. Commentaries on news consultants, including those of Powers, Edward Barrett (1973), Gary Deeb (1977, 1978), and Lloyd Grove (1983), are among the classics in news-media criticism. As well, news consultants influenced the career of Cronkite, who started as a dispassionate national newscaster. By making a public issue out of consultants, he rose alongside CBS colleague Edward R. Murrow as a conscience of 'good journalism'. Cronkite (1976) condemned news consultants as 'demagogues' and 'fly-by-nights' whose commercial tendencies were making 'suckers' out of compliant news directors. News consultancy lacks 'permanent advantage', he insisted, and soon would disappear as a 'fad'.

On that point Cronkite, 'the most trusted man in America', was proven wrong—and with meaningful consequences. This is because the main current of news criticism continues to be led by people like Cronkite: alienated journalists-turned-commentators, newspaper and magazine columnists, and others sympathetic to the news media. These popular critics have been instrumental in bringing the consulting function to the public's attention. Yet, writing with an interpretative, preachy, and often reformist slant, they typically overlook the immutable relationship between commercialism and news. This has instilled in news, in a volume of popular literature attacking news consultants, showcase criticism that has had little practical effect. Only recently have scholars diverted from this literature and begun examining matters with a more distanced view.

This is not to say that popular criticism of news consultants lacks good intent. Critics are rightfully bothered by several components of the consulting process, not least that 'code of silence' stemming from the consultants' proprietary relationships with competing newsrooms. Although the consultants have recently assumed a more active public posture and are no longer likened to agents of the CIA, much of their activities is hidden. Also troubling is the consultants' research pedigree: the founders of the consulting industry and many who populate it have no journalistic experience. Yet another anxiety is the power news consultants wield over those who seek journalistic careers. With immense talent banks, consultants often determine which news directors, anchors, and reporters get what jobs.

Yet no issue is more exasperating than simply the spectre of outside advisers turned loose inside newsrooms. Because the traditional concept of journalism is cornerstoned by 'freedom of the press', some popular critics have likened consultants to the communists who overran Eastern Europe. While debates remain as to who actually possess the freedom, journalists or the owners and managers who hire consultants, there is no question that news consultants espouse commercial values and force those in newsrooms to go along. News consultants readily concede audience-building and profit-making. And while they steadfastly deny allegations that they influence news content, and say they only 'package' the news, several academic studies clearly suggest a content-determining role (Maier 1986; Hartshorn 1980; O'Donnell 1978). In one study by Betsey Peale and Mark Harmon (1991) news consultants were associated with patterns of content, including a de-emphasis on government and politics and a stress on crime-related coverage, weather-reporting, and 'news you can use'.

Besides this, scholars have connected news consultants to format elements that determine news content. It was one of the news consultants, McHugh & Hoffman, which invented the so-called 'soundbite'. This, visualization, and reporter involvement can decide in advance what news is reported. Further, what to many may be a 'smoking gun' is published evidence that consultants do assess content in their research and indeed advocate topics generating the greatest commercial return (Berkowitz, Allen, and Beeson 1996).

Content control remains the headline concern. The first exposés were not merely critiques of consultancy practices but outright demands that news consultants leave content alone. Arguing that sales staff had committed a 'heist' of the news, Powers, in *The Newscasters*, demanded that journalists and others step forward and 'clean up the mess' (1977: 1, 238). Led by Marvin Barrett, who warned that news consultancy 'is going to have a long-term impact on the moral and intellectual fiber of this nation', the banishment of consultants was once the crusade of the DuPont–Columbia University organization, the sponsor of broadcast journalism's most prestigious awards (M. Barrett 1975; Henninger 1976). A resolution demanding that local TV stations suspend contracts with consultants was almost approved by the Radio–Television News Directors Association (RTNDA), the field's major trade organization (Johnson 1974). For a time, it appeared these pleas were having a significant effect. Several media did fire consultants, including Miami's WTVJ. Its news director, Ralph Renick, generated national headlines and became a folk hero in the campaign when he removed his station's Magid contingent by threatening physical force (Anderson 1974).

This Renick episode illustrates the extreme passions news consultants can kick up. Yet far more remarkable has been the blasé reaction of the consultants, who today have risen to global stature while critics continue to drag them through the mud. Again: what limits the criticism? Why are consultants still around? Part of the reason, eventually admitted many years later by Renick, is a tradition in popular criticism of emotionalizing the sanctity of journalism, to the point where commercial requirements go unrecognized. A colleague of Renick who became prominent in TV news for chairing the RTNDA's many investigations of consultants, a Houston news director named Ray Miller, finally agreed: 'The easiest thing in the world is to raise a fuss about news consultants. . . . [But] this is a red herring. As long as we have a commercial media, we're going to have commercial values in news' (personal communication, 10 September 1995).

Ultimately, the news consultants' ubiquitous research function best explains that industry's imperviousness to criticism. Again, it is the research, not the advising, that makes news consultancy so attractive to its clients. In affirming this, Frankola (1990) and Jacobs (1990) suggest that, because research is not part of the critical agenda, consultants have had an open field for making the claim that by coordinating research and disseminating its results they serve a socially desirable purpose. It is a claim not without merit or substance. That the public should be given a voice in the affairs of the media has been a goal elsewhere in media criticism. Further, the Federal Communications Commission's (FCC) critically acclaimed 1960 community ascertainment policy, which required broadcasters to collect public input through a research process, actually helped inspire the consultancy industry (Allen 1996). Accordingly, consultants have defused controversies by contending that journalists free to report whatever they want can overlook subjects non-journalists and the public at large deem important. Some scholarly studies bear out this possibility. In examining consultancy-using newsrooms, Dan Berkowitz (Berkowitz, Allen, and Beeson 1996) has observed marked differences between the news content journalists personally prefer and that which they are compelled to report. Then there are the studies of Richard Coleman (1983; 1995), who has found news preferences divided on class lines: those (including journalists and critics) in the upper-middle class, which comprises 20 per cent of the US population, have different values from those in the lower-middle and upper-lower classes, a 70 per cent group whose use of the media has been shown to be homogeneous, whose preferences are more simplistic and whose IQs are lower.

In news criticism, more attention needs to be given to characteristics of the mass audience, the greatest constituency of TV news. As Stanley Greenberg (1996) maintains, '[P]rogressives do not adequately understand the lives and struggles of working- and middle-class families.' Thus when upper-middle-class critics complain that consultants 'give the public not what it needs but what it wants', they may actually be saying, 'We're not getting what *we* want.' Most of the public may be getting what it needs after all.

Whatever the case may be, clearly meaningful in moving issues overseas has been the effective use of the 'we hear the audience' argument in winning over American newsrooms. Contact with news consultants increasingly is second nature even to news professionals inclined to oppose such interaction, an effect documented in scholarly studies of newsworkers who can't tell the difference between journalistic and commercial values (Berkowitz 1993; Stone 1987). Peter Hoffman, co-founder of McHugh & Hoffman, feels foreign expansion would not have been possible without this professional legitimacy at home. 'We were opposed in newsrooms at first,' he notes, 'but . . . we told clients, "You can't [convert] souls in an empty church," that journalism means little without an audience' (personal communication, 10 June 1994). As Frank Magid further explains: 'Our foreign clients recognized that there was no television system more competitive than in the United States. So it was quite apparent that those in foreign countries would come to the United States, and to us, because we had been accepted in 200 newsrooms and had the research expertise they had to have' (personal communication, 10 July 1995).

Global impact: four opening cases

In 1995 I began examining the global impact with opening studies of Great Britain, Germany, Greece, and the Czech Republic, four countries where American news consultancy was early to arrive (Allen 1997; 1998). Results suggesting patterns of both commercialization and Americanization can help propel further discussion. Before this, though, more about the context of international news consulting needs to be said.

The reason Magid was right, that those overseas do seek American expertise, has been spelled out in a loosening of government controls on the media, the result today a profusion of new privately owned media in virtually every country. This began in the early 1990s. While mostly unknown in the US, privatization is perhaps the most significant development in the non-US media since the invention of the printing-press in Europe five hundred years ago. Prior to 1990, practically every country had a one- or two-channel broadcasting system, with government-supported 'public' services the model for media development. This changed and privatization burst forth when governments realized they could not control the distribution of video recorders, satellite services, and other new media. Policies protecting public media were retracted and competitive markets opened.

A seminal event in both global media privatization and news consultancy was the public-to-private conversion of the British media as mandated in a 1988 White Paper by Margaret Thatcher's government (Home Office 1988). Under this plan, the franchising of Great Britain's then heavily regulated ITV system was thrown open to competitive bid. In exchange for large, one-off fees, winning bidders were given latitude for maximizing profits and instigating competition with the BBC. Upon entering the franchising phase, several companies turned to the United States and hired Magid for research and consulting that would improve their positions in the bidding. At the conclusion of this historic 'auction' in 1991, twelve of the sixteen ITV affiliates became Magid clients (Davidson 1992: 221–40). In 1992 Magid joined the London-based company Independent Television News (ITN), a consortium responsible for the news seen on the main national ITV network and its companion Channel Four.

Another harbinger of privatization was the rise of democracy and the institutionalization of market systems in the former Eastern-bloc nations of Europe. Germany, where the fall of the Berlin Wall symbolized this change, moved rapidly to deregulate what had been a two-channel public system in West Germany and a one-channel communist-based system in East Germany. After reunification in 1990, the German government continued to respond both to business interests seeking expansion in the region and to the demands of citizens that more TV be available, the latter an impetus for the democratic revolutions that occurred in Germany and several other Eastern European countries around this time. To take shape were five new private networks, the largest being RTL. In 1992, RTL began a second network, RTL 2, and it subsequently hired AR&D for research and consultancy that would give RTL 2 an advantage over a targeted older competitor called Pro 7.

It was shortly after staking these positions in Great Britain and Germany that the consultants moved into Greece and the Czech Republic. In 1990, Greek television was officially privatized, the first licensee being a network called Antenna, which enlisted Magid in 1992. The third major US consultancy firm, McHugh & Hoffman, was the first to enter a former communist country when it was hired by the new Czech network Nova in 1994.

Of all countries, Great Britain and Germany continue to afford the greatest opportunities for study because of the size and sophistication of their competitive systems. In Britain during the mid-1990s, newscasts on the Magid-backed Channel Four competed in prime time with the news on non-consultancy BBC 1. Similarly in Germany, AR&D client RTL 2 competed against non-consultancy Pro 7. Because of these arrangements, the two British and two German newscasts could be matched, with a framework of consultancy newscast traits, derived from studies performed in the United States, appropriate for comparisons. Analysed were British newscasts in January 1996 and German newscasts in November 1995.

Great Britain Given its extensive inroads into Britain's ITV system, it was perhaps no surprise that Magid's presence was easily observed. While non-consultancy BBC 1 had lengthy individual stories often of two minutes' duration, consulted Channel Four had shorter pieces, the average story being only 61 seconds. While both newscasts balanced 'talking-head' stories with those laden with pictures and reporter involvement, the consultancy newscaster, Channel Four, had an additional format, the commercial 'tease', which instructed viewers to 'stay tuned' and comprised 12 per cent of total airtime. While BBC 1 heavily concentrated its coverage in and around London, including Parliament, Channel Four's coverage was spread throughout Great Britain where the majority of viewers reside. In the studies, short stories, souped-up formats, and localized coverage provided definite clues to the level of Magid's activities.

Yet more was learned in the analyses of story topic. It is known from past US studies that consultants reject news that is remote from and abstract to viewers and favour stories which are proximate, timely, interesting, gut-level, and which best fit the description of 'news you can use.' From these findings researchers have developed a twelve-topic framework, in which six topics—government, politics, national business and the economy, education, distant wars, and disasters—are designated 'non-consultancy' traits. The other six—crime, personal economic matters, health, human interest, weather, and sports—are designated 'consultancy' traits. In the UK, the non-consultancy network excelled in 'non-consultancy' topics, and the consultancy network excelled in 'consultancy' topics, in eight of the twelve items. A key item was government, a subject consultants are known not to favour. Only 6 per cent of the Channel Four newscast was concerned with government, this comparing to 16 per cent at BBC 1. Channel Four did carry more political news than the BBC, and this was unexpected. Yet at Channel Four, one-third of the news consisted of unrest, health, human interest, and personal economic matters, more evidence that Magid had been there.

Besides the content, differences in the on-air 'look' of the programmes provided some of the best indicators. BBC 1 maintained a conservative approach devoid of frills, one intent on minimizing distractions and channelling the substance coming from the newscaster. In contrast, the newscast on Channel Four was steeped in aesthetic elements and an approach more eye-catching, urgent, immediate, and personable. Attention was given to the regularity with which main newscasters appeared. BBC 1 featured different newscasters and otherwise adhered to what Europeans call the 'presenter' system. Channel Four had adopted fixed news anchors, a male and a female, a definite trait of consultancy newscasts in the United States. Particularly visible were differences in the newscasts' studio settings. Viewers tuning to BBC 1 saw before a panorama of dark blue a huge studio desk large enough to seat ten newscasters, although only one appeared. In contrast, viewers of Channel Four saw a more intimate setting in which the anchors were in close proximity, as in local newscasts across the US.

Germany When the studies turned to Germany, effects became more apparent. Once again, the consultancy newscast had shorter stories, AR&D client RTL 2 keeping its items to an average of forty-seven seconds, compared to one minute on non-consultancy Pro 7. In the formatting, RTL 2 devoted only 18 per cent of its news to 'talking heads', compared to 40 per cent at Pro 7, and it carried three times as much visual material and material in which reporters in the field were heard and seen. Especially telling in Germany were the geographical analyses. RTL 2 devoted almost 50 per cent of its airtime to regional developments and used only 20 per cent to report happenings in Bonn and Berlin. At Pro 7 the numbers were reversed. A sidelight at both RTL 2 and Channel Four, one which may further suggest American influence, was not overwhelming but marked notice of news from the United States; on consultancy newscasts, stories from America outnumbered stories from the nearby EU countries by almost two to one. Notable were the newscasts of 4 October 1995, in which RTL opened with a series of reports from Los Angeles on the acquittal of former US football star O. J. Simpson, whereas Pro 7 carried only one short item on the verdict.

The analyses of story topic also fit the expected pattern. In Germany, the non-consultancy network excelled in 'non-consultancy' topics, and the consultancy network excelled in 'consultancy' topics, in eleven of the twelve items. RTL 2 devoted 10 per cent of its news to government and 9 per cent to politics, compared to more than 30 per cent for the two at Pro 7. Further, RTL 2 cast substantial proportions of its newscast around human interest (17 per cent), crime (16 per cent), and sport (11 per cent), this again in line with the consultants' apparent emphasis on proximate, gut-level content and/or 'news you can use'.

In the meantime, differences in the on-air styles of the two German newscasts were striking. In the studies, Pro 7 maintained a classic BBC-style no-frills approach. It rarely showed the entire studio and used instead head-and-shoulders shots of the newscaster, this seen throughout the newscasts. As well, Pro 7 featured rotating presenters, anathema to American consultants. In contrast, AR&D's RTL 2 had an anchor team; a red, white, and blue colour scheme; a background diorama containing a multi-coloured map of the world; and a five-piece modular studio, lit from underneath, which permitted the main anchor to interact with other individuals. Titled *Action News*, RTL 2's national newscast was almost indistinguishable in form from local newscasts in the United States.

Greece The consultants' movement into Greece represented different circumstances from those in Great Britain and Germany. Greece is smaller, and, while it is not a developing nation, its per capita income of $9,500 (relative to $20,000 in the UK and $28,000 in the US) and its political unrest approximate conditions in countries which are. The Magid–Antenna relationship was of further interest because many of its details had been publicly reported. Magid, for example, disclosed the subcontracting to an Athens firm of the first extensive audience research in Greece. It was also known that teams of Magid consultants were on-site for several weeks at a time and advised on newsgathering investments, marketing, and the hiring of news personnel. Magid recommended a 'star' anchor as a counter to the rotating presenters seen on ERT, Greece's government-run channel, and used focus groups to select this person, a radio disc jockey named Terrence Quick. He was counselled by Magid talent coaches in Athens and eventually flown to Magid headquarters in Iowa for more extensive instruction.

Antenna newscasts during September 1995 were examined. Because most of the results paralleled those already observed in the UK and Germany, more can be related here through description. That summer the worldwide news agenda had been headed by war in Bosnia, a four-hour car ride from Greece. While news from nearby Bosnia was included, never was it the lead story. It was the third item on one Antenna programme, preceded by a report about a Greek national basketball star who had signed a new contract, and another about a construction accident in downtown Athens that threatened to snarl the next day's road traffic. On a typical night at least two-thirds of the coverage was from inside Greece; while political news did receive three to four minutes during the half-hour programmes, more time was devoted to crime, unrest, personal money matters, and features, the same pattern as previously seen.

Similar to Channel Four and RTL 2 was the style of presentation Antenna had adopted. Each night a dozen different reporters contributed reports, all with extensive visual material, many live, and few longer than ninety seconds. While within these items were numerous 'talking heads', many were everyday people reacting to reported events. An example was a story about the government's decision to fund a new railway system, in which citizens weighed the benefits against higher taxes and fares. This attempt at steering coverage away from ministers and politicians and having it hit at gut level was consistent with the consultants' apparent disdain for raw government news. Also prominent were aesthetic elements that almost seemed lifted from the US. In addition to a news–weather–sports pattern identical to American local newscasts, Antenna's programme revolved around a male–female co-anchor arrangement, with Quick the dominating personality. On numerous occasions he was seen chatting with reporters and others on the news set. This air of informality, which balanced Quick's otherwise serious delivery, suggested that Magid's efforts at talent coaching had achieved the intended effect.

Czech Republic As the research continued, the fourth early beachhead, the Czech Republic, had two key attractions. While like Greece not a developing country, its per capita income of $10,000 set it apart from the West. Above all, as a former communist country, it has had a tradition of resisting news from the United States. It is there that McHugh & Hoffman is consultant to that start-up commercial network known as Nova.

Because of what became a high level of popular acceptance, Nova has received much attention in the West and many of the details of its relationship with McHugh & Hoffman have been reported. This included the main finding of the research, that Czechs were unhappy with the drab, monolithic news presentations on CST, the former communist monopoly, and had an intense desire for what they perceived as a more liberating US news style. McHugh & Hoffman advised on marketing factors and in the hiring of news personnel, with plans for news centred on male–female co-anchors. Further, a local newscast called *Eyewitness News* seen on WABC-TV in New York served as a model. Nova staff studied recordings of *Eyewitness News* and eventually were flown to New York to observe the WABC production.

The first Nova newscasts during May 1994 were examined. Three of every four news items pertained to events in the Czech Republic, and of these nearly half were regional rather than occurring in Prague. While much of the content dealt with money matters, consumer issues, and coping with daily life—the familiar 'news you can use'—spot crime, manhunts, and unrest were heavily treated. In addition, Nova stressed investigative reporting. In one investigation, a reporter unveiled a scandal at an elite Prague athletics club. Another exclusive exposed a pornography industry which had taken root in Prague shortly after the revolution and which was booming five years later.

The styling resembled that on the three other consultancy newscasts, in which a large number of field reporters contributed heavily visual 'action' reports. Aesthetically, Nova largely met the requirements of the New York local newscast on which it had been patterned. Although not technically refined, Nova was distinctive because it originated not in a studio but in a working newsroom, a technique widely employed by local TV stations in the Americas, Germany, Indonesia, and elsewhere. In this busy setting the anchors were the centres of attention, and they tempered serious reporting with informal chit-chat, this particularly visible in their introductions of the weather forecast and sports news. And, no doubt on the instructions of McHugh & Hoffman, the anchors wielded yet another on-air device, one probably unthinkable under communist rule. At every appropriate moment they smiled.

Spreading abroad: where and why

While the studies were limited to just four countries, they paint a fairly consistent picture of what scores of millions of viewers typically see on news presentations orchestrated by US news consultants. Before bringing the discussion back to the critical plane, it is important to note that much occurred during and shortly after the studies, including accelerated sales activities that had brought the consultants numerous additional clients. At hand was an opportunity not just to map the consultants' overseas outreach, but also to ask some of the principals why this growth had occurred.

Just ten years after their first foreign forays in 1990, American news consultants could be found in sixty-five overseas news organizations in twenty-five countries, very small American ventures, temporary contracts, and disclosure restrictions limiting an exact count. Magid currently operates entire divisions from bases in London and Kuala Lumpur, and it was out of London in 1998 that it pulled off a significant feat. After eventually ending its relationship with ITN, Magid joined ITN's competitor, the BBC. Long celebrated around the world for epitomizing quality journalism, the BBC's hiring of Magid was likened to the Vatican assembling atheists to pick the next Pope. In truth, though, the Magid–BBC relationship was no real surprise in the newly privatized British system that forced the BBC to compete.

Magid's other clients include the twelve ITV affiliates in the UK, TV 2 in Norway, MTV 1 in Finland, TV 3 in Malaysia, RTB in Brunei, RCTI and SCTV in Indonesia, BiTV in India, Singapore Military TV, YTN in South Korea, TVNZ 2 in New Zealand, and the Ten Network in Australia. AR&D now competes with Magid at Great Britain's Channel 5, its other clients the two RTLs in Germany, RTL 4 and RTL 5 in the Netherlands, and additional outlets in Luxembourg, France, and Australia. McHugh & Hoffman has positions in Germany (1A), Romania (Media Pro), Slovenia (Pro Plus), the Ukraine (Gravis), Finland (MTV3), Brazil (SBT), Puerto Rico (Teleonce), and Colombia (Caracol).

Other US consultants add to the number of relationships. The Minnesota-based Atkinson Research consults TV One, the public network of New Zealand, while Kansas City's Shannon Communications advises a new private channel called Bophuthatswana TV in South Africa. A New York firm called Storyfirst Communication, originally set up to advise local broadcasters in the US, recently acquired part-ownership of both the ICTV network in the Ukraine and the CTC network in Russia. In 1998, a US-styled newscast on CTC entered into competition with the forty-year-old *Vremya* on Russia's public ORT, the former television mouthpiece of the Soviet Communist Party. According to Storyfirst executive Tom Battista, 'When you see someone like Magid inside the BBC and an American company challenging a Russian institution like *Vremya*, it's obvious the times have changed' (personal communication, 15 November 1997).

The consultants' openness in discussing details is part of this change. They concede recommendations for shorter stories, fewer 'talking heads', visual material, and proximate news coverage, and they confess that many of the consultancy programmes do 'look American'. And as overseas media rush to privatize and compete, there is little mincing of words about the imperative of profitability. While consultants complain that overseas television viewers are not as TV news-attuned as those in the US, and that this affects the ratings count, their concepts have proven their commercial worth. Magid's activities eventually coincided with increases of up to 10 per cent of the audience in Britain's ITV system. In Germany, AR&D client RTL 2 went on to add about 30 per cent to its audience share. Near zero at the time of Magid's arrival, that Greek network Antenna wound up claiming half the national news audience. Most dramatic has been the commercial success of that Czech newscast on Nova, which went on to command 70 per cent of Czech viewers and reduce the former communist public channel, CST, to slivers. 'All of Eastern Europe is tuning into the saga of Nova TV,' the *Wall Street Journal* reported in 1997 (Frank).

The consultants explain their good fortune in terms of that same 'we hear the public' ideal introduced in the United States. Reading the public, they say, ensures both a profitable and a better news source. As AR&D's Ed Bewley recounts, 'We came to Europe because of our research experience. Prior to this there was no need for research because there was no competition . . . [But] once privatization hit, clients had to have a channel of communication with their audience' (personal communication, 10 June 1996). Speaking from London, Brent Magid emphasizes that news in the UK had changed little in thirty years. 'You saw an older man read news stories with few visuals or production effects,' he states. Rather than with 'warmth and interest', programme elements such as 'segments [that] concluded with "End of Part One", "End of Part Two"', repelled viewers, according to Magid, and the firm's Charles Munro saw this in the research: 'When we arrived, everything they covered were the machinations of government. It was so extreme that we called their newscasts "MPs parade"'. As Brent Magid further explains, 'The first thing we did when we got here was to go out and ask the people whether they preferred newscasts that were livelier, more human, and gave you more of a reason to tune in.' The affirmative responses coupled with increasing ratings, maintains Magid, 'have started to alter the concept of TV news in every country we have entered' (personal communications, 15 July and 9 October 1995).

Professional acceptance has not been a foregone conclusion. Magid encountered intense opposition upon entering ITN, unresolved disagreements between the consultants and programme producers the reason why the ITN–Magid relationship was severed. Yet of the overseas newsworkers contacted in the studies, few disparaged the consultants and most were positive in their remarks. 'The Americans try very hard and they help us make the news stronger. They always have ideas and are easy to work with,' commented Marion Gruntman of Germany's 1A (personal communication, 19 December 1995). Another German newsworker who asked to remain anonymous feels US input is 'necessary' because 'they are up to date'. An ITN newsworker named Clive Jones concurs: 'Consultants are helpful because when you are close to a project you sometimes can't see the wood for the trees. They often tell you things you already know, but they can help you confirm your own prejudices and instincts' (Miller 1993).

Vic Reuter, director of news for RTL, is especially candid. Speaking from RTL headquarters in Luxembourg, he noted RTL's restlessness with its ratings and an initial 'mistrust [of consultants] by the news members' when the AR&D representatives first appeared. 'We had never had any coaching, and we were not used to the role-playing AR&D said would help us adapt to the people's needs,' Reuter recalls. But because the consultants spent long hours working individually with staff members, 'things got better'. He insists that all the discussions with newsworkers were keyed to research AR&D had conducted. Further, once relations had stabilized, a sort of 'halo effect' followed the consultants, simply because they were Americans. 'Everybody asked, "Why did you go to the States [for help]?" Then everyone realized, "That's the country of TV,"' relates Reuter (personal communication, 31 January 1997).

Underlying these comments is an expectation that international news consultancy, while new, is permanent. Magid, for example, anticipates that by 2010 half of all its news consultancy business will be conducted overseas. As Reuter puts it, 'No TV in Europe can now be allowed to operate without news consultants.' Moreover, at least for the foreseeable future, this expertise seems certain to come exclusively from the United States.

News criticism in a new news age

To the legions weaned on straight, functional, state-supported newscasts, a first encounter with 'action news' is rarely less than memorable, and critics have not sat back. Yet to date, and in another repeat of events in the United States, analysis of news consultants has been governed by popular sources. The result, a body of criticism more seething than penetrating, has been visible in Canada, where the magazine *Starweek* assailed the McHugh & Hoffman 'formula', the 'everyday stuff from weather tips to sports reports, the stock market, sex and sudden death . . . [and] how to trim off 10 pounds' (Bawden 1994), a comment little more original than that in the Netherlands, where *TV World* blames RTL 4, the AR&D client, for 'downgrading the traditional [high-quality] strengths' of Dutch TV news (Fuller 1993). In New Zealand, the national magazine *Metro* has accused American consultants of instituting 'Barbie and Ken dual-anchor teams' (Atkinson, 1994), while in Great Britain an outpouring of newspaper comment has invoked more spicy if condescending anti-consultant terms. 'News doctors', 'fever charts', 'cult of personality', and 'dumbing down'—first heard many years ago in the United States—have become the new buzz words overseas (Miller 1993; 'Stars Without Stripes' 1993; Greenslade 1992).

Again, popular criticism does have a place. By exposing the hidden complex of news consultancy, its grey flannel suits and briefcases, its cost–benefit equations and data spews, it brings reality to a modern journalism more complicated than when Walter Cronkite simply read the news. Yet too often consultants are a convenient target for writers who want good copy and who do not understand or appreciate the underlying reasons why consultants exist, namely the profit, competitive, and audience-demand motives endemic in commercial media. Worse still, the impulse to mock consultants and belittle their research function has left the incorrect impression that they are an aberration in the system, if not dilettantes who will someday go away. Starting with Cronkite's false 1976 assessment of news consulting as a 'fad', the literature has done little to sober the field to that which today is seen: globalized, privatized media with deep roots in the US, in which the twin forces of commercialism and research-consultancy will steer the process of news. What, then, are some of the meaningful issues scholars should probe, discuss, and debate? If critics cannot change the system, what can they do to improve it? How can they reach those inside it?

One way is by raising the issue of Americanization, more definable now than ever even though fears about US media dominance, those which first inspired debates over 'cultural imperialism' (UNESCO 1980), have subsided. As globalization accelerates, the image of the 'ugly American' is, rightfully, less of a concern (Hamelink 1995; Golding and Harris 1997). Still, there remains something odd about American advisers entering so many overseas newsrooms. At the outbreak of the debates twenty years ago, C. C. Lee (1980: 87) drew attention to the potential spread of American advisers and envisaged a 'practice perfectly consistent with the imperative and logic of the American expansionist era'. The consultants are sensitive to this. They themselves note that, particularly in less developed countries, even subtle effects such as adding music and male–female co-anchors can change both the culture of news and a country's information flow. Under pressure to privatize and make a quick profit, they concede, at least some of their innovations abroad are actually framed by audiences in the United States. Add to this the fact that consultants do not concentrate in certain locales but have networked together newsrooms all over the world, and even more questions about Americanization ensue. So far, though, little of this has come to anyone's attention, and the consultants have been fairly free to do as they please.

Another concern is the 'power' nature of their relationship with client news media, the one issue that did bring a measure of reform in the US. When the RTNDA investigated news consultants, it stopped short of a resolution aimed at banishing Magid and the others. Yet in the process the RTNDA issued guidelines that have since compelled media owners to involve news directors in decisions to hire and fire consultants. While many argue that the guidelines have put consultants and news directors on friendlier terms, they nevertheless have leavened the influence of the consultants, if only in a small way. Outside the US such codes do not exist, nor is there a professional organization analogous to the RTNDA that could study and evaluate the consultants' activities. Are commercial consultants best suited to the role they have assumed, that of teaching journalists overseas the American process of news? Are they denying an opportunity to real educators and others who might be better equipped?

Beyond these questions is another issue, one that has long rattled inside the TV news industry. It is the estrangement of the upmarket audience component in a consultancy news system inexorably devoted to the masses. This matter rarely comes to light in criticism for the reason given earlier by Stanley Greenberg, that intellectuals and progressives typically are not attuned to 'the masses'. In US journalism, moreover, the idea of a single American 'public' is almost a professional and critical creed. The consultants, of course, beat a path to the high-school-educated, middle and lower classes, their struggles, those Greenberg identifies, the script for practically everything that is seen on TV news. This may be good for the masses, and yet as Eileen Meehan (1990) correctly points out those higher on the ladder, the 25 per cent in the US with college degrees, 'don't count'. While it can be argued that numerous newer media do include the upper and upper-middle classes, in almost a discriminatory fashion this is not true in news. Elites have struggles, too. Given that most news consultants have MAs or Ph.D.s, the fact that they have not established an upmarket newscast alternative has always been surprising, particularly so today because of the likelihood that such a venture would succeed in a crowded marketplace and probably prove economically sound.

Finally, the consultants' movements abroad are an occasion to lend attention to the one component of news that operates outside the journalism–commercialism conundrum. This is non-commercial public broadcasting, which until privatization served as the bedrock of broadcast news and information in most countries. Around the world, public broadcasting has not been the stepchild it is in the United States. Mandated to educate and uplift the public, it has had a broad following even in the lowest social strata. Today, though, it is in danger. Newscasts on public networks are proving easy prey for American consultants, while Magid's hiring by the BBC, the world's most eminent public system, is a harbinger of things to come. The case for public media is no different from that for public libraries and schools. Still, given the possibility that non-commercial media may completely disappear, be that in name only, the effort should be made.

Suffice it to say that much more needs to be known. Representatives at Magid, for example, do not expect their international activities to come to fruition until well into the twenty-first century. Of greatest interest in the years ahead will be the push into less-developed, former Third World countries, where consultants will either fail resoundingly or leave their most significant marks.

An important opportunity for the critical community lies in sorting this out. For better or worse, gone are the days of Walter Cronkite, when goodly types were hailed as visionaries for speaking their minds about commercial intrusions in news. As the world shrinks, so does the size of the choir the do-gooders can preach to, at a time when news globalization is opening new lines of understanding and debate. Journalism's nemesis may still be the consultants. Even so, the 'demon' now may be useful in helping us better evaluate new issues in the global media.

References

Allen, C. (1996). 'Mandate to News Consult: The Untold Story of the FCC's 1960 Community Ascertainment Policy'. Paper presented to the Association for Education in Journalism and Mass Communication, Anaheim, CA.

—— (1997). 'Sold American: The influence of U.S. news consultants on newscasts in Great Britain and Germany'. Paper presented to the Association for Education in Journalism and Mass Communication, Chicago.

—— (1998). 'American News Values Abroad: The Spread of U.S. News Consultants in the Wake of Privatization'. Paper presented to the International Communication Association, Jerusalem.

Anderson, J. (1974). 'Channel 4, Renick Flee Era of Franchise News'. *Miami Herald*, 14 October: 14.

Atkinson, J. (1994). 'Hey Martha! The Reconstruction of One Network News,' *Metro*, April: 94–101.

Barrett, E. W. (1973). 'Folksy TV News'. *Columbia Journalism Review*, November–December: 16–20.

Barrett, M. (1975). *Moments of Truth?* New York: Crowell, 1975.

Bawden, J. (1994). 'Morning Glory'. *Starweek*, 5 October: 4–5.

Berkowitz, D. (1993). 'Work Roles and News Selection in Local TV: Examining the Business–Journalism Dialectic'. *Journal of Broadcasting & Electronic Media* 37: 67–81.

Berkowitz, D., Allen, C., and Beeson, D. (1996). 'Exploring Newsroom Views about Consultants in Local TV: The Effects of Work Roles and Socialization'. *Journal of Broadcasting and Electronic Media* 40: 447–59.

Bock, M. A. (1986). 'Smile More: A Subcultural Analysis of the Anchor/Consultant Relationship'. Unpublished MA thesis, Drake University, Des Moines, IA.

Coleman, R. (1983). 'The Continuing Significance of Social Class to Marketing'. *Journal of Consumer Research*, 10: 265–80.

—— (1995). *American Social Classes in the Middle Nineties* (Marketing Monograph no. 1995–1). Manhattan, KS: Kansas State University Department of Marketing and International Business.

Cronkite, W. (1976). Keynote speech to Radio–Television News Directors Association [text and audio recording], Iowa City, 13 December: RTNDA archive.

Davidson, A. (1992). *Under the Hammer: The Inside Story of the 1991 ITV Franchise Battle.* London: Heinemann.

Deeb, G. (1977). 'It's the Press 1, Technology 0'. *Chicago Tribune*, II, 18 May: 16.

—— (1978). 'How Television Plugs into Our Tastes' [series]. *Chicago Tribune*, 6–8 March.

Frank N. Magid Associates (1996). *The Magid Institute*. Marion, IA: FNMA.

Frank, R. (1997). 'U.S.-styled TV Station is a Hit among Czechs'. *Wall Street Journal*, 30 April: 1, 8.

Frankola, K. (1990). 'Who Uses Consultants and Why?' *RTNDA Communicator*, August: 12–15.

Fuller, C. (1993). Public humiliation. *TV World*, April: 23.

Golding, P., and Harris, P. (1997). *Beyond Cultural Imperialism*. London: Sage.

Greenberg, S. B. (1996). 'Private Heroism and Public Purpose'. *The American Prospect*, September–October: 34–40.

Greenslade, R. (1992). 'Sorry, I Missed the Point'. *The Times* 11 November: 32.

Grove, L. (1983). The Bland Leading the Bland. *Washington Post*, 6 November: 18–20.

Hamelink, C. (1995). *World Communication: Disempowerment and Self-empowerment*. London: Zed.

Hartshorn, G. G. (1980). 'The Impact of Consultants on Local Television Stations'. Unpublished MA thesis, University of Maryland, College Park, MD.

Henninger, D. (1976). 'Doctoring the Evening News'. *National Observer*, 17 February: 17.

Home Office, UK. (1988). *Broadcasting in the '90s: Competition, Choice, and Quality*. London: HMSO.

Jacobs, J. (1990). *Changing Channels*. Mountain View, CA: Mayfield.

Johnson, R. (1974). 'Consultants . . . Praised, Damned, Feared'. *RTNDA Communicator*, June: 8.

Lee, C. C. (1980). *Media Imperialism Reconsidered*. Beverly Hills, CA: Sage.

Maier, R. D. (1986). 'News Consultants: Their Use by and Effect upon Local Television News in Louisiana'. Unpublished MA thesis, University of Southwestern Louisiana, Lafayette, LA.

Meehan, E. R. (1990). 'Why We Don't Count', in P. Mellencamp (ed.), *Logic of Television*. Bloomington, IN: Indiana University Press, 118–37.

Miller, J. (1993). 'How the News Doctors Make Breakfast More Palatable'. *Sunday Times*, 1 October: 17.

O'Donnell, M. J. (1978). 'Newscast Content of Six Iowa Television Stations: News Consultant-retaining Stations Versus Non-consultant Stations'. Unpublished MA thesis, Iowa State University, Ames, IA.

Peale, B., and Harmon, M. (1991). 'Television News Consultants: Exploration of Their Effect on Content'. Paper presented to the Association for Education in Journalism and Mass Communication, Boston, MA.

Powers, R. (1977). *The Newscasters*. New York: St Martin's Press.

'Stars Without Stripes' (1993). *Scotland on Sunday*, 17 January: 2.

Stone, V. A. (1987). 'Changing Profiles of News Directors of Radio and TV Stations, 1972–1986'. *Journalism Quarterly* 67: 984–91.

UNESCO (1980). *Many Voices, One World*, 254–69, *passim*. Paris: UNESCO.

Wittstock, M. (1992). 'Brooke tells BBC Use Licence Fees to Fund Changes'. *The Times*, 25 November: 1–2.

Chapter 7

From Flick to Flack: The Increased Emphasis on Marketing by Media Entertainment Corporations

Matthew P. McAllister

MEDIA practitioners may well remember May 1998 as the month of 'Seinfeld versus Godzilla'. This designation is not because of the dramatic excellence of either the final episode of the popular NBC TV sitcom or the blockbuster Sony film. Both were uniformly trounced by critics. Rather, the competition between the two entertainment behemoths came in the form of massive publicity and marketing.

The last episode of *Seinfeld*, for instance, was promoted on the cover of numerous magazines months before it aired, including *Time*, *Rolling Stone*, and several covers of *Entertainment Weekly*, *People*, and *TV Guide*. Talk shows such as *Charlie Rose*, *Live with Regis and Kathie Lee*, and *The Late Show with David Letterman* devoted special interviews or segments to the show. A plotline in the rival ABC sitcom *Dharma and Greg* centred on the popularity of the final *Seinfeld* episode. NBC itself touted the episode through promotions aired during other programmes and news segments discussing the show's passing. Product advertisements mentioned the last episode, including an ad for Pond's Clear Pore Strips ('Bye-bye Seinfeld! With Jerry gone, use Thursday nights to get rid of blackheads.') and a TV commercial for Macintosh declaring Jerry Seinfeld an innovator of Gandhi-esque stature.

Similarly, the producers of *Godzilla* found that 'Size Does Matter' not only for the monster, but also for the marketing campaign. Spending as much as $50 million on advertising (a record amount for a movie), Sony began running teaser previews in theatres a year in advance of the movie's release (Eller 1998; Welkos 1998b). The studio also used giant urban billboards to compare landmarks to the beast—'His footprint is as big as Wrigley Field.' Around 300 merchandisers, licensees and promotional partners signed on to sell the giant lizard's likeness, including Taco Bell's $60 million tie-in advertising campaign (Elliott 1998; Welkos 1998a).

And Jerry and Godzilla were not alone in their marketing visibility that summer. The promotional blitzes for *Armageddon*, *The Truman Show*, *The X-Files* movie and cable television networks like ESPN, among many others, were also impressive.

A major premise that justifies the existence of modern media systems in a democracy is the separation of media content from advertising. According to this premise, advertising—as the major funding system of the mass media—should not unduly influence the non-advertising content. The news stories, entertainment programmes, opinion pieces, and films are to be autonomous from the influence of any one group, and that includes advertisers. As media critic Ben Bagdikian describes this theoretical separation in the print media, 'It has been a sacred edict in official newspaper ethics that church and state—news and advertising—are separate and that when there is any doubt each is clearly labeled' (Bagdikian 1997: 163).[1] Although this quotation refers to newspapers, entertainment as well as journalistic media have an obligation to build and maintain a wall between content decisions and advertising influence.

Without this separation, stories and images that are critical of specific advertisers, as well as advertising and commercialism generally, may be rarely if ever found. Conversely, pro-advertiser and commercial messages may find themselves inserted in the non-advertising media content if advertisers have too much influence over it. Its tone may be altered, as advertisers prefer media content that is light, non-disturbing, and with an emphasis on happy endings. Textual features of advertising—its look, pace, sounds—may be copied by other forms of media without the wall that divides (Andersen 1995; Bagdikian 1997; Baker 1994; McAllister 1996).

What happens, though, when a media company *becomes* an advertiser? How can one company build a wall between parts of itself?

This essay explores the growth of motion-picture and network-television marketing by mass-media conglomerates and the implications for such growth. I shall first explore the evidence for this expansion, then the reasons for it, and finally the implications such activity may have on the role of modern media in a democratic society.

The recent increase in entertainment marketing

The promotion of new films and television programmes is, of course, not new. The advertising of films in local media began practically with the birth of the film industry in the mid-1890s, and national advertising by the movie studios was occasionally used by 1915 and routinely used by the 1930s (Staiger 1990). Movie trailers—the coming attractions shown in cinemas—and public-relations tactics like opulent premieres, film celebrity magazines, and publicity stunts also were developed early in films' history (Staiger 1990; Hiebert, Ungurait, and Bohn 1991). Walt Disney showed in the 1950s how symbiotically created television programmes (*The Mickey Mouse Club; Disneyland* on ABC) can be used to promote films and other entertainment holdings like theme parks (Brooks and Marsh, 1995). The studios increasingly emphasized television advertising for 'event' films after 1975, when the success of *Jaws* illustrated the value of 'saturation' advertising (Hiebert, Ungurait, and Bohn 1991). In the 1970s and 1980s, films like *Star Wars* and *Batman*

---

[1] Bagdikian (1997) of course argues persuasively that the theoretical separation between media content and advertising is violated frequently and fundamentally. Other scholars who have made similar claims include Andersen (1995); Baker (1994); and McAllister (1996).

paved the way for using merchandise and cross-promotional partners not just for additional revenue streams but also for publicity (Kaplan 1997; Meehan 1991).

With network television, on-air promotional spots have long been a routine technique. Originally such spots were done on film, often just by editing a previously shot scene from an episode; by the mid-1970s the advantages of video tape were being exploited, with original material increasingly produced specifically for on-air promotions. Print media like *TV Guide* and local television listings are also established tools for television marketing. The pressure to market television shows successfully increased as audience-ratings techniques became more sophisticated, as with the implementation of overnight ratings on the West Coast in the mid-1970s, and the demographically sensitive people-meter ratings in the 1980s (Cowles and Klein 1991).

But in recent years media conglomerates have placed even more emphasis on the marketing of entertainment films and programmes. This heightened emphasis can be illustrated in several ways. First, the amount of advertising money spent by entertainment conglomerates is significantly increasing. Possible ways to measure an increase include comparisons of advertising spending by media companies to the spending by earlier media companies and to advertisers in other industries. Tables 7.1 and 7.2 list the entertainment corporations among the Top 100 US advertisers, across all industries, by advertising dollars spent in 1987 and 1997, respectively. Comparing the two, it is obvious that entertainment corporations have become larger and more numerous. The average rank for entertainment advertisers in the Top 100 in 1987 was 63rd, with these four entertainment corporations spending an average of $229 million on advertising (adjusted to match the 1997 inflation equivalent). In 1997, there were two more corporations listed in the entertainment category and the average rank for these six corporations was 31st, or twice as high as a decade earlier. In addition, the latter companies spent on average $757 million on advertising, or over three times as much as the earlier ones, even when the earlier average is adjusted for inflation.[2] Looking at the growth in entertainment advertising from 1994 to 1995, the 34 per cent increase in entertainment advertising was surpassed by only one other industry, computers and electronics (Reina 1996).

Increased advertising for both film and network-television properties is largely responsible for the above increase. Studios spent nearly $1.7 billion on advertising in 1996, an increase of 20 per cent on the year before (Levin 1997a). The average wide-release 'event' movie budgets about $25 million for advertising (Jensen 1997b). The jump in advertising and marketing costs has prompted studio executives to wonder if these costs are 'galloping out of control' (Weinraub 1996), while *Variety*

---

[2] Table 7.1 lists all corporations designated as 'Entertainment and Media' by *Advertising Age* for 1987, while Table 7.2 lists all corporations designated 'Movies and Media' for 1997. The trade journal did not include General Electric as a media company in 1987, but did in 1997, even though GE's purchase of RCA (and thus NBC) occurred in 1986. Even if GE were factored into the 1987 table, the average ranking for 1987 would be 57, and the average amount spent would be $237 million, still significantly below the 1997 figures of 31 and $757 million. Seagram, the owner of MCA/Universal, was not listed as a 'Movies and Media' company in the 1997 table. Obviously, some of the corporations that were included also have significant non-media holdings that factor into their advertising spending.

TABLE 7.1 Advertising spending by entertainment corporations ranked among the top 100 advertisers for 1987

Overall ranking	Corporation	Amount spent (US $ million)	Adjusted for 1997 inflation (US $ million)
36	Walt Disney Co.	250	353
45	Time Inc.	197	278
79	Warner Communications	110	155
93	MCA Inc.	91	128
Total		648	914

Source: Adapted from 'Top 100 Advertisers by Primary Business' (1988).

TABLE 7.2 Advertising spending by entertainment corporations rnaked among the top 100 advertisers for 1997

Overall ranking	Corporation	Amount spent (US $ million)
7	Walt Disney Co.	1,250
11	Time Warner	1,013
20	Sony Corp.	778
22	Viacom	745
49	News Corp.	459
75	General Electric	298
Total		4,543

Source: Adapted from 'Sales per Ad Dollar by Most-Advertised Segment' (1998).

called the amount spent to market 1997 theatrical releases 'unprecedented' (Johnson and Petrikin 1997: 1).

Network television is also spending at exceptional levels to market itself. The networks spent as much as $500 million during fall 1996 to promote their new programmes (Elliott 1996), including an NBC spot for *The Jeff Foxworthy Show* that cost $240,000 to produce, a record for a network promo (Levin 1996*b*). TV networks use themselves as a medium for promotion. NBC allocated the equivalent of nearly $500 million of its own airtime for programme promos during the 1995–6 season (Dupree 1996). This figure probably increased for the next season. The number-one advertiser during the 1996 Olympic broadcasts was NBC, which aired 552 commercials for itself, more than the next two heaviest advertisers—Coca-Cola and General Motors—combined ('Leading Olympic advertiser? NBC', 1996). The networks also use other media. Their spending on billboards nearly tripled from 1991 to 1995 (Hudis 1996). For the fall 1998 season, ABC placed advertising stickers on 15 million bananas that were distributed nationwide (Egan 1998).

Besides the heavy promotion for individual shows, one buzzword for network promotion in the middle to late 1990s is 'branding', or the establishment through advertising of a network identity (Dupree 1996; Levin 1996*b*). By pounding the same advertising theme, the networks hope to establish a favourable image of themselves and the programming they provide. NBC attempted to capitalize on its mid-1990s ratings dominance through the slogan 'Must See TV'. CBS, the network of familiar faces like Bob Newhart, Bill Cosby, Gregory Hines, Bryant Gumbel and Candice Bergen, comforted viewers with 'Welcome Home'. The off-beat, yellow-motif 'TV Is Good' summers of 1997–98 campaign for ABC, at a $40 million price tag, attempted to woo younger viewers (Kim and McCarthy 1997).

However, the amount of money spent on 'measured' advertising by movie companies and television networks greatly underestimates their marketing activities. With both groups, perhaps a more significant source of promotion is their licensing and cross-promotional activities. Licensing involves the tie-in merchandise such as T-shirts, toys, and games that feature characters or other icons from a movie or TV show. Cross-promotion involves a joint advertising or promotional campaign with another marketer, such as a fast-food restaurant, in which often the ads are paid for by the non-media partner (McAllister 1996).

In 1992, the movie industry was buzzing about the licensing and cross-promotional deals of the anticipated *Batman Returns*. Based on the publicity generated by the licensing of video games and action figures and the cross-promotion with McDonald's (for Batman cups) and Choice Hotels, that movie generated the equivalent of $65 million in paid advertising, none of which Time Warner had to pay (Magiera 1992). Such a figure, impressive in 1992, would be seen as paltry five years later for such a high-profile release. With tie-in deals, the 1997 instalment of the action series *Batman and Robin* generated nearly twice as much free publicity, $125 million, as the earlier sequel (Benezra 1997). And, pushing the envelop even farther, this franchise pales in comparison to Universal's *The Lost World*, for which $30 million was spent in advertising and marketing, but which generated the equivalent of $250 million in tie-in deals with Burger King, Mercedes-Benz, and General Mills (Jensen 1997a). Long-term deals between studios and non-entertainment marketers also point to the centrality of cross-promotion. Disney's ten-year deals with both McDonald's and General Motors ensure publicity through the year 2006 (Feder 1996; Gelsi 1996). As one studio executive explained, movie studios look for 'promotions that penetrate the culture' (Jensen, 1997a : 52).

CBS and NBC began systematic cross-promotional activities with advertisers in 1989, with ABC acquiescing in 1996 (Levin 1996a). The networks use such marketing tactics to tout both the premiere of the fall season and sweeps months (when local advertising rates are set). The latter goal has resulted in such stunts as the distribution of more than 38 million pairs of 3-D glasses in Wendy's (ABC) and Little Caesars Pizza (NBC) for the May 1997 sweeps (Schneider 1997).

Why has the entertainment industry turned so strongly to marketing activities in the 1990s? The answers have to do with changes in technology, production costs, and corporate ownership.

Reasons for increased entertainment marketing

New promotional media   One reason for the increased emphasis on entertainment marketing is the implementation or maturation of different media that both need promotion and can be used for promotion. The continued increase in the number of cable channels, for example, means more specialization. These specialized channels then seek to 'brand' themselves with individual promotional identities and can deliver demographically targeted audiences to other advertisers, including entertainment firms (Weinraub, 1996). ESPN's award-winning *This Is SportsCenter*, which has been called 'Felliniesque', features irreverent and hip promos with a mock documentary feel (Jensen 1996). Other cable channels have sought similar promotional success. As one executive for the Discovery Channel explained, 'We got to the point where we discovered that we were in the brand-building business, not the cable business' (Murphy 1997: 16). As regards using cable as an advertising medium, from 1995 to 1996 Viacom increased its advertising spending on cable networks by over 64 per cent, Walt Disney Co. by over 71 per cent, and Time Warner by over 108 per cent (Top 25 cable networks advertisers, 1997). Even the networks use their cable competitors to promote programmes. Both NBC and CBS have formed cross-promotional deals with Comedy Central to market the broadcast networks' situation comedies (McAllister 1996).

Video tapes have also become a pre-eminent source of revenue and promotion. The 1986 video of *Top Gun* featured the first cross-promotional ad on a video tape for a movie, in this case for Pepsi; the video ad was worth about $8 million in promotional perks to Paramount, *Top Gun*'s studio (Wasko 1994). Videos now routinely include trailers for other movies and even television shows. As an example of the second use, a promotion for ABC's 1996 Saturday Morning line-up appeared on the video of *Toy Story* (Ross 1996). Movie studios increasingly have an incentive to promote the sale and rental of video tapes as well. Although the film industry made $5.9 billion at the 1996 box office, the rental and sales of videos generated around $16 billion (Matzer 1997). Such revenue potential explains why Paramount spent $50 million to promote the video release of *Titanic*, more than it had spent to promote the cinema release (Fitzpatrick 1998).

A third medium that has increased both the need for promotion and the venues for promotion is the Internet. *Advertising Age*, the industry trade journal, marks October 1994 as the birthdate of Internet advertising with the creation of the sponsored HotWired web site (Williamson 1996). Most event films now require their own Internet location, often with expensively designed games and graphics, to promote the film. *The Game*, a 1997 Polygram film, was promoted through an elaborate Internet web site that drew 850,000 hits a day (Jensen, 1997c). ESPNET SportsZone receives about 20 million hits a week, and is among the top ten of all Internet sites in advertising revenue (Jensen 1996). However, SportsZone is also heavily advertised itself on ESPN and ESPN2. Disney is a heavy advertiser *on* the Internet, spending as much as $100,000 a month for 'banner' placement on Internet search engines (Rich 1996).

Production costs, production glut An additional factor in the growth of entertainment marketing is the increased cost, and increased competition, of mainstream films and network television programmes.

With movies, this means that production for studio releases is getting more expensive, and therefore more economically risky, while competition for screen space has become fierce. Movie-makers have found themselves in a classic 'Catch 22'. To secure financing, they must build 'bankable' elements into their sales pitches. Unfortunately, such bankable elements—big stars, action adventure scenes, elaborate special effects—are expensive, and so increase the price of movie-making. As Table 7.3 shows, from the early 1970s to the late 1990s the costs of producing and marketing a mainstream studio film have increased tenfold, after adjusting for inflation, from $7.5 million in 1971 to $75.6 million in 1997. Ten movies released or in production in 1997 had production costs over $100 million, including the $200 million price tag for *Titanic* (Johnson and Petrikin 1997; Weiner 1997). As one Fox executive said about putting together the proposed budgets for films, 'Every day I have two choices. One is to make a series of absolutely insane deals and the other is to make no movies at all' (Masters 1996: 58).

What exacerbates the financial risk of these costs is the high demand for screen space. The number of movies released by the major studios rose from 141 in 1992 to 212 in 1995 (Black, Bryant, and Thompson, 1998). Wide releases, or movies that are released on more than 3,000 cinema screens, have also increased (Klady 1997). This means that producers feel more pressure to perform well quickly—such as having a big opening weekend—to keep their many cinema managers satisfied and their movies on the screen.

Advertising and marketing are perceived as the way to do this. The studios cite research showing that 80 per cent of decision-making about motion pictures is influenced by TV ads (Jensen 1997*b*). Because so many films are based on the same premise (big stars surrounded by special-effects action), saturation advertising is needed to differentiate one movie from another. Ironically, though, the use of heavy advertising to ensure a big opening weekend adds to the glut of movies. By using expensive national advertising, studios increase the need to push for a wide release to make the ad campaign cost efficient (Hiebert, Ungurait, and Bohn 1991). So the wide release is viewed as justifying large marketing campaigns, and large marketing campaigns are viewed as justifying the wide release.

TABLE 7.3 Rising costs of producing and marketing a studio film, 1971–97

	Cost (US $ million)	Adjusted for 1997 Inflation (US $ million)
1971	1.9	7.5
1980	13.9	27.1
1995	54.1	56.8
1997	75.6	75.6

Source: *Adapted from Black, Bryant, and Thompson, 1998: 158.
**Adapted from Bart (1998).

Network television is facing similar competition and cost issues, raising the need for heavy advertising as a strategy for economic predictability. For the first time in television history, the Big Three networks (ABC, NBC, CBS) saw their combined share drop below 50 per cent, in the 1996–7 season (Levin 1997*b*). With the increased popularity of cable networks and the relatively new broadcast networks (Fox, UPN and WB), a traditionally comfortable oligopolistic TV network system is not quite so comfortable for the Big Three.

This ratings competition has prompted production costs to rise, as the broadcast and cable networks look to provide 'prestige' or flashy programming for bored viewers. The 1996 season saw per-episode fees in the $1 million range for *new*, untested sitcoms, but ones that featured such stars as Michael J. Fox, Bill Cosby, Ted Dansen, and Arsenio Hall (Flint 1996*a*). In order to keep the top-rated *ER*, NBC agreed to pay $13 million per episode in 1998, nearly twice the previous record for a television series (Carmody 1998). High-profile motion pictures command top dollar for their network television debut. The Fox network spent $80 million for the television rights to *The Lost World*, the most at that time for the TV rights to a film (Rice and Higgins 1997). Sports programming is also increasingly expensive. Fox, ABC, CBS, and ESPN shocked the television and sports industries with a collective $17.6 billion deal for the rights to broadcast National Football League games through 2006, double the amount that the League had got in its previous contract (Shapiro and Farhi, 1998). Similarly, CBS paid $1.7 billion for the rights to the NCAA men's basketball tournament through the year 2002, and NBC's exclusive broadcast coverage of the Olympics from 1998 to 2008 will cost the network $3.6 billion in fees (Schlosser 1997). These fees are only for the rights to the broadcasts. The costs of the actual production are additional. Cable and broadcast networks, seeking to recoup such costs through advertising revenues and to prevent further ratings erosion, turn to increased advertising and marketing.

Corporate synergy A final factor that has led to the increased emphasis on entertainment marketing is the mega-corporate context of these studios and networks. Conglomerates like Time Warner, Disney, Viacom, and News Corp. have built their media empires upon the philosophy of corporate synergy, whereby the whole of the corporation is greater than the sum of the parts. The conglomerates acquire smaller organizations that complement and can contribute to the other holdings of the corporation.

Just taking Disney's sports holdings (a relatively small part of the entertainment conglomerate) as an example, the corporation owns ABC's *Monday Night Football* and that network's rights to other sports; the Mighty Ducks hockey team in Anaheim, CA; the Anaheim Angels baseball team; four US cable sports networks (ESPN, ESPN2, ESPNEWS and ESPN Classic); two international cable networks (ESPN Latin America, ESPN Pacific Rim); the ESPN Radio Network (with 420 affiliates), ESPN SportsZone Internet site, ESPN Sports Club in Walt Disney World, and ESPN *Magazine* (Jensen, 1996). The strategy is that each of these holdings exploits and is exploited by the others.

Media critics have raised serious concerns about the control of information,

diversity of information, and impact upon democracy of the media megacorporations (Aufderheide *et al.* 1997; Bagdikian 1997; McAllister 1996; McChesney 1997;
Meehan 1991). Corporate executives, obviously, are excited about the synergistic
possibilities. When the same corporation owns related outlets, they can use each
other to move content and promote themselves. Along these lines, the synergistic
corporate ownership of media outlets has encouraged increased entertainment
marketing activities in at least four ways.

The first way is that one corporate holding may be encouraged to buy advertising
on another. Although certainly such ad buys have to achieve the goals of the advertiser, when advertising is kept in-house so is the revenue. In the mid-1990s, News
Corp. subsidiaries increased their spending on the Fox TV network by nearly 300
per cent (Mandese 1997). In a similar vein, the Disney-owned ABC promoted its
1996 children's line-up with advertising in *Disney Adventures*, *Disney Magazine*,
direct mailings to Disneyland and Disney World annual pass-holders, and preview
guides distributed in Disney retail outlets (Ross 1996).

A second, more significant incentive is the creation of synergistic licensing deals.
As Meehan (1991) explains, corporate buy-outs often deplete a corporation's cash
assets, and one advantage of synergistic ownership is that the development of
content is made more cost-efficient as the same characters, stories, and symbols can
be moved through a variety of corporate holdings. Thus, cross-promotion activities
are enhanced when two media companies are owned by the same parent. One of
the most successful early examples of this was Warner Brothers' *Batman* in 1987,
when the conglomerate (pre-Time Warner) used such holdings as Warner Books,
Warner Records, and DC Comics to create both alternative streams of revenue and
multi-media publicity for the original movie (Meehan 1991).

In the late 1990s, such activity is a corporate given (McAllister 1996). One
Columbia executive says that 'We look in our own backyard first. Then we look to
see if other kinds of things are there that we could do with advertisers' (Sharkey
1994: 23). The connection between books and films offers an illustration. Harper-
Collins publishing, owned by News Corp., has an office on the Fox movie studio
lot, also owned by News Corp., and has published such News Corp. properties as
X-Files books and calendars. Disney's Hyperion Press awards authors bonuses if
the authors sell rights to their books to other Disney divisions (Petrikin 1996).

In such licensing deals, a formal contract details the financial arrangement
defining the licensing activity, even when it is between subsidiaries of the same
conglomerate. A third way corporate ownership increases entertainment
marketing—promotional plugs in content—involves no such official document.
This form tends to be influenced more by a corporation's public relations departments than by its advertising departments, and affects the news/information
divisions as well as the entertainment divisions. Stories about fictional or real
'Twisters' appeared on the cover of the Time-Warner-owned *Time* and *Entertainment Weekly* in May 1996, the same month the Warner Brothers' movie *Twister* was
released in cinemas (Synergy 1996). Episodes of the ABC's sitcoms *Roseanne*, *Step
By Step*, and *Boy Meets World* in 1996 were set on Walt Disney World during that
park's twenty-fifth anniversary (Mandese 1997).

Finally, a last way that corporate synergy may increase entertainment marketing is through the corporation's overall promotional ethos. Conglomerates like Disney are promotionally minded and expect their holdings to be promotionally minded as well. Such philosophies can filter throughout the corporation, influencing organizational policies to be more favourable to marketing activities. For years ABC resisted establishing cross-promotional deals with advertisers. At one point in the early 1990s, Mark Mandala, the network president, even publicly attacked the idea of cross-promotional deals with advertisers and called for less commercial time on television (Brown 1992). Four years later, 'in a clear sign of new owner Walt Disney Co.'s influence on the Alphabet web', the network announced it would seek cross-promotional tie-ins with advertisers. This move puts ABC more in line with Disney's corporate philosophy. As one advertising executive asked, 'How can you not have marketing tie-ins when you're a division of Disney?' (the above two quotations from Levin 1996a: 39).

This discussion has focused on the nature of media ownership, but to a lesser degree the above incentives also apply to cooperative production deals between media giants. McChesney (1997) points out that the eight largest media conglomerates have joint ventures with an average of four other mega-media conglomerates and many more with smaller firms. Such joint ventures include co-production or distribution of films between studios, such as the cooperation between Fox and Paramount on *Titanic* (Brodie and Busch 1996); and of television shows between studios, such as Warner and Universal's *Cloak and Dagger*, aired briefly on ABC in 1997 (Stanley 1996). Like ownership synergy, joint-production arrangements encourage cross-promotion and the widespread use of both conglomerates' resources to market the product.

Given the growth of entertainment marketing and the reasons for it, what are some possible implications of this growth? How might the stress on marketing activities affect the kind of ideas we as audiences receive? The next section focuses on three related implications: the increase in high-concept entertainment, the increase of advertising, and the blurring of advertising into non-advertising content.

Implications of increased entertainment marketing

Privileging the promotionally friendly One implication of the emphasis on entertainment promotion is that movies and TV programmes that are easy to promote—those 'high-concept' entities whose plot can be boiled down to a thirty-second spot—may be given the green light much more easily than more complex but also more promotionally difficult material.

With film, this may discourage the adult-oriented, character-study movie. As one Fox executive noted, 'They are not the easiest concepts to digest from a trailer or one-sheet' (Brodie and Busch 1996: 85). As a result, the studios may be more eager to promote movies that have visually dramatic messages such as 'Giant Monster Destroys America' or 'Meteor Hits Earth'. These messages *are* digestible. Even actor preference may be affected by promotion. Some Hollywood stars avoid modestly budgeted films and lean toward more high-concept ones, as the latter 'will be a high priority for the studio's marketing machine' (Brodie and Busch 1996 : 85). Although other economic factors certainly have encouraged the prominence of 'super-blockbusters'—such as their ease of translation for international markets and attractiveness to movie-going teenagers—the marketing niche of these films is also relevant.

The pressure to create 'event' television episodes is also promotionally driven. In the search for marketing hooks, producers of TV series are encouraged by the network to come up with 'gimmick' episodes. Television viewers were inundated with such episodes in 1997, especially during sweeps periods. The episodes took the form of live production (*ER*); reverse chronological storytelling (*Seinfeld*); musical numbers (*The Drew Carey Show*, *Chicago Hope*); theme nights (like NBC's 'Blind Date Monday' in fall 1997); 3-D episodes (*Third Rock from the Sun*); and cross-overs from different or old programmes (*Homicide*'s characters on *Law and Order*) (Berger 1997). The episodes are then highly promoted, as such promotion becomes simpler and more immediately attention-getting. It is easier to highlight with a soundbite an episode produced in 3-D than solid storytelling and good character-ization.

The stress on event films and event TV shows has implications for both quality and creator autonomy. High-concept films become less a compelling human drama and more a roller-coaster ride. Focusing on the television 'event,' one critic bluntly argues, 'Shows that are based on stunts and novelties are usually awful' (Berger 1997: AR37). Television creators may feel that they have no choice but to generate technological gimmicks or integrate stunts into the plots to satisfy the networks. They want their shows promoted. As one producer said, 'I suppose you have the option to say no, but it's probably not a feasible option' (Berger 1997: AR41).

More ads A second implication of the increase in entertainment marketing in the 1990s is the overall increase in advertising that viewers experience. Media users are exposed to less content and more advertising. Television especially highlights this increase.

The number of TV programme promotions has increased since the 1980s. One study found that ABC aired around 7,000 promos for its programmes in 1990, nearly twice what it had produced a decade before (cited in Eastman and Otteson 1994). A more recent study, summarized in Table 7.4, found that, when compared to 1991, three of the four major networks had increased the time for programme promos in prime time, devoting about four and a half minutes per hour to touting their own programmes (Fleming 1997). A third study found that advertising and promotion time tends to be even higher during local news, late-night and daytime programming, reaching nearly twenty minutes in the last slot (Farhi 1998).

In fact, Table 7.4 *under*estimates the number of promotions in primetime net-work television. Two common genres in primetime TV, news magazines, and sport include many promos within the programmes themselves. ABC's *Monday Night Football* routinely offers presenter Al Michaels previewing the network's

TABLE 7.4 Time devoted to programme promotion and product advertising per hour. Four largest broadcast networks in prime time, November 1991 and November 1996

	1991			1996			Total Change 1991–6 (minutes per hour)
	Promos	Ads	Total	Promos	Ads	Total	
ABC	3:50	9:00	12:50	3:44	11:26	15:10	+2:20
CBS	4:17	9:10	13:27	4:21	10:29	14:50	+1:23
Fox	3:49	11:03	14:52	4:25	11:40	16:05	+1:13
NBC	3:47	9:57	13:44	4:35	10:33	15:08	+1:24

Source: Adapted from Fleming (1997).

Wednesday night line-up; the anchors on primetime news magazines similarly tout forthcoming programmes before going to break. As will be shown in more detail below, much of the media content not coded by the above study as 'promotion' may have been influenced by entertainment marketing. Just about any ad-free space is viewed as fair game for promotion. In 1994, NBC began a promotional unit called 'NBC 2000' which implemented such strategies as the placement of programme promotions on a split screen at the end of a programme while the credits for that programme go by (Mandese 1994). Now other networks do the same.

This increase in programme promotion has been accompanied by an increase in product advertising. The study summarized in Table 7.4 shows that time devoted to product commercials on the four biggest broadcast networks increased. The combination of promos and product advertising on all networks in 1996 reached 'an all time high' (Fleming 1997: 19). At least a small part of the increase in product advertising may be due to the increase in entertainment marketing. Spending on TV ads for theatrical films increased by 35 per cent from 1995 to 1996 (Levin 1997a).

If the television networks are increasing the number of promotions for their programmes and advertisements for consumer products, something must be being squeezed out. Time devoted to Public Service Announcements PSAs and the programmes themselves has decreased in this enhanced promo-commercial environment. PSAs have decreased from 1991 (an average of eight seconds per hour) to 1996 (six seconds per hour) on the four largest broadcast networks. Fox, which in 1996 devoted four and a half minutes per hour to self-promotion and over eleven and a half minutes per hour to product commercials, designated two seconds per hour to PSAs. UPN averaged zero seconds of PSAs in 1996 (Fleming 1997).

Although many advertisements are occasionally entertaining, they are not the primary reason why viewers participate in media consumption. Viewers watch for the programmes. A common argument from broadcast television executives is that television is 'free' to viewers. As they point out, unlike subscription-based media, broadcast television is not 'pay-per'. However, to assume therefore that TV is free also assumes that viewers' time is not valuable, because viewers pay for TV with their time. For every forty-five minutes of programme, we have to tolerate fifteen minutes of commercials. Jhally (1987) even goes so far as to argue that a TV viewer is a type of 'labourer' in the political economy of television. Viewers 'work' by watching commercials in exchange for a 'salary' consisting of entertainment and information programming. Applying this metaphor to the current discussion, television is now demanding increased productivity with an accompanying cut in pay! In the 1990s, time devoted to programmes like situation comedies has decreased by one to two minutes on each of the national networks (Flint 1996, 1997). Even if one rejects the labour metaphor, the above increase still highlights the increased time that viewers must spend with explicitly promotional media if they are to watch network television.

Ads embedded in media content I began with a discussion of the wall between media content and advertising. A major effect of increased entertainment marketing is to wear this wall down. Such erosion has occurred both because media content is looking more like advertising and because advertising is looking more like media content. In this section I shall focus on the first half of this trend.

Both information media content and entertainment media content can become more ad-like when media systems self-promote. This trend is manifested in three ways: product placement, synergistic corporate promotion, and the piggybacking of media products on the promotional efforts of other media products.

First, when entertainment marketers establish cross-promotional partnerships with advertisers, a major benefit the entertainment companies receive is the publicity provided by the cross-promotional advertiser. But the advertisers want something too. They want the 'glamour' of being associated with Hollywood icons and access to the audiences of these icons. These goals may be achieved through product placement deals, often a major clause in cross-promotional contracts.

Product placement occurs when brand-name products appear conspicuously in films or television programmes in exchange for economic or promotional compensation. Product placement has been much discussed by critical scholars (see Andersen 1995; Fuller 1997; McAllister 1996; Miller 1990; Wasko 1994), often stressing this practice as an alternative source of revenue for film and of advertiser goodwill for television. However, as important as the revenue—if not more so—is the publicity for entertainment corporations that accompanies the practice. As media companies emphasize the marketing benefits of cross-promotion, they are willing to offer themselves as advertising vehicles. One 1996 trade-journal article argues that as a result of the growth of cross-promotional alliances 'there's no doubt we'll be seeing more big brand names woven into the fabric of TV and film scripts' (Matzer *et al.*: S9). Indeed, talent agencies like William Morris, which traditionally broker deals for the likes of Brad Pitt and Julia Roberts, have begun representing marketers like Pepsi and MBNA America Bank hoping to integrate them into the biggest movies and TV programmes, just as they would the biggest Hollywood star (Johnson 1996).

Examples of product placement in movies and television programmes are common. Kellogg's cereals appeared in the kitchen of *Seinfeld* at the same time as Jerry Seinfeld and other NBC stars appeared on 125 million boxes of cereal (Andersen 1995; McAllister 1996). When Mercedes-Benz promoted *The Lost World* at its car dealerships and in its print advertising, its new M-Class all-activity vehicle was being chased on screen by T.rexes (Jensen 1997*a*). Val Kilmer's title character in the movie *The Saint* drove a Volvo C70 coupé, as Volvo ads explained (Gelsi 1997). BMW ads, on the other hand, bragged that their car was the choice of James Bond in *GoldenEye*; the superspy also appeared in globally distributed Heineken point-of-purchase displays, while he crashes a car into a Heineken truck in *Tomorrow Never Dies* (Arndorfer 1997). Ray-Ban sunglasses helped save the world in *Men in Black*, as the ads for the product bragged (Jensen 1997*b*).

With the routine placement of products in entertainment as a source of revenue and publicity, critics wonder about the degree to which this activity influences media content. Product placers have sued when a scene featuring a product ended up on the cutting-room floor, and other companies are selective about the proper 'environment' for their product's cinematic appearances (Wasko 1994). Scenes added to spotlight products, happy endings, movies set in the present, and a general pro-commodity/consumption orientation are some of the occurrences that a reliance on product placement may encourage (Wasko 1994; Miller 1990).

Besides product placement, a second factor of entertainment marketing that has encouraged media content to take on characteristics of advertising is the synergistic pressure for one media product to promote another media product with the same corporate owner. When a media corporation owns a television network, a movie studio, sports teams, magazines, and other communications holdings, it can use one subsidiary to promote another. Television provides many clear examples of how this promotional strategy may pervade programme content.

Sometimes this promotion manifests itself in trivial references in one programme to another programme, both owned by the same corporate parent. In the 1996 season premiere of *Murphy Brown*, one character, network executive Stan Lessing, is caught watching an actual programme by a network rival, the WB's *Pinky and the Brain*. 'It's funny,' justifies Lessing (Elliott 1996). How can this be an example of synergy, given that *Murphy Brown* is a CBS programme? *Murphy Brown* is produced by Warner Brothers television, a Time Warner sibling to the WB.

Sometimes this promotion manifests itself in whole plotlines, as illustrated by a May 1997 episode of *The Parent 'Hood*, a programme on the WB Network. Eight-year-old Nicholas decides to submit an entry to an essay contest with the theme 'Why I Love Bugs Bunny'. The airing of the episode, besides its sweeps-month date, coincided with the release of the Bugs Bunny commemorative stamp, and the first prize in the contest is a visit by Bugs Bunny (or at least someone in a Bugs Bunny suit) and a poster-size replica of the stamp. Nicholas wins the contest, but only because another character in the show, the adult Wendell, writes the essay for him. When Bugs Bunny and the judge in the contest (a Time Warner executive?) show up at Nicholas's house to award him the prize, Nicholas confesses that he did not write the essay.

The confession scene revolves around pure adoration of Bugs. Nicholas tells the judge why he really loves Bugs Bunny: 'When I started first grade, I was really, really scared. But then I just thought of Bugs. He isn't scared of anything. Even when Elmer Fudd tries to shoot him, he just kisses him on the nose and says, "What's up, Doc?" I didn't kiss anyone on the nose, but I made a whole lot of friends. And I owe it all to Bugs Bunny.' Despite the messy issue of the plagiarism, Nicholas nevertheless wins the contest. Bugs Bunny is still, of course, a heavily licensed character, with merchandise sold in Warner Brothers stores and other outlets and appearances in movies like *Space Jam. Looney Tunes* merchandise, in fact, generated $2 billion in revenue in 1994 (Curan, 1995). The plotline for *The Parent 'Hood* thus became a Warner Brothers love-fest, in which one Time Warner product was used to promote another.

Sometimes this promotion manifests itself in whole programmes. An elaborate example is ABC Saturday Morning television during the 1996–7 season. *The Mighty Ducks* is an animated TV series about a team of ice-hockey-playing alien ducks who fight crime and battle against the evil character Dragaunus. The series was also shown in syndication and a direct-to-video movie-length version is available for purchase, as are Mattel toys featuring *Mighty Ducks* characters.

The level of corporate promotion that sparked this programme is amazing. The cartoon toys were, in essence, a commercial for *The Mighty Ducks'* multi-commodity franchise. *The Mighty Ducks* was originally a 1992 cinema film which spawned two sequels—a series, not coincidentally, known for its successful product placement (Fuller 1997). All three films are available for sale on video, and are shown on pay-cable via the Disney Channel. The Mighty Ducks is also the name of an Anaheim-based ice-hockey team owned by Disney. The cartoon Ducks are, like the real team and Disneyland, located in Anaheim. One episode of the cartoon series guest-starred the likeness and voice of Guy Hebert, the goalie for the real hockey team. The opening sequence of the cartoon features a song that says the name 'Mighty Ducks' nine times. The uniform logo is the same for the movie team, the NHL team, and the cartoon team. In addition, licensed merchandise (jerseys, hats) with this logo is sold in sports outlets and Disney stores. *The Mighty Ducks* cartoon, then, is an obvious example of Disney using its children's programming expertise to cultivate brand loyalty for future adult sports fans.

Another Disney programme created to promote Disney holdings is ESPN's *NFL Prime Monday*, aired during the 1997–8 football season. It was essentially a ninety-minute lead-in to a programme on another channel, ABC's *Monday Night Football* (*MNF*). The whole point of the programme was to analyse the game, and to inform viewers what to watch for during the ABC broadcast. Personalities were shared between *NFL Prime Monday* and *MNF*. The *Prime Monday* host 'interviewed' Dan Dierdorf, one of the trio of announcers on *MNF*. Later in the programme, Chris Berman, the ESPN celebrity and host of *MNF*'s halftime show, was also spotlighted, but on the *MNF* rather than the ESPN set. And in an even more obvious promotional plug, *NFL Prime Monday* asked a trivia question (such as 'Which offensive lineman holds the record for most career yardage?') which was then answered on ABC's *MNF*. In the synergistic world of corporate television, audience 'flow' is now structured to be a multiple-channel experience.

The pressure to promote entertainment programmes on the same network or within the same corporation also affects news programming. Not only was NBC the heaviest promoter *during* the Atlanta Olympics, but it was also the heaviest promoter *of* the Olympics, the most frequently covered news story on NBC for 1996, though not even in the top ten stories of the year for the other broadcast networks

(Herman and McChesney 1997). The network morning news programmes have since their beginnings been promoters of the network primetime schedule, and this practice continues today. A January 1998 instalment of *CBS News Saturday Morning* featured host Susan Molinari[3] interviewing actor John Dye of that network's *Touched by an Angel*; when Matt Lauer of NBC's *Today Show* interviewed John Lithgow on an October 1997 morning, the 'hook' of the story was that *Third Rock from the Sun* had moved to a new slot.

Part of the reason the final *Seinfeld* was such a publicity monster may have been that it plugged into the promotional apparatuses of two news-oriented corporations. GE/NBC was able to promote the show with news reports on NBC (via *The Today Show*, *Dateline* and *NBC Nightly News*) and various programmes on CNBC and MSNBC. Nearly twenty-seven minutes of news time of the 12 May 1998 *Dateline*, well over half of the total, was devoted to the last *Seinfeld*. Similarly, Time Warner owns Castle Rock Entertainment, the production company that made *Seinfeld*. The corporation aired numerous stories on its subsidiary CNN as well as cover stories in *Time*, *Entertainment Weekly* and *People*, magazines that the corporation also owns. The pressure to publicize increases such practices.

A last way that media content may take on the look of advertising because of entertainment marketing is the ratings benefits one media entity siphons from another through shared publicity. The 'plugola' that occurs when local stations create news stories for their eleven o'clock news around a highly publicized network programme or made-for-TV movie may be the clearest example of this (Benson and Alden 1995; Waxman 1996). As newsrooms are bombarded with increased public relations information about a hot movie or series, especially from the station's own network, and can exploit the publicity efforts of these entertainment products, they are more tempted to create stories around these efforts.

Such activity occurred with the much-hyped 1997 live season premiere of *ER*. The local affiliate in Roanoke, VA, connected not just one but two news stories to this episode, one the night before the episode and one the night after. 'News Channel 10 gives you a behind-the-scenes look at NBC's *ER*, where they're preparing for their live one-hour show tomorrow night,' enthused the local news anchor. The promo was accompanied by the music of *ER*, scenes of actors rehearsing a scene, and a brief soundbite from actor George Clooney. The second story was advertised as even more *ER*-like, and also piggybacked off the networks' promotional efforts. In the on-air promotions for this story, the affiliate copied the look of the network's *ER* promotion, editing in segments of the promotion, tinting the reporters' camera resolution to look like the promotion, and even appropriating the language of the promotion. Trying to duplicate the 'work without a net' feel of the special episode, a reporter breathlessly asked viewers to 'join me after NBC's live broadcast of *ER* where we'll be in an actual emergency room where events happen unrehearsed and anything can happen'. This promo was aired before and during the *ER* broadcast.

One study of a New York City affiliate found eleven and a half minutes of

---

[3] Molinari is an example of the blurring of the cross-pollination of politicians as media celebrities, as discussed in the introduction to this book.

'plugola' in an hour-long local 5 p.m. newscast (Benson and Alden 1995). Such activities are used to increase the ratings of the local news, exploiting the heavy promotional efforts of the networks and movie studios. At the very least, such activities skew the content of news towards entertainment-oriented topics, letting the networks and other entertainment organizations influence the news agenda. But another effect is the further blurring of advertising and media content, made especially ubiquitous by the complementary trend of the use of media characters and symbols in product advertising.

Media content embedded in advertising As noted above, when advertisers cross-promote with entertainment corporations, they are not being philanthropic; they want their products promoted as well, and often demand access to the symbols of the programmes/movies. One manifestation of this demand is product placement. Another is the use of entertainment symbols in the product advertisers' cross-promotional ads. An effect of this appropriation is that advertisements for such activities often look like programme promos, or even the programmes/movies themselves.

Sometimes what the advertiser wants is simply a scene or two from the movie to edit into the cross-promotional ads. The advertiser can then construct a faux dialogue between the commercial's narrator and the movie scenes. In a summer 1997 Sprint/*Men in Black* tie-in commercial, for instance, the narrator touted a special offer whereby the viewer could receive a special long-distance rate (Sprint is a long-distance phone service provider) and free *Men in Black* movie tickets. 'You can see it for free,' said the narrator, and Will Smith's character, in a scene interspliced from the movie, responded, 'What's the catch?' The use of scenes of the movie was so strong that the commercial at first appeared to be a movie trailer rather than an ad paid for by Sprint.

Other cross-promotional ads take the appropriation of entertainment symbols a step further by producing new footage featuring movie and television characters, rather than just using existing scenes. Here, the entertainment icons truly become characters in the commercials. A tie-in commercial that aired in 1997 presented two characters attacked by a *T.rex* even as one character admired *The Lost World*/Burger King watch of the other. The appearance of the dinosaur seemed to have been filmed specifically for the commercial, and was not just from a scene from the movie. Another example pushes this promotional cooperation even further. During the re-release of *Star Wars* in early 1997, a cross-promotional commercial for Pepsi was aired. In a very appropriate symbol for the type of cooperation between product advertisers and media creators, it portrayed Darth Vader literally reaching through a movie screen to grab hold of a Pepsi. And such original product-pitching by Hollywood icons is no longer limited to computer-animated characters. Pierce Brosnan, the suave 007 in *Tomorrow Never Dies*, replayed his role in a Visa commercial to cross-promote the film (Busch 1997).

Such manipulation of entertainment signs also occurs in cross-promotion and licensing advertising involving television characters. The cast of *Friends* appeared in Diet Coke ads, essentially playing the characters they do on TV (Benezra and

Stanley 1995). Sarah Michelle Gellar, who plays the title character in *Buffy, the Vampire Slayer* on the WB network, was featured in MCI (like Sprint, a provider of long-distance phone services) cross-promotional ads (Stanley 1997). During the 1997 Super Bowl for Budweiser's 'Bud Bowl', Fox commentators Howie Long and Ronnie Lott appeared as Fox commentators, holding Fox Sports-flagged microphones, in a commercial which followed appearances by Long and Lott on the pregame broadcast. On Saturday Morning television, young audiences can see their favourite live-action Teenage Mutant Ninja Turtles both in the programme, and in the commercials for the turtle action figures.

The appropriation of entertainment symbols in product commercials will continue to increase. 'Cast commercials', such as the *Friends*/Diet Coke ads, will become more prevalent as the producers of television programmes (Walt Disney Television; Warner Brothers Television) are also the network distributors of television programmes (ABC and the WB, respectively) (Levin 1996a; McAllister 1996). This integration of production and distribution of network broadcast television was prohibited by legislation—specifically, the Financial Interest and Syndication Rules—until the mid-1990s. Because the networks are typically the ones who negotiate directly with advertisers, the fact that more networks are producing their own shows means closer access to television production by advertisers. In addition, the long-term cross-promotional deals between product advertisers and media producers, such as Disney's decade-long deals with McDonald's and General Motors, encourage such integration as marketing relationships solidify.

The combination of advertising embedded in media content and media content embedded in advertising affects the viewers' ability to evaluate mediated information. One valuable skill that critical viewers have is the ability to determine when media messages are trying to sell something. When we know a message is designed around a persuasive intent, we evaluate the information in that message differently from a message without an obtrusive persuasive intent. Of course, all mass-produced messages have some level of persuasion built into them. Television programmes, because they are commodified via the ratings system, have a strong incentive to persuade us to watch. This logic is built into every second of commercial television. The promotional function of entertainment marketing adds another layer of persuasive intent. And as this layer is masked by programmes becoming more ad-like, and ads becoming more programme-like, our ability to understand and separate the layers of persuasion is made more complicated.

Take the *Mighty Ducks* example previously discussed. At one point during a typical episode, the ABC programme faded into a commercial break. A programme separator, used to signal the transition from programme to commercial, then appeared. On children's television, such separators are designed to let young viewers understand clearly that a series of messages with persuasive intent will now appear, and these messages are distinctly different from the programming. However, during the 1996–7 season, the programme separator employed by ABC was a series of vignettes featuring the characters from Disney's *Toy Story*. This 'separator' was then followed by a commercial. During one episode, the commercial that followed the programme separator was a cross-promotional ad for Fruit of the

Loom children's underwear with Disney's *Hercules*. The Disney-based nature of all these images broke down critical distinctions of symbolic types. In the flow of *Mighty Ducks*, *Toy Story* and *Hercules* images, even the most savvy viewer would have had a difficult time distinguishing the programme from the programme separator from the programme promo from the product advertisement.

Conclusion

Media companies are finding themselves in an increasingly costly, competitive, conglomerate-oriented environment, in which economic logic encourages heavy promotion by these companies, often using themselves to do the promotion. Such strategies encourage the production of easily marketable entertainment products, the amount of advertising viewers are exposed to, and the merging of advertising and media content.

Both our ability to evaluate media phenomena and the choices available to us are compromised. As the wall between advertising and content erodes, the aptitude required to understand the functions and design of media content becomes more complex. Techniques such as product placement makes movies and television programmes less ad-free, and may even alter the ideas available in these forms. Advertising itself begins to appropriate the icons and formulae of media content. Indeed, the distinction between what is an ad and what is entertainment may become irrelevant in this new promotional environment.

As far as viewer choice is concerned, certain non-promotional ideas may find fewer and fewer production outlets. Fox, Disney, and Warner Brothers' creators may introduce content ideas that have less to do with what viewers will find useful and entertaining, and more to do with the promotion of other corporate holdings. Movies and TV episodes that are easy to promote are given preference over other types of content. When the local and network news programmes fill their news time with promotional items, they must inevitably exclude other items which may be less persuasively valuable but more informationally or democratically valuable.

So as media entities toot their own horn, we must wonder what tunes are being left unplayed.

References

Andersen, R. (1995). *Consumer culture and TV programming*. Boulder, CO: Westview Press.

Arndorfer, J. B. (1997). '007's Sponsor Blitz'. *Advertising Age*, 28 July: 24.

Aufderheide, P., Barnouw, E., Cohen, R. M., Frank, T., Gitlin, T., Lieberman, D., Miller, M. C., Roberts, G., and Schatz, T. (1997). *Conglomerates and the Media*. New York: The New Press.

Bagdikian, B. (1997). *The Media Monopoly* (5th edn.). Boston: Beacon Press.

Baker, C. E. (1994). *Advertising and a Democratic Press*. Princeton, NJ: Princeton University Press.

Bart, P. (1998). 'Trapped atop a Tentpole'. *Variety*, 16 March: 4, 82.

Benezra, K. (1997). 'Dark Knight Ascendant'. *Brandweek*, 20 January: 1, 6.

Benezra, K., and Stanley, T. L. (1995). "Nice to have "Friends"'. *Adweek*, 25 September: 4.

Benson, J., and Alden, B. (1995). 'The Plugola Problem'. *Columbia Journalism Review*, May–June: 17–18.

Berger, W. (1997). 'The Year of the Gimmick'. *New York Times*, 21 December: AR37, AR41.

Black, J., Bryant, J., and Thompson, S. (1998). *Introduction to Mass Communication* (5th edn.). Boston, MA: McGraw Hill.

Brodie, J., and Busch, A. M. (1996). 'H'Wood Pigs Out on Big Pix'. *Variety*, 1 December: 1, 85.

Brooks, T., and Marsh, E. (1995). *The Complete Directory to Prime Time Network and Cable TV Shows 1946–Present* (6th edn.). New York: Ballantine Books.

Brown, K. (1992). 'ABC's Mandala Calls for Less Commercial Air Time on TV'. *Adweek*, 8 June: 2.

Busch, A. M. (1997). 'Shaken and Stirred Up over Endorsements'. *Time*, 15 December : 34.

Carmody, J. (1998). 'NBC puts its Money on ER'. *Washington Post*, 15 January: B1, B6.

Cowles, S. B., and Klein, R. A. (1991). 'Network Television Promotion', in S. T. Eastman and R. A. Klein (eds.), *Promotion and Marketing in Broadcasting and Cable*. Prospect Heights, IL: Waveland Press, 168–85.

Curan, C. M. (1995). 'Licensed Products have Warner Bros. Laughing All the Way to the Bank'. *Daily News Record*, 26 May: S26–7.

Dupree, S. (1996). 'Give Ourselves a Hand'. *Mediaweek*, 3 June: 38, 39.

Eastman, S. T., and Otteson, J. L. (1994). 'Promotion Increases Ratings, Doesn't it? The Impact of Programme Promotion in the 1992 Olympics'. *Journal of Broadcasting and Electronic Media*, 38, 307–22.

Egan, M. (1998). 'ABC Tries a Novel Approach'. *Buffalo News*, 4 August: 4C.

Eller, C. (1998). 'Early Maneuverings for a Monster Hit. *Los Angeles Times*, 9 January: D4.

Elliott, S. (1996). 'A TV Season where Image is Everything'. *New York Times*, 20 September: D1.

—— (1998). 'Marketers Sweat a Bit as "Godzilla" Disappoints at the Box Office'. *New York Times*, 10 January: D7.

Farhi, P. (1998). 'Plenty of Words from the Sponsors'. *Washington Post*, 14 May: A1, A18, A19.

Feder, B. J. (1996). 'Disney Talking to McDonald's about Alliance for Promotions'. *New York Times*, 11 April: D1, D7.

Fitzpatrick, E. (1998). 'Paramount Foresees 4Q Surge with "Titanic" video'. *Billboard*, 20 June: 6.

Fleming, H. (1997). 'PSA Slice Shrinks as Commercial Pie Grows'. *Broadcasting and Cable*, 31 March: 19, 22.

Flint, J. (1996*a*). 'TV Trauma: Will it Open?' *Variety*, 2–8 September: 1, 77.

—— (1996*b*). Intro course focus: How to stop surfing. *Variety*, 23 December 1996–5 January 1997: 31, 32.

Fuller, L. K. (1997). 'We Can't Duck the Issue: Imbedded Advertising in Motion Pictures', in K. T. Frith (ed.), *Undressing the Ad: Reading Culture in Advertising*. New York: Peter Lang Publishing, 109–29.

Gelsi, S. (1996). 'Lights, Cars, Action'. *Brandweek*, 2 December: 1.

Herman, E. S., and McChesney, R. W. (1997). *The Global Media: The New Missionaries of Global Capitalism*. London: Cassell.

Hiebert, R. E., Ungurait, D. F., and Bohn, T. W. (1991). *Mass Media VI: An Introduction to Modern Communication*. New York: Longman.

Hudis, M. (1996). 'TV Loves the Great Outdoors'. *Mediaweek*, 16 September: 9.

Jensen, J. (1996). 'Cable TV Marketer of the Year'. *Advertising Age*, 9 December: s1, s2.

—— (1997a). '"Jurassic" Sequel Set to be Promo Monster'. *Advertising Age*, 10 February: 1, 46.

—— (1997b). 'High Hopes for "Men in Black," and Ray Bans'. *Advertising Age*, 14 April: 1, 52.

—— (1997c). 'PolyGram Uses Intrigue to Tease "The Game" Debuts'. *Advertising Age*, 25 August: 3, 29.

Jhally, S. (1987). *The Codes of Advertising: Fetishism and the Political Economy of Meaning in the Consumer Society*. New York: Routledge.

Johnson, T. (1996). 'Agents Rep Banks, Trucks, but Where's the Bucks?'. *Variety*, 30 September–6 October: 15, 17.

Johnson, T., and Petrikin, C. (1997). 'Studios get Summer Sweats'. *Variety*, 24 February–2 March: 1, 62.

Kaplan, D. A. (1997). 'The Force is Still With Us'. *Newsweek*, 2 January: 52–6.

Kim, H., and McCarthy, M. (1997). 'TBWA's ABC makeover'. *Adweek*, 21 July: 4.

Klady, L. (1997). 'Burnout Blisters Pix'. *Variety*, 14–20 July: 1, 57.

'Leading Olympic Advertiser? NBC'. (1996). *New York Times*, 6 August: D7.

Levin, G. (1996a). 'Mouse Clout Promotes ABC Ad Tie-in'. *Variety*, 15 January: 39, 42.

—— (1996b). 'Kill 'em with laughter'. *Variety*, 19 –25 August: 25, 26.

—— (1997a). 'Biz Blurb Spending Spree'. *Variety*, 24–30 March: 9, 14.

—— (1997b). 'Promos: No "Slogans" Heroes'. *Variety*, 23–29 June: 1, 109.

Magiera, M. (1992). '"Batman Returns"—Licensees Cheer'. *Advertising Age*, 1 June: 1, 29.

Mandese, J. (1994). 'NBC Entertains New Viewer Hook'. *Advertising Age*, 5 September: 8.

—— (1996). 'NBC's "Seinfeld," "ER" Hit Record $1 Million Minute'. *Advertising Age*, 16 September: 1, 52.

—— (1997). 'Ad Efficiencies Often Thicker than Blood'. *Advertising Age*, 12 May: s30.

Masters, K. (1996). 'Hollywood Fades to Red'. *Time*, 5 August: 58–60.

Matzer, M. (1997). 'The Pictures Got Smaller, the Opportunities Got Bigger'. *Brandweek*, 3 March: 33–5.

Matzer, M., Grimm, M., Underwood, E., Gelsi, S., Spethmann, B., Khermouch, G., Benezra, K., Lefton, T., and Mehegan, S. (1996). 'The Demand Curve'. *Mediaweek*, 27 May: S8–S12.

McAllister, M. P. (1996). *The Commercialization of American Culture: New Advertising, Control and Democracy*. Thousand Oaks, CA: Sage.

McChesney, R. W. (1997). *Corporate Media and the Threat to Democracy*. New York: Seven Stories Press.

Meehan, E. (1991). '"Holy commodity fetish, Batman!": The Political Economy of a Commercial Intertext' in R. E. Pearson and W. Uricchio (eds.), *The Many Lives of the Batman: Critical Approaches to a Superhero and his Media*. New York: Routledge, 47–65.

Miller, M. C. (1990). 'End of Story', in M. C. Miller (ed.), *Seeing Through Movies*. New York: Pantheon Books, 186–246.

Murphy, I. P. (1997). 'TV Stations Extend Reach through Retail Outlets'. *Marketing News*, 6 January: 1, 16.

Petrikin, C. (1996). 'Is H'wood Learning to Go by the Book?' *Variety*, 16 December: 1, 99.

Reina, L. (1996). 'Great Together'. *Editor & Publisher* 31 August: 22–3.

Rice, L., and Higgins, J. M. (1997). '"Lost World" Finds Home on Fox'. *Broadcasting and Cable*, 9 June: 31.

Rich, L. (1996). 'Disney's New Attraction: Banners'. *Adweek*, 30 September: 4.

Ross, C. (1996). 'ABC Enlists Disney's Help on Fall Promo Blitz'. *Advertising Age*, 2 September: 1, 35.

'Sales per Ad Dollar by Most-advertised Segment' (1998). *Advertising Age*, 28 September: s47.

Schlosser, J. (1997). 'Big Deals for Big Tickets'. *Broadcasting and Cable*, 28 April: 20.

Schneider, M. (1997). 'Networks' Gimmick Gives Sweeps a New Dimension'. *Advertising Age*, 5 May: 20.

Shapiro, L., and Farhi, P. (1998). 'ABC Keeps Mondays in Record NFL Deals'. *Washington Post*, 14 January: A1, A10.

Sharkey, B. (1994). 'Who is Running Hollywood's Show?'. *Mediaweek*, 28 March: 22–4.

Staiger, J. (1990). 'Announcing Wares, Winning Patrons, Voicing Ideals: Thinking about the History and Theory of Film Advertising'. *Cinema Journal* 29/3:3–31.

Stanley, T. L. (1996). 'Stylish Action Revival at 8'. *Mediaweek*, 7 October: 12.

—— (1997). 'WB's "Buffy" gets an important call'. *Mediaweek*, 6 October: 4–5.

'Synergy'. (1996). *Forbes*, 17 June: 20.

'Top 100 Advertisers by Primary Business'. (1988). *Advertising Age*, 28 September: 152.

'Top 25 Cable Networks Advertisers'. (1997). *Advertising Age*, 29 September: 5:56.

Wasko, J. (1994). *Hollywood in the Information Age: Beyond the Silver Screen*. Austin, TX: University of Texas Press.

Waxman, S. (1996). 'The 11 o'Clock Ruse'. *Washington Post*, 23 January: E7.

Weiner, R. (1997). 'Budgetary Bedlam'. *Variety*, 10–16 March: 1, 97.

Weinraub, B. (1996). 'Entertainment Studio Executives are Alarmed by a Surge in the Costs of Marketing Movies'. *New York Times*, 12 August: D7.

Welkos, R. W. (1998a). 'There will be no escaping "Godzilla."' *Los Angeles Times*, 14 May: F49.

—— (1998b). 'How to Make or Break it at the Box Office'. *Los Angeles Times*, 15 June: F1, F6.

Williamson, D. A. (1996). 'Web Ads Mark 2nd Birthday with Decisive Issues Ahead'. *Advertising Age*, 21 October: 1, 43.

Part III

Advertising and Culture

Introduction

BEGINNING in the 1920s, advertising soon came to occupy a central position in American culture. Americans are inundated with up to 3000 marketing messages a day, rarely escaping contact with corporate logos and product images, at home, at work, or at school. Advertisements are a ubiquitous part of the city street scene, and all too often intrude upon the natural environment. One recent proposal is for the commercialization of outer space by placing commercial messages in orbit, 'branding' the sky. Promotional culture now penetrates almost every aspect of life, but nowhere is it more prevalent and insistent than in all forms of media culture. As the media become ever more dominated by advertising through such innovations as 'infomercials' and product placement, the commercial media environment has become naturalized to a new generation, one which does not remember a time when not every message was tied to the sell.

The intersection of American media and other national formats creates new genres of hybridity; cultural forms that emerge out of the cultural mix. In 'US Voices on UK Radio', Nancy Morris details one such union of American commercial voices and styles on local radio in Britain. The meanings associated with various accents may differ from culture to culture, but the strategy of employing them in the service of profit remains constant.

In 'Intoxicating Consumption: the Case of Beer Commercials', Lance Strate argues that beer commercials make special appeals to cultural conceptions of masculinity, reinforcing stereotypic depictions of gender. At the same time they employ the resources of commercial culture to promote products whose abuse poses health and safety risks. Both the product and the symbolic culture that surrounds it mutually reinforce entrenched social problems.

In 'Road to Ruin: the Cultural Mythology of SUVs', Robin Andersen examines one of the most stunning and successful advertising campaigns in the history of American marketing. Commanding nearly 50 per cent of market share, Sport Utility Vehicles are bought by one out of every two American families. Many owners believe themselves to be environmentally conscious, yet SUVs consume more gas and emit more greenhouse gases than cars, and in general cause enormous environmental and safety problems. Andersen argues that these contradictions are not apparent because the highly persuasive advertising is not contradicted in media owned by large corporations and dependent on advertising revenue.

Katherine Fry examines how advertising and marketing strategies shape taste cultures and coffee-consumption patterns in 'Starbucks Coffee: Cultivating and Selling the Postmodern Brew'. Using images of an exoticized other, the retail coffee chain mystifies the production and global relations of coffee distribution and consumption, even as it functions as an identity marker in late-twentieth-century capitalism. Starbucks' efforts at market distinction represent a larger pattern whereby advertising and marketing closely align with reproduction of a social and global order identifiable partly through race and geography, and increasingly through habits of consumption. All of this illustrates the overarching argument that advertising is fundamental to the spread of the marketplace into ever more facets of our everyday life as single markets continue to expand globally.

New technologies are often surrounded by utopian narratives, providing the last frontier of redemption to a media all but lost to debased entertainment and celebrity gossip. In 'Scalable Hype: Old Persuasions for New Technology', Dan Weisberg takes a close look at the new media as products, through the familiar formats of TV genre advertising. He examines the utopian narratives and depictions, and questions the social function of such representations and their match with technology's ability to offer a better social and economic world.

Chapter 8

US Voices on UK Radio

Nancy Morris

THE relationship between local media and local communities is a prominent topic of contemporary media analysis. Commercialization and international-ization have brought charges that globalized media are losing their local specificity (Kleinsteuber 1992; Martín Barbero 1997). In this essay I examine a small corner of this issue, asking why US accents are so commonly used in station identification announcements in UK commercial radio, and explore the implications of this practice.

Spoken accents—variations in the pronunciation of words—can not only dis-tinguish a speaker's origins, but also evoke value judgements and stereotypes once a listener hears only a few words (Giles and Coupland 1991: 58; Edwards 1994: 93). The immense power of accents is manifest in the United Kingdom, with its tremen-dous range of speaking styles linked to both geography and social status. Numerous studies have shown that British listeners rank speakers as more or less intelligent, trustworthy, disagreeable, and so on, based solely on which variety of English the speakers use (Aitken 1984: 526–7; Brown 1997; Giles and Coupland 1991: 48; Giles and Sassoon 1983).

The standard prestige dialect of English, characteristic of those from the upper social strata, is commonly termed 'received pronunciation' (RP), or at times 'The Queen's/King's English'. It is also known as 'BBC English', for in the early years of radio broadcasting the British Broadcasting Company adhered to a pronunciation policy recommending what a linguist has called 'broadly speaking, traditional RP' (Gimson 1984: 46).[1] The 1971 *BBC Pronouncing Dictionary of British Names* noted that until the Second World War, all announcers 'spoke the variety of Southern English known as Received Pronunciation'. Although regional accents began appearing on BBC in the 1960s (Leitner 1983: 65), in 1971 the editor of the *Pro-nouncing Dictionary* commented that '[e]ven today, the old style is still regarded as having an important place in broadcasting' (Miller 1971: v). Nearly twenty years later, a British professor of education observed that 'there is still a widespread public expectation that certain aspects, at least, of radio and television broadcasting should be transmitted in a standard accent' (Honey 1989: 32–3).

Since the establishment of local commercial radio in the UK in 1973, however, regional accents have been increasingly heard on the airwaves. One of the purposes of instituting local radio broadcasting was to serve particular communities, and

Nancy Morris, 'US Voices on UK Radio' from *European Journal of Communication*, 14/1 (1999), by permission of the publisher.

[1] Another linguist has described RP as 'loosely, old-style "BBC English"' (Miller 1996: 129).

local stations are legally bound to 'cater for the tastes and interests of persons living in the area' (United Kingdom 1990). A conspicuous way to be local is for the on-air voices to be recognizably of the community. Yet, while many commercial radio presenters sound local, many stations' identification announcements do not. Despite the vigorously local orientation of commercial stations throughout Britain, many of them feature 'drop-ins'—pre-recorded station identifications and slogans—delivered in unmistakably North American accents by voice-over artists from the United States.

The prevalence of US voices for this key image-establishing element of radio output seems initially surprising in the accent-conscious United Kingdom. In contrast to radio, television stations throughout the country feature mainly British voices on their voice-overs and announcements, as well as for news and programme presenters. Given the well-established links between language and identity (Edwards 1985; Giles and Coupland 1991: 94–108; Morris 1995: 82–4), the widespread concern about the relationship between identity and mass media (Morley and Robins 1995; De la Garde, Gilsdorf, and Wechselmann 1993; Tomlinson 1991: 34–67), and the space that local broadcast media can provide for the 'celebration of cultural distinctiveness' (Meech 1996: 81), the role of imported voices on local radio stations merits consideration.

Background

Commercial radio is relatively new in the United Kingdom. Until 1972, the only holder of a radio transmitting licence was the British Broadcasting Corporation, a non-commercial public-service broadcaster funded through compulsory annual fees paid by radio—and later TV—owners. Before the Second World War, British radio consisted of two BBC stations broadcasting mixed programming. While adapting some US formats and ideas for British audiences, the BBC was wary of the US style of broadcasting (Camporesi 1994: 626–7). After the war, it expanded its service to three national and six regional stations. The three national stations featured a varied output of music and talk, and became increasingly differentiated over time (Crisell 1986: 25–6; Briggs 1995), but none was solely dedicated to popular music; for this, UK listeners tuned in to several stations that transmitted from continental Europe, notably Radio Luxembourg (Crisell 1986: 33–4).

With little outlet on British radio for the burgeoning of rock 'n' roll, several unlicensed 'pirate' radio stations began broadcasting alternative pop and rock music in 1964. Operating from ships anchored just outside Britain's territorial waters and flying non-British 'flags of convenience', Radio Caroline, Radio London, Radio Scotland, and others may have been perceived as the domain of rogue hippies, but in fact they were successful businesses whose profits came from paid advertising. The pirate stations were largely modelled on US popular music stations. Their claims that they were providing a desired service to an underserved audience were validated by their popularity—they quickly attracted an enormous listenership (Crisell 1986: 33–4; Venmore-Rowland 1967: 108–10).

The pirate stations faced ongoing legal threats. As proposed anti-pirate legislation being considered by Parliament would affect British citizens only, offshore radio stations increasingly hired foreign on-air and support staff (Venmore-Rowland 1967: 119; Baron 1975: 49). Of fifty-two DJs whom John Venmore-Rowland (1967: 131–50) profiled in Radio Caroline, eighteen were from the United States or Canada or had spent considerable time there, and another eight were from Australia or New Zealand.

In 1967, the UK government forced the pirate stations to shut down by enacting the Marine Broadcasting (Offences) Act, prohibiting offshore transmissions aimed at Britain. The BBC, meanwhile, had got the message. It reorganized its three national stations and added a fourth. Aimed at a young audience, Radio One, the new service, was 'Britain's first legal popular music station' (Brand and Scannell 1991: 205). As another element of its 'rapidly compacted response to the radio pirates' (Tunstall 1983: 33), the BCC began establishing local radio outlets in addition to its six regional stations (Briggs 1995: 621, 623, 639–40).

A far more fundamental change was the opening up of the airwaves in 1973 to local commercial radio. Local radio stations were to be independent—that is, not linked to the BBC or any other central body—and, for the first time, licensed radio in Britain would carry advertising. Such a move had been under discussion for many years, and it was implemented upon the Conservative Party election victory in 1970. By the mid-1980s there were some fifty commercial stations throughout Britain, and by the mid-1990s that number had grown by another hundred stations.

UK radio today

In 1998, five BBC radio stations broadcast to the whole of the UK, each with a different programming focus: new and alternative rock music and youth-oriented programming; 'light' melodic music and programming aimed at the babyboomer age group; classical music and arts programming; news and information; and a new AM service of sports, news and talk. Additionally, regional BBC stations offer a mix of programming geared to local areas. The commercial radio market consists of 193 stations, with more licences to come. Three commercial stations broadcast across the UK; the others are restricted to local areas. In 1995 the BBC lost its market lead; for the first time, commercial radio accounted for more than half of all UK radio listening (Snoddy 1995).

The vast majority of commercial stations are aimed at young audiences. Of the 190 local commercial radio stations listed in the 1997 *Radio Authority Pocket Guide*, 159 describe themselves as playing some combination of contemporary hits and/or golden oldies, with varying amounts of talk, news, and sports. Of the remaining thirty-one stations, fourteen broadcast ethnic-interest or minority-language programming, three feature country music, and one offers religious programming. Some local stations are independently owned; many are part of large media conglomerates. Thirty are members of groups of three to six stations. Two companies own forty-six stations between them, nearly reaching the upper limit of permitted concentration of ownership.[2] Jointly owned AM/FM operations are common, with the AM typically playing oldies and targeted toward the 35+ age group and the FM featuring chart hits targeted at the 15–35 group.

The overall sound of UK commercial radio is often considered very American. Jeremy Tunstall (1983: 45) has commented that '[a]lthough the pirates lost the battle, what they represented—American style Top Forty radio with commercials—won the war'. During the twenty-five years of commercial radio in the UK, its US counterpart has provided a ready reference point as well as a source of personnel and material. The increasing outrageousness of present-day British breakfast radio, for example, owes much to United States 'shock jocks' such as Howard Stern, although the British version is tame by US standards.

For many stations, particularly FM contemporary music stations, sounding American in the 1990s is achieved in part by using American sounds. For example, listeners to an Edinburgh station periodically hear a forceful male US voice proclaiming 'continuous hits with less talk: simply the best, 97.3 Forth FM'. When US voices are used for such drop-ins, they are usually authentic US accents, rather than British voices attempting a US accent, or the hybrid 'mid-Atlantic' mixture of US and UK pronunciation that is often perceived as characteristic of some British popular music and media personalities (Honey 1989: 66–7).

While it is not possible to know precisely how many UK commercial radio stations use US voices for station identifications and other drop-ins, as this changes all the time, such usage is quite common.[3] One station executive commented in an interview that US voice-overs have 'become so widespread now they have become like the acceptable benchmark'. Another described her station as 'bucking the trend of a lot of commercial radio' by avoiding US accents. The head of an audio production house that supplies radio voice-overs and promos stated that a 'huge majority' of UK contemporary music stations use US accents for their voice-overs.

Curiously, this practice has attracted little attention in UK radio operating textbooks (Redfern 1978; Wilby and Conroy 1994; McLeish 1994; Kaye and Popperwell 1992).[4] Accents and local forms of speech receive mention in *Radio Production* when the communicative roles of programme presenters are discussed (McLeish 1994: 7). *Broadcast Journalism* cautions aspiring newsreaders that 'out-of-town intonations may not find favour with a local audience' (Boyd 1988: 136). *Radio Production*'s section on pronunciation focuses only on getting place names right (McLeish 1994:

[2] Under UK ownership rules, no individual or company is allowed to accumulate commercial stations whose share of the total listening audience for commercial radio totals more than 15%.

[3] Those stations that do use US voices get them through production houses or agencies, some in the UK, some in the US. One radio executive explained: 'There are a variety of people that you can call upon to do them . . . several competing agencies and production companies that supply voices'. They may buy jingle and promo packages made to their specifications. Or they may contract with an individual voice-over artist. A Welsh station executive described this process: 'We have a guy—I believe he's in L.A.—that we fax over drop-in lines—a number of them, a full page of them—from time to time and he [records them and] sends them back. They would be breakfast idents, weather idents, anything to do with maybe sponsorship'.

[4] One academic examination of radio criticizes the 'sexist mode of address' of speech on UK commercial radio, but does not mention accents (Lewis and Booth 1989: 102–3).

106); *Making Radio* mentions the importance of pronouncing people's names correctly (Kaye and Popperwell 1992: 55). *The Radio Handbook* states that voice-overs provide a station the opportunity 'to promote a particular identity that is appropriate for the target audience: an excited voice that oozes with enthusiasm for a young listenership, a mature, friendly and "educated" voice for a 40-plus, professional audience, and so on' (Wilby and Conroy 1994: 56). Yet, despite the ubiquity of US-accented drop-ins, the care taken in delineating appropriate voices for different audiences does not extend to accent. Overall, although station identifications and other drop-ins are discussed in these textbooks in terms of their purposes, uses, and production, the accents employed in them are not considered.

The study

To explore this issue I interviewed nine executives of UK commercial FM contemporary-music radio stations who had decision-making power over on-air sound. I also spoke with the head of an audio production house and one Scottish radio presenter. The radio executives represented sixteen stations: two of them held management posts at FM operations, six were responsible for joint AM/FM operations, and one oversaw two FM stations. As US voice-overs are more frequently used on youth-oriented FM stations, the interviews concentrated on FM outlets, but AM stations were also discussed. Of the ten FM stations considered here, five are in Central Scotland and five elsewhere. The Scottish stations were selected because their partially overlapping broadcast areas mean they are to varying degrees in competition with one another, and because they offered a clear contrast, since three of them use US accents for voice-overs and two do not. The other stations were chosen from a list of UK broadcasters to provide a selection of stations from across the rest of the UK. This sample was intended not to be statistically representative, but rather to provide a broad overview of commercial youth-oriented radio.

The FM stations all describe their formats as 'contemporary hits' or 'adult rock' (Radio Authority 1997). They feature lively announcers, frequent small-scale competitions, and contemporary popular music interspersed with talk, sports coverage, and listeners' phone calls. All of them link broadcast segments with pre-recorded voice-over announcements ranging from the name of the station to sung jingles to punchy slogans ('Clyde One FM—the best in the West'). Six of the ten FM stations represented in this study use US accents for station identification announcements and slogans.

Accents on UK radio

Interviewees distinguished between the desirable qualities of on-air voices used for presenters, newsreaders, advertisements, and drop-ins. The preference for local presenters was pronounced. Cool FM in Belfast was the only station that had a North American presenter:

Northern Ireland: One of our DJs here [is] a Canadian girl, which in Northern Ireland, it wouldn't really make any difference whether it's Canadian or American, you know? It's sort of seen as an American accent. . . . That sort of stands out and . . . we see it as an advantage in the fact that it is something slightly different from the other stations.

A contrasting perspective was expressed by a Scottish interviewee:

Scotland 1: It's a funny thing that everybody who wants to be a disc jockey thinks they should put a mid-Atlantic accent on. But the reality is, whenever you hear a tape with a mid-Atlantic accent, you go, 'Oh God no, not again!'

The importance of presenters having local accents was mentioned by several station executives:

Scotland 3: The people who you recruit on air are local people who speak with various forms of accent in the various forms of colloquialisms, which are recognized, which actually show that we are distinct and different . . . and that we are proud of our area and that we care for it.

Scotland 4: We would hope that we have a kind of local sound and not necessarily sound mid-Atlantic as some of the other stations tend to do.

England 2: We really are trying to sound as much like a Lincolnshire radio station as possible. . . . I have continued saying no to American voices.

A manager at an English station mused on the thought processes of radio station decision-makers:

England 1: I think a lot of . . . programmers would shy away from hiring a main-line presenter from the States. . . . I think they are a little afraid of the acceptability in the UK marketplace, and will think: 'OK, what is my average listener going to think? Is he going to think: "American voice, yes, I am going to tune in, listen longer"? Or is he going to think: "Oh, hang on a minute, that sounds different . . . I am a bit afraid of *different* so I am going to retune to the other station down the road"?' . . . I think there is a differentiation between [presenters and drop-ins]. . . . And I think . . . as long as the programming is knitted together with a UK voice they'll be OK.

Among interviewees, the preference for local accents did not apply solely to presenters. Two of the Scottish managers specifically mentioned that they preferred local voices for newscast anchors as well.

Scotland 3: The newscasters . . . have that lovely Scottish burr in their voice which we think is so important . . . So, yes . . . we like to preserve the way they communicate with the audience and because we think it's important to show that we are local. We can do that through accent.

Scotland 2: I prefer us to have Scottish [news] readers, that's for sure.

The greatest range of accents on British commercial radio is heard in advertisements, which feature a multiplicity of types of UK regional speech—Cockney, various Scottish, RP, and many others—as well as Irish, Australian, North American, and genuine or feigned accents of non-native speakers of English.[5] Several interviewees commented on the use of accents in advertisements. In this case, the emphasis was on the 'fit' between the product advertised and the type of voice used to advertise it.

Northern Ireland: Is it something that needs to be a bit wacky? And, you know, upbeat? Then they would tend to go for either like a game-show voice locally, or an American voice . . . something to pick it up a wee bit more.

Wales: I did some work for an American doughnut franchise. . . . And we did some radio commercials for them and we used an American voice because the fit was good. . . . It was all about American flavour, the blueberry dip . . . and the strawberry. But his delivery of those names! 'Straw-ber-ry'.

While interviewees had no qualms about using US accents for advertisements if they were appropriate to the product, it was clear that in this context the choice of US voices was a calculated decision. The same cannot be said of the use of US accents for drop-ins.

The use of US accents for drop-ins

The precise awareness of variations in pronunciation exhibited by programming executives when they talked of presenters and advertisements is indicative of the care taken in defining the 'sound' of a radio station. Voice-over recordings and drop-ins (also called 'sweepers') are vital components of a station's sound, linking together programme segments, and repeating crucial information—the station's name, slogan, and wavelength. Yet, when asked why they used US accents for drop-ins, several executives did not have a ready answer. One interviewee's comment that 'It seems that it's always been done that way' (England 3) indicates that US voices on drop-ins were simply taken for granted as part of commercial radio. Discussing this question, interviewees came up with three groups of explanations for their use. US voices set station identification announcements apart; they evoke favourable associations with US popular culture; and they are a historical remnant of the early days of British commercial radio.

Distinctiveness

A distinctive voice for drop-ins was preferred in order to differentiate station logos from other on-air material. The production-house executive suggested that this separation of audio elements was fundamental:

Having an American accent and a different voice separates the station ID from the commercials. . . . Of course people don't want to pay huge amounts of money to make a voice exclusive. So the easy and cheap answer was to use American voices. As far as I know, most

---

[5] See Montgomery (1995: 73) for a discussion of the use of accents in British television advertising.

people use Americans that are based in America; certainly all the voices I supply are from America.

Such differentiation was cited by the Welsh station executive as a factor in his choice of US voice-over artist:

The guy we use obviously doesn't present any form of programme, so any work that he does stands apart. . . . It doesn't pale into normal programming.

Other interviewees confirmed that using a non-local accent was seen as a quick way to differentiate station announcements. But, of course, this need not necessarily be a United States accent. One of the Scottish stations uses an English voice for drop-ins, somewhat surprising given the general antagonism to the English in Scotland.

Scotland 4: When you have drop-ins like that, throughout the programming, it is always best to have a voice which isn't on air anyway.

Asked whether an English accent was an issue in Scotland, he replied, 'I don't think it's tremendously important what particular kind of voice you use for something like that as long as it's radio-friendly.' Other station executives were less open to using accents from other regions. They provided several reasons for bypassing the vast repertoire of UK accents in their attempts to achieve auditory distinctiveness.

Wales: In Wales, why don't we use an English drop-in? . . . I think it's just the Americanness, for want of a better word, it's just the unique delivery and it's the way that it's put across.

A Scottish executive stated that he might use a 'flat' or neutral English accent, but not an accent that was very strong and locally specific.

Scotland 3: What I wouldn't do is have a Yorkshire or a Geordie [Newcastle] accent or a Liverpool accent . . . because that is . . . so unbelievable and so wrong.

Nor, he continued, alluding to RP, would he use a 'toffee-nosed accent which might get up a lot of people's back because it brings with it a consciousness of class, and it brings with it that kind of problem.'

The interviewee from the Northern Ireland station explained the choice of a US accent as one that would be understood across a great range of local Northern Irish accents which were not necessarily mutually intelligible:

There are so many different regions here, there are so many voices you can't actually use, because . . . it's a very, very thick brogue and people wouldn't really understand it. So we tend to use voices that would be a lot clearer.

The lack of appeal of UK regional accents because of their local specificity and whatever associations they may evoke makes non-British accents attractive by default. But radio stations could use any number of accents, such as Antipodean or Caribbean or Indian, not to mention, say, the voices of Italians or Russians or other non-native speakers of English. They choose US accents for other reasons: the perceived appeal to younger listeners of US-style delivery and the popular culture it is linked to; relatedly, the perceived intrinsic superiority of US voices for radio; and the established history of US voices on UK commercial radio.

Style

A particular style of radio delivery—brash, emphatic, and male—was perceived to have originated in the United States and thought best achieved by US voices. This was linked to a sense of the United States as a source of much youth-oriented popular culture, a connection felt to be a positive one for the stations' target audiences.

Wales: There is so much in this country that has come across from America. I mean, at kids' level, the skateboard, wearing your cap back-to-front, a hundred other things the kids can associate with that, so on FM when they hear an American voice, it's cool, it's good, you know?

Northern Ireland: We use [US accent] quite often actually in [drop-ins] because it gives a . . . sort of youthful image. . . . The AM station is mainly into the thirty plus audience, where the FM would be the fifteen- to thirty-four-year-olds. . . . The American accents [on FM] tie in with youth popular culture.

Wales: FM just is perceived—the younger generation. We feel that the voice extols youth. . . . We do use it on AM, but ask [the voice-over artist] to sort of calm down the delivery.

Scotland 1: The voices that you are talking about, the jingles and promotions and things like that, that is more to do with the style, to do with the trend, to do with fashion, to do with what the kids on the street go with. For instance, they'll buy Levi's, they'll move with something, one particular thing, or sound, and it is all to do with feeling sexy, feeling right, feeling in touch with a sort of happening scene.

England 1: These British voices are good but sometimes don't reflect these real contemporary values that these programmers need and enough attitude, do you know what I mean? And I think that it's sometimes the attitude angle that the radio stations are looking for and again it becomes a first choice to have these American sweepers. . . . Those great-big American voice-overs . . . are very nineties contemporary, cutting-edge.

This executive then spoke of his previous post at another radio station:

In my last job . . . I chose . . . for my sweeper packages a UK voice. He is very good, a very deep voice, very punchy, quite attitudinal. That was, for me . . . one step shy of going for an American voice-over.

Vocal power

This appreciation of US style was also linked, in some cases, to the notion that US voices were more powerful and US accents carried more authority, or were more convincing, than British ones. Several interviewees commented on the actual quality of the voices, at times conflating the sound of vocal delivery—a product of genetics and training—with the accent that those voices speak in.

Scottish DJ: It's that kind of butchness which a Scottish accent doesn't really accommodate. I mean, if I did it, I'd just sound ridiculous . . . an American accent at least sounds fairly convincing. . . . People think, 'Oh, must have some authority' . . . because it's so deep and because it's so resonant.

England 1: The texture and tone of the voices are just right and I think that the American markets have become so, so—refined, if you like—that these main-line voice-over artists working in America have got it down to a fine art.

Scotland 3: When you are trying to develop a sense of credibility and a sense of warmth, there is a very recognizable technique which is basically using a very rich, deep American voice which somehow or other seems to be the norm.

Wales: The strength of the voice that he's offering is something. . . . It's the accent, I guess. . . . I think it's a mixture of the voice, the quality.

English production-house head: People . . . love the big American lines and the big production values which would sound stupid with English people saying them . . . and it's very difficult to find English voices anywhere that have some sort of power to them. . . . To a British ear, hearing a British person saying something that's supposed to be cool never sounds as good.

Statements about the inherently superior tonal quality and power of US voices can be easily refuted by citing renowned British actors such as Laurence Olivier or Sean Connery. The unexamined assumptions about US voices may be due to the other key determining factor of the sound of British drop-ins: the presence of US influence from the beginnings of UK radio.

Precedent

When commercial radio began in the UK, with pirate broadcasting and later with legally sanctioned commercial broadcasting, radio entrepreneurs looked to the United States for ideas (Baron 1975: 98), as had BBC personnel before them (Camporesi 1994). The US was seen by interviewees as the originator of commercial radio and of the particular style of fast-moving, fast-talking radio that many UK youth-oriented stations emulate.

Scotland 1: Commercial radio basically grew up in America and so many of the ideas that have come into UK radio has just been us catching up. . . . In the pirate days when all the pirate stations needed jingles . . . quite a few of them stole American jingle packages! . . . The only people that existed were the American ones.

Scotland 3: I think we wouldn't actually have these accents if we had had commercial radio at the same time as the States. . . . When commercial radio was first starting up here, we were consuming American-style commercial radio because that is where it had established a base. And American DJs were shipped into the ships. There were all these characters who . . . were passing on: 'This is how you do it, chum.' So there was a transatlantic feel about that.

Scotland 4: Radio has been around a lot longer in that form in America than it has in this country. So . . . they have had time to naturally develop. What's been done here is that people have gone across to the States on holiday, or for work, and they have heard these stations and they've come back and they've thought: 'Well, maybe we should try this.'

Wales: I think . . . within radio, in this country, and to people who work in radio, there is a high regard for radio in America, which is where, obviously, radio is huge.

England 3: They heard it sound great over there and want it to sound great over here.

England 2: I kind of feel that it all dates back to when commercial radio first started in this country . . . and of course Americans have been doing it for years and a lot of people who started in commercial radio then felt, well, the Americans know what they are doing, there's a lot of people will listen to Americans. I mean, we all listen to American radio when we can; it is seen as . . . the birthplace of how to do pop commercial radio.

This perception that the US is the source of this style of radio brings with it the impetus to imitation. Similarly, since the 1960s, many British rock musicians have not only borrowed rhythm and blues styles from the United States but have also imitated US accents in their singing. Linguist Peter Trudgill (1983: 144) suggests that their adoption of a US form extends beyond purely musical elements because it is felt to be 'appropriate to sound like an American when performing in what is predominantly an American activity'. This observation is equally applicable to radio.

The avoidance of US accents for drop-ins

Of the ten FM stations represented in this study, four—two in Scotland and two in England—did not use US accents. Executives cited various reasons for this choice. The programme-controller of a small Scottish station that uses an English voice for some announcements explained that these voice-overs were recorded by an English employee of another radio station owned by the same company, and therefore did not cost his station anything to produce. In contrast, one well-resourced English station does not use US accents because 'we are part of the GWR radio group and they have gone for a highly processed, less American-sounding voice'. GWR is one of the two largest radio groups in Britain, and has a group-wide policy guiding on-air sound. The other large radio group, EMAP, does not have a group-wide policy for voice-overs, but, according to an interviewee from an EMAP station, most EMAP stations use US voices for station identification.

Executives at the other two stations that did not use US accents made this decision because of their explicit concern with creating a local sound.

England 2: We are a local station, therefore we want to sound local. And I don't really see the point of trying to sound American.

This interviewee added that her station does buy jingles from US production houses, but 'we have them resung by English singers. . . . I mean, accents are quite important.[6]

The other Scottish station that does not use US accents plays heavily on its Scottishness, from its name—Scot FM—to slogans such as 'The station for our nation' and 'The voice of Scotland'. Although it did have some US-accented drop-ins when it first went on the air in 1994, it has moved away from this, perhaps due to the shuffling of decision-makers. The station executive interviewed explained that 'It just doesn't sound right to have an American saying, "This is Scotland's station"'. But, he noted, it had not been easy to find a satisfactory Scottish voice for drop-ins.

The problem that causes us, then, is just to find the right voice. We found somebody but he is difficult to use because he is far away and he doesn't have facilities so it's costly. It is inconvenient but there doesn't seem to be a better option. . . . He's actually an actor, he is not a voice-over artist at all. He was spotted on [TV] . . . and we thought 'Oh, let's give that a try.' I mean, he wasn't particularly good at doing the voice-over and took a lot of coaching to get what we wanted. And it was hard work.

The interviewee explained that there are not many Scottish voice-over artists, and that those who are established 'do the commercial circuit'. The station does not want to use a voice for station identification that is also heard on commercials, 'because he is our sound of the station, if you like'.

The difficulty of finding appropriate local voices, or 'talent', as on-air presenters are termed in the business, was confirmed by other interviewees. The programme-controller of the Scottish station that uses an English announcer for its drop-ins stated, 'It's difficult to find a good Scottish voice for something like that'. Both the interviewee from the English station that does not use US accents and the Welsh station executive concurred:

England 2: I can imagine that they have trouble finding Scottish voices. I mean, I can't find that many good Lincolnshire voices.

Wales: You find that a great deal of the talent within Wales moves out of Wales . . . or goes into television, where the better-paid jobs are.

Despite any difficulties there may be finding local vocal talent, there are signs that UK commercial radio's utilization of US voices is on the wane. Interviewee Scotland 4, from the Scottish station that uses an English voice as a cost-cutting measure, was not particularly enthusiastic about US accents and said that, even if he could afford to use them, he would be disinclined to do so: 'I don't see the great attraction to American voices'. Perhaps the use of US accents is a fad that is approaching the end of its cycle of popularity. Interviewee England 1, from the GWR radio group, implied as much when he said that his station's use of a 'less American-sounding' voice-over artist 'does actually make a refreshing change from some of the voices that you hear on all the radio stations at the moment'. The interviewee from a Scottish station that makes extensive use of US accents for drop-ins made it clear that his station was open to change:

Scotland 1: If it works we are happy to go for it. So the fact that it is American is neither here nor there. . . . Although it probably sounds sexy to have that, I don't know, but it certainly is

---

[6] So important are accents that, when making the jingle that is played underneath this station's weather forecasts, an elaborate arrangement was undertaken. The interviewee explained that the station's broadcasting area straddles two areas that have different pronunciations of the word 'forecast'.

'We had a bit of a dilemma . . . so we have got a four-track thing, and two people are on it singing "forecahst" and two people singing "forecast". So whichever you say, hopefully, that is the one you hear. . . . That is important to us, just getting that sort of thing right'.

effective. . . . We have a fair degree of research that goes on and I'll not go beyond that because I don't want to reveal too much about what techniques we use. . . . It works at the moment so we'll use it, but we are always looking at different ways of . . . making good, entertaining, exciting radio for our target audience.

Several interviewees spoke of an increasing self-confidence in the UK, attributing it variously to the new political climate brought about by the election of a Labour government; to the ascendance of London, in particular, in the world hipness sweepstakes and, in Scotland, to the recent moves toward political devolution. This confidence has, they say, brought with it a desire to reduce the use of US accents. The executive from an English station that does not use US accents said, 'I think it's only fairly recently that perhaps we've had the confidence in our product to actually make it sound local to us.' A similar sentiment was expressed by a Scottish radio executive, who said he was trying to move away from the use of US voice-overs.

Scotland 3: I think [the use of US accents] is diminishing. I think also there is a greater sense of confidence in attitude . . . not only what we do on air but within the community itself. . . . It's difficult to research that, but it's just a feeling you get.

Since the time of the interview, this station, while continuing to air numerous drop-ins by a US announcer, has added a new jingle. Ending with that most American of phrases, 'Have a nice day', the jingle is sung by evidently English singers in ferocious Britpop style.

The head of an audio production house, writing in a trade magazine of the recent switch from US to UK voice-overs by two major London stations, said, 'There are still strong arguments both for and against US voices.' He stressed that US voices were a significant way of ensuring that station identification did not 'merge with the commercials and DJs on the station'. But using British voices, he countered, can evoke 'the "We're once again the world's coolest city" feel-good factor that's doing the rounds' (Sandman 1997). Perhaps related to this resurgence of 'cool Britannia', a reverse trend is perceptible. In an interview, the audio production-house director mentioned that he is now 'getting an awful lot of calls from American stations looking for English voices and that's happening in a lot of big markets now. In Los Angeles particularly is where it started. I'm now supplying English voices to America and American voices to England.'

As is increasingly being pointed out, cultural influences flow in many directions, if not always as visibly as they flow outwards from the United States (Sokolov 1991; van Hemel, Mommaas, and Smithuijsen 1996). Imitation is commonplace when forms originating in one culture are adopted into another. Staying in the realm of accents, it is not only British rhythm 'n' blues singers who mimic the accents that come with the musical form. US musical groups, to cite just one other example, often affect Jamaican intonation when singing reggae songs. This pattern of imitation of elements that accompany cultural forms also helps explain 'the quasiEnglish accents adopted by American Shakespearean actors even when acting in plays set in, for example, Verona' (Trudgill 1983: 145). It is easy to overlook such examples of cultural influences entering the US, rather than issuing from it, just as some UK radio executives take for granted the source of the voices they put on the air. But it is worth noting that the flow of cultural influences is not unidirectional.

Discussion

Interviewees frequently cited the longstanding identification of commercial broadcasting with the United States as a primary cause of the use of US voices for station identification. Since the beginnings of British commercial radio, station executives have regarded US radio as a fundamental frame of reference and source of ideas. One chronicler of pirate radio has suggested that '[t]he most important thing about the pirate era was that it showed the people what commercial radio could sound like' (Baron 1975: 55). In addition to the historic influence of the United States, interviewees identified the auditory distinctiveness provided by a different accent and the allure of a 'showbusiness' sound as reasons for the use of US voices. Beneath these explicit reasons, I would suggest, lie two others: in the context of the UK, this type of voice is perceived as class-free, and in the context of present-day youth culture the voice verges on being nationality-free as well.

First, US accents may serve a purpose specific to the UK by bypassing the social inequalities coded in British speech (Honey 1989: 72). Thus, a radio station can identify itself with a voice that does not alienate potential listeners by evoking negative responses based on the perceived class of the speaker. This may also explain in part the choice of US accents over, say, Caribbean ones, which carry implied lower status in British society. This class-evading function was alluded to by some interviewees.

Second, in addition to the absence of social-class markers, US accents also seem to transcend nationality. Interviewees were forthright and nearly unanimous about the positive associations with contemporary youth culture of the voices they choose for drop-ins. Honey (1989: 72) argues that 'the American accent is to some extent glamorized' by the film and television industries, to which we can add, as interviewees did, its association with Coke, Levi's, trainers, baseball caps and countless other youth-oriented products. But British enthusiasm for the United States is ambivalent. Given the sometimes derisive attitudes in the UK toward various aspects of the US, its inhabitants, its media, and its cultures, using US accents may be risky for an audience-dependent medium. However, the glamorous associations attributed to US voices attach neither to a randomly selected US voice, nor to an identifiable US regional accent. They attach, rather, to a particular style: forceful and exaggerated—or, in interviewees' words, 'great-big', 'attitudinal', 'punchy', 'butch'—carried in regionally non-specific tones. This energetic style of delivery has been associated with US announcers since as early as the 1930s, when a BBC magazine noted 'the full-blooded zest' of a US presenter's 'approach to the microphone' (*Radio Times*, cited in Camporesi 1994: 627). With the spread of US media products, a generic US accent coupled to a high-powered vocal style seems to have shed specific national associations, becoming instead a sort of 'free-floating international accent' (Mike Cormack, personal communication, 1998), indexing youth, commercialized popular culture, and modernity. This vocal style is part of a complex of experiences, advertisements, and products of 'Americanised yet international youth culture' (Meyers 1998: 35). A study of responses to advertisements for such products as Levi's and trainers, for example, showed that, for South Asian teenagers in London, 'Being "cool" . . . is a matter of detachment from specifically local, territorially based styles' (Gillespie 1995: 182). Radio identifications are in a sense advertisements for the station, and in this context it makes sense that they are put forward in the US voice and vocal style that I will term 'international pop-speak'.

Using this 'international pop-speak' rather than local voices for station identification announcements was, for interviewees, a way of plugging into youth culture, which is seen as global. The trend for commercial radio stations even in non-English-speaking Western European countries to use drop-ins in the English language by US voice-over artists[7] indicates the powerful presence of 'international pop-speak' in commercial youth-oriented radio.

These findings could be taken to substantiate fears that the import or imitation of US-originated popular culture threatens to override local forms of expression, and that an over-reliance on US-derived forms may encourage importing communities to undervalue their own cultures (Schiller 1976; Katz and Wedell 1977; International Commission for the Study of Communication Problems 1980; Starowicz 1993). The extent to which interviewees took for granted the use of US accents for drop-ins in UK radio was striking. Even more notable was some interviewees' muddling of vocal quality and accent, apparently reflecting a sense of inadequacy concerning British voices.[8] However, the unquestioning acceptance by some UK radio executives of this form of 'pop-speak' did not extend to programme presenters; for most interviewees, US accents were acceptable only within the restricted framework of drop-ins and advertisements.

It could be argued that British commercial radio stations uphold the distinctiveness of the communities they serve—and profit from—by being sensitive to local concerns, and by providing local weather, news, traffic information and advertisements—features often highlighted as keys to local radio service (Wilby and Conroy 1994: 46–7; Barnett and Morrison, 1989: 54–61; Briggs 1995: 631). To critics like Hans J. Kleinsteuber (1992: 149), who has described European radio content as 'pseudo-local', this is not sufficient because 'the most local elements of this programming might be the DJ's local dialect . . . and the commercials for local businesses'. But such a critique does not take into account the enormous power of accent, which is perhaps one of the strongest ways of establishing a local identity. These stations are not the community open forums called for by advocates of a more participatory model of community broadcasting, but they do retain a local

---

[7] I have confirmed such usage in Italy, Germany, Greece, Turkey, and Israel.

[8] Linguists have demonstrated that speakers of non-standard regional language varieties in the UK and elsewhere tend to evaluate standard language varieties more favourably than their own manner of speaking (Miller 1996: 128; Giles and Coupland 1991: 48). In *The Eclipse of Scottish Culture*, Beveridge and Turnbull (1989: 15) observed a tendency in Scotland to regard 'specifically Scottish culture' such as language 'as inferior to metropolitan styles'. The authors thoroughly rebut various discourses that they say contribute to a negative Scottish self-image.

identity. UK radio sounds local precisely because of the local accents and vocabularies that prevail in the presenters who introduce the music, interact with listeners on the telephone, and link together programme elements.

In the face of much concern about imported media and identities, some recent analyses have suggested that local communities are not becoming homogenized, but rather are expressing their distinctiveness through both adhering to their own traditions and devising local versions of international styles (Dowmunt 1993; McQuail 1996). British commercial radio provides an example of this 'localization of the global' (Tehranian and Tehranian 1997: 157). US influence is reflected in the style of many programmes and in the US voices announcing station names in 'international pop-speak'. Yet, hearing its versions of breakfast and talk radio, its homey phone-ins, and its particularities of music and humour, no listener could deny the underlying Britishness of British radio. An analysis of early UK radio similarly concluded that, even when BBC programmes were copies of US formats, the final product still remained peculiarly British (Camporesi 1994: 636). There are specifically British reasons for the present-day prominence of US voices on UK radio, as well as reasons that are associated with the position of the United States as the dominant exporter of media and popular culture. The intersection of these reasons, and the adaptation of a US form to a British foundation, has resulted in the particular amalgam that is British commercial radio. Interviewees' insistence on British presenters highlights the role of US voices as different, and as having the function of punctuating the programming and advertising the station rather than dominating broadcast output. Local culture remains conspicuous in UK radio, even when communicated with elements of a commercial form that was developed in the United States.

Acknowledgements

I am grateful to the interviewees for their time and insights. I would also like to thank Suzy Angus, Mike Cormack, Gillian Doyle, Stephanie Marriott, Peter Meech, Jonathan Ray, Philip Schlesinger, and Deborah G. Stinnett for helpful comments, and William Dinan, Deirdre Kevin, and Richard Haynes for innumerable favours.

References

Aitken, A.J. (1984) 'Scots and English in Scotland', in P. Trudgill (ed.), *Language in the British Isles*. Cambridge: Cambridge University Press, 517–32.

Barnett, S., and Morrison, D. (1989). *The Listener Speaks: The Radio Audience and the Future of Radio*. London: HMSO.

Baron, M. (1975). *Independent Radio: The Story of Commercial Radio in the United Kingdom*. Lavenham, Suffolk: Terence Dalton.

Beveridge, C., and Turnbull, R. (1989). *The Eclipse of Scottish Culture: Inferiorism and the Intellectuals*. Edinburgh: Polygon.

Boyd, A. (1988). *Broadcast Journalism: Techniques of Radio and TV News*. Oxford: Heinemann.

Brand, G., and Scannell, P. (1991). 'Talk, Identity and Performance: The Tony Blackburn Show', in P. Scannell (ed.), *Broadcast Talk*. London: Sage, 201–26.

Briggs, A. (1995). *The History of Broadcasting in the United Kingdom*, vol. 5: *Competition 1955–1974*. Oxford: Oxford University Press.

Brown, D. (1997). 'Courts "Deplore" Brummie Accent'. *Guardian*, 25 September: 7.

Camporesi, V. (1994). 'The BBC and American Broadcasting, 1922–55'. *Media, Culture and Society*, 16/4: 625–39.

Crisell, A. (1986). *Understanding Radio*. London: Methuen.

De la Garde, R., Gilsdorf, W., and Wechselmann, I. (eds.) (1993). *Small Nations, Big Neighbour: Denmark and Quebec/Canada Compare Notes on American Popular Culture*. London: John Libbey.

Dowmunt, T. (ed.) (1993). *Channels of Resistance: Global Television and Local Empowerment*. London: British Film Institute.

Edwards, J. (1985). *Language, Society and Identity*. Oxford: Basil Blackwell.

——(1994). *Multilingualism*. London: Penguin.

Giles, H., and Coupland, N. (1991). *Language: Contexts and Consequences*. Milton Keynes: Open University Press.

Giles, H., and Sassoon, C. (1983). 'The Effect of Speaker's Accent, Social Class Background and Message Style on British Listeners' Social Judgements'. *Language and Communication*, 3/3: 305–13.

Gillespie, M. (1995). *Television, Ethnicity and Cultural Change*. London: Routledge.

Gimson, A. C. (1984). 'The RP Accent', in P. Trudgill (ed.), *Language in the British Isles*. Cambridge: Cambridge University Press, 45–54.

Honey, J. (1989). *Does Accent Matter?* London: Faber and Faber.

International Commission for the Study of Communication Problems (1980). *Many Voices, One World*. Paris: UNESCO.

Katz, E., and Wedell, G. (1977). *Broadcasting in the Third World: Promise and Performance*. London: Macmillan.

Kaye, M., and Popperwell, A. (1992). *Making Radio: A Guide to Basic Radio Techniques*. London: Broadside.

Kleinsteuber, H. J. (1992). 'The Global Village Stays Local', in K. Siune and W. Treutzschler (eds.). *Dynamics of Media Politics*. London: Sage, 143–53.

Leitner, G. (1983). 'The Social Background of the Language of Radio', in H. Davis and P. Walton (eds.), *Language, Image, Media*. Oxford: Basil Blackwell, 50–74.

Lewis, P. M., and Booth, K. (1989). *The Invisible Medium: Public, Commercial and Community Radio*. London: Macmillan.

Martín Barbero, J. (1997). 'Cultural Decentring and Palimpsests of Identity'. *Media Development*, 44/1: 18–21.

McLeish, R. (1994). *Radio Production: A Manual for Broadcasters* (3rd edn.). Oxford: Focal Press.

McQuail, D. (1996). 'Transatlantic TV flow: Another look at cultural costaccounting'. In A. van Hemel, H. Mommaas, and C. Smithuijsen (eds.), *Trading Culture: GATT, European Cultural Policies and the Transatlantic Market*. Amsterdam: Boekman Foundation, 111–25.

Meech, P. (1996). 'The Lion, the Thistle, and the Saltire: National Symbols and Corporate Identity in Scottish Broadcasting'. *Screen*, 37/1 68–81.

Meyers, C. B. (1998). 'Global Marketing and the New Hollywood: The Making of the "Always Coca-Cola" campaign'. *Media Information Australia*, 86, February: 27–37.

Miller, G. M. (ed.) (1971). *BBC Pronouncing Dictionary of British Names*. London: Oxford University Press.

Miller, J. (1996). 'Language Attitudes and Scottish Inferiority'. *Scottish Affairs* 15: 128–33.

Montgomery, M. (1995). *An Introduction to Language and Society*. London: Routledge.

Morley, D., and Robins, K. (1995). *Spaces of Identity: Global Media, Electronic Landscapes and Cultural Boundaries*. London: Routledge.

Morris, N. (1995). *Puerto Rico: Culture, Politics, and Identity*. Westport, CT: Praeger.

Radio Authority (1997). *Pocket Guide*. London: Radio Authority.

Redfern, B. (1978). *Local Radio*. London: Focal Press.

The Sandman (1997). 'Voicing an Opinion'. *X-Trax: The Magazine*, December 1997–January 1998: 188.

Schiller, H. L. (1976). *Communication and Cultural Domination*. White Plains, NY: M. E. Sharpe.

Snoddy, R. (1995). 'Commercial Stations are Winning'. *Financial Times*, 20 September: 36.

Sokolov, R. (1991). *Why We Eat What We Eat: How the Encounter between the New World and the Old Changed the Way Everyone on the Planet Eats*. New York: Touchstone.

Starowicz, M. (1993). 'Citizens of Video-America: What Happened to Canadian Television in the Satellite age', in R. de la Garde, W. Gilsdorf, and I. Wechselmann (eds.), *Small Nations, Big Neighbour: Denmark and Quebec/Canada Compare Notes on American Popular Culture*. London: John Libbey, 83–102.

Tehranian, M., and Tehranian, K. (1997). 'Taming Modernity: Towards a New Paradigm', in A. Mohammadi (ed.), *International Communication and Globalization*. London: Sage, 119–67.

Tomlinson, J. (1991). *Cultural Imperialism*. London: Pinter.

Trudgill, P. (1983). 'Acts of Conflicting Identity: The Sociolinguistics of British Pop-song Pronunciation', in P. Trudgill (ed.), *On Dialect: Social and Geographical Perspectives*. Oxford: Basil Blackwell, 141–60.

Tunstall, J. (1983). *The Media in Britain*. London: Constable.

United Kingdom (1990). *Broadcasting Act*. London: HMSO.

Van Hemel, A., Mommaas, H., and Smithuijsen, C. (eds.) (1996). *Trading Culture: GATT, European Cultural Policies and the Transatlantic Market*. Amsterdam: Boekman Foundation.

Venmore-Rowland, J. (1967). *Radio Caroline*. Lavenham, Suffolk: Landmark Press.

Wilby, P., and Conroy, A. (1994). *The Radio Handbook*. London: Routledge.

Chapter 9
Intoxicating Consumptions: the Case of Beer Commercials
Lance Strate

HOWEVER problematic late capitalism's culture of consumption may be, it is still possible to make distinctions among the commercial products that are consumed. Some products we may judge to be relatively innocuous, others downright harmful; in this way, we might engage in a kind of sociocultural triage, and give particular attention to those products that pose marked health and safety risks. And while we may not always want to control or prohibit such products, either for reasons of preserving individual freedom, or simply because such efforts are not worth the time, energy, or cost, we still may question whether we want to permit their promotion. In the United States, we have already said no to tobacco advertising, at least on television, and further controls on non-broadcast marketing and promotions are forthcoming. Few would argue that these measures are inappropriate, outside the tobacco industry and their advertisers. If anything, the past few years have seen the tobacco industry's stonewall topple nearly as fast as the Berlin Wall, and we have learned how it, quite cynically, has pursued strategies to promote its products among children and teenagers, and in full knowledge of the associated health risks (see Jacobson and Mazur 1995, for a discussion and analysis of tobacco advertising).

American firearms manufacturers and retailers generally limit themselves to fairly modest local campaigns, but can you imagine a nationally aired series of commercials romantically depicting the use of high-powered rifles, machine-guns, and pistols to blow away human-shaped targets? Or gun ads depicting homeowners firing at would-be burglars, or billboards extolling the destructive power of hollow-point and teflon-coated bullets? Should the gun industry be allowed to continue, let alone extend its promotional efforts that target children (see Herbert 1999, for a critique of such practices)? Knowing that we pay a heavy price in human life for our right to bear arms in the US, might not gun control also include restrictions on advertising? Is there a point at which the risk to public safety and security outweighs commercial rights to freedom of speech?

Along the same lines, given the problem of gambling addiction, should race-tracks and state-sponsored lotteries be allowed to promote these activities, as they do in much of the United States and elsewhere? The problem is not one of virtue and vice; it is a matter of public health and safety. Moreover, the issue I am addressing here is not whether these practices and products ought to be outlawed, but instead whether they should be encouraged. The question is one not of prohibition, but rather of promotion. It is true that in the United States the First Amendment affords some protection for commercial speech, but we are also within our rights to regulate and limit advertising messages (e.g., truth in advertising laws), especially those that are carried via publicly owned airwaves.

Like tobacco, firearms, gambling, and prostitution, alcohol is a product associated with considerable health and safety risks, including addiction and disease, death and injury due to drunk driving, and sexual abuse, rape, and other forms of violence connected to intoxication. Of course, it is also a product that is in many ways socially acceptable, pleasurable, possibly healthy in small amounts, and in some instances required for religious observances. How, then, can we discourage abuse, short of altogether prohibiting use? One thing that we can do is simply put an end to advertising for these products. Over ten years ago, I served as part of a research team that examined the messages of beer commercials and their relationship to the social problem of drunk driving; in our report, (Postman *et al.* 1987), my colleagues and I recommended banning or restricting beer commercials in the United States, not as a panacea, but as one of a number of steps that need to be taken in order to foster change.

After all, the presence of beer advertising, especially on television, implies that the product is no different from toothpaste, candy, or soda pop. Eliminating the commercials would more clearly indicate that this is an adult product, and one that is potentially dangerous. Given the ban on cigarette commercials and the voluntary abstinence on the part of the hard-liquor industry, a ban on the broadcast advertising of beer, and perhaps all alcoholic products, would establish a more consistent policy than we have now. Also, the sheer number of beer commercials works against any attempts at social marketing. Public-service campaigns can achieve only limited results when competing with the 'Don't worry, be happy' advertising of the beer industry. Unless equal time were provided, banning beer ads would be the only way to give social marketing a chance. Influenced in part by our study, the Department of Health and Human Services (1988: 29) recommended that advertisers should not 'portray activities that can be dangerous when combined with alcohol use', or 'use celebrities with a strong appeal to youth'. These efforts did lead to some modification of the industry's behaviour, including its sponsorship of public-service spots advocating responsible drinking, but the changes were small and short-lived. Addicted as they are to sales and profits, the alcohol industry and its advertisers simply cannot be trusted to act in the interests of public welfare. And, given the enormous political power wielded by the alcohol lobby, there is little motivation to do so (Massing 1998).

At the same time, direct efforts to deal with health and safety issues, such as law enforcement, medical and psychological services, information programmes, and persuasive campaigns, all have enjoyed limited success. These efforts should not be abandoned, but alone they are not enough. Curtailing the problems associated with alcohol abuse will require more than modifying behaviours, increasing knowledge, and changing attitudes; it will require cultural change. As the anthropologist Mary Douglas (1987) demonstrates, drinking is both a social activity and a cultural construction. This indicates that alcohol-related problems are culture-specific, and in

large part culturally produced. In the case of societies characterized by late capitalism, that culture is permeated and often produced by cultural industries that
include the mass media (Jameson 1991; Schiller 1989). Under such circumstances,
agents seeking to generate cultural change do not face the same barriers as exist in
more traditional societies. Advertisers and the mass media are in the business of
instigating continuous cultural change and upheaval. And sometimes these modifi-
cations and mutations favour the interests of public health and safety—witness the
changes regarding tobacco use that have occurred over the past few decades. But
even advanced technological cultures are far from easy to change, and cultural
problems can be reinforced in a variety of ways. Advertising is one such way, and
my own research indicates that alcohol advertisers will incorporate pre-existing
cultural values, beliefs, and attitudes to drinking in order to sell their products, and
without regard to the role those values, beliefs, and attitudes play in perpetuating
alcohol-related problems; in other words, alcohol advertisers reinforce these problems as a means of promoting their products (Postman et al., 1987; Strate, 1990,
1991, 1992a, 1992b).

The American alcohol industry spends over $1 billion a year on advertising in
order to influence the beliefs and behaviour of consumers and to promote the sale
of its products (Jacobs 1989). Alcohol advertisers argue that the purpose of their
advertising is only to reinforce brand loyalty and to increase their share of a pre-
existing market for alcohol consumption. The US tobacco industry made similar
claims, which have recently been shown to be false, and we have no reason to grant
any greater credibility to the alcohol industry; if nothing else, it is hard to believe
that so much money is being spent in pursuit of so modest a goal as market share.
Whether their claims are true or not is ultimately irrelevant, however, because they
refer only to the intentions of advertisers, not to the results of their activity. They
may, for example, claim that images of attractive young women in bikinis are used
solely to attract the viewer's attention, but the result is that a strong message about
the role of women is sent to the audience. Or consider the following brief analysis
of a magazine advertisement for B and B Brandy included by my colleague Robin
Andersen in *Consumer Culture and TV Programming* (1995: 109):

A young, affluent couple in evening clothes is shown in a hotel room. The man leans over
the woman, grinning somewhat lasciviously as he clutches her hand. She sits at a table on
which a drink is displayed, and her position of vulnerability is emphasized by the giggly look
of intoxication on her face. It is the end of an evening and she holds the 'Do Not Disturb'
sign in her hand. He is poised to take action; she is perhaps the unwitting target.

The image is a clear invitation. It appeals to the masculine need for power, providing a
fantasy of female vulnerability and the implicit approval of domination. We cannot evaluate
this image without taking into consideration the cultural association of sex and power—and
ultimately, that of sex and violence—which bring to mind the issue of date rape.

As Andersen points out, statistics show that drinking is significantly associated with
date rape. This does not mean that advertisers are intentionally promoting violence
towards women, although they may be using pre-existing notions that alcohol
increases sociability and lowers inhibitions in an effort to sell their product. The

point is that, like drugs, advertisements have side effects, effects that may be unintended but quite devastating.

Alcohol advertisers will also tell you that their messages are intended for adults, but again such claims were falsely made by the tobacco industry, and otherwise are of little relevance (see Jacobson and Mazur, 1995, for a discussion of tobacco and alcohol advertisers' appeals to under-age populations). Young people may constitute an unintended audience, but they *do* receive the messages of alcohol advertisers, and they do so quite frequently. Children and teenagers spend more time attending to the messages of television and other media than they do in any other activity aside from sleeping (Postman 1979), and they do not confine themselves to children's programming. Everything on television, including alcohol advertising, is easily accessible to children, and is watched by children; in this sense all television is children's television. Alcohol advertising reaches young people, and it teaches young people. Say 'educational television' and most people will think of Mr Rogers, not Miller Beer; Big Bird and Oscar the Grouch, not Spuds MacKenzie and Louie the Lizard; Captain Kangaroo and Mr Greenjeans, not Frank Bartles and Ed Jaymes. But commercials are more efficient educators than either *Sesame Street* or the traditional schoolroom. As Peter Drucker (1989: 249) notes: 'There are more hours of pedagogy in one thirty-second commercial than most teachers can pack into a month of teaching. The subject matter of the TV commercial is secondary: what matters most is the skill, professionalism, and persuasive power of the presentation.' It is no accident that a survey conducted by the Center for Science in the Public Interest (1988) found that the average eight- to twelve-year-old child can name more alcoholic beverages than presidents of the United States. These results are a testimonial to the effectiveness of the alcohol industry's curriculum.

The lessons taught by advertisers are quite different from those taught in the schoolroom, however. Commercials do not teach reading, writing, and arithmetic, but they do teach values, attitudes, and behaviour. The advertising curriculum is devoted not to science and history, but to images and lifestyles. Commercials contribute nothing to book learning, but are quite conducive to social learning, the process by which we learn the roles that we are expected to perform, and the rules and norms, ideals and aspirations, and fears and prejudices of our society. In essence, social learning is the learning of culture, and one of the ways in which this is accomplished is by internalizing a set of myths. In using the term 'myth', I am not referring to a falsehood or fairy tale; rather, myths are uncontested and generally unconscious assumptions about the world that we live in (Barthes 1972; Fiske and Hartley 1984; Williamson 1978). Myths provide ready-made answers to universal human questions, questions about ourselves, our relationships with others, and our relationship with our environment. For example, every culture has a set of myths that explain the differences between children and adults, and between men and women. These differences are rooted in biology, but only culture can provide their meaning. Only through social learning can a child understand what it means to be a man. And those myths that are associated with masculinity are of special relevance here. After all, it is well known that the majority of beer-drinkers are men, that most beer advertising is aimed at a male audience, and that the problems related to alcohol abuse often disproportionately involve men; young males are particularly associated with safety problems such as drunk driving. Therefore it is worthwhile to consider the relationship between this at-risk group and our culture's assumptions about masculinity.

In the traditional myth of masculinity, men are characterized by their ability to handle stressful situations. Masculine identity is established—that is, a male proves that he is a man—by risk-taking. Men seek out or create challenges in order to demonstrate their strength, courage, and skill. The challenge is a test of the individual's ability to control his environment, and himself. When facing a challenge, some element of danger is often desirable, for it magnifies the risks of failure and the significance of success. While physical challenge is the archetype, it can be supplemented by other types of challenges, including the economic, the intellectual, and symbolic challenges such as games and contests. In meeting a challenge, victory is desirable, but there is no shame in losing; after all, we all eventually lose in our confrontation with the ultimate challenge, death. The only cause for shame is if the individual fails to confront the challenge. (For an extended study of the agonistic component of masculinity, see Ong 1981.)

My intention here is not to condemn the myth of masculinity in its entirety, but rather to note some of its more troubling characteristics, especially as they relate to drinking and getting drunk. Alcohol is associated with masculinity because it threatens self-control. Its effects on physical coordination, mental efficiency, and emotional stability serve as a challenge against which men can demonstrate self-mastery by 'holding their drink'. The man's man suffers no ill effects from drinking, and to admit to having drunk too much is to violate this masculine ideal. The individual who tries to live up to this archetype will claim that he 'knows when to say when', even if he doesn't; to admit that he doesn't 'know when' would be a sign of weakness and lack of self-control. The individual who tries to live up to this ideal will also tend to overestimate his ability to 'hold his drink.' And this is why Budweiser's 'Know when to say when' public-service campaign, while certainly better than nothing, was a weak appeal: the vagueness of the slogan, the fact that 'when' is never specified, allows individuals who do *not* know 'when to say when' to continue to believe that they *do*.

Still, it would be odd for the beer industry to contradict the myth of masculinity in its public-service announcements, since they rely on it so heavily in their advertising. I should note at this point that advertisers did not invent the myth of masculinity. It can be found in the stories and jokes that we tell, in the games that we play, and in the way we act out our social roles. Advertisers simply utilize pre-existing myths in order to sell their products. This is no minor role, however, as Marshall McLuhan (1951: v) argued: 'Ours is the first age in which many thousands of the best-trained individual minds have made it a full-time business to get inside the collective public mind. To get inside in order to manipulate, exploit, control is the object.' Rather than rely on logical arguments and claims that might be evaluated as true or false (and therefore subject to truth in advertising laws), advertisers rely on evocative images and themes. As Tony Schwartz (1974: 24), one of the first to use this soft-sell strategy, puts it: 'The critical task is to design our package of stimuli so that it resonates with information already stored within an individual and thereby induces the desired learning or behavioral effect.' In other words, advertisements are designed to evoke meaning in the minds of the audience. Messages need not be stated explicitly, but instead simply suggest their meaning, depending on the audience to fill in the missing pieces. The images and themes are drawn from our shared culture, and therefore tend to evoke similar meanings in many different people. While this same process holds true for all forms of communication, advertising, especially television commercials, tries to elicit the most meaning from the least amount of information.

Advertisers use the cultural meanings evoked by mythic themes and images to sell products, and in doing so also reinforce and reshape those myths. Thus, beer commercials are perhaps the most concentrated source of information on what it means to be a man in our culture; they constitute a veritable manual on masculinity. And they stress the association between masculinity and alcohol to a greater extent than any other single source. Of course, the ads never explicitly state that beer should be used as a means of testing manhood. To do so would be suicidal for the beer industry. Instead, they associate beer-drinking with other types of challenges, often presenting their product as a reward for meeting those challenges. The ritual of drinking after facing a trial is seen as appropriate because alcohol itself poses a challenge. Drinking, then, becomes a way to symbolically re-enact the earlier test. The association between beer and challenge is, in a subtle way, an equation between drinking and challenge (Postman *et al.* 1987; Strate 1990; 1991; 1992*a*, *b*; see also Mort 1996; Savan 1994).

For example, one of Budweiser's most frequently aired spots during the 1980s featured a young Polish immigrant and an older American foreman. In the opening scene, a union hall dispatcher was reading names from a clipboard, giving workers their assignments. Arriving late, which earned him a look of displeasure from the foreman, the nervous young immigrant took a seat in the back. When he was finally called, the young man walked up to the front of the room, corrected the dispatcher's mispronunciation of his name, and was given his assignment. The scene then shifted to a montage of the day's work; by the end of the day it was clear that he had earned the respect of his co-workers. The final scene was in a crowded tavern; the young man walked through the door, and made his way to the bar, looking around nervously, until someone called his name, and the foreman handed him a beer. In both the first and last scene, the immigrant began at the back of the room, highlighting his outsider status, and moved to the front as he was given a chance to prove himself.

Having mastered the initial challenge of work, the reward of beer is an invitation to re-enact his feat symbolically. By working hard and well, he gained acceptance in the work world; by drinking the beer, he also gained acceptance into the social world of the bar. Here, the myth of masculinity was bound up with the ideal of the American Dream of economic success and upward mobility, and the theme of initiation: initiation into American society, initiation into the workplace, initiation into the bar-room, and ultimately, given the immigrant's youth, initiation into adulthood. Initiation always involves challenge; otherwise, membership in the group would not be valued.

The theme of masculine challenge and initiation is also present in a 1998 commercial for Coors beer, featuring Lee Ermey reprising his role as a drill instructor from the 1987 Stanley Kubrick film, *Full Metal Jacket*. Addressing a platoon of men, Ermey angrily announced: 'During a surprise inspection of your barracks this afternoon I found this,' and he held up high a six-pack of Coors Light. The men looked nervous as the sergeant continued, 'I want the soldier who belongs to this beer to step forward—NOW!' No one moved, so the sergeant went on sarcastically, 'What's the matter? Do you miss your precious Rocky Mountains, dipping your tootsies into an ice-cold Rocky Mountain stream, fraternizing with some snow bunnies?' As he said this, one soldier imagined that he and his fellows were skipping through the wilderness, then that he was running barefoot into a stream, and finally that he and a comrade were sitting in the stream with two beautiful women in bathing suits, each of them holding a bottle of Coors Light. The young man's reverie was interrupted by Ermey screaming, an inch from his face, 'Do you, Kowalski?' As Kowalski squirmed, the drill instructor turned to the platoon and screamed, 'I want to know whose beer this is right now!' The men suddenly came to attention, their eyes fixed on an officer who had entered the vicinity but remained off camera. Ermey was unaware of the new presence until he heard, 'It's my beer, Sergeant.' The voice was John Wayne's, and the commercial cut to a cinematic image of Wayne playing a two-star general in the 1962 film *The Longest Day*, brought into this advertisement by the innovation of digital video editing. The drill instructor looked Wayne up and down, awestruck, grinning sheepishly at the sight of his idol, and said, 'You put this here?' Wayne responded, 'I certainly did, and I checked on 'em.' Cowed, Ermey answered, 'I wasn't going to take it, sir.' Wayne then uttered one of his trademark terse replies, 'I'll bet!' The sergeant held out the six-pack to him and said, 'No really, look, it's still cold.' Wayne took one bottle and affirmed, 'You're right!' Still not satisfied, he went on, 'Now, what'd'ya do with my pretzels?' Ermey snapped back into drill-instructor mode, turned to his platoon and yelled, 'Well, don't just stand there, find the general's pretzels.' The men scattered in all directions at exaggerated speed in their haste to follow their sergeant's orders, and the commercial cut to the printed slogan, 'Tap the Rockies'.

In this advertisement, the young men were being trained to be soldiers by an older drill sergeant, and being taught how to claim full membership in the hyper-masculine world of the military. Contrasted against the youth and immature masculinity of the platoon, we had the American archetype of the man's man, John Wayne. His presence removed any doubt that we were fully immersed in discourse concerning masculinity. Moreover, despite the integration of women into the military, the motif of the army retains a powerful association with manhood, and this is borne out by the fact that there were no women in the platoon depicted in the ad. From time immemorial, physical combat has been one of the main methods by which men have proven their masculinity. While hunting may serve as a substitute, warfare is the ultimate test. The challenge that must be met is in part a physical one, based on strength, speed, and skill; in part it is a cognitive challenge, requiring strategy and cunning; but ultimately it is an emotional challenge, forcing men to face their fears, manage their anger, and take control of (and suppress) their feelings (Rushing and Frentz 1995). The purpose of boot camp is initiation into the ways of warfare as practised by adult males. In order to prepare soldiers to face the challenges of battle, the training incorporates agonistic rituals, as well as tasks exercising physical and mental discipline. The drill instructor's hazing is a direct challenge to self-control, and the appropriate behaviour in our culture is for men to keep their emotions in check.

The sergeant in the ad functioned as a challenge to the trainees' discipline and self-control in general, but the content of his calling-out was also of great significance. Why did the presence of beer in the barracks pose a problem? Presumably, it was a violation of regulations, but Ermey made it clear that it is more than that—it is a challenge to the Spartan mindset of the fully initiated soldier. Thus, the target of his derision was hedonism: taking pleasure from the sensuous experience of nature, women, and alcohol. Each posed a challenge to self-control, and therefore to the attainment of full masculine identity, at least in the drill instructor's eyes. Between the polar opposites of the platoon's immaturity and desire, and the sergeant's authority and discipline, John Wayne's star persona served as a mediator. Apart from his implicit credibility as a traditional role model, his status as general gave him full command over the situation, affirming the basic tenets of the myth of masculinity. Against the extreme Puritanism of the drill instructor, however, he exhibited almost childlike behaviour in his concern over his pretzels, and in his use of phrases like 'I'll bet!' He elicited similar behaviour from Ermey in the form of youthful hero worship. The lesson imparted was that pleasure is acceptable if it is earned by hard work, and by successfully facing up to challenges. Boys will be boys, and men can be boyish as well, as long as they have established their masculine identities.

In this advertisement beer was identified with nature, as it is generally in the campaigns of Coors and many other manufacturers. The company's campaign slogan, 'Tap the Rockies', along with its long-standing emphasis on its use of Rocky Mountain spring water, implies that the beer is a natural resource, not a mass-produced industrial product. While this is a semiotic strategy commonly employed in advertising (Williamson 1978), in this case it resonates with the belief held by many drinkers that beer is a kind of health food; it also helps to disguise the fact that beer is an addictive drug whose effects on judgement and coordination are potentially dangerous. In many other beer advertisements (as with the ads for SUVs analysed elsewhere in this volume) nature is depicted as a challenge to be met and overcome, i.e., taming the wilderness, and the identification of beer with nature suggests that beer too can serve as a test of manhood (Postman *et al.* 1987; Strate 1990, 1991, 1992*a*, *b*). In the Coors commercial, nature was unthreatening, and the challenge it posed was one of temptation. The vision of a Rocky Mountain paradise threatened to turn fighting men into nature boys, resulting in a loss of discipline and self-control. The identification of nature and beer implied that the pleasures of drinking posed the same type of threat to military training and initiation into the adult world of warfare.

The presence of women in this advertisement was not insignificant. As noted, there were no female soldiers in the platoon, just two women in bathing suits in the soldier's Rocky Mountain daydream; that this reinforced traditional gender stereotypes is quite obvious. The inequality was further reinforced by the fact that the men were dressed not in bathing suits as well, but in their fatigues. The scene itself showed the women and men socializing while immersed in the stream, all holding bottles of beer. This reinforced pre-existing notions concerning alcohol as a facilitator of interaction between the sexes, and the stream itself may have functioned as an unconscious symbol of sexual relations. As a male fantasy, scenes of this sort resonate with the very real relationship between alcohol and date rape noted above. But far from being portrayed as victims, in this commercial the women were identified with nature and beer as temptations that challenged the men's discipline and commitment. The Rocky Mountains were portrayed as Edenic, and the unnamed bathing beauties were cast in the role of Eve. This coincides with the myth of masculinity, in that the challenge to the male is to remain cool and calm in the presence of beautiful women. The ladies' man typically suppresses any sign of interest or excitement in the opposite sex; he is Joe Cool. Oddly enough, Budweiser's canine mascot, Spuds MacKenzie, fitted this profile, insofar as he was treated as a human being in his ads; Spuds never lost his cool, even when he was fawned over by women attractive enough to make other males salivate like Pavlov's dogs. In the case of dogs of war such as Ermey and Wayne, such restraint is second nature. For young men not yet fully initiated into masculinity, femininity and desire alike must be subjected to control and repression, be they manifested in others, or in themselves.

Ultimately, the Coors commercial did not endorse Ermey's extreme Puritanism, as abstinence interferes with the sale of alcoholic beverages. Rather than avoid the pleasures of drinking in an effort to maintain self-control, the advertisement implied that the man's man can successfully meet this challenge. John Wayne is no less a masculine archetype, no less in control, for his fondness for beer and pretzels. And, as far as the commercial was concerned, alcohol consumption had no bearing on the tasks required for military training and actual combat, such as using firearms or driving jeeps and tanks, and it likewise had no bearing on physical endurance, or on the ability to follow orders or plan strategies. As a challenge that the fully initiated male can readily resist and overcome, it served as an easy way to demonstrate mature masculinity.

The theme of control was also apparent in a commercial for Lite Beer from Miller that was aired in 1998. Part of a series that combined stylistic aspects of low-budget educational, industrial, and documentary films with an avant garde, ironic tone, this advertisement featured a retro, 1960s look. It opened with a printed disclaimer that 'Not everyone in this ad will have a Miller Time. But *YOU* might', which was read by an off-camera voice. The commercial cut to a still image of a can of Lite Beer, with the slogan 'Miller Time', and then the action began with an Indian scientist in lab coat holding a chewtoy, a nearby dog staring at it expectantly. His voice-over told us 'We all know how a dog reacts when it sees something it really likes.' The dog was allowed to grab the toy at this point, and the camera showed a close-up of his wagging tail. Cut to a second Indian scientist, his voice-over revealing, 'Unexpectedly, I've noticed the same behaviour on this young man.' The camera revealed the young man, who nodded to us; he was standing in the laboratory, and was somewhat short, with long but neat hair and a beard, dressed in a suit. The voice-over continued with 'Look at this . . . ' and the scene shifted to a party; we saw a 45 rpm record placed on a turntable and heard early-1960s-style music. The young man was waiting in a queue with other men, and received a bottle of Lite Beer. He brought it to his mouth, but before he could complete the action his arm began to move uncontrollably back and forth, wagging like the dog's tail; as a consequence, beer flew all over the place, wetting the young man, his suit, and the surrounding area. The music, which was largely instrumental, intermittently included the exclamation 'I can't control my arm!' The commercial cut to another point during the party. The young man was seated, talking to a very attractive young woman; she was elegantly dressed, her hemline provocatively short. A waiter brought the young man a Lite, which elicited the same reaction, the beer flying all over the woman as well. She was surprised and turned away to avoid getting wet, but she did not seem entirely displeased with this turn of events. Back in the laboratory, the scientists had the young man holding a bottle with a hand-written sign that said 'Other Beer'; he showed no reaction. He then picked up a bottle with a sign that said 'Miller Lite' and his arm began to flail about once more, this time accidentally hitting one of the scientists on the nose, and knocking him down. On the voice-over, the other scientist said, 'Can you turn this into something good?' As if in answer, he taped drum sticks to Lite Beer bottles and handed them to the young man, who suddenly began to play drums like a professional.

Despite the ad's absurdist qualities, it incorporated some of the central elements of the myth of masculinity: A young man was plagued by a lack of self-control, unable to meet the challenge posed by alcoholic consumption. He was finally aided by two mature males (who obviously do not suffer from the same loss of control), authority figures who taught him not to avoid the problem-causing substance, but to take command of it. The choice of ethnicity for the two scientists was somewhat offbeat for an American advertisement, as images of Indians and other Asians are not all that common. It did, however, contribute to the ad's retro sensibility, given the 1960s fads for things 'Indian', such as sitar music, transcendental meditation, and Hare Krishna; it also played on the stereotype of Indians as nerds. As non-whites, as victims of the young man's inadvertent attack, and also given the relatively low-tech state of their laboratory (appropriate for the 1960s), the two were unthreatening, if not servile. At the same time, as scientists they were in a position of authority, and were able to solve the young man's problem in the end. Moreover, the scientists remained impassive throughout the commercial, thereby demonstrating appropriate masculine restraint.

The young man, overtly labelled a 'young man', was naturally characterized by immaturity. The fact that he was something of a freak, in that he behaved like a dog, was also of interest. Dogs are symbols of masculinity, and they have been used as mascots by beer companies such as Budweiser. But they are also animals, and as such are characterized by a lack of self-control relative to human beings. The young man's problem was both childish and animalistic. There were also strong psycho-sexual overtones. The beer bottle was a phallic symbol, and the act of shaking up its contents and then letting it explode out clearly parallels ejaculation. Thus, the young man's lack of control might suggest a lack of genital self-control, i.e., mas-turbation and premature ejaculation. The scene in which he doused the young woman was titillating, vaguely paralleling rituals from wet-T-shirt contests and hard-core pornographic films; in this sense it was also degrading, and approvingly linked alcohol with loss of control and the victimization of women.

In this ad, male sexual anxiety was coupled both with an attack on a woman and with breaking the nose of another man. The violence was not intentional, and was played for laughs, thereby downplaying the seriousness of the actions themselves. This subtly reflected the tendency to excuse or downplay antisocial behaviour that is associated with drinking—'I was only drunk!' The American legal system has moved away from this position as regards problems such as drinking and driving, but the attitudes persist within the culture, particularly among young males. Coup-ling dangerous behaviour with a lack of consequences may sell beer, but it is an irresponsible message. That the young man's dilemma was easily solved also served to downplay the problems involved. An alcohol-related problem was turned into something good! In this ending, tape was the symbol of discipline and restraint, the drum sticks reinforced the phallic nature of the bottle, and the young man demon-strated his newfound control and power through a drum solo. His skill would not have been discovered had it not been for the beer; alcohol acted as the vehicle of his talent, reinforcing misconceptions about alcohol enhancing coordination and dex-terity. There is no question that the commercial was clever and funny, but the underlying social reality that it connected to was unfortunately quite serious.

Let me turn to one final beer commercial from 1998, this one for Bud Light. We saw a young man peering into a refrigerator which was empty, apart from a carton of milk and a stalk of celery. He said to his roommate, 'I thought you were going to buy some Bud Light.' The roommate entered the kitchen and responded, 'Do you see any Bud Light?' The first fellow answered, 'No.' 'Well, then,' responded the roommate, and then his buddy left. Now alone, the roommate reached down and tugged, revealing the view of the empty refrigerator to be merely a photograph on a window shade. As it rolled up, the real interior of the fridge stood exposed, full of bottles and cans of Bud Light. The ad cut to the slogan 'Make it a Bud Light', as a voice-over said, 'For the great taste that won't fill you up and never lets you down, make it a Bud Light.' We returned to the roommate, now sitting on a couch, watching football. The first young man asked, 'Where'd you find that one?' The roommate responded, 'Behind the milk.'

The scene here was a bachelor pad. Presumably, the two young men were short on domestic skills and responsibilities, but placed a great deal of importance on keeping beer in stock. The roommate took on the quality of the trickster archetype, e.g., Prometheus, or the Amerindian coyote deity. The challenge was one involving cunning, as he put one over on his friend. While this may seem somewhat unfair, as there was plenty of beer for both of them, masculine relationships are character-ized by a degree of ribbing, joking, insulting, and sometimes bullying. This is an alternative to genuine displays of emotion, which threaten a loss of emotional control—real men do not show their feelings about each other. Instead, they pose symbolic challenges to each other, which tests self-control: can you take it? As the test is not all that hard, the typical effect is to reaffirm masculine identity for each other. In this case, the first young man failed the test, thereby appearing somewhat less than fully masculine: something of a wimp, you might say. The roommate demonstrated his manhood successfully, showing that he was the alpha male in this two-pack. Again, beer served as the medium for proving masculinity, but there was something even more disturbing about this ad. The secretiveness and selfishness, the hiding of alcohol and the denial of reality, all are behaviour associated with alcoholism. That the roommate drank his beer in the presence of his friend countered the stereotype of the alcoholic who drinks alone; moreover, we were present with him, as the commercial teamed us with him by letting us in on the trick, while the first young man remained unaware of what was going on. The roommate's lack of desperation, and the absence of any other ill-effects kept us from associating his behaviour with alcohol addiction, and reinforced the misconception that it cannot happen to a beer-drinker, or simply that 'It can't happen to me.'

Rather than recognizing the problems associated with intoxication and alcohol abuse, advertising associates drinking with masculinity in numerous ways, and thereby exacerbates a major social problem. Themes of challenge of control abound, as do images of speed, movement, and even driving! While it might be possible to limit beer-marketing to simple name identification, the surest way to avoid the kind of dysfunctional messages discussed here is to eliminate alcohol advertising altogether, as I have argued. Also, I should point out that the myths found in beer commercials could be the focus of public-service campaigns. Social marketing and media advocacy could be used in an attempt to disassociate the concept of challenge and masculinity from the practice of drinking (Wallack, Dorfman, Jernigan, and Themba 1993). Also, public-service spots could actually criticize or parody the dysfunctional elements of specific commercials, in an attempt to inoculate the audience against beer commercials. Ultimately, alcohol advertising perpetuates the problem of drinking and driving, and reducing the potency of this advertising would go a long way towards effecting cultural change, and saving lives.

References

Andersen, R. (1995). *Consumer Culture and TV Programming*. Boulder, CO: Westview Press.

Barthes, R. (1972). *Mythologies*, trans. J. Cape Ltd. New York: Hill & Wang.

Center for Science in the Public Interest (1988). Kids are as aware of booze as presidents, survey finds. Washington DC: CSPI news release, 4 September, 1988.

Douglas, M. (ed.) (1987). *Constructive Drinking: Perspectives on Drink from Anthropology*. Cambridge: Cambridge University Press.

Drucker, P. (1989). *The New Realities*. New York: Harper & Row.

Fiske, J., and Hartley, J. (1984). *Reading Television*. New York: Methuen.

Herbert, B. (1999). 'America's Littlest Shooters'. *New York Times*, 2 May: 17.

Jacobs, J. B. (1989). *Drunk Driving: An American Dilemma*. Chicago: University of Chicago Press.

Jacobson, M. F., and Mazur, L. A. (1995). *Marketing Madness: A Survival Guide for a Consumer Society*. Boulder, CO: Westview.

Jameson, F. (1991). *Postmodernism, or, the Cultural Logic of Late Capitalism*. Durham, NC: Duke University Press.

Massing, M. (1998). 'Strong Stuff'. *New York Times Magazine*, 22 March: 36–41, 48, 58, 72–3.

McLuhan, M. (1951). *The Mechanical Bride: Folklore of Industrial Man*. New York: Vanguard Press.

Mort, F. (1996). *Cultures of Consumption: Masculinities and Social Space in Late Twentieth Century Britain*. London: Routledge.

Ong, W. J. (1981). *Fighting for Life: Contest, Sexuality, and Consciousness*. Ithaca, NY: Cornell University Press.

Postman, N . (1979). *Teaching as a Conserving Activity*. New York: Delacorte Press.

Postman, N., Nystrom, C., Strate, L., and Weingartner, C. (1987). *Myths, Men and Beer: An Analysis of Beer Commercials on Broadcast Television, 1987*. Washington, DC: American Automobile Association Foundation for Traffic Safety.

Rushing, J. H., and Frentz, T. S. (1995). *Projecting the Shadow : The Cyborg Hero in American Film*. Chicago : University of Chicago Press.

Savan, L. (1994). *The Sponsored Life: Ads, TV, and American Culture*. Philadelphia: Temple University Press.

Schiller, H. (1989). *Culture, Inc.: The Corporate Takeover of Public Expression*. New York: Oxford University Press.

Schwartz, T. (1974). *The Responsive Chord*. Garden City, NY: Anchor.

Strate, L. (1990). 'The Mediation of Nature and Culture in Beer Commercials'. *New Dimensions in Communication, Proceedings of the 47th Annual New York State Speech Communication Association Conference*, 3: 92–5.

—— (1991). 'The Cultural Meaning of Beer Commercials'. *Advances in Consumer Research*, 18: 115–19.

—— (1992a). 'Beer Commercials: A Manual on Masculinity', in S. Craig (ed.), *Men Masculinity, and the Media*. Newbury Park, CA: Sage, 78–92.

—— (1992b). 'Beer Commercials, Masculinity, and Drunk Driving: A Dysfunctional Relationship'. *Drinking and Driving Prevention Symposium Proceedings*. Ontario, CA: Automobile Club of Southern California: 37–46.

US Department of Health and Human Services (1988). *Surgeon General's Workshop on Drunk Driving Proceedings*, Washington, DC.

Wallack, L., Dorfman, L., Jernigan, D., and Themba, M. (1993). *Media Advocacy and Public Health: Power for Prevention*. Newbury Park, CA: Sage.

Williamson, J. (1978). *Decoding Advertisements: Ideology and Meaning in Advertising*. London: Marion Boyars.

Chapter 10

Road to Ruin: the Cultural Mythology of SUVs

Robin Andersen

THE Toyota 4 runner sits off-road in the middle of a fern-laden forest. The Ad copy announces: 'THE ANSWERING MACHINE FOR THE CALL OF THE WILD.

'From a rugged mountain vista to deep in the plush forest, nature calls out for us. And the 1997 Toyota 4 wheel drive, is one of the only machines capable of answering that challenge. With a powerful 183-hp V6 engine and the highest ground clearance in its class, you'll be able to handle almost anything nature may throw at you. And with 4Runner's roomy interior and available leather seats, civilization is never really far away. The 1997 Toyota 4Runner. Your answer for the call of the wild.'

At the end of the twentieth century, in an age when environmental destruction is widely recognized, at a time when public sentiment turns towards the preservation of some of the few wild ecosystems left on the globe, Sport Utility Vehicles (SUVs) have come to occupy the central cultural space that celebrates the wonders of that diminishing natural world. SUV advertising of the 1990s created a plethora of fantastical imagery celebrating the Earth, its wilderness areas and the wild creatures that inhabit those landscapes. Through advertising, the SUV has been symbolically constructed as a mythical commodity, the vehicle through which the wonders, joys, and dangers of the environment can be freely experienced, once the sticker price has been paid. This essay maps the imagery of SUVs, its effects on consumer behaviour, and the contradictions that emerge between the symbolic geography of SUVs and the actual impact they have on global landscapes.

The popularity of SUVs

The long and complicated romance between the automobile and American culture is now a full-blown love affair with trucks. Since the late 1980s, sales of 'light trucks', the vehicular classification which includes Sport Utility Vehicles as well as Mini-Vans, have risen at double the pace of cars. In 1975, trucks, vans, and four-wheel-drive vehicles (4×4s) accounted for 21 per cent of all light vehicles sold. But with high profits, cheap gas, and the most aggressive marketing campaign in American history, light trucks now take almost 50 per cent of market share. By 1997, five of the top ten selling vehicles in the US were light trucks and SUVs. Manufacturers claim they don't make money on cars any more, only on trucks.

Profits on the massive gas-guzzling Chevy Suburban can run to an astonishing $10,000.

And the bigger the better. Sales of full-sized pickup trucks have nearly doubled since 1991, while sales of compact pickups have fallen. In April 1997, 21,000 buyers chose the Ford Expedition, weighing in at 5,174 lb and sitting a whopping 31 inches (78.74cm) off the ground. Ford car sales fell 10 per cent that month (Meredith 1997). By 1997, sales of the biggest SUVs had quintupled in six years (Bradsher 1997*b*).

The promise of nature

Public desire for these vehicles is driven by the promise that the wonders of nature can be had by sitting high above the ground in a sport utility vehicle. This powerful persuasive association between SUVs and the environment is communicated through some of the most stunning imagery of the natural world ever seen in American advertising. In this visually enhanced television environment, during innumerable primetime commercial breaks, one of these vehicles can be seen charging through Africa surrounded by endangered species, perched atop the spire of an awesome natural formation in the middle of a desert, elevated on a coastal ridge above the pounding surf, or bouncing through an evergreen forest amid shafts of brilliant sunlight.

One television advertisement for Jeep shows two people sitting at a campsite overlooking the desert wilderness below. Their peaceful reverie in this off-road locale is disturbed by the shouts of another Jeep-owner on a similar formation across the gorge. Accounting for his jubilance, the couple comments that 'This is his first time.' One of advertising's favourite attention-getting devices, the double meaning, in this case offers a sexual significance which ties such pleasures to the commodity. The ad text also refers to the fact that he is a first-time Jeep-buyer who has driven into the wilderness and is ecstatic. The couple in the ad, on the other hand, have grown accustomed to having such natural beauty and excitement brought to them through the habitual use of their off-road vehicle.

Such scenes of 4×4 owners ensconced in the natural world are reproduced in glossy magazine layouts, also visually enhanced to make the wilderness appear even more delightful. One two-page layout shows a Jeep framed by a line of tall evergreens in a clearing surrounded by a range of majestic snow-covered peaks. A high-sierra tent and a full backpack sit amid smooth rocks, wild flowers, and lush grasses. No road is visible, and the Jeep has managed to bring its occupants to this pristine location without crushing or destroying any vegetation. The truck is simply part of the wilderness, the effect underscored by the way the vehicle blends with the wild area, depicted in the same tones and reflective light. Even though rich blues, greens, and violet hues are visible, the scene is a night-time landscape. A campfire glows yellow and orange. The Jeep-owners have been transported to another world, a vastly different place constructed as an escape from the urban and suburban environments they mostly inhabit. The text reads, 'Of all the things that can keep you up nights, Cherokee's payments won't be one of them.' Coming from out of the forest are the sounds of wild animals, 'squawk, caw, howl, hoot, crunch, ker-plunk, thump . . . '

In one advertising layout a treacherous mountain slope shows big-horn sheep clinging to the side of the cliff; the ad points out that an SUV is also managing to traverse the difficult terrain. These vehicles occupy the wilderness in the same ways animals do; within the depiction they attain the status of a biological phenomenon. No longer a machine or the product of human endeavour, they become a natural part of the ecosystem. As part of nature, another ad announces, 'It's only fitting that nature point out the changes to our latest 4×4.' Majestically backlit, the machine dominates a pile of jagged rocks, light radiating around it. Among a number of other attributes, 'nature' tells us that the machine has 'Quadra-Drive—Our Most Advanced 4WD System Ever'.

The wonders of wildlife

In one of the most imaginative television scenarios, a 4×4 drives through a land-scape that morphs into great, powerful animals. The magical transformations take place as the truck passes over the terrain; an elephant's dry surface materializes out of a desert landscape, and cactus branches become the horns of an antelope that takes full form and turns to look at the viewer. The animals become visible only with the help of the truck, as if the tyres of the SUV have brought them to life. In the last scene a huge grizzly bear rears up out of the wilderness.

When the Nissan Pathfinder 'went on safari', opening the African campaign during the Super Bowl of 1996, the earth's large mammals became tied for ever to 4×4 vehicles. Hippopotamuses were shown in the water, seen through spectacular underwater photography. Footage of the majestic awkwardness of giraffes in motion occupied the same frames as the Pathfinder, as if it were also part of the ecosystem.

By the end of the decade, SUVs had confronted water buffaloes and sunk into jungle swamps, only to emerge unharmed. Elephants had cleaned the outsides of these vehicles and small monkeys had explored their interiors. Wolves had chased them though the temperate forests of north America, and bears had kicked their tyres. In a television advertisement aired in 1999, on safari once again, zebras fell into formation, running in a straight line, the SUV as one of their number, across the wild African savanna amid clouds of dust.

The inspiration of nature, its solitude, the escape it offers from urban environ-ments, and the opportunity it affords to see large intriguing animals are all essential to the persuasive messages that surround 4×4s. Through the quality of 'iconicity', (Messaris 1997) the visual messages create powerful associations, using a represen-tational mode of communication whose persuasive powers are augmented by a grounding in subjective experience. In one sense, then, nature is the denotative referent, effectively provoking a desire for the experience of awe that wilderness landscapes afford. To a certain degree advertisements do speak literally about nature, and some consumers do take SUVs off-road into wildland areas. But even for the 13 per cent of drivers who do, and certainly for those who never go off-road, the advertising imagery enhances and mythifies the experience of nature. While the imagery gains legitimacy through its representational mode, it is still a mediated experience of nature, an enhanced social construction, complete with the mythic dimensions created by advertising persuasion.

Advertising can only promise the natural world through images, but in what sense are those images made tangible through the purchase and use of 4×4s? To put it another way, how do the desires evoked by the representations mesh with owners' experience of SUVs? Their purchase and use has continued to escalate for over a decade, and yet very little real experience of nature is made manifest through their use. In what way, then, do they fulfil the promises they make, and how is such a cognitive feat performed? To begin to answer these questions, we must turn to the history of automobile mythology.

The automobile as metaphor

The fast, powerful machines of the twentieth century have been the stuff of cultural fantasy and mythic representation from the moment they rolled off the assembly line. Automobiles, like other mass-produced and -marketed commodities, are social markers; they speak about the identities, dreams, and social status of their drivers. As Wernik (1989: 202) notes, 'Out on the road they carry that same sense of class/ cultural identification into the wider cultural domain.' Cars, like clothes constitute a 'kind of third skin for ambient industrial man. Like clothes, too, as markers of identity within an anonymously circulating public they readily become subject to the fashion dynamics of competitive display, which manufacturers themselves have naturally encouraged to accelerate obsolescence and sales' (Wernik 1989: 202–3). The metaphors that turn these machines into the expressive icons of the moment have, of course, changed over time. Marshall McLuhan (1951) first noticed the psychocultural sexual fascination with the disembodied engines on pedestals and the curvaceous 'Bodies by Fisher'. Early on, the red sports car, descended from the racing car, communicated male sexual prowess, 'an almost perfect symbol for the masculinist technology values racing itself celebrates: a male identified machine, shaped like a bullet, and experienced from within as an exhilarating rush towards orgasm, death, and the future' (Wernik 1989: 204). And cars have been the symbolic vehicles of individual freedom. The empty highways of the dry, open landscapes of the American West are the final uncharted frontiers, the last places where rules are suspended as the sleek machines of independence head out of the confines of social convention. Social discontent and rebellion are part of the mythic narratives played out in the cultural space of the combustion engine (Andersen 1995).

A little security in an insecure world

The three-pronged association of freedom, sexuality, and the automobile has given way in the 1990s to a new psychocultural construct, one whose symbolic language includes not only escape, but a sense of security through power and control, potent guarantees of 4×4 capabilities. As one analyst noted, 'trucks give drivers a feeling of mastery over an uncertain and threatening world' (Treece *et al.* 1994: 76). While SUVs promise comfort in the midst of uncivilized terrain, it is primarily psychological comfort their owners seek. The assertion of control is often the actual promise, the site of emotional emulation. In this sense, the environment is a metaphor. It provides a symbolic space for the cultural expressions of the need for control in a world where such socio-economic satisfactions are in short supply. This process of dislocation has created a set of complicated and often contradictory messages about nature.

While nature is depicted as beautiful, stunning and awe-inspiring, it is also threatening and unpredictable, a force to be reckoned with, a challenge to be answered, a world to be conquered in your SUV. Desires for control and power are best played out against an environment that is symbolically constructed as hostile. (This theme is also evident in the advertising of beer: see Chapter 10.) In SUV ads this is done in a number of ways.

SUVs are situated in exotic, unknown and dangerous places. They take you to places so colourful that 'even the fever is yellow'. SUV advertising has appropriated the action/adventure narratives of neo-colonial fascinations, once the territory of films like *Indiana Jones and the Temple of Doom*. The mini-narratives of advertising scenarios reference an entire genre, very familiar to media consumers. One magazine ad proclaims that the 'legendary' Land Rover Defender 90 'has deftly transported adventurers deep into the Amazon jungle. Up the Atlas mountains of Morocco. Down the Copper Mines of Zambia. Through the whirling Sands of the Sahara. A 14-gauge steel chassis and 3.9 liter V-8 engine enable it to outmuscle and outmaneuver any other open-top 2-door on the road today. Or off the road today. And in the gorge tomorrow. What better way to become one with nature?' Becoming 'one with nature' is a fun adventure, but it can also transport the driver over a threshold to a world that is threatening and dangerous. The Defender sits in the middle of a remote jungle. An old-fashioned bush helmet sits on top of a circular patch of sand just outside of the open door. Outside the protection of the 'extraordinarily powerful' 4×4, the driver has been swallowed up by an inhospitable natural environment. The need for the protective '14-gauge steel chassis' is confirmed. Without it, untamed nature has done its worst. It has sucked him down.

Once advertising's dislocation has rendered nature dangerous, images of mud, dirt, and water spraying out from under the tyres as 4×4s tear through wilderness areas confirm that nature must be mastered. The small print at the bottom of a page of advertising proclaims that the Jeep Cherokee Sport is 'a gutsy four-wheel drive sport utility vehicle with the ability to plow through just about everything and anything except, quite thankfully, your savings account. Jeep. There's Only One.' In another magazine ad, the endangered black rhino is charging a Pathfinder in Kenya's 'wildlife mecca'. The ad copy promises that you'll 'enjoy the additional challenge of numerous animal species that would like nothing better than to make you their next meal. Or, at least, send your car to the body shop for a little fender work.' And with regard to extreme temperatures and bumpy roads, 'simply adjust the Pathfinder's automatic climate control to a suitably humane temperature'.

As the danger/adventure games are played out SUVs assume the role of mechanical security blankets. As one researcher explained, 'It doesn't matter what nature throws at people. They can go anywhere, do anything. You turn that key, and you feel you're in total control of the environment' (Treece *et al.* 1994: 76). The loss of mastery over a menacing world has been deflected onto a fantasy of mastery over the environment. As the Chevy Blazer ad beckons, 'a little security in an insecure world'.

SUV advertising gives symbolic form to a variety of psycho-social fears. Often gendered as female,[1] as in a television ad when bad weather threatens, 'she will freeze you, she will burn you, she will try to blow you away', Nature is dangerous, and trucks are the vehicles that will triumph over that threat. The road has become a cultural battleground where a disempowered public seeks victory on the last frontier. We no longer seem able to rule our lives, but we can rule the road. Nothing speaks freedom like these new, improved image-enhanced vehicles of cultural mythology. As one perceptive analyst noted, 'it's the frontier, the concept of taming the land. We still believe we can tame the world through these machines' (Treece *et al.* 1994: 76). SUV advertisements assure buyers that the best way to relate to nature is to run over it. In this we see a prolific cultural imagery firmly ensconced in nineteenth-century formulations of human civilization depending on the taming and domination of nature. The names of sport utility vehicles evoke the conquering adventures of the American frontier: Blazer, Explorer, Pathfinder, Laredo, Cherokee. The sad irony is that the celebration of nature in SUV advertising as a source of inspiration and awe has morphed over time. Ever more connected to the need for power and control, this latest marketing construct reasserts an old, familiar hegemony of domination of the natural world, one that has led to much environmental destruction. In addition to the negative ideologies these advertisements convey, the product itself, and its use, destroys the natural world.

The actual effects these vehicles have on the environment are buried under advertising fantasies of vehicle that will 'go farther', and take them 'off-road' to the freedom of the wilderness. But for the 13 per cent of 4×4s owners who do use them off-road, the environmental consequences are dire. As tyres tread across unpaved, mostly public lands, intense soil disruption causes a disastrous combination of erosion and compaction, destroying wild plant species. The loose dirt thrown from under the tyres leaves deadly deposits on plants growing nearby. A favoured image is driving across a stream bed, a quintessential depiction of a remote wild place. When 4×4s traverse creeks and streams they cause destructive

---

[1] For a more complete discussion of the gendered rendering of 'mother nature' and its symbolic consequences, see Andersen (2000).

ruts that erode stream banks, increasing water turbidity detrimental to the fish and other organisms. Indeed, use of the dirt roads themselves creates ruts and causes destructive run-off on public lands (Wright 1995). They fragment and destroy the habitat of the animals they depict with such fascination. Ironically, as the celebration of the wilderness is tied to 4×4s, their sale and use have prevented conservation of wild areas. A western Massachusetts group called Friends of Rivers blocked a US Park Service plan to designate the upper reaches of the Farmington river a federally protected 'wild and scenic river'. Friends of Rivers included the owners of an oil distributor and off-road-vehicle dealership (Burke 1994).

Becoming one with nature in ads often includes coming into contact with wild animals. Most animals avoid noise, which increases their metabolism and interferes with their hearing. Turtles have been run over and wolves and antelope have left areas frequented by noisy 4×4s.

Consumer identities

While drivers play out fantasy encounters with nature, their 'station wagons of the 90s' are mostly used to run errands in urban and suburban settings. Consumer research shows they have little to do with 'utility', even though those in the know now call them 'utes'. Over the last decade trucks have been transformed from a blue-collar need to a mass-market want. Luxury interiors and image-marketing provide the comfort which allows truck consumers to make personality statements. As one 4×4 owner noted, these vehicles are a bigger status symbol than a luxury car: 'A friend of mine sold her BMW to get an Expedition. Since when did it become an embarrassment to drive a BMW?' Because of their large engines and heavy frames, Sport Utilities are notably less fuel-efficient than the cars they are replacing. Yet consumers buy and drive them as if they were cars, with little concern for gas mileage. An Amoco researcher noted, 'They drive recreational vehicles for errands. They're looking for comfort, size and performance—not mileage' and 'Many owners of less fuel-efficient vehicles say they gladly pay more for the pleasure of sitting high above the traffic and knowing they have four wheel drive' (Salpukas 1995: A25).

Gas guzzlers

In the midst of the country's Bronco fever, the *New York Times* discovered that the demand for gasoline had increased dramatically by 1995, up 5 per cent from the year before. 'The only plausible explanation, according to some oil industry economists, is Americans' growing use of sport utility vehicles, pickup trucks and mini vans' (Salpukas 1995: A25).

As one car salesman observed, when customers shop for a vehicle like the Chevy Tahoe, they don't even look at the sticker that says it does twelve miles per gallon in city driving. 'They don't ask about the mileage. It's irrelevant to most of them'

(Salpukas 1995: A25). This pleasure is made affordable by a gas-pricing system held artificially low which does not incorporate environmental destruction in its calculations. In 1995 the cost of gas was only 6 cents for every mile travelled, compared to 9 cents in 1973 (after adjusting for inflation). Oil exploration, drilling, and shipping all damage the environment so stunningly depicted in the advertising. Oil extraction in Alaska's last wilderness areas will disrupt the ecosystem and break up the habitat of large animals such as bears and wolves, and of migrating herds of caribou, moose, and elk. If consumption of fossil fuels decreased, the demand to tap the Alaskan reserve would be unnecessary. If the advertisements were not so effective in creating the demand for these vehicles, the habitats and animals depicted would not have to be destroyed in order to keep them running.

As noted above, the vast majority of light trucks are not used for work. This of course reveals the falsity of industry arguments used to lobby against increased fuel efficiency—that the engines have to be bigger to do all that hauling. Nor are light trucks subject to the same federal regulations as cars for emissions standards and safety equipment. SUVs create two and a half times the emissions of cars, contributing heavily to the greenhouse gases that cause global warming. In spite of industry lobbying, that may be about to change. The US is setting the worst example for energy use on the globe, helping prevent international treaties to reduce greenhouse gases. 'Even measured by the yardstick of fulfilling the voluntary commitment the US made in Rio in 1992 to reduce its greenhouse gas emissions to 1990 levels by the year 2000, US policy has been an unambiguous failure' (Retallack 1999). SUVs are tied directly to US policy failures, as Retallack (1999: 112) points out: 'New-car fuel economy in the US is now declining, due partly to greater use of sport utility vehicles and the absence of meaningful mandatory automobile fuel economy standards. For every dollar of public funds given to public transportation, the automobile receives $7.'

The symbolic geography of advertising eclipses the operative cultural awareness that sport utility vehicles destroy the Earth. Ironically, light-truck buyers conceive of themselves variously, as practical, flexible, nonconformist or 'environmentally conscious' (Treece et al. 1994: 73). And herein lies the beauty of advertising culture. In the fantasy world of postmodern promotional associations, the impulse to dominate does not clash with the desire for environmental conservation. The construction of identity through consumption allows environmentalism to sit comfortably next to environmental destruction. As Meister (1997: 232) points out, 'When nature becomes a commodity, the emphasis is always on the gratification of human needs, without any attention paid to the non-human needs of nature. Such needs are transformed into human needs/greeds and apparent through images of consumer environmentalism. We can shop at the "nature store," and in owning the Jeep Cherokee, park nature in our suburban driveways.' The rugged individualism, mass-marketed to a consumer public, allows drivers to feel nonconformist as they conform to adverting persuasions. These contradictions are unified through the use of a visual language that persuades precisely because it does not make overt claims. Visual persuasion has only to place SUVs in pristine settings. It is through the lack of a logical connection that they are accepted at an aesthetic level (Baudrillard

1983). Because of 'syntactical indeterminacy' (Messaris 1997) the contradictions fail to emanate from the image. The photograph reveals not the essence of the machine and its use (Benjamin 1968) but only the stylistic elements that appear on advertising's glossy surface (Ewen 1988). Indeed, consumers are reluctant to contemplate pleasing images in a way that would cause psychic distress (Haineault and Roy, 1993). The unpleasant connections between gas consumption and the destruction of the globe remain obscured behind the stunning imagery. And of course, those connections are blocked by advertising influences on media content. Off-roading remains the activity of play; it's all in good fun.

Deadly pleasures

Sport Utilities are designed with very high ground clearance to get over rocky, rutted unpaved roads. The popular Ford Expedition has a bumper height of 31 inches (78.74cm). Even though most will never drive over rocks (most consumers don't want to dent their expensive status symbols) the height that makes their drivers feel powerful and in control also makes them deadly. The pleasure of sitting high above the traffic has its consequences.

'More Americans now die in crashes involving a car and a light truck than in crashes involving two cars' (Bradsher 1997a,: A1). When cars and light trucks collide, car occupants account for 80 per cent of deaths. That means you are four times more likely to die if you are unfortunate enough to be the driver of the car colliding with a 4×4. And these vehicles are driven very aggressively. Why wouldn't they be? They have been designed and advertised as the very essence of rugged individual power.

Cars are designed to meet federal crash standards that test a car's ability to 'withstand a collision with a similarly shaped vehicle within 500 pounds of its own weight' (Bradsher 1997a: A1). Yet a light truck outweighs a car by, on average, at least half a ton. The stiff steel-framed underbodies of light trucks tend to hit cars very high, in places not designed to take the impact. In some accidents SUVs ride up over the bonnet of a car. The structurally weak lightweight steel of a car's unibody shell is no match for 5,000 lb of belligerent force, bearing down on you, looking for something to dominate. Side-impact collisions are worse, because the heavier SUVs are so high that they cause injury to the upper body, head and neck, the type of injury most likely to be fatal. The odds that the driver of the car will die in a side-impact crash with an SUV are 27 : 1.

As SUVs began to target the female market share, advertising focused on the safety features of the vehicles, often depicting them avoiding road hazards and manoeuvring through bad weather. But SUVs are more likely than cars to roll over and kill their occupants. In addition, the steel frame of an SUV has a deadly effect when the driver runs into a stationary object. Because the stiff steel does not crumple, it transfers the impact to the driver inside the car. And because federal safety standards for trucks are more lenient than those for cars, their brakes are generally not as efficient. 'Large sport utility vehicles and pickups account for an unusually large share of pedestrian deaths, apparently because of their weaker brakes and lack of maneuverability' (Bradsher 1997c,: A1).

But manufacturers complain that making SUVs safer will affect their profit margins: 'putting lower bumpers on light trucks would ruin the rugged boxy look that so many buyers find attractive' (Bradsher 1997a,: D20). At this point changing the design would take many years and cost billions of dollars. Answering criticisms of the dangers of fleet incompatibility, manufacturers say the best way to reduce traffic accidents is to make people wear seatbelts, improve highway construction and crack down on drunk drivers. But if a drunk driver runs a light in New York City his or her car will be confiscated. The legal basis of such action is the *potential* to do harm. SUVs have demonstrated their potential to do harm in much greater numbers than other vehicles. According to the legal logic for drunk drivers, then, SUVs should be confiscated. Regulators need to question market priorities which continue to place drivers of smaller cars at such risk. The continued growth in the number, size and weight of light trucks will only increase the hazards to smaller cars in the future.

Sitting in traffic on New York City's West Side Highway I had time to study the Toyota 4Runner billboard. Clear Mountain water poured out of the big open sidedoor of the boxy vehicle. Superimposed on the interior was a beautiful pristine vista of clean air, high mountains and glassy water. 'FOLLOW YOUR DREAMS', it commanded. Looking at the urban jam, with SUVs towering all around me, I wondered about the nature of those dreams. Certainly the advertising was effective, and accounts for the initial popularity of these vehicles. The cognitive mindset evoked through the ads undoubtedly, at least at first, provides a pleasurable adventure/nature fantasy that affords emotional satisfaction. Advertisers call this phenomenon 'added value', mental fantasies that enhance the emotional satisfaction derived from the use of the product. But such mental states wear off in the face of the commonness of everyday use. Undoubtedly many owners had the same experience as one who confided, 'I feel really stupid for buying this car [a SUV]. I feel had by the marketing. This thing costs me a fortune, and I don't even like driving it anymore.' Now however, many are making 'defensive buys', choosing SUVs because it is dangerous not to (Lombardi 1997). As the owner of a new Ford Explorer boasted, 'Hey you're not going to intimidate me with your big truck anymore' (Treece et al., 1994: 77). With the proliferation of intimidating trucks on the road—all those people expressing their need for power and control—who wants to own an anonymous econo-box that's going to be on the losing end of that Suburban. Weighing in at 1,962 lb, the Geo Metro is no match for those vehicles. Ford Escorts and Toyota Corollas are each 16 inches (40.64cm) off the ground. With this loss of the highway commons, the collective good is abandoned to a spurious sense of personal empowerment. Along the way, the Earth continues to be destroyed.

Commercialized media

New York Times correspondent Keith Bradsher, along with a few other print and broadcast journalists, has published reports about safety issues surrounding SUVs, fleet incompatibility, fatality rates, and crash-test research released by the National Highway Traffic Safety Administration and the Insurance Institute for Highway Safety (Bradsher 1998). But broader environmental issues associated with SUVs' role in global warming and ecological destruction go unmentioned. Car dealers and manufacturers account for a huge portion of media ad revenues, and they have been successful in closing down the public debate. With the car industry paying the bills, would-be truck buyers are not going to hear about the environmental impact of the over-extraction of fossil fuels, the mass environmental destruction caused by roads, the greenhouse gases building up from vehicle emissions and causing global warming, or the depletion of the ozone layer caused by the air-conditioning units of the climate-controlled luxury cabs (Burrington 1994).

In the 1990s, when the Pathfinder went on its television safari across the African savanna, Shell Oil also went to Africa to find the fuel to keep the 4×4s running. The extraction of fossil fuel led to the destruction of tribal lands. When local villagers became environmental activists and protested against such destruction, they were brutally repressed by Nigeria's military dictatorship, which in November 1995 executed nine activists, including Nobel prize-winner Ken Saro-Wiwa. One of the top news stories identified by Project Censored as underreported for that year was Shell exploitation of Ogoniland in Nigeria. The environmental activists were protesting against the devastation of their farms and homes by the Royal Dutch/Shell group. Ninety per cent of Nigeria's foreign revenue comes from oil exports, and Shell, headquartered in Houston, Texas, imports almost 50 per cent of Nigeria's annual oil production. Aaron Sachs (1996) author of the *World Watch* article 'Dying for Oil', told Project Censored, 'The consumer ought to know—indeed, has a right and a responsibility to know—the consequences of his or her actions and decisions . . . you might want to know if some of the profits from the gas you regularly buy for your car (and buy more of for your truck) are going into the pockets of an unelected dictator who is committing environmental genocide within his own country' (Phillips and Project Censored 1997).

'Both the US government and Shell—as well as a few other major oil companies—benefit from the lack of (media) attention. The car/oil lobby is the largest and richest interest group in Washington, and [President] Clinton has refused to impose sanctions on Nigeria largely out of fear that he would alienate Shell and friends and that gasoline prices might rise a few cents' (Phillips and Project Censored 1997: 34).

Major media organizations and newspapers refused to print ads by Amnesty International exposing Shell's destruction and involvement in the military repression of Nigerian activists. The effective elimination of information allows such destruction to continue. More recently, Chevron's role in the destruction of Nigerian wetlands made the censored-news list for 1999. 'For decades, the people of the Niger Delta have been protesting the destruction of their wetlands. Discharges into the creeks and waterways have left the region a dead land, resulting in the Niger Delta becoming one of the most heavily polluted regions in the world' (Phillips and Project Censored 1999: 57). Chevron was obliquely involved in the deaths of student demonstrators protesting the destruction. On 28 May 1998 'Nigerian soldiers were helicoptered by Chevron employees to the Chevron owned oil facility off the coast of Nigeria in order to attack student demonstrators who had occupied a barge anchored to the facility' (Phillips and Project Censored 1999: 57). Two students were killed and many more were wounded. Investigative reporter Amy Goodman (1998), producer of a noncommercial documentary about the incident, caught up with Chevron's chief executive at the April 1999 shareholders' meeting in Florida. She asked him directly if he would guarantee that Chevron would not be involved in more killings of Nigerian students. He boldly replied, 'No' (Goodman and Scahill 1999). And why should he? When information regarding the devastating consequences of First World oil consumption is unavailable to the vast majority of American consumers, corporations involved in such global destruction have little incentive to change.

The incredible proliferation of car and truck advertising, and direct industry influence, blocks the discussion of environmental issues. As advertising exalts the wilderness, it promotes an ideology and practice that destroy it. Ads sent out in an information vacuum reassure buyers that the worst excesses of car culture can co-exist with the yearning to preserve what's left of the natural world. Nothing needs to change. We can have it all—rapacious oil-drilling, the wholesale slaughter of wildlife and its habitats, the pollution of Africa, the killing of those who protest against it—and still find spiritual communion with a sanctified Earth.

Advertising censorship affects the most important aspects of public debate by excluding a whole array of discourse considered unacceptable to corporate sponsors. Oprah Winfrey is not going to have a show titled, 'How I was Horribly Maimed and My Family Wiped Out when my Geo Metro was Hit by an Expedition on the Way to the Supermarket'. Barbara Walters is not going to interview someone from Transportation Alternatives. And Exxon, with a thirty-show hit-list of unacceptable programmes (Lawrence 1989), will not support a primetime investigation about how the oil and automobile industries lobby to keep fuel efficiency down, and money spent on highways up, and lobby against subsidies for public transport (Greenpeace 1992). And the blackout of all this information results in a near-total lack of public debate on transportation. We did not hear much about Texaco's devastation of the Ecuadorian rain forest a few years ago either. Without such information, there will never be public demand for environmentally responsible corporate policies, nor will elected officials be induced to legislate for better fuel-efficiency standards and emission control to reduce greenhouse gases. Only an informed citizenry can contest advertising's make-believe world. But in this brave new world of advertising censorship, long-cherished democratic traditions, the last hope for social and environmental justice, give way to fantasy persuasions and dream worlds of adventure.

There is some hopeful indication that the media blackout may no longer be possible. A February 1999 article on the front page of the business section of the Philadelphia Inquirer actually raised environmental issues. Ford's new Excursion will do only 12 miles (19.2 km) to the gallon. The article reported criticisms by two environmental groups, the Sierra Club and Friends of the Earth: 'basically it's a garbage truck that dumps into the sky' (Akre 1999: D1). The caption to the accompanying photograph read, 'The Sierra Club has a campaign against the 19 foot-long, gas-guzzling Ford Excursion. The slogan: "The Ford Valdez. Have you driven a tanker lately?"' (Akre 1999: D1). Ironically, the new chairman of Ford, William Clay Ford Jr., is a self-styled 'lifelong environmentalist' who has promised to be an industry leader in developing clean vehicles. But the powerful forces of market relationships clearly make that impossible. Ford will make $12,000 to $20,000 profit on each SUV sold. Public education and environmental regulation are the only possibilities for changing this downward trend toward global destruction.

Conclusion

The SUV is the quintessential commodity fetish. When we buy it, it does not speak of the corporate practices of global domination, or the vast environmental degradation it causes. Corporate censorship is now essential in keeping these hidden relations from entering public discourse. The suppression of information is essential for advertising effectiveness. Advertising fantasies resonate only as long as no contending information shatters their illusions.

When advertising helps truck-buyers express their 'green' identity, who's ever going to want to take the train? This remarkable advertising campaign has mapped a symbolic world where SUVs not only can co-exist with nature, but are naturalized within the wild geographies of the places they inhabit. This, in itself, is a phenomenal example of the persuasive power of visual discourse. Such persuasions also illustrate the creation of cultural mythologies utterly dislocated from the consequences of the actual destructive practices that they engender. In the context of this popular symbolic culture, human activities have no consequences.

Consumers must place advertising within the framework of critical thought. Part of that project is to reconnect the aesthetic and social–psychological meanings to the tangible material and environmental relations from which they have sprung, or, in the case of four-wheel-drives, from the jungle sink-holes their operation has created, and from which they do not ascend unsoiled.

References

Akre, B. (1999). 'Environmentalists Seeing Smog over Ford's New Giant SUV'. *Philadelphia Inquirer*, 27 February: D1–7.

Andersen, R. (1995). *Consumer Cultural and TV Programming*. Boulder: Westview Press.

—— (2000). 'Selling "Mother Earth": Advertising and the Myth of the Natural', in

R. Hofrichter (ed.), *Reclaiming the Environmental Debate: The Politics of Health in a Toxic Culture*. Boston: MIT Press.

Baudrillard, J. (1983). *Simulations*, trans. P. Foss, P. Patton, and P. Beitchman. New York: Semiotext(e).

Benjamin, W. (1968). 'The Work of Art in the Age of Mechanical Reproduction', in H. Arendt (ed.), *Illuminations*, trans. H. Zohn. New York: Schocken Books, 217–52.

Bradsher, K. (1997a). 'Collision Odds Turn Lopsided as Sales of Big Vehicles Boom'. *New York Times*, 19 March: A1, D20.

—— (1997b). 'A Deadly Highway Mismatch Ignored'. *New York Times*, 24 September: A1, D6.

—— (1997c). 'Further Problems of Safety Found for Light Trucks'. *New York Times*, 12 December: A1, D17.

—— (1998). 'Insurers Saying Sport Utilities Need Redesign'. *New York Times*, 10 February: A1, A16.

Burke, W. (1994). 'The Wise Use Movement: Right-Wing Anti-environmentalism', *Propaganda Review*, 11/spring: 4–10.

Burrington, S. (1994). *Road Kill: How Solo Driving Runs Down the Economy*. Boston: Conservation Law Foundation.

Ewen, S. (1988). *All Consuming Images: The Politics of Style in Contemporary Culture*. New York: Basic Books.

Goodman, A., and Scahill, J. (1998). 'Drilling and Killing! Chevron and Nigeria's Oil Dictatorship'. Audiotape. *Pacifica Radio's Democracy Now!*

—— (1999). 'Chevron and Nigeria', in *The 6th Annual Project Censored Awards*, held at Fordham University, New York, 29 April.

Greenpeace (1992). *The Environmental Impact of the Car*. Seattle: Greenpeace.

Haineault, D., and Roy, J. (1993). *Unconscious for Sale: Advertising, Psychoanalysis and the Public*. Minneapolis: University of Minnesota Press.

Lawrence, B. (1989). 'Advertisers Hit Lists of Network Shows Grows Longer'. *Washington Post*, 22 June: E1, E6.

Lombardi, K. S. (1997). 'Too Big? Depends on Where You Sit'. *New York Times*, 16 November Section 14: 1, 4.

McLuhan, M. (1951). *Mechanical Bride: Folklore of Industrial Man*. New York: Vanguard Press.

Meister, M. (1997). 'Sustainable Development' in visual imagery: Rhetorical function in the Jeep Cherokee'. *Communication Quarterly*, 45/3: 223–4.

Meredith, R. (1997). 'Ford Sales Fell 4.3 per cent in April as Big 3 Lost Share to Foreign Makers'. *New York Times*, 6 May: D1.

Messaris, P. (1997). *Visual Persuasion: The Role of Images in Advertising*. Thousand Oaks, CA: Sage Publications.

Phillips, P. and Project Censored (eds.) (1997). *Censored 1997. The News that Didn't Make the News*. New York: Seven Stories Press.

—— (1998). *Censored 1998: The News that Didn't Make the News*. New York: Seven Stories Press.

—— (1999). *Censored 1999: The News that Didn't Make the News*. New York: Seven Stories Press.

Retallack, S. (1999). 'How US Politics is Letting the World Down'. *The Ecologist*, 29/2: 111–18.

Sachs, A. (1996). 'Dying for Oil', repr. in P. Phillips and Project Censored (eds.), *Censored 1996. The News that Didn't Make the News*. New York: Seven Stories Press.

Salpukas, A. (1995). 'As Rugged Vehicles Take to the Streets, Gas Prices Take Off'. *New York Times*, 25 June: A1, A25.

Treece, J., Anderson, S., Sandler, G., and Murphy, K. (1994). 'Trucks: Why We Love 'em'. *Business Week*, 5 December, 70–80.

Wernik, A. (1989). 'Vehicles for Myth: The Shifting Image of the Modern Car', in I. Angus and S. Jhally (eds.), *Cultural Politics in Contemporary America*. New York: Routledge, 198–216.

Wright, D. (1995). *The Road Ripper's Guide to Off-road Vehicles*. Houghton, MI: ROAD-RIP.

Chapter 11

Starbucks Coffee: Cultivating and Selling the Postmodern Brew

Katherine G. Fry

L EAFING through the pages of the April 1992 issue of *Sunset*, an upscale regional lifestyle magazine published and distributed in the western regions of the United States, one encounters a two-page ad for Starbucks coffee. Featured in the ad is New Guinea, one of the countries from which Starbucks purchases its speciality coffee beans. The two-page spread includes a photo on the left-hand page, with ad text on the right. The photo is an extreme close-up of a native New Guinea man. His face, which fills the entire frame, is painted a vibrant red. White paint is streaked around his eyes and mouth and across his nose; his cheeks and chin are dotted white. The Konmei Man, the bottom caption says, wears a red band overlaid with puka shells round his forehead. His eyes and mouth recede into the background, barely visible because of the paint and the way the photograph is lit. The façade, all this bright paint on Konmei Man's face, is overwhelming. The imposing photo portrays to *Sunset*'s readers a human being vastly different from themselves. Perhaps he could even be called exotic and mystical. The Konmei Man is a person these readers could never know the way they know their neighbours or fellow magazine-readers. It is likely the only way they will come close to him or his culture is by purchasing the coffee produced in his country. The ad's text on the facing page doesn't mention Konmei Man at all, yet it complements his mystique.

The text describes the coffee grown in New Guinea, how Starbucks feels about purchasing and roasting it, and how the reader can obtain the final product. 'The spirit lives in every Starbucks bean,' it begins. It goes on to explain that this land where coffee beans are grown, and purchased by foreign coffee-buyers, is a place where 'spirits shadowdance with reality. Where the forces of nature and the power of myth write an ever changing story.' The text continues by describing the finicky bean-buyers at Starbucks and how in roasting, regarded here as an art form, 'we unlock the hidden magic in every bean'. It includes information about how to purchase, by mail order, this coffee that originates 'In the rich, ancient soil of some of the world's most exotic lands.' Several small yet colourful visual images are interspersed among the words. The one at the top is an inset of a flattened globe; at the end of the text is a replica of a stamp featuring a colourful toucan bird, a symbol of New Guinea. At the bottom, supporting all the rest, a bag of Starbucks coffee with the now-familiar green and white mermaid logo bursts open and coffee beans spill out of the top.

The subtext of the ad is difference. It invites American magazine-readers to gaze upon a native, an exotic, mystical other, at the same time as it literally offers a taste of the other through the purchase of coffee, a product not widely grown in the United States.[1] While the Konmei Man and toucan images indicate symbolic difference, the map on the upper left side of the text page indicates geographic difference. The flattened globe inset reminds readers that the place from which this coffee has been purchased is far, far away. But you, dear reader, can visit vicariously through your purchase of coffee beans carefully chosen and artfully roasted by Starbucks. The text and photo 'exoticize' New Guinea and its culture for *Sunset* in an effort to appeal to the refined tastes of a readership which yearns for travel and appreciates fine speciality coffees. The ad freezes this culture in the past and, referring to the forces of nature and myth, relegates New Guinea and its native peoples to another era, less developed than that of the implied *Sunset* readership. The native's painted face suggests a savage culture and people steeped in ritual equated with the past, a sort of nostalgia that is particularly useful here to sell coffee. The exotic and mystical attributes assigned to Konmei Man, New Guinea and the coffee bean work well as advertising strategies because they appeal to that portion of American consumers attracted to New Age mysticism or neo-paganism. Under the New Age rubric are assembled a mixed bag of ideas about 'native' spirituality and non-Western ways of thinking. Remnants of New Age thought appear throughout popular culture, and lately tend to concentrate in advertising and marketing efforts. In this Starbucks ad, the people and history of New Guinea are cultural signifiers presented in such a way as to appeal to the New Age mindset. Yet the culture is actually submerged in the ad, subordinated to the demands of the international coffee market, and specifically the Starbucks Corporation.

The Konmei Man as the 'face' of coffee in this early Starbucks ad can be compared with another, more familiar advertiser-created face. Juan Valdez, whose image has been used in print and television ads for '100% Colombian Coffee', is a familiar icon to US consumers. Some interesting comparisons can be made between the two contrived figures. Juan Valdez, like Konmei Man, is an exoticized figure representing a less-developed country which grows and exports coffee, mostly to developed countries, particularly the United States, which is the world's leader in coffee imports (Schapiro 1994). Wearing a traditional sombrero, he sports a blanket and leads a donkey weighted on both sides with sacks of carefully selected and roasted coffee beans for waiting (white) consumers. Juan Valdez is more overtly associated with coffee than is Konmei Man. In fact, in numerous television commercials he appears in the homes, indeed the kitchen cupboards, of middle-class suburban couples, surprising them in the morning when they enter the kitchen and discover him there, ready to prepare their morning brew. Always smiling, kind and ready to serve, Juan Valdez has been used for years to sell mass-marketed Colombian coffee to Americans. While at one time he was, for American consumers, an exotic figure, that is no longer the case. The smiling man with the sombrero has become too familiar; his image is appropriately attached to mass-marketed coffee.

---

[1] For an account of how the other has been situated temporally, and especially how the non-white other has been used for publicity purposes among European and American traders and travellers for centuries, see Duncan 1993.

Konmei Man is exotic. His image represents the unknown and mysterious to those sophisticates seeking the remote and the untouched. Konmei Man delivers. He does nothing in the Starbucks ad to sell coffee beyond showing his face. He is completely passive, displaying his exotic self to the camera in order to sell specialized coffee to an elite crowd in a specialized leisure magazine.

While the two figures are similar, in that they are male images representative of countries where coffee is widely grown and exported, how they appear in their respective ads, and what they do or don't do, is emblematic of the different taste cultures to which they are targeted. Understanding distinctions among the ads and where they appear, and especially how they fit into a larger scheme—the history of the coffee industry and the contemporary practices of imaging and promoting coffee—is vital to answering some of the questions I attempt to answer here. How did Starbucks coffee rise so quickly from obscurity to near-ubiquity in the late 1990s in the United States? In what ways has speciality, or gourmet, coffee become a symbol of status and a means of creating identity? What do the practices of promoting and consuming Starbucks coffee reveal about contemporary capitalism? How can Starbucks be called the postmodern brew?

To answer these questions, let us first return briefly to Juan Valdez and Konmei Man. The exotic other has been used as an advertising tool in Europe and the United States since before the nineteenth century. To appropriate the images of racial, ethnic, even gender difference in advertising is part of what John Urry (1990) calls constructing the tourist gaze. By whose authority are these images created? Who partakes in them, gazes upon them, and what realities lie behind the faces and bodies of those appropriated for the sale? The fictional Juan Valdez represents the small coffee farmer of Colombia who takes pride in his beans and works hard to produce the best that he can, taking care to preserve the land, and hoping to sell for a fair market price. The reality behind Juan Valdez is that the small Colombian coffee farmer has been all but obliterated, replaced by large corporate plantation owners who have driven out smaller farmers, hired workers at very low wages, and damaged the land by growing coffee using full-sun methods as opposed to shade-grown methods of farming, significantly damaging the fragile surrounding ecosystem (Schapiro 1994; Tangley 1996). In addition to mistreating the environment, corporate owners mistreat their workers. Strenuous working conditions and low wages keep them poor, unhealthy, and constantly at the mercy of imposed corporate values. Despite the realities of life for workers in coffee-producing countries like Colombia, the image of Juan Valdez persists, and we Americans who like to drink the mass-marketed 100 per cent Colombian beverage are none the wiser. As a sales tool, the image is appealing. It works, but it is a lie.

So it is with Konmei Man. In New Guinea, coffee was introduced as an agricultural cash crop in the 1940s and 1950s by whites who moved there mostly from Australia, Britain, and the US. In his 1964 book *The Stone Age Island*, about his work in New Guinea, visiting film-maker Maslyn Williams refers to coffee-growing in New Guinea as the 'touchstone of progress' (p. 218) and the hope of an integrated relationship between highland tribesmen and white settlers. He went on to explain that New Guinea natives in the 1950s were born primitive, but that the activity of raising and exporting coffee was a 'civilizing' factor (p. 220). In fact, the introduction of coffee in the highlands of New Guinea also changed the environment and the economy, nearly erasing traditional family gardening rituals. Someone else had come in and imposed their progress on the 'natives', changing the social organization in that part of New Guinea. Later in the book Williams explains, in what he considers glowing terms, that 'By their [the whites'] example, and the creation of a transport and marketing system, they have helped to lift the highland tribesmen onto the threshold of the twentieth century in a single step' (p. 256). Today coffee is an important source of income in the highland area of New Guinea, but a small number of local capitalists own the largest plantations, controlling this dominant export crop, having long ago driven out the smaller clan producers, affecting not just their economy but their whole way of life (Wheeler 1988). We don't know, from the Starbucks ad, whether Konmei Man is a highlander or not, whether he is a coffee grower, or whether he has any association with coffee whatsoever. Likely there is no connection, but he is, presumably, a native of New Guinea.[2] And in New Guinea, a relative newcomer to mass coffee export, farmers produce arabica beans, the high-quality beans purchased by Starbucks and other speciality coffee companies. Therefore, Konmei Man's image is newer, more exotic, and more removed from the experience of most Americans than that of the familiar Juan Valdez. Konmei Man's passivity and his removal are appealing. His inactivity renders him symbolically malleable. He appears at once all-knowing and innocent, threatening but not too threatening. Because he has been photographed at such an intimate distance he is vulnerable to semiotic exploitation. Readers of the ad, those who have come to appreciate the finer coffee brewed from arabica beans, and who want, especially, to display their knowledge and their good taste can interpret the image to suit their own preferred fantasy of the man and the place he represents.

French sociologist Pierre Bourdieu (1984) has examined the significance of taste as a marker of social class. Taste, he argues, is a guide for lifestyle creation as well as a marker of social class. Bourdieu uses the term 'habitus' to describe the taste structures of class fractions. Habitus is a key structuring element in class-based society. It is the unconscious, or naturalized, system of rules dictating food, clothing, product, entertainment, and other lifestyle choices made within class-based groupings. Continual adherence to this system of rules reinforces the habitus, even as the habitus reinforces the choices themselves. Bourdieu argues that among the class fractions who have the most economic and cultural capital (vast resources of either money or education, but not necessarily both), everyday items and practices are removed from practical use, sometimes raised to the level of 'art'. That is, they are often divorced from their function, with emphasis placed on their form. Today product and service advertising is largely lifestyle-oriented. In some ads the lifestyle context created around a product such as an automobile emphasizes its practical use, and in others the elegance or 'good life' qualities surrounding, or promised

---

[2] None of my research on New Guinea has led me to any tribe or peoples called Konmei. Neither have I found the term used in any context, as a name or a label, associated with the people of New Guinea. Giving Starbucks' ad agency at the time, EvansGroup, the benefit of the doubt, perhaps it is an obscure term they unearthed in their own research.

with, the use of that automobile. Bourdieu points out that in capitalist society the class-based system is determined and maintained not only economically and politically, but also symbolically. Lifestyle choices as markers of one's taste are symbolic choices indicating class membership. Class boundaries are maintained, then, partly through lifestyle choices. These choices become naturalized as 'good', 'bad', or 'vulgar' taste, usually a determination made by the ideologically dominant classes, but accepted tacitly by the majority.

The mass media, particularly advertising, are crucial to late capitalism's maintenance of class-based habitus. Both the venues for and the content of print and broadcast media advertisements signal the population groups to whom they are aimed. The difference between Juan Valdez and Konmei Man as advertising icons represents, on one level, the difference between taste groups for coffee, but on a broader level it reflects changes within advertising and marketing of many consumer products as capitalism itself changes. Juan Valdez, advertising mass-marketed '100% Colombian Coffee' on broadcast television, reaches a wide audience and diverse market segment. In the ads Juan is selling and serving his coffee to the general population of middle-class consumers for breakfast. The coffee is a practical, habitual every(white)man's beverage in these ads. In contrast, the Starbucks ad's Konmei Man is removed, passive and more exotic. He is associated with the beans via mystique. The ad refers to the mythical nature of the place from which the beans have come. New Guinea, a small country colonized much later than Colombia, is still a mystery to most Americans. Therefore, in the effort to market its produce, native New Guinea culture can be readily appropriated, recast, even transformed, to appeal to the desires of the right market niche. This is coffee for a refined taste.

John Urry (1990) builds on Bourdieu's ideas about social maintenance and the habitus, but adds what Bourdieu leaves out: the maintenance of a class-based system via symbolic lifestyle choices along the lines of class, race, and geography. Urry's 'tourist gaze' concept refers primarily to the leisurely travels of the monied classes who venture to new places, consuming them visually through picture-taking, but also physically through consumptive presence on the land. The tourists' desire to consume, both Urry and Boorstin (1961) argue, is the impetus for their travel. The foreign peoples and places of consumption are also the objects of the traveller's gaze, implying a less powerful position on the part of those gazed upon: the objectified v. the objectifier. Most often this unbalanced relationship occurs along the lines of race or ethnicity. The typical scenario is light-skinned people touring 'exotic' less-developed countries where darker-skinned people cater to all their needs, desires and expectations. Urry further complicates the concept of tourist gaze by distinguishing the collective gaze from the elitist gaze, which he says is more Romantic, a gaze sought mostly by the educated elite. It is more ascetic, seeking magnificent scenery and solitude. His distinction between the mass and elitist gazes fits Bourdieu's concept of habitus: that different choices are made by different class fractions. In his discussion of differing gazes, Urry points out that distinctions have arisen as a result of changes in the economics of tourism which parallel changes in overall capitalist consumption. The movement overall has been from mass to specialized. Old tourism, he argues, was about packaging and standardization, but new tourism is more segmented, flexible and customized.

While on one hand Urry is talking about physical travel, on the other he includes the gaze as constructed through photographs and other media. One need not physically travel to exotic places in order to gaze upon the exotic other. The mass media and advertising, he argues, act as culture's mediaries, contributing enormously to our ability—through photographs, video and film—endlessly to reproduce and visually consume the other. In the United States, television commercials and print ads, and their surrounding programme and editorial content, persist in objectifying other peoples and places. They participate in the ongoing creation of consumption needs, but they also segment needs into smaller market niches à la contemporary marketing and advertising logic. Media and consumption habits have become more distinctive, both creating and accommodating differing tastes. One clear vehicle of distinctive consumption is the consumer lifestyle magazine.

Sunset is a standard-bearer of good taste and a means by which to travel, even vicariously, both nationally and internationally. This glossy regional lifestyle magazine is filled with ads and editorial content about fine foods, entertaining, home decorating, gardening and travel. Advertisements perfectly complement editorial content about lifestyle choices for those with the economic and cultural capital to live, in their leisure, as *Sunset* invites them to. In fact, ads are barely distinguishable from editorial content. Both reflect a logic of consumption whereby text and photographs, ads and articles, are constructed to sell to the right demographic regional niche market. The readership of *Sunset* has a mean average income of about $80,000, and 67 per cent hold professional or managerial positions.[3] The readership is solidly middle- to upper-middle class. The Travel section of the issue in which the Starbucks ad appears includes promotional ads and articles about visiting California's Big Sur for scenery; Utah for mountain biking; Australia; Victoria, British Columbia and Papua New Guinea. The brief article about travel to New Guinea is an interesting complement to the Starbucks ad featuring New Guinea in that same section. The article (pp. 46–7), only text without accompanying photos, describes for the reader the possibility of a twelve-day journey on which to experience 'the stone-age cultures of Papua, New Guinea'. Anthropologist guides on the trip explain local customs and offer tours through stilt villages. All of this can be yours, the article explains, at a cost of $3,290 through the travel agency Abercrombie & Kent. This article, though patronizing, is a straightforward offer of exchange to the reader; the nearby Starbucks ad, in comparison, veils the commodity exchange by mystifying both the culture and the coffee bean.

This Starbucks ad was one of the company's first forays into print advertising.[4]

[3] These figures based on information available in 1993 from a telephone interview with research analyst Ray Petsche at *Sunset* magazine. While figures for race and ethnicity of readership are not available, one can surmise, by glancing at the text and images of the magazine, that the magazine caters to a majority white readership.

[4] The ad was produced by EvansGroup of Seattle, Washington.

Of significance is the fact that the ad appeared only in the Northwest edition of *Sunset*, one of three area editions of the magazine.[5] Most likely this is because Starbucks began operation in Seattle, Washington, and in 1992, the year it went from private company to public corporation, it was still selling coffee beans largely in local retail establishments and by mail order, as the ad indicates. At that time the speciality coffee industry was growing, but still wasn't nearly as big as it became in the late 1990s, so national advertising then would not have been cost-effective. For reasons that have to do partly with geographic import/export shipping possibilities, and partly with its unique social traditions, the north-western United States is the contemporary national leader in offering speciality, or 'gourmet' coffee. From San Francisco, Portland, and Seattle, the trend has slowly spread east.[6]

Anthropologist William Roseberry (1996) explains in a detailed analysis how the international coffee trade was dominated for some time after the Second World War by a few mass importers, most notably General Foods and Procter & Gamble, for mass supermarket sales.[7] This was the period of standardization and concentration within the coffee trade. Its peak sales years were in the 1950s and early 1960s, and since then sales have steadily decreased. Currently it struggles to create new markets to offset a drop in daily coffee consumption, particularly among young adults. Standardization within the trade was possible in part because of trade regulations and international import treaties the US had signed with major coffee-producing nations such as Colombia. The treaties enssured that a certain quantity of beans would be purchased from particular suppliers each year, and that a certain price would be paid. By the early 1980s these treaties had expired and the industry began to experience growth among smaller, speciality importers and roasters who buy from a wider array of producers. The new roasters want to capitalize on the differences in beans and roasting methods to suit different tastes. Such differences had been masked in the heyday of mass importing, roasting and distribution. In those days, bean varieties were blended and roasting methods were so similar that most coffee was prepared the same way and tasted much the same. Speciality coffee roasters helped move the industry away from standardization. Roseberry explains how speciality marketers actually shaped consumer taste by creating niche markets for higher-quality, more expensive, or what he terms 'yuppie' coffee. He compares changes within the coffee industry with those pertaining to capitalism at large.

Roseberry's emphasis on the changes in trade and capitalism is similar to Urry's (1990) discussion of shifts in contemporary capitalism towards the creation of specialized markets and consumption habits. Andrew Wernick (1991) describes the same phenomenon, but in different terms. Juan Valdez and Konmei Man illustrate how advertising's form, forum, and content all contribute to creating and distinguishing taste cultures, but Wernick argues that advertising is only part of a

[5] The two other regional editions of *Sunset* are the Central West and Southern West editions.

[6] See Roseberry (1996) for a more detailed account of the earliest days of speciality coffee retailing in San Francisco, Portland, and Seattle.

[7] According to Roseberry, in the early 1980s fewer than two hundred roasters and processors operated in the United States, and only four controlled 75 per cent of the entire coffee trade.

larger promotional culture, or culture of commodification. 'Promotion' is the term he uses to describe how the larger culture is engaged, more and more, in activities geared to imaging and selling: goods, services, people, and much more. According to Wernick, promotion is a rhetorical form that cuts across all communicative and social phenomena. We've reached the point, he argues, where imaged commodities have become advertisements for themselves, and 'the range of cultural phenomena which . . . serve to communicate a promotional message has become, today, co-extensive with our produced symbolic world' (1991: 182). Clearly he's talking about more than just advertising. He is describing a condition wherein all mass- and many non-mass-media messages, produced goods, and even human actions aim to 'sell' in some way. It seems much of our symbolic world is caught in capitalism's web of logic. When everything promotes something, when the goal is to create desire and consumption by putting a price, even a social or symbolic one, on all choices, it is only logical that clear distinctions must be made among those choices. The places we travel to, the range of media we consume, the types of messages we choose, even the coffee we drink, are all sold to us in a way that acknowledges our membership in narrowly defined niche market groups. Promotion permeates, choices abound. But ironically all these choices have a homogenizing effect. Wernick explains that on the surface it appears we have the ability to choose. We can choose between this pair of shoes and that pair, between Mexican food and Thai, between Hawaiian Kona coffee and dark French roast coffee, but underneath these choices are all structured for us. We aren't choosing from a universe of possibilities; we're choosing from a predetermined menu of available items, many of which are not inherently different. We suffer from what Boorstin (1961) calls 'extravagant expectations'. That is, we expect more than can be delivered to us. We have, in our media and other cultural practices, created illusions that lead us to believe we can have everything, that the world is filled with surprises and adventure, but that we also have complete control of the world. According to Boorstin (1961: 5), 'The making of the illusions which flood our experiences has become the business of America, some of its most honest and most necessary and most respectable business.' Since everyone's involved in the same business, it's become nearly impossible to encounter the truly new or authentic. The illusion of specialized choices means more distinctions made between the same things. This is why promotional activities must be rhetorical. The logic of promotion dictates that imaging is the way to create the veneer of choice.

The Starbucks Corporation has successfully imaged itself as a unique company with unique products. Since Howard Schultz purchased and began running the company in 1987, he has worked to distinguish Starbucks as a company that retains its 'smallness' even as it continues to grow, quickly becoming a large corporation, and notably the largest speciality coffee roaster, distributor and retailer in the United States. By 1997 there were about 1,200 Starbucks retail operations across the US, with new ones opening every week. And its reach is extending beyond national borders. Starbucks hopes that by the year 2000 they will have 2,000 stores in the United States and internationally (Cuneo 1997). These figures do not even take into account additional supermarket product sales, corporate contracts or other promotional tie-ins.[8] Despite its incredible corporate reach, Starbucks presents itself as a small, caring company concerned about its employees, about the good feelings customers get when they enter a Starbucks establishment and order their cappuccinos and double lattes, and even concerned about the coffee farmers and coffee-producing countries from which they purchase their beans. The corporation's promotional activities have helped to hone an image that corresponds to a hip, New Age, politically correct, 'feel good' lifestyle—something that appeals to the young and young-thinking (see McDowell 1996). According to Goodby, Silverstein & Partners, the ad agency with whom Starbucks signed in 1996, 'We have an opportunity to redefine what coffee means to a generation' (Jensen 1996: 1). Economically, that Starbucks can successfully market itself and its coffee as a feeling and/or a lifestyle choice is possible in part because of recent changes in the international coffee trade as outlined above. Ideologically, its marketing success is based on an ability to match a product or group of products with taste groups in a social/economic milieu where promotional activities and corresponding image creation are accepted, even naturalized, methods of presentation; where consumption choices and identities intermingle; and where geographic, ethnic, and class differences can be exploited to create images and promote consumption.

Starbucks' hip yet caring image permeates each facet of the business, from management to employees, to retail atmosphere, to product tie-ins. Employees trained to work in retail establishments are called 'baristas'. Each barista is given a twenty-four-hour intensive training seminar at the beginning of their employment where they learn everything from 'brewing the perfect cup', to 'calling' the drinks, to sharing feelings about selling coffee, relaxing, and boosting each other's and each customer's self-esteem (see Reese 1996). Among management they are officially referred to not as 'employees' but as 'partners', or simply as 'human beings'. Many of Starbucks' human beings are young, college-educated adults who have, by default, landed in the retail service industry because that is where, in the current job market, they could easily find employment. The emphasis on feelings works well with this group of young people who possess not economic capital but a good deal of what Bourdieu refers to as 'cultural capital'. Starbucks presents itself as much more upscale a chain than McDonald's or WalMart, whom Starbucks' management detest being compared with because they see their mission as 'elevating the coffee experience' (Reese, 1996: 6), not as becoming a ubiquitous, cut-throat corporation bent on putting smaller retailers out of business. The upscale image is appealing to young employees with more educated, refined tastes than those employed by perceived 'downscale' fast-food and other retail chains. Starbucks has successfully transferred an image not only within its own ranks, but also among its customers and within the communities it serves.

Starbucks engages in a number of activities that promote its goodwill within the communities where it opens its chain of stores. In his autobiography, *Pour Your*

---

[8] Starbucks sells its own brand of ice cream and its frappuccino drink in many supermarkets, and tests its own supermarket brand coffee in some US areas. It also has corporate contracts with Hilton Hotels, Nordstrom, and United Airlines (Cuneo 1997).

Heart Into It (1997: 281), chief executive Howard Schultz describes Starbucks' charitable activities.

In communities troubled by our entry, we have met with local leaders to understand local concerns. . . . Starbucks managers have the power to allocate donations to local causes like ballet and opera companies, AIDS organizations, food banks, schools, and PTAs. In every city, all eight-day-old coffee beans are donated to food banks . . . in fiscal 1996 we gave away more than $1.5 million in cash and kind, equaling about 4 percent of our net earnings.

He continues in the same paragraph, 'Since we don't exploit these actions for public relations, a lot of our customers don't even know about them.' But since Schultz's book is displayed in almost every Starbucks store, many customers will know about these activities if they didn't know already. Clearly these are the types of promotional tactics engaged in by numerous corporations. Such tactics work to promote goodwill, and by doing so increase the bottom line, allowing corporations further to increase their reach, often creating a monopoly within a given area under the pretext of community concern. Starbucks takes its community goodwill even further. They feature in their stores literature that describes their partnership with CARE, an international relief organization that provides assistance to less-developed countries such as Guatemala, Indonesia, Kenya, and Ethiopia. These are some of the many countries from which Starbucks purchases its coffee beans. The promotional literature in the stores features the smiling faces of the natives from each country who have presumably benefited from the CARE/Starbucks partnership, but whose lifestyles do not afford them luxuries like tourism or even the choice to consume gourmet coffee. The photos are not unlike the photo of Konmei Man: the objects of our gaze and another sales tool for Starbucks.

The niche of customers targeted here—some of whom may directly associate Starbucks with its community activism, some of whom may not—is made up of savvy gourmet coffee consumers who, if they possess the good taste and ability to discern, recognize that Starbucks has become nearly synonymous with fine coffee roasts and beans available from exotic places the world over. Starbucks, like other speciality roasters and retailers, has been concerned about getting and keeping young coffee drinkers, but would also like to promote coffee consumption among other age groups. A sure way to do that, Starbucks realizes, is to become associated with a range of cultured items, thereby proving that it is not only a caring corporation but also a corporation 'in the know.' This means it hopes to cultivate an image of hipness. More specifically, it wants to be linked with the latest cultural trends, and particularly the trends associated with its desired market segment. Proof of this can be found on the shelves of the Starbucks retail stores. Marketing ploys include producing and selling a blues CD, *Blending the Blues*, which features music heard in some coffee stores, displaying and selling upscale coffee and tea drinking paraphernalia, and recently signing a deal with Oprah Winfrey to promote and display 'Oprah's Book Club', both the list and book choices, usually right next to Schultz's own autobiography. Of course this cultivated image is really rampant merchandising which increases significantly the corporate bottom line. Schultz (1997: 262) reflects on the desire to create an image as corporation-in-the-know when he writes about the latest ideas sprung from Starbuck's head of marketing: 'Scott believes that Starbucks should be a "knowing" company: in on the latest jokes, the latest music, the latest personalities, up to date about politics, literature, sports, and cultural trends.' The entire store, beyond the goods displayed on the shelves, is planned with an ideal consumer in mind. That Starbucks understands the good taste, if not affluence, of its customers, is reflected in this passage (Schultz 1997: 307): 'Many of our customers are sophisticated and discriminating, and they expect us to do everything with taste, not only our coffee preparation but also the esthetic design of our stores and packaging. When they come into our stores, they're after an affordable luxury, and if the setting doesn't feel luxurious, why come back?'

Essentially, Starbucks' marketing and promotion efforts have crafted a consumer niche. The customers' good taste has been carefully cultivated. Starbucks understands the need to sell coffee not as a product of good value, but as representative of a lifestyle and signifier of good taste. Starbucks' New Agey philosophy, so attractive to many who fit this 'good taste but low on cash' market niche, is reflected in the latest television ad campaign, whose theme 'coffee, tea and sanity' promotes Starbucks as a haven in a world of manic pressure.[9] Many who have exposed themselves to the ad campaigns past and present, who regularly visit a Starbucks retailer for speciality brews, or who enthusiastically consume the latest marketing tool— Howard Schultz's autobiography—perhaps find it hard to resist its appeal. The entire promotional package has afforded Starbucks broad cultural licence to become the largest speciality coffee retailer in the USA, opening stores all over, and often right next to or down the street from established smaller gourmet coffee retailers.

But Starbucks is not without its detractors. One of the ironies of late capitalism, an irony that parallels Wernick's argument that choice is the façade of homogeneity, is that creating a market niche for a product is often accompanied by a desire to expand to near ubiquity. If we're so successful within this niche, why not keep expanding and gobbling up new markets? Starbucks' desire to expand has met with resistance among some speciality coffee rivals and some consumer and political groups who have launched a Starbucks backlash of sorts. This backlash has taken the form of protests in some American and Canadian cities, often outside newly opened Starbucks stores, and an anti-Starbucks pitch by owners and customers of some smaller coffee retailers.[10] In an effort to respond, and ever mindful of retaining its image as small and caring, beginning in the summer of 1997 Starbucks launched the 'coffee, tea and sanity' television ad campaign, which includes animated creatures, both human and animal, who find relief and transformation when they sip their Starbucks beverages. The campaign underscores Starbucks 'feelgoodness', just as Schultz's autobiography does. No doubt the timing of its publication was also meant to offset the backlash. An entire chapter, entitled 'You Can Grow Big and Stay Small', is a defence of Starbucks' national expansion and its

---

[9] A full description of this ad campaign can be found in Cuneo (1997).

[10] Starbucks protests have been reported in Linden Hills, Minnesota, in the United States, and in Vancouver and Montreal in Canada (see Solomon 1996; McGugan 1996).

international aspirations; the title itself belies one of the tenets of current New Age thinking: 'small is beautiful'. Schultz explains at length why the company is not to be blamed for some of the retail and consumer problems and concerns that have arisen in areas where it has opened stores. He refers to many of these as 'misunderstandings' among those unclear about the Starbucks company values. Clearly this chapter, coming as it does near the end of the book, is meant as a reminder that Starbucks need not be feared, but ought to be celebrated as a triumph of entrepreneurial capitalism. However, while Schultz is quick to promote Starbucks' good intentions, he briefly acknowledges the growing fear of retail homogenization in neighbourhoods and towns in the USA, and even global corporate homogenization. But his words only reinforce an image. Starbucks does not change the situation of homogenization; it reinforces it.

Starbucks' retail success is but one example among many illustrating the logic of late capitalism. Starbucks offers us much, but delivers really very little. It promises an opportunity to travel to exotic worlds of speciality coffee—to Guatemala, Ethiopia, even New Guinea—all without having to leave our familiar, comfortable surroundings. The more stores that open, the easier it is for us to venture away, and to indulge our unique sense of style. But we needn't physically go away; we need merely fix our gaze on the likes of Konmei Man, one image among many chosen to promote exoticism and mysticism for those of us who desire to consume the other, both visually and in liquid form.

Since we have the good taste to discern fine coffee, we understand and accept that Starbucks affords us just one line of consumer products among many in our cultural cache of lifestyle accoutrements. Of course it is so much more than coffee. It is art, spirituality, hipness and political correctness. 'The underlying foundation of this company is not about growth.' Schultz explains at the very end of his book (1997: 332). 'It is about the passionate, soulful connection we have with our people, our customers, and our shareholders.' Since we know the Starbucks image, its mission statement, and its good deeds, how can we feel anything but elation about our good taste and our good sense? The postmodern brew is an image and it tends to delude us, but no more than it deludes itself. We are all part of the same system of promotional logic. Boorstin argues that our extravagant expectations dictate our constant search for adventure and authenticity, which is only an illusion—merely an attempt to make the exotic familiar. The modern American, he says (1961: 79–80), expects that the exotic can be made to order. 'He [sic] has come to believe that he can have a lifetime of adventure in two weeks and all the thrills of risking his life without any real risk at all.' We all understand the logic of promotion. The only rule of the game is to sell, and sell to the right market group. If we are part of that group, we're told we can go anywhere—indeed, we feel as though we've gone everywhere. The fact is, we've really gone nowhere. Konmei Man is still only an image in the magazine and we are exactly where we started.

References

Boorstin, D. J. (1961). *The Image: A Guide to Pseudo-events in America.* New York: Atheneum.

Bourdieu, P. (1984). *Distinction: A social critique of the judgement of taste* (R. Nice, Trans.). Cambridge, MA: Harvard University Press.

Cuneo, A. Z. (1997). 'Starbucks Breaks Largest Ad Blitz'. *Advertising Age*, 19 May: 1.

Duncan, J. (1993). 'Place, Time and the Discourse of the Other', in J. Duncan and D. Ley (eds.), *Place/Culture/Representation.* London: Routledge, 39–56.

Jensen, J. (1996). 'Sharing Starbucks Quandary at AAF'. *Advertising Age*, 10 June: 4.

McDowell, B. (1996). Starbucks is Ground Zero in Today's Coffee Culture: Brand Goes Beyond Cup by Embodying Attitude'. *Advertising Age*, 9 December: 1.

McGugan, I. (1996). 'Attack of the Killer Cappuccino'. *Canadian Business*, December: 149.

Reese, J. (1996). Starbucks: Inside the coffee cult. *Fortune*, 134/4: 190.

Roseberry, W. (1996). 'The Rise of Yuppie Coffees and the Reimagination of Class in the United States'. *American Anthropologist*, 98: 762–75.

Schapiro, M. (1994). 'Muddy Waters: The Lore, the Lure and the Lowdown on America's Favorite Addiction'. *Utne Reader*, November–December: 58–65.

Schultz, H. (1997). *Pour Your Heart into it: How Starbucks Built a Company One Cup at a Time.* New York: Hyperion.

Solomon, J. (1996). 'Not in My Backyard: Starbucks is Doing Great, but Is a Backlash Beginning?' *Newsweek*, 16 September: 65.

Tangley, L. (1996). 'The Case of the Missing Migrants'. *Science*, 274: 1299.

Urry, J. (1990). *The Tourist Gaze: Leisure and Travel in Contemporary Societies.* London: Sage.

Wernick, A. (1991). *Promotional Culture: Advertising, Ideology and Symbolic Expression.* London: Sage.

Wheeler, T. (1988). *Papua New Guinea: A Travel Survival Kit.* Berkeley, CA: Lonely Planet Publications.

Williams, M. (1964). *The Stone Age Island: New Guinea Today.* Garden City, NY: Doubleday.

Chapter 12

Scalable Hype: Old Persuasions for New Technology

Dan Weisberg

> People here communicate mind to mind. Not black to white.
> There are no genders. Not man to woman.
> There is no age. Not young to old.
> There are no infirmities. Not short to tall.
> Or handsome to homely.
> Just thought to thought. Idea to idea.
> Uninfluenced by the rest of it.
> There are only minds. Only minds.
> What is this place? Utopia? No. No.
> The Internet. The Internet. The Internet . . .
>
> MCI Communications Corp., television advertisement, 1997

IT needs no long argument to prove that there was a lot of technology on the hearts, minds, and lips of Americans at the turn of the millennium. Technology products, executives, and stock prices are constant topics in national, financial, legal, and scientific news sources. In December 1997, *Time* magazine named Andy Grove, chief executive of Intel Corp., its Man of the Year,[1] and *Spy* magazine, in its annual '100 Worst People, Places, and Things!' issue, labelled the Internet 'the Most Boring Subject in the World' ('The Internet' 1997: 24).

This essay primarily discusses technology ads on TV and only secondarily examines the technology itself, because advertising is easy to understand and technology isn't. Technological progress is too complicated, inevitable, and, as Jaques Ellul calls it, 'ambivalent', meaning that no matter how technology is used, on both a global and a personal level, 'it has of itself a number of positive and negative consequences' (Ellul 1990: 35). In other words, all technology, and probably all progress of any kind, is both good and bad simultaneously (though not necessarily in equal measure), despite Andy Grove's assertion that 'Technology happens. It's not good, it's not bad' (quoted in Isaacson 1997: 50).

There has also been a dramatic increase in the quantity of technology advertisements on television over the last few years. Technology companies spent $492 million for TV airtime in 1996, up 23 per cent on 1995, and more than double the

---

[1] For a man whose 'mantra' is supposedly 'Only the paranoid survive', Grove keeps a pretty high profile, offering *Time* 'unprecedented access to his life and work', and granting a lengthy interview to CNN's Beverly Schuch.

$208 million spent in 1994 (Armstrong 1997). This mass of ads promises that the products (or, as the ads call them, the 'solutions') will solve many of our personal, familial, professional, and social problems. At the same time, these advertisements are almost identical to countless others—for products like beer, cars, dishwashing liquid, life insurance, sneakers, and psychic hotlines.

Americans have decades of experience both watching Budweiser ads and actually drinking Bud. We know that, unfortunately, it will take more than a twelve-pack to transform our lives into the fantasy we see in the ad. We've spent years both watching car ads and actually driving cars. We know that we can't solve our day-to-day problems simply by shutting the door of our luxury sedan, even though the guy in the ad does. However, we are still learning about things like the Internet and e-mail, not to mention e-business, scalability, network computers, anti-hacker fire-wall security devices, and the year 2000 problem.[2] And we are just beginning to understand the claims and representations technology companies are making in their advertisements. Can we really use the Internet and other technologies to become smarter, better informed, less racist, closer to our families? If so, would we even want to?

A closer look at some specific ads, below, will illustrate the similarities between technology ads and all others. But one important difference should be understood first. Unlike the dishwashing-liquid and car ads, technology commercials seem to be fairly literal in their claims. The MCI ad at the beginning of this chapter is not meant to be ironic. It seriously compares the Internet to a utopia where people are judged not on their gender, age, race, or looks, but strictly on the quality of their thoughts, ideas, and minds. That's a strong claim. According to this and other spots, new technology will dramatically alter the ways we communicate, learn, and work. Technology will mediate the most important events of our lives—even the birth of our children. These claims are probably already true. Further, a partnership of the good intentions of humans and the power of technology will solve our most perplexing problems, such as how best to educate our young, strengthen our families, and break down the barriers that separate rich from poor. This is not yet true, and probably never will be. How seriously are we meant to take these claims?

If the ads are accurate, in the real world, not just the world of TV commercials, we'll soon be better employees, managers, salesmen, and consumers. We'll be better thinkers, doers, parents, husbands, and wives. We'll be less racist and sexist, and more understanding of our fellow humans. Basically, we'll all be ready for 'that multimedia application called life', as human existence is now known in certain circles (specifically, in a Philips Magnavox television advertisement aired during 1997).

It's always hard to take anything on a TV screen too seriously—not just commercials, but even supposedly important things like news, politics, and technology.

---

[2] Even Bill Gates still had mixed feelings about the Internet as late as November 1995, until Goldman Sachs took Microsoft's stock off its Priority Recommend buy list because Microsoft lacked a comprehensive Internet strategy. A few weeks later, Gates, for the first time, publicly committed his company to the Internet (Wallace 1997).

And, in the long run, the future of technology products and their corporate owners will depend mostly on what they can and can't do in our homes and offices, and little on what they can do for the characters portrayed in their ads. But, in the short term at least, technology commercials, like all other ads, are mirages that can temporarily distract the viewer from the actual products and companies being advertised—hiding flaws, distorting motives, and making unnecessary products as appealing as an ice-cold Mountain Dew soda after a long day of extreme sports. Because in technology ads, as in all ads, the value of the product equals the values of the viewing audience. In other words, advertisers show us exactly what they think we want to see, not just in the product, but in ourselves.

Before analysing the ads themselves, one more question should be addressed: why are there suddenly so many of them on TV? *Business Week* suggests (Armstrong 1997: 113) that technology companies are switching their advertising budgets from print to television because the public is having a hard time differentiating among the glut of brand names, as

high-tech products are becoming commodities. Personal computers and printers, for example, have become all but indistinguishable, except for the name on the box. Internet service providers offer the same access, for the same price. And the barriers for entry in cyberspace are so low that Web companies are scrambling to build a brand name faster than their competitors so they won't be cyberhistory. 'It's just like beer, or cars,' says Karen Edwards, Yahoo! Inc.'s director of brand management. 'The products are similar enough that image has a lot to do with why people buy one instead of the other.'

It's refreshing that a director of brand management is willing to state for the record that image has a lot to do with why people buy things. But if consumers did not understand this fairly obvious trade secret, it is doubtful that executives like Ms Edwards would explicitly state it. Following her line of reasoning, it seems to be understood and accepted by both advertisers and consumers that ads attempt to create an image, recognition, and demand for a specific product. For advertisers and brand managers, the product's actual quality or necessity is less important than its image, or brand recognition.

Brand recognition is built by creating an aura around a product. This can be done by identifying one easily understood aspect—such as a unique feature or a low price—that differentiates the product from the pack of competitors. It can also be done by paying an admired (or notorious) celebrity to endorse the product, or by portraying the product against a backdrop of images that most of the target audience will find pleasing, to create good vibes around something that consumers might naturally find harmful or threatening, or just not care about.

Although the heads of a number of technology companies have become both admired and notorious celebrities, technology ads, by and large, follow the last marketing strategy. As in other ads, people just like you happily use the product in idyllic surroundings, or the product transforms a negative or sceptical person into a more satisfied true-believer (that is, a consumer). As mentioned above, the sophisticated audience of the late 1990s has learned not to take these ads too seriously. We're just happy when dishwashing liquid gets our dishes clean. We know it won't change our life; we don't expect it to. But the chances are that consumers have significantly higher expectations of, and a high financial investment in, a state-of-the-art computer. Therefore, we might expect computer ads to be more rational and specific about features, and less hyperbolic and generally insulting to our intelligence.

Of course, we'd be wrong. Advertisers are so conditioned to overhype the same impossible promises wrapped in the same vague imagery that it's too late to change now. The funny thing is that much of the new technology really is amazing, and all the unnecessary hype only raises consumers' expectations to levels above what the product can deliver. Now, without any further unnecessary hype, some specific examples.

Philips WebTV

In 1997, Philips produced an 'infomercial' to promote its version of the WebTV Internet Terminal.[3] Like most infomercials, it used a combination of 'celebrities' (in this case, Ron Barr, host of the nationally syndicated radio talk show *Sports Byline USA*, who revealed, 'I've always said that I think information is power') and once-sceptical, now true-believer regular folks, who represented the viewing audience.

Keep in mind that this was an infomercial for a sophisticated piece of technology, produced by one of the largest and best-known consumer electronics companies. But, based on the vague promises that the product would make your life better, bring your family closer together, and maybe even help you land a job so you wouldn't be watching infomercials at 3 a.m. any more, Philips had obviously borrowed heavily from the juicers, psychic hotlines, and other pioneers of the infomercial frontier.[4]

'For those who are afraid of the Internet, for whatever reason,' said a gentleman with long hair and beard, poised on a motorcycle, 'all I can tell you is, I was the same way.' A mother recalled that 'One day, it [presumably, WebTV] just happened to have the choice on there for "Kids Search," and when I clicked in on that, it just gave me all these different things for little kids. You know, games and colouring pages.' The woman was amazed by, and thankful for, these new-fangled activities she could now share with her daughter.

Another woman told us, 'I have a granddaughter. We get on [WebTV] together. Um, it's interesting, because I can show her how to get around, and then we both share the experience.' Yet another mom added: 'My kids, uh, they use it for research, for papers that they do at school.' As she shared this bit of information, we

---

[3] WebTV Internet Terminals are manufactured by Philips Consumer Electronics Company and Sony Electronics. In August 1997, WebTV Networks, Inc. was acquired by Microsoft Corporation. For $199.95, WebTV lets users hook up to the World Wide Web through their television and phone line. They can surf the Web using a cordless remote control, and can write e-mail using a cordless keyboard, sold separately.

[4] Actually, this Philips infomercial aired at a more civilized, weekend afternoon hour, on WPXN-TV 31, New York.

saw her two children biking into the driveway. Then the kids, sitting on the lawn in front of their bikes, testified. 'This one site,' the older one said, as a screen-shot of an erupting volcano was shown, 'they have things on volcanoes, a whole bunch of different things, like all on history and things.' 'It's cool,' his little brother summed up. (The ad did not state how much of the boys' striking intellect was directly attributable to their use of WebTV.)

In commercials, computers, like other commodities, are very frequently portrayed bringing families closer together. Generation gaps are closed as multimedia experiences are shared. This theme has less to do with computers than it has with how Americans feel about families: we like them, and if a product can make our family stronger, we'll probably like it, too. On a more practical level, many products are marketed as being simultaneously cool and pro-family, so that when kids clamour for the item, parents can feel good about acquiescing. These products hit a nice marketing exacta.

Even in Philips's own infomercial, many of the compensated users (assuming they were not scripted actors, which, for the sake of their careers, hopefully they weren't), had difficulty going into any sort of detail about why WebTV is beneficial, or differs from a board game or an encyclopedia. We instead learned that WebTV is 'about' sharing quality time with your kids, without having to expend much energy or imagination yourself. Your children might even be tricked into enjoying homework, because computers blend education and entertainment into a cool hybrid. This claim that computers have the power to make children actually enjoy school was made more explicitly in a Microsoft ad. The spot showed children using computers in the classroom to learn about Ancient Egypt, play chess, and watch a shark devour another fish. At the end of the ad, four children shrieked, 'It's cool to be smart!'[5]

Returning to the Philips ad, if we weren't totally convinced yet of WebTV's value, some old-fashioned, just-folks logic from a wizened, Middle America, senior citizen type should seal the deal. 'I really believe in it,' he said. 'I think it's a great investment, and if I didn't think so, I wouldn't say so. As far as I'm concerned, that's the best money I've spent since I bought my horse!' This man was obviously sceptical about computers. Judging from his high regard for his horse, he was probably sceptical about the automobile, too. But he had decided to buy WebTV anyway, and was more than satisfied with the product. His common-sense approach to technology was an attempt to provide what all ads, computer and otherwise, desperately want: credibility.

In *Brandweek* magazine, Len Sellers (1990: 20) writes that 'the big "C" in new media isn't computer, content or context. It's credibility, the one thing that will ultimately keep and increase the number of real life users. A belief in the worth of computers . . . is what people really buy into, and misrepresentation is the surest way to damage that faith.'

Advertisements like this WebTV infomercial—which is actually the most rational

---

[5] Microsoft Corporation, television advertisement, 1997. For a comprehensive analysis of this 'learning as a cool activity' syndrome, see Postman (1985, 1987, 1988).

and least ridiculous ad discussed in this chapter—are a sure way to kill off new technology's credibility, because they sell computers with the same vague, hyperbolic language and imagery with which other ads sell psychic hotlines and all the other products at which most people laugh. If the technology does not meet the advertised representations—and it's still very unclear if it does—then, as Sellers predicts, credibility will be lost.

Sellers adds that, 'Increasingly, ads about computers, the Internet and Web sites have a strong element of dishonesty. Selling the sizzle is one thing; selling something that isn't there smacks of Three-Card Monty.' For example, he doubts the ability of current web sites to offer TV-level capabilities, and questions whether most people will be able to use their computers as effortlessly and productively as the users in the ads do. Even Bill Gates's demo of a new Microsoft product at a major 1998 technology show crashed, to the amusement of the audience.

Bob Garfield (1997: 49), in *Advertising Age*, asks why the MCI ad quoted at the beginning of this chapter must 'so compulsively overstate, overhype and oversell?' He points out that

Nobody's saying the Net isn't a remarkable medium and a priceless resource, but like any other technological advance, it is just that. MCI's comparison notwithstanding, it is not utopia. It is not a panacea. And it certainly is not as heroically humanizing as MCI would have us believe. There is ample utility and promise in this technology to fill a thousand commercials with a sense of awe, wonder and concrete benefits [without resorting to such levels of hype].

Garfield (1997: 49) writes that when he first saw the MCI ad, it was so overdone he assumed it was 'one of those bracing, austere Nike commercials . . . that idealizes and melodramatizes the importance of sports to girls', before realizing that 'it's actually a bracing, austere MCI Communications Corp. commercial . . . that idealizes and melodramatizes the importance of the Internet to democracy' (the MCI ad was directed by Sam Bayer, who also directed some Nike ads).

In a 'Personal Computing' column in the *New York Times*, entitled 'An Industry that Shrugs Off Errors', Stephen Manes (1998) wrote that

problems with personal computers are clearly becoming the rule, not the exception. As someone who has long been fiddling with hardware and software for a living, I am no longer flabbergasted or even surprised at the number of products I try that do not work as advertised or do not work at all . . . 'Good Enough' has become the computer industry's pervasive standard of quality . . . that allows companies to ship products with known problems while planning to fix them in the next release. It is what keeps users clicking, cursing and waiting on hold as they attempt to work or play with their hardware and software instead of having to repair it.

Scott Rosenberg (1998), senior technology editor of the online publication *Salon Magazine*, suggests that technology companies 'ship products that don't work to seize market share so that some other company can't get a foothold. Or to be able to tell business customers that your company offers a full suite of services. Or to placate impatient investors. "Does it work?" has always been fairly low on the computer industry's list of important questions.'

It is, in part, the intense pressure to raise brand awareness and market share that leads vendors to announce the imminent release of products that aren't nearly ready (called 'vapourware'), then rush the products to market, before all the bugs are worked out, and overstate their features in commercials. Once the consumer starts to equate computer ads with all the others (if he or she hasn't done so already), the technology will have lost a lot of credibility, and theoretically it will be a lot harder to sell consumers such expensive products. In reality, though, technology companies have made a fortune by using our dissatisfaction with their merchandise to drive the sales of upgrades and new products.

IBM e-business solutions

In 1997, the computer industry coined the phrase 'e-business'. Before that, technology companies used 'e-commerce' to refer to Internet-based transactions. Despite the fact that analysts expect electronic, or online, commerce to jump from an estimated $10 billion in 1997 to more than $220 billion in 2001, the industry considered the scope of e-commerce too limited. So, while e-business includes e-commerce, it also encompasses e-inventory, e-customer service, e-human resources, intranets (a mini-Internet only used inside an organization), and extranets (intranets that can be accessed by a company's customers, suppliers, and partners). In other words, IBM and many other vendors are encouraging companies to shift most of their business operations over to the Internet, largely by implementing full-service web sites, and groupware (sophisticated e-mail programmes) and other Internet-based software. As if that weren't ambitious enough, e-business can also save Christmas, at least for technically savvy little girls and their clueless parents.

In one IBM ad, aired a few days before Christmas 1997, the Nutcracker Suite played in the background as Mom and Dad helplessly searched for the assembly instructions for their daughter's new bicycle. 'She's been wanting this for a long time,' Dad cried. 'She'll be so disappointed.' It appeared all hope was lost until the pyjama-clad girl, unable to sleep on Christmas Eve, saw the scene from the top of the stairs. She glimpsed the bike company's web address, 'kidsbike.com', printed on the box. The girl then scurried into her room, went to the customer-support page on the Kidsbike web site, and printed out the instructions, which she then tossed down to her parents. 'Oh, *here* they are!' said Dad, still oblivious, but at least now able to assemble the bike (hopefully). 'Be there when your customers need you. IBM e-business solutions', read the final graphic.

Of course, countless ads use the Spirit of Christmas to sell products, and this ad's message seems to be that if a turn-of-the-millennium girl can't believe in Santa Claus, at least she can believe in the Internet. But the commercial was targeted not at the girl or even at her parents, but rather at the executives of the fictitious competitors of the fictitious Kidsbike company. It was selling a new concept and the phrase that now defines that concept: e-business. Executives were shown one potential benefit of turning their business into an e-business. What was not hinted at is that such a transformation may completely change the way a company and its competitors operate. A 1999 survey by the American Management Association (Franklin 1999) reported that over 60 per cent of the companies that laid off workers in the last half of the 1990s did so because of changes within the companies, automation, or new technologies. The layoffs of the early 1990s, by contrast, were driven by slumping demand and financial difficulties. Many workers feel their jobs are threatened by new technology, and this commercial tries to calm those fears. So, we got a happy family celebrating Christmas, with the help of an e-business solution.

Philips Isis

Continuing the family motif is a spot for Philips Isis, a mobile phone with an extra-long-lasting battery as its key differentiator. After the commercial's narrator said vaguely, 'Today, neither time nor distance can keep us from sharing our lives,' we saw a guy working on what looked like an isolated oilrig, somewhere in the middle of a large body of water. The man was on his Isis mobile phone, talking to his wife, who was lying in a hospital bed, and who had just gone into labour. After explaining that he was 'in the middle of nowhere,' and wouldn't be able to attend the birth of their baby, he coached her through the delivery process, just as they probably practised in Lamaze class when the hectic, modern world allowed them to spend some time together. Six hours later, with father and mother both still on the phone (thanks to the power of the Isis battery, obviously), the baby was delivered. 'I love you honey!' the guy said. 'Honey?' At this point, his wife's voice was replaced by the sound of his newborn child crying, and the proud dad was overcome by the miracle of life.

The fact that Philips was confident that most people would find this ad cute and heartwarming is disturbing. The ad equates a mobile phone call with witnessing the birth of one's child, which is *almost* the definition of tasteless. (It would be more tasteless, for example, to joke that this commercial ended before the audience saw the mother and newborn baby killed on their way home from the hospital, in a head-on collision caused by a driver who took his eyes off the road to make a call on *his* Isis phone.) The ad's logic implies that the man and his wife should be grateful for technology like the phone, which allowed the man to fulfil his responsibilities as a good husband and father. This logic, which is used in many technology ads, rests on the late-1990s assumption that all working Americans are always 'swamped'.

Our wretched shortage of discretionary time helps us justify the lifestyles and values we've adopted during the bull 1990s, when we seem to consider thinking and talking about public issues temporally impossible. In *Salon Magazine*, Todd Pitock (1998) wrote that 'In an era of conspicuous production and suffer-to-earn bravado, ["swamped" has] become the adjective of the decade. People are proud to earn and spend money. You earn time off, too, but time spent not earning money is almost like an unconventional sexual desire. If it's not actually something to be ashamed of, it's nothing to be advertised, either.' Swamped Americans, Pitock continued, often use the term 'Must be nice.' This is 'another woe-is-me 1990s lamentation,' delivered with mock self-pity but obvious pride when other people reveal that they indulge in a non-money-making activity. For example, 'You read a book last week-end? Must be nice.' Or, 'You were at your wife's side to experience the birth of your daughter? Must be nice.' Whether we really are as swamped as we claim is debat-able, but, to the extent that we are excessively busy, technology is more often the cause of our affliction than the cure.

Swamped or not, a mobile phone has nothing at all to do with childbirth, just as e-business has nothing to do with Christmas (apart from encouraging us to buy stuff). But because many people are still unsure whether or not they like mobile phones and e-business, but *are* sure they like childbirth (or, at least, children) and Christmas, ads like these get made. And they get worse.

Compaq Presario 4800 Series

To wit, this Compaq ad. A white couple sat in an office in an adoption agency, talking to the black administrator. 'Scared?' she asked the couple. The looks on their faces and the way they nervously clutched each other's hands let us know that, yes, they were scared. 'This should help.' The administrator turned to her computer, and opened an e-mail message, 'From: Asia. Subject: Taylor Family.' The e-mail contained streaming video of a newborn Asian baby. 'The new Compaq Presario 4800 Series with Intel Pentium II Processor can change the way you look at life,' overstated the narrator. The woman turned back to face the couple, who were now too thrilled to be scared. 'Say hello to your new daughter.'

This ad is a snapshot of what we wish America could be like, racially speaking. And perhaps, if computers can all just get along, it doesn't matter whether or not we humans can. But the proliferation of technology is magnificently designed at least to spark and at most to force massive debate on race, education and schools, language, culture, business, free speech, law, and privacy. In fact, the Internet, e-mail, and other new technologies supply not only the impetus for discussion, but the means with which to discuss. Without a doubt, much debate exists, and new technologies have inspired and facilitated a lot of it. But it remains unclear whether the Internet will meet the same fate as the radio: born and raised by scientists and hobbyists, then enriched by many voices who are eventually tuned out by limited commercial interests. The Internet's current vitality and variety are encouraging; ads like the ones discussed here are ominous. Either way, the debate on how this technology is best implemented should be extended to the many who—whether due to lack of interest or lack of means—have never intentionally typed three *w*s in a row. And the meaningless, privately funded and motivated, rhetoric of the ads described here must be kept separate from and unequal to non-commercial, pub-licly motivated language real people use in real life.

Oracle network computers

If it seems a bit of a stretch to discuss racial issues in computer commercials, reread the MCI ad at the beginning of this chapter. The Internet is advertised as a great liberator and equalizer, because it gives all of us access to vast amounts of information. Thanks to the Internet, the playing-field is now level, and there is nothing holding anyone back from success. Many ads show women and minorities running their own start-up companies on their desktop personal computers. However, even the limited public debate on technology has produced some fears about the 'information have-nots': people, schools, and neighbourhoods that are not yet online. The information have-nots, otherwise known as the poor, will be left behind because they lack the skills and resources needed to compete in the Information Age.

In his 1998 State of the Union Address, Bill Clinton yearned for 'An America where every child can stretch a hand across a keyboard and reach every book ever written, every painting ever painted, every symphony ever composed.' The president, using words that could have been lifted straight out of a technology ad, implied that the government is concerned about bringing the information have-nots up to code. 'We should enable all the world's people to explore the far reaches of cyberspace,' he said.

According to the Oracle Corporation, this is one problem the president need not worry about. One of Oracle's commercials for its network computers started with the same assumption as Clinton's: we all know the Internet is an unparalleled tool for general self-improvement. But, the commercial's narrator worried, what about people who 'can't afford personal computers? Fortunately, as of today, we'll never have to ask that question again. Network computers allow *everyone* to join the information age. And, we'd like to say, "Welcome." Oracle: enabling the information age.'

Only a TV commercial could ask an important and troubling social question, then immediately answer that 'we'll never have to ask that question again'. The Oracle web site claims that 'the network computer allows absolutely everyone in the world to tap into the massive power to entertain, enlighten, email—to do anything you and a computer are possible of achieving.' Wow, absolutely everyone in the world? Well, anyone with a TV, and $200 down and $20 a month.

In the TV ad, a young boy named Mikey was sitting in his living room, using his network computer. However, he did not live in the idyllic surroundings seen in most other ads, because Mikey was a poor, urban kid of indeterminate race. We saw a grim cityscape outside his apartment window. Before network computers, Mikey could never have afforded access to the Internet. Thus, instead of electronically learning and socializing with his more economically fortunate friends from the safety and solitude of his living room, who knows what antisocial behaviour he might have become involved in? Now, he was off the streets, learning about whales.

This ad is another example of a positive aspect of technology being inflated to ridiculous proportions to fulfil the viewers' hopes for, and to equate a product with, the way things *could* be. Network computers, because of their lower price, do allow more people to get online. But to suggest that everyone in the world is now free to join the information age, or even that this fact in and of itself means anything, is obviously misleading. The spot could be seen as an underhand attempt to end one of the most contentious technology debates going today (namely, universal Internet access), by claiming that the problem is solved, so we can all stop feeling guilty about poor kids like Mikey who can't afford a computer. It's more likely, though, that the ad is less nefarious. Complexity is not television's strong suit. If network news shows hesitate to cover complex issues in depth, it's unfair to ask commercials to do so.

The year 2000 problem

By the time this book is published, the world will know whether the Y2K was, in fact a problem—technologically, biblically, whatever. At the time these words were written, though, all we had to go on was the frightening warnings of professional and amateur Year 2000 experts, the comforting assurances of the financial and airline industries, and NBC's production of *Y2K: The Movie* ('What if they're right?'). Well, if they *were* right, this book probably didn't make it to publication. If anyone is actually reading this, hopefully things didn't turn out too badly.

A different Y2K problem, in the months leading up to the Big Day, was that when someone mentioned new technology and the new millennium in the same sentence, chances are he or she was not trying to put some perspective on where technology is taking us as a society, but was instead a panicked technology manager trying to figure out how to save the corporate network before time ran out.

Jaques Ellul (1990: 348) suggested that 'Frequent reiteration of messages eliminates critical reaction.' Nothing frequently reiterates a message quite like advertising. The proliferation of new technology raises some important, critical questions, and we as consumers and citizens need first to figure out what they are, and then to ask them.[6] We're already being told that one such question—What will happen to people who can't afford computers?—never has to be asked again. That's a comforting answer, but if it and other similar commercial answers to critical questions are accepted, the result could be disastrous.

The elimination of critical reaction and dissent, combined with a lot of hype, quickly leads to widespread belief that, even if there is no reason for a product, or a law, or a situation to exist, there is also no reason for it *not* to exist. The product, law, or situation achieves Andy Grove's beloved 'it's not good, it's not bad, it just happens' non-value. With computers and other technologies now mass produced

---

[6] Neil Postman (1998) suggests the following six questions: What is the problem that this [new] technology will solve? Whose problem is it? What new problems will be created by solving an old one? What people and institutions will be most seriously harmed? What changes in language are occurring as a result of technological change? What new sources of economic and political power will emerge?

and marketed, many new products are being made available to the public. Ellul (1990: 350) wrote that often

People do not easily see the use of such an object, but they are ready to react as obedient consumers. There has to be mass consumption of high-tech products. Indeed, these are the key to all economic development . . . [Technology] can continue its triumphant march only if the public follows, buying the maximum number of computers, tape recorders, videos, photocopiers, high-definition televisions, microwaves, and compact disks. For every new technical advance there has to be a public that is ready to buy the latest product.

In other words, technology products, like other products, are primarily created simply to be purchased, and secondarily and often only coincidentally to make us smarter, or better parents, or less racist. Products that make us smarter but aren't profitable disappear, while those that make the buyer stupider and the seller's bottom line blacker thrive.

So when technology executives say they 'believe' in the Internet, their belief is really in their ability to market and sell us large quantities of brand-name Internet products. But when technology ads demand that we, too, believe in the power of the Internet, we must do so with the same fervour with which we believe in spending time with our family and communicating with our friends, or learning, or being good at our job and making money. If we believe in these things (and who doesn't?), then technology *must* be a big part of our life and our budget.

This is true not just of technology commercials, but of most ads for any product. That's why the ads all contain the same messages and, in many ways, an advertisement for one product might as well be an ad for any other commodity. Once advertisers (often using focus-group testing) identify the most-favoured images, emotions, and values of the target market, they can confidently advertise those images, emotions, and values, and simply superimpose the dubious product over them, whether that product is a computer, a car, or a candidate.

In another Oracle commercial, a young technology manager suggested to his company's chief executive that the company invest in network computers. The executive liked what he heard about the product, but asked the technology manager why he hadn't recommended buying network computers last year. There was a long pause, as the other managers looked nervously at their colleague. 'They, uh, didn't exist,' he finally replied. The boss was impressed, and so were we. In advertising, something that is new, whether it's a new lemon scent or a new way to communicate, is more valuable than something that is old. If it isn't, there is no reason for us to buy it.

But while most commercials can only sell a false concept of newness, in technology ads, newness and the product are identical. Because it's not just that the Internet is the adjective 'new'—like a new lemon scent or this year's model of a car—it's that the Internet is the noun 'newness'. Despite the blind denials of some technology critics, computer companies produce products that create rare opportunities to change ourselves, our businesses, and (why not say it?) the world. The gimmick of newness is not necessary. And yet, as illustrated, this technology is advertised as if it were just one more stupid product that maybe we could be convinced to buy, as long as we can be suckered into thinking it's the latest and greatest.

Perhaps advertisers assume that consumers—rendered sceptical and virtually numb by the millions of commercial exposures they have endured over the course of their life—are unwilling or unable to understand the real thing when they see it. Maybe advertisers realize they have promised us so much newness for so long, and delivered so little, that now they are afraid to advertise, and we are afraid to recognize, a product or an idea that isn't just new, but can really change things. In other words, we want to see black women helping white couples to adopt Asian babies; poor, urban kids safely learning and socializing; and grandmothers exploring the Internet with their granddaughters. At least, we want to see all these things in commercials, where they are only the old, familiar, false promises of a million other ads, not to be taken too seriously and not meant to reflect reality, or even the advertised product.

In ads, the future is already here, and it doesn't require any new thought, emotion, debate, or policy. It doesn't really require any change—we just have to buy. It is our *buying*, not the product itself or our use of it, that creates the future and fulfils the ad's promise. We are happy to buy this commercial version of newness while technology stuns us, and upgrades itself.

References

Armstrong, L. (1997). 'Cars, Beer, and Web Browsers'. *Business Week*, 12 May: 113.

Ellul, J. (1990). *The Technological Bluff*, trans. G. W. Bromiley. Grand Rapids, MI: William B. Eerdmans.

Franklin, S. (1999). 'The Load at Work is Getting Heavier'. *Chicago Tribune*, 26 October, Section 3: 1.

Garfield, B. (1997). 'Is Internet Utopia? Good Heavens, No' [Bob Garfield's Ad Review]. *Advertising Age*, 20 January: 49.

'The Internet Prolongs its Cybermitzvah'. (1997). *Spy*, December: 24.

Isaacson, W. (1997). 'Man of the Year'. *Time*, 29 December: 50.

Manes, S. (1998). 'An Industry that Shrugs off Errors'. *New York Times* [online], 13 January.

Pearlstine, N. (1997). 'The Man and the Magic'. *Time*, 29 December: 8.

Pitock, T. (1998). Swamped. *Salon Magazine* [online], 26 June.

Postman, N. (1985). *Amusing Ourselves to Death*. New York: Penguin.

—— (1987). *Teaching as a Conserving Activity*. New York: Dell.

—— (1988). *Conscientious Objections*. New York: Alfred A. Knopf.

—— (1998). 'Technology and society'. Address delivered at Calvin College, Grand Rapids, MI, 12 January.

Rosenberg, S. Scott (1998). 'They Know what's Best for You'. *Salon Magazine* [online], 16 January.

Sellers, L. (1997). 'Hype, Meet Reality'. *Brandweek*, 14 April: 20.

Wallace, J. (1997). *Overdrive: Bill Gates and the Race to Control Cyberspace*. New York: John Wiley & Sons.

Part IV

Commercial 'Diversity?'

Introduction

SOME scholars have noted that marketing practices validate certain subgroups within the larger culture. Because no market segment or subculture is excluded from the marketing mix, they are transformed into lifestyle consumption groups and become important targets for advertising. Advertising images speak to the needs, preferences, and sensibilities of a variety of market segments, turning the total market into the sum of its diverse parts. The validation of subcultures is thought to be a positive if unexpected side effect of marketing practices. But other scholars point out that the positive impact of representations of certain subgroups may be mitigated precisely because of the targeted nature of such images in publications and programmes not likely to be seen by, and therefore not challenging to, members of other subgroups or a mass audience. In addition, the content and context of advertising representations of different subgroups must be taken into careful account in assessing their interpretive significance to the larger culture. We offer here three essays that address the marketing strategies and advertising images targeted at three different marketing segments; women, teenagers and African Americans.

The emergence of the supermodel as a distinct category of celebrity over the past few decades is based in large part on a shift in advertising strategy, as models have been transformed from nameless mannequins into stars. Accompanying this shift is the commodification of modelling, and the introduction of the supermodel as a brand name for both celebrity image and fashion product. Using textual analysis as their primary methodology in 'Image Culture and the Supermodel', Delicia Harvey and Lance Strate argue that, while supermodels have gained important recognition as individual personalities, such mediated subjectivities are based on traditional representational modes of objectification.

Robert M. Entman and Constance L. Book offer an extensive content analysis of the representation of African Americans in US advertising in 'Light Makes Right: Skin Colour and Racial Hierarchy in Television Advertising'. Their approach offers an important contribution to the analysis of the changing representation of African Americans in advertising culture, especially the increasing prevalence of images of black athletes.

In 'Talking Back to Calvin Klein: Youthful "Targets" Confront their Commercial Image', Lauren Tucker's research exemplifies another methodology for documenting and understanding image culture. She has conducted focus-group interviews with teenagers and young adults who offer their own interpretation of Calvin Klein advertising and the controversy raised by its depiction of youthful sexuality. She also explores the implications of the controversy by analysing the ways it has been discussed in other media formats.

Chapter 13

Image Culture and the Supermodel

Delicia Harvey and Lance Strate

THE origin of the model is lost to antiquity, but is no doubt tied to the development of visual media. By having a human being pose for a drawing, painting, or sculpture, artists could obtain better results than when working from imagination or memory. The use of models has multiplied geometrically with the development of perspective in the visual arts during the Renaissance; the invention of the printing-press in the fifteenth century and the development of engraving; nineteenth-century innovations such as steam-powered printing, photography, chromolithography, and the motion picture; and twentieth-century innovations such as television and computers. More visual media require more visual content, and human beings have always had a narcissistic fascination with the human image. As communications technologies have set the stage for contemporary image culture, not only the demand for but also the interest in models has grown dramatically.

But burgeoning numbers alone do not tell the whole story. In the past, there were two types of model. The first was the famous person, chosen or self-selected as a model because of that very fame. In this case, the depiction might enhance or extend the individual's fame, but did not confer notoriety in and of itself. The second type was the anonymous model, chosen on the basis of appearance. Like an actor playing a role, this model might be used to depict a fictional character, or a figure whose true appearance is unknown (for instance, Moses, Jesus, or Mary). Or the model might remain nameless, a pure image. A third type of model has recently emerged, however—the supermodel. In this case, the model starts out as anonymous. Unlike most unnamed models, however, the supermodel rises to the top of the profession and gains fame through modelling itself. Supermodels like Cindy Crawford, Naomi Campbell, Claudia Schiffer, Kate Moss, Vendela, and Elle Macpherson now take their place in our cultural pantheon alongside the stars of television, film, popular music, and sport, as well as the leaders of the political, industrial, religious, and military sectors of society.

The technologies of visual communication set the stage for the supermodel, and media commercialism provides the cues. Models are used in a variety of contexts, but none is more prominent than the display and promotion of clothing, cosmetics, and other related products and services dedicated to the enhancement of the individual's appearance. Fashion is about looks, but of course it is also about money. The fashion industry has long been associated with the rise of consumer culture (Ewen 1976, 1988; Ewen and Ewen 1982). After all, fashion sales depend upon advertising and marketing to convince consumers to replace items that are entirely functional, for reasons that are entirely symbolic. Fashion is the paragon of conspicuous consumption (Veblen 1979), and women have traditionally served the dual function of conspicuous consumers and the conspicuously consumed, as status symbols for men and the site/sight of pleasure for the patriarchal male gaze (Berger 1977; Goffman 1979). Similarly, fashion models are salespersons, but are also the product being sold.

Thus, while supermodels model fashion, they themselves are models of commercialism, simultaneously playing the role of consumer, product, and promoter. To put it another way, in advertising products, they themselves become the products of advertising. We can therefore trace the emergence of the supermodel to changes in fashion advertising since the 1960s (what follows is a summary of research reported in Harvey 1997).

From coat hanger to supermodel

The fashion advertising of the 1960s emphasized the product, the clothing working to minimize the role of the model by hiding her under the big, shaped suits, hats, and gloves. Leslie Rabine (1994: 60) describes this concealing fashion as displaying the '"Jackie Kennedy" style of stiff, boxy trapeze suits and dresses, prim and perky in their elegance'. The exception to the hidden and unknown models of the 1960s was, of course, Twiggy. Indeed, the fact that Twiggy did become so well recognized may have something to do with the fact that her fame came in association with the miniskirts and small dresses of the Mod culture which she brought to America in 1967 (DeLibero 1994). The clothes in which she was seen naturally highlighted her unusual thinness, making her much more recognizable.

Advertisers employed a minimalist approach as regards setting and environment in this period, allowing for what Rabine (1994) describes as a world that seemed hermetically sealed from the outside world. Such settings removed the models from the real world and real people, while relatively less active poses in comparison to today's fashion photography also contributed to the look of a 'sealed' world. It follows that the less realistic the setting, the more likely the model is to be viewed as a mannequin, rather than a memorable and significant individual. Often, advertising text in the sixties emphasized the fabric of the clothes, rather than the model wearing them, and many designers advertised together with a fabric or fabric manufacturer. The model was simply one of many tools used to photograph an item of clothing.

The 1970s brought slight degrees of change. In terms of clothing type, images began to advertise more revealing and form-fitting garments. As more of the model's body was being photographed, more attention was paid to her size and figure: her body was becoming a more prevalent feature, distinguishing one model from the next. Hence, the status of the model was somewhat elevated. Also important was the gradual increase in the use of close-ups, making models' faces increasingly visible. Images of models on a runway began to become common during this period, adding to their recognizability, establishing them as professionals with a job to do, and thereby making them appear more 'real'. All these factors contributed to a slight shift toward focusing on the model and 'her' clothes, rather than on the more utilitarian connection between clothing and the consumer. Theme and story also became more developed during this decade. As advertising text began to employ narrative formats, settings became more detailed, varied, and realistic, models' poses included more activity, and more men appeared in advertising for women's clothing as a component of the storyline.

The attention paid to elements outside the product was evidence of a shift in focus that allowed for new forms of commercial celebrity. During the 1970s Ralph Lauren appeared in his own advertisement (a photograph of himself in close-up). This was part of a series which he had begun in 1974, according to Deyan Sudjic (1989), and was part of the creation of the Lauren mystique, making him one of the most recognized designers. The campaign assumed that readers did not want to see the clothes; rather they wanted to see the Ralph Lauren image, the designer who represented the lifestyle. What Lauren did for designers, Cheryl Tiegs did for models. Her breakthrough came when she posed for *Sports Illustrated* in 1978 in a see-through fishnet bathing suit. Steven Aronson (1983: 26), noting that the photograph was not significantly different from one that might appear in *Playboy* magazine, states: 'With the politician's awareness of a constituency, Tiegs had elected to show off in *Sports Illustrated* rather than in *Playboy*, realizing that if she were to be marketed as the girl next door, she couldn't afford to sit in the center of *Playboy*. A *Playboy* bunny does not live next door.' Her calculated self-display brought Tiegs an unprecedented level of fame for a fashion model, including an appearance on the cover of *Time* magazine in 1978; her issue was the second highest in news-stand sales for that year, eclipsed only by the cover featuring the Jonestown massacre, and outselling issues whose covers featured Muhammad Ali, Pope John Paul I, and John Travolta. The cover story's title was 'A Famous Face is Now a Name', and, by achieving name recognition, it became possible for her to go from modelling products to endorsing them. The carefulness she showed in her act of self-display is, according to Aronson, what allowed her to become a spokesperson for the conservative Sears, Roebuck corporation, and ultimately launch her own brand of clothing. As Lauren moved from designer to model, Tiegs went from model to designer, both converging in the realm of celebrity.

Tiegs's breakthrough came at the end of the 1970s, and it is therefore the eighties that are most often referred to as the period during which the supermodel emerged. For example, a search for the topic 'supermodel' in research databases like Lexis/Nexis, the database of newspaper, journal and magazine articles dating back to 1980, lists the topic 'supermodel' only in articles from 1985 forward. Michael Gross (1995) also argues that no models achieved a higher success level than those who emerged in the late eighties. During that decade, the trend toward smaller, tighter clothing continued, as Susan Faludi (1981) points out; she also mentions that designers pushed towards the 'little girl' look and the 'slender silhouettes' during this period. The seemingly lesser emphasis on the look of the clothing allowed for more movement or 'action' on the part of the models. The idea of branding, or advertising that associates the product with a non-product image or idea, had become prevalent by the mid-1980s. Thus, some models became supermodels by becoming brands themselves: part of selling the image of the designer meant selling the face of a certain model. Increases in advertising length also allowed for the selling of a certain aura or world associated with the product. Sudjic (1989: 77) explains the effect of these longer ads: The Ralph Lauren 'image', for example, 'features a regular cast of models who reappear month after month. They live in a curiously timeless world made up of images pieced deftly together out of a past that is not exactly the 1930's, nor the 1950's.' These longer advertisement series, then, not only sold a particular image or idea, but also allowed particular models to be seen over and over again in a set of pages. Hence, the appearance of early supermodels such as Paulina Poriskova and Christie Brinkley coincides with a less product-focused, more branded form of advertising.

The 1990s have only continued with these trends that highlight the model or designer image. Text has changed in advertisements to emphasize elements other than fabric, and designer or brand name seems to be the most important. Models are occasionally named in clothing ads and very often named in cosmetic advertisements. Hence, the trends in clothing, text, setting, and advertising type over this decade have led the model to be a more central focus of these images. She no longer represents a *way* to advertise a product; she is the face of the product. A further extension of the supermodel craze evident in the images of 1996 is the crossover between film and TV celebrities and models in the fashion magazines. For example, the actress Carrie Otis was used as a model for Donna Karan in 1996 ads, and the same designer more recently used both Demi Moore and Bruce Willis in a series of ads, while Melanie Griffith was chosen as the new Revlon girl.

Even more revealing is the extent to which supermodels have crossed over to sectors outside fashion. Some of the larger publishing houses have recently been climbing over each other in order to publish the next supermodel story. As Robert McCrum (1996) wrote in the *Guardian*, 'Today, almost all the major literary houses, who once took pride in publishing international writers, are using the [Frankfurt Book] fair less to trade rights on the next García Marquez or Gunter Grass, and more to chase hectically after ready-made bestsellers like Naomi Campbell's *Swan*, the hot book of 1993' (p. T17). Naomi is not the only supermodel who has realized how to cash in on her own celebrity. Claudia Schiffer had her own autobiography published entitled *Memories* (1995) and Pavillion Books published *Kate* (Moss 1995), a photo-biography of Kate Moss. Cindy Crawford continued the trend as the main attraction at an American Booksellers Association convention where she was promoting *Cindy Crawford's Basic Face* (Crawford, Kashuk, and Boyes 1995; McCrum 1996). The book includes her own make-up tips for young women. The presence of so many 'ready-made' bestsellers to which publishers seem so willing to attach their names proves that the life of a model has moved to a new level of celebrity.

The evidence of supermodel mania continues as one turns to another medium of popular culture: movies. The fashion industry is the latest background against which many directors have moulded their stories. What began with Robert Altman's satirical look at the industry, *Ready to Wear*, in 1994, has continued to the supposedly more serious (due to their documentary style) insider's view of the fashion world. *Unzipped* (1996) was a well-received documentary following a fashion season with New York designer Isaac Mizrahi which hosted a number of supermodel stars. The next film to be produced could be considered the apex of supermodel fame. *Catwalk* (1996) was an entire film devoted to following supermodel Christie Turlington through her semiannual fashion circuit of Milan, Paris, and New York (Phinney 1996). There is also a project in the works for a Charlie's Angels film featuring Claudia Schiffer, Tyra Banks, and Vendela (Bark 1996). Supermodels have also managed to appear in films unrelated to fashion. Naomi Campbell can be seen in *Miami Rhapsody* (1995) and *Girl 6* (1996); Elle Macpherson can be seen in *Sirens* (1994), *If Lucy Fell* (1996), and *Jane Eyre* (1996), and Cindy Crawford made her debut in *Fair Game* (1996). While none of these films has recorded ticket sales of blockbuster proportions, the mere popularity of fashion as a subject adds to the celebrity status of modelling and the supermodels' appearances in so many recent films prove their heightened popularity.

Television has also done its part to cash in on the audience pull of movies about modelling. What began with model roles such as that of Vanna White's on *Wheel of Fortune* and developed into the introduction of the 'spokesmodel' category on the television programme *Star Search*, has clearly continued its popularity with television audiences (Strate 1995). As Janet Ozzard (1996: S4) of *Women's Wear Daily* discovered when speaking with Dave Cussaro of the cable channel E!, 'Fashions clearly stick out as one area that's often requested by advertisers.' This is true because of the draw of both a male and a female audience; males who want to see the supermodels and women who want to see the fashions and emulate the objects of male desire (Ozzard 1996). Of course, in addition to E!'s *Fashion File* and *VideoFashion*, a host of other fashion news programmes exist. CNN's fifteen-year-old *Style* with Elsa Klynch has begun to be crowded out by some of the other cable channels now following fashion. MTV's *House of Style* has a reputation as one of the more unusual of the many shows because of the faster pace that MTV productions usually have. VH1's *Fashion Television* also concentrates on the runways of the world, together with a new network coming to cable viewers, the Fashion Network, a twenty-four-hour outlet for style coverage. It is evident from the outburst of fashion television that the obsession with supermodels is not limited to a handful of women's fashion magazines. As Ginia Bellafante (1996: 68) of *Time* writes, 'Given pop culture's unabating fascination with designers, models and the celebrities who worship them, it's not surprising that TV has finally taken a focused interest in fashion.'

The hype of the supermodel has not only been written about and broadcast, it has also been sung. Probably the most famous drag queen in America, Rupaul, produced a popular recording and video for his song 'Supermodel (You Better Work!)' (Cronin 1996). Singer Jill Sobule wrote and performed a song entitled 'Supermodel' that was included in the soundtrack for the film *Clueless* (Justin 1995). Terence Trent D'Arby also came up with his own addition to the supermodel song with 'Supermodel Sandwich', which was included on the *Ready-to-Wear* soundtrack. Whether the songs are out of admiration or annoyance, it appears that the music industry is well aware that the fame of these few select models has risen to almost epic proportions, placing them higher on a list of subjects to be sung about.

Supermodels also loom large on the Internet, be it on professional sites with a fashion focus (here Crawford again dominates), amateur tribute (or satirical) sites, or on sites that are pornographic purveyors of real and fake images of the women in various stages of undress (further reinforcing their objectification). And, while perhaps not considered one of the more popular media, there is a final example of just how well known models have become in the last decade. It comes in the form of a doll. Three supermodels, Naomi Campbell, Claudia Schiffer, and Karen Mulder, have all had children's dolls fashioned in their likeness. Instead of Barbie, little girls can play with a miniature supermodel of their choice (Philoppannat 1996).

The supermodel as celebrity

What one realizes, by reading about the various media that have all in one fashion or another paid tribute to the supermodel craze, is that supermodels are celebrities. Books are written by them or about them; films are made about them, songs titled after them, and television shows feature them as part of the regular cast. They are cross-marketed, just like the rest of the megamedia landscape which unites shopping with celebrity entertainment. They also have, like all other celebrities, learned to exploit and use their celebrity to make additional earnings, for example by having a doll modelled after their face or figure; they therefore have gained a form of agency. But, like that of most celebrities, their fame is unearned. According to Daniel Boorstin (1978: 57), 'the celebrity is a person who is known for his well-knownness'. Unlike heroes, who are famous for their accomplishments, celebrities are manufactured, products of media, hype, and publicity. But a less judgemental perspective can be taken by tracing the links between changing conceptions of the hero and changes in media environments such as the shifts from orality to literacy, and from print to electronic communication (Strate 1994, 1995). In this way, the celebrity can be viewed as the type of hero that emerges in an electronic media environment, one that is characterized by image and personality. Whereas in oral and typographic media environments, name recognition comes first and is primary, visual communication technologies have made face recognition minus name recognition common among electronic heroes (Cathcart 1994). Whatever perspective is taken, it is hard to overlook the ordinariness of the celebrity as opposed to traditional heroes. That the supermodel's fame is a result of simply appearing in the media, not of any significant accomplishment, is quite apparent; the focus is on their lifestyles and gossip about their personal lives. Because they do little more than dress up and pose, supermodels become the target of ridicule, often directed at their intellect. They may also be mocked for their emphasis on thinness ('Eat something!'). In this, they are not only ordinary, but at times ironic figures who seem to be less in control of their lives than their audience (Monaco 1978).

It is important to emphasize that media celebrity is very much a part of media commercialism. Sudjic (1989) discusses the role of consumerism in the manufacturing of celebrity, as well as the concomitant role of celebrity in promoting consumer-ism. From an entirely different perspective, Rein, Kotler, and Stoller (1987) provide a how-to manual for obtaining high visibility, noting how celebrity increases earning potential; making the individual's image into a product not only allows the model to rise to the top of her profession, for example, but also vaults her into an entirely different arena, the celebrity industry. Like many celebrity entertainers, super-models are distinguished by the affluence they derive from their profession. While the emphasis on lifestyle may be part of the hype, the money they have earned to afford that lifestyle is substantial. Media depictions of the supermodel may there-fore invoke the American dream of upward mobility, emphasizing her success story, which is typically one of discovery. For example, Gross (1995) writes about how Kate Moss was just another teenager until she was magically spotted by an agent on a plane trip. The rewards for being chosen are enormous, but this also means that the stakes are high and the competition fierce, as C. Wright Mills points out (1956: 74):

The movie stars and the Broadway actress, the crooners and the TV clowns are celebrities because of what they do on and to these media. They are celebrated because they are displayed as celebrities. If they are not thus celebrated, in due time—often very short—they lose their jobs. In them, the panic for status has become a professional craving: their very image of self is dependent upon publicity, and they need increasing doses of it.

As self-fulfilling prophecies, supermodels' sole focus must be media attention. As products, supermodels represent 'the maximum amount of profit' 'produced from investment in the smallest number of performers; these are the "stars". Stars exist only to be checks to the majority of artists practicing their art' (Sennett 1977: 292). In other words, they are the product of manipulation, and must tread a fine line between maintaining their fan base and avoiding overexposure. Manufactured, manipulated, supermodels are at once characterized by the ordinariness of every-day reality, and the extraordinariness of hyperreality.

The supermodel as simulation

Boorstin (1978) refers to celebrities as human versions of pseudo-events, media events manufactured to seem more compelling than actual events. Similarly, Baudrillard (1983) uses the term 'simulation' to refer to technologically manu-factured phenomena that appear to be hyperreal, that is, more real than real. Rather than representing something in the real world, simulations are originals that are artificially constructed. Rather than maps that depict a territory, they are models that serve as the blueprints for the real world. That supermodels are in a sense unreal creations of communication technology is quite apparent; that they also are objects of emulation and imitation is equally clear. As Gary Gumpert (1987) argues, the media create a perception of perfection that is impossible to duplicate in reality. In the case of models, this occurs through photographic retouching, airbrushing, or computer manipulation (Ewen 1988), or more directly through plastic surgery, the object of which is to create a more photogenic or media-friendly look, as opposed to enhancing appearance to the naked eye (Aronson 1983). Simulations, according to Baudrillard, are products of postmodern consumer culture, and it is the pursuit of mediated perfection that forces the model into the complete commodification of the self.

As highly successful and visible women, supermodels are also role models, and this makes their hyperreality especially problematic as their ideal forms set up unrealistic expectations. Supermodels and models in general, precisely because they are not models of the rest of us, are a great source of anxiety for women, and this anxiety serves advertisers well as a spur to further consumption. The ideal of thinness that supermodels represent is, ironically, a scarce commodity, one that is all but impossible to achieve, but which leads to the consumption of diet foods, programmes, and exercise products and services. Most women only see what they consider their faults or deficiencies when faced with the image of the latest super-model. Naomi Wolf (1991) cites a 1985 survey in which 90 per cent of the female respondents thought they weighed too much. Rita Freedman (1986) writes about the flesh-loathing that women feel in response to this idealized standard. She cites (p. 24) a psychologist's study which asked women, who were carefully chosen women of no history with eating disorders nor mental illness, to evaluate photo-graphs of themselves. 'None of these women were overweight, none were emotion-ally disturbed, yet all were dieting, all were self-rejecting, and all suffered from a poor body image.'

In addition, the supermodel celebrity has a unique relationship to the female audience in comparison with the way they relate to other celebrities. Women can relate to and share in the everyday ordinariness of other types of celebrities because one occasionally sees flaws or hints of their own reality in these people. Actors are seen in unattractive roles in films or television and sports heroes are sometimes photographed at their moment of defeat or while performing a less-than-attractive sport action. Models, however, while they may attempt to show the real Cindy or Linda, are always overshadowed by their image. Unlike actors or singers, beauty is their field and they are never seen in any other light than a beautiful one. So, the supermodel simulation remains a constant reminder of what Wolf (1991) calls 'the beauty myth' despite the fact that there may be more to the person than the persona.

Why does it matter? The result of the rise of the supermodel is that, while fashion advertising and imagery has always legitimized the beauty myth, now celebrity does so as well. Suddenly the image is a reality because we 'know' her and therefore the beauty standards are supposedly achievable. For example, an explanation of how she does this can be found in the many workout tapes and beauty-tip books (like Cindy Crawford's mentioned earlier) put out by these models. By capitalizing on their fame in this way, they send a message that with these beauty tips, or with this workout routine, the impossible beauty standards put forth by their image and others are attainable. Furthermore, by capitalizing on her fame in such a manner, the supermodel celebrity strengthens her role as commodity; and while other celeb-rities capitalize on their fame by associating themselves with products, the super-model commodity more directly works against positive images of strong women.

The supermodel who says that she will not get out of bed for less than $10,000 a day confirms that she is a product with a high price. But what is dangerous about presenting herself as something that is bought and sold is that it works to bring back notions that feminists have been working against: women as dispensable, like all the other products.

An implication of the supermodel celebrity's unique relationship to the female audience can be found in their role or lack of role as an example to young girls. In other words, while heroes were worshipped for their deeds and entertainers came to fame through some talent or action, supermodels can only be worshipped for their image. As an ideal upon which to model oneself, there is no moral code, good deed, or particular talent or accomplishment that they represent. Are those who idolize them aiming for beauty as their goal? Holly Brubach (1997: 56) wrote that in the past it was 'most likely a girl would have modeled herself on a female relative or on a woman in her community'. Celebrating the female fashion model creates a somewhat vacuous heroine for young girls, and trying to measure oneself against such standards of beauty can lead to negative psychological and physical effects. Mary Pipher (1994) gives the reader evidence of both. She writes that, more than anything else, young girls worry about their weight. They are psychologically worse off because of the peer pressure to be thin. In terms of the physical, she writes, on any given day in America half the female teenagers are dieting and one in five has an eating disorder. It remains evident that while supermodels alone cannot be the cause of such negative effects on women and young girls, there are other types of heroine who would allow for healthier role models.

Like other celebrities, the supermodel lends her name to an endless list of products (in her case most of them are beauty products), adding to her omnipresence. She is at once real and ordinary, and the image of hyperreal perfection. As a result, the supermodel comes to represent a duality to the women who read and see her images: while she has become an important example of the modern-day heroine, the celebrity, she is also a dangerous role model if we look to her as the standard of beauty. The danger of the supermodel celebrity can be overcome, however, in a world where possibilities for opposing messages about what defines beauty and success are all around us. To address it, however, one has to make sure opposing messages exist. Within our media of communication the message must be clear that beauty is about more than the physical. The less support supermodel messages get from the public, the more likely it is that advertisers and media professionals will receive the message. It will take action on the part of audiences to stop watching, reading, and listening to the supermodel hype.

References

Aronson, S. M. L. (1983). *Hype.* New York: William Morrow.

Bark, E. (1996). 'Next Stop, Petticoat Junction?' *The Record*, 2 June: 004.

Baudrillard, J. (1983). *Simulations*, trans. P. Foss, P. Patton, and P. Beitchman. New York: Semiotext(e).

Bellafante, G. (1996). 'Absolutely Fatuous: Fashion Isn't Boring, but the Spate of Cable Programs Devoted to it Could Make You Long for a Show about Cute CPAs'. *Time*, 3 June: 68.

Berger, J. (1977). *Ways of Seeing*. London: BBC.

Boorstin, D. J. (1978). *The Image: A Guide to Pseudo-events in America*. New York: Atheneum.

Brubach, H. (1996). 'Heroine Worship'. *New York Times Magazine*, 24 November: 55–7.

Cathcart, R. (1994). 'From Hero to Celebrity: The Media Connection', in S. Drucker and R. Cathcart (eds.), *American Heroes in a Media Age*. Cresskill, NJ: Hampton Press, 36–46.

Crawford, C., Kashuk, S., and Boyes, K. (1996). *Cindy Crawford's Basic Face*. New York: Broadway Books.

Cronin, M. (1995). 'Dragtime—It's No Secret why Drag Performers are Gaining Mainstream Popularity: They Put on a Good Show'. *Seattle Times*, 5 September: F1.

DeLibero, L. (1994). 'This Year's Girl: A Personal History of Twiggy', in S. Benstock and S. Ferris, (eds.), *On Fashion*. New Brunswick, NJ: Rutgers University Press, 41–57.

Ewen, S. (1976). *Captains of Consciousness: Advertising and the Social Roots of Consumer Culture*. New York: McGraw-Hill.

—— (1988). *All Consuming Images: The Politics of Style in Contemporary Culture*. New York: Basic Books.

Ewen, S., and Ewen, E. (1982). *Channels of Desire: Mass Images and the Shaping of American Consciousness*. New York: McGraw-Hill.

Faludi, S. (1981). *Backlash: The Undeclared War against American Women*. New York: Cross Publishers.

Freedman, R. (1986). *Beauty Bound*. Lexington, MA: Lexington Books.

Goffman, E. (1979). *Gender Advertisements*. Cambridge, MA: Harvard University Press.

Gross, M. (1995). *Model*. New York: William Morrow.

Gumpert, G. (1987). *Talking Tombstones and Other Tales of the Media Age*. New York: Oxford University Press.

Harvey, D. (1997). 'The Fashion Model as a Celebrity: From Coat Hanger to Supermodel'. Unpublished MA thesis, Fordham University, New York.

Justin, N. (1995). 'Jill Sobule Profits from Penchant to Kiss and Tell'. *Minneapolis Star Tribune*, 4 August: 1E.

McCrum, R. (1994). 'Beautiful Prose: The Frankfurt Book Fair Used to Be about Literature. Now . . . it's the Naomi, Claudia and Brigitte Show'. *The Guardian*, 10 October: T17.

Mills, C. W. (1956). *The Power Elite*. London: Oxford University Press.

Monaco, J. (1978). 'Celebration', in J. Monaco (ed.), *Celebrity*. New York: Delta Books, 3–14.

Moss, K. (1995). *Kate*. New York: St Martin's Press.

Ozzard, J. (1996). 'Scene: Fashion Coverage on Cable Television'. *Women's Wear Daily*, 17 May: S4.

Philipponnat, V. (1996). 'Valley of the Dolls'. *TopModel*, July–August: 50–8.

Phinney, S. (1996). 'Models Take Licks in Catwalk'. *Austin-American Statesman*, 5 July: E11.

Pipher, M. (1994). *Reviving Ophelia*. New York: Ballatine Books.

Rabine, L. (1994). 'A Woman's Two Bodies: Fashion Magazines, Consumerism, and Feminism', in S. Benstock and S. Ferris (eds.), *On Fashion*. New Brunswick, NJ: Rutgers University Press, 59–74.

Rein, I., Kotler, P., and Stoller, M. (1987). *High Visibility*. New York: Dodd, Mead.

Schiffer, C. (1995). *Memories*. London: Mandarin.

Sennett, R. (1977). *The Fall of Public Man*. New York: Vintage Books.

Strate, L. (1994). 'Heroes: A Communication Perspective', in S. Drucker and R. Cathcart (eds.), *American Heroes in a Media Age*. Cresskill, NJ: Hampton Press, 15–23.

—— (1995). 'The Face of a Thousand Heroes: The Impact of Visual Communication Technologies on the Culture Hero'. *New Jersey Journal of Communication*, 3/1: 26–39.

Sudjic, D. (1989). *Cult Heroes: How to be Famous for More than Fifteen Minutes*. New York: W. W. Norton.

Veblen, T. (1979). *The Theory of the Leisure Class*. New York: Penguin. Originally published 1899.

Wolf, N. (1991). *The Beauty Myth: How Images of Beauty are Used Against Women*. New York: Doubleday.

Chapter 14

Light Makes Right: Skin Colour and Racial Hierarchy in Television Advertising

Robert M. Entman and Constance L. Book

Anthropologist Mary Douglas (1970) argues that every culture develops potent symbolic associations and rituals organized around the polar opposites of purity and pollution. Although the two realms may at times intermingle (Stallybrass and White 1982), some things, peoples, events, practices are consistently linked to the pure and good, the ideal end of the continuum, and others are associated with the dangerous, unclean, polluting end. Entman and Rojecki (1997) suggest that American culture contains an implicit hierarchy of racial desirability. Those persons categorized as White are implicitly associated with the preferred, pure pole, while Blacks implicitly occupy the less desirable portion of the spectrum, associated with dirt and danger. At one time, African Americans were unambiguously linked in American culture with the negative pole, and this was reflected in their virtual absence from mainstream cultural products, including advertising, except for a few stereotypes that recalled Civil War-era images (Kern-Foxworth 1994; Pieterse 1992). But Blacks now appear in over a third of primetime television commercials (Entman and Rojecki 1997), and frequently take major roles in movies and television programmes. They dominate most popular sports and large swathes of the music industry. Does this mean the cultural order and its racial hierarchy have been transformed? Yes and no. In this essay we employ a careful content analysis of television advertising in order to gauge change in the cultural political economy of race.

We focus on advertising because of its central purpose and methods. In an effort to engage viewers and buyers, advertisers attempt to create visually appealing scenarios of society; to do this, they tap into the targeted audiences' emotions, desires, and prejudices. The average American household has its television set on for six hours a day, of which about an hour consists of commercials. Messages embedded within television advertising are likely to have significant socializing effects; we also know they have significant economic effects, helping to transform desires and anxieties into willingness to spend on goods and services (Messaris 1997; Turow 1997; Goldman and Papson 1996; O'Barr 1994; Williamson 1978). All this makes television ads a fertile arena for exploring the political economy of cultural change and racial representation.

Few advertisers wanted to link their products in the dominant, White buying public's minds with persons symbolizing pollution or danger. But in recent decades, as both a product and a cause of the civil rights revolution, Blacks have arguably moved to an intermediate position on the spectrum of acceptability, as evidenced by the high visibility of African Americans in many mainstream cultural products, including advertisements. This does not mean that Black persons have equivalent cultural status in America, and research suggests that, if the intensely negative stereotypes of old are now rare, more subtle images that codify racial separation and hierarchy remain (Entman and Rojecki 1997; Rojecki 1996; Entman 1992). Blacks are now *liminal* in American culture. As a category Black persons are in an ambiguous transition from their former status as a distinctive lower caste (Ogbu 1978). Not fully accepted as equivalent to Whites, still widely seen by Whites as fundamentally different and often inferior and fearsome, Blacks nevertheless occupy a far less negative place in the symbolism of American culture than they once did.

We suggest that advertising is a barometer of the transition: how far it's come and how far it has to go. Darkness has long evoked danger and dirt, so the mental associations of the colour black and the words 'Black person' may be negative for the dominant group. In these circumstances, we might expect the use of actors with dark skin to be a matter of real concern among advertisers. On the one hand, Black persons comprise a significant sector of the consuming audience, and firms face both economic and political pressures to include them in advertising scenarios. On the other, the majority audience is White and harbours continuing fears, resentments, and other negative emotions toward Blacks, the kinds of feelings advertisers do not want associated with their products. Moreover, Blacks themselves may have internalized dominant cultural ideals in ways that make their responses to cultural stimuli more similar to Whites' than might be expected. These conditions could produce an unstable, uneasy compromise: the frequent use of Blacks in advertising, but perhaps under unconsciously evolved yet consciously applied rules about the types, numbers, roles, and product associations of Blacks. Entman and Rojecki's (1997) results suggest as much. In this essay we seek to extend their work to the subtle but highly charged realm of skin colour.

Our basic idea is this: light is better than dark; light is associated with purity, dark with danger and pollution. Research shows the White majority appears more accepting of light-skinned Black females; those with more 'Caucasian' features are considered more desirable and more beautiful (Neal and Wilson 1989). Skin colour is also related to health among African Americans (Klag *et al.* 1991; Gleiberman *et al.* 1995); researchers hypothesize this impact arises in part from the extra stress imposed by US society on those with darker skins.

Even among Blacks, research has documented the existence of intraracial prejudice based on skin colour. Hall (1995) argues that Blacks have internalized light skin as an ideal because of their inability to fight the dominant culture. Researchers have used face cards with varying degrees of skin colouration to assess colour ideals among Black males, finding more favourable associations with lighter skin. (Hamm, Williams, and Dalhouse 1973; Sciara 1983). When Blacks were asked to self-report skin colour and these findings were compared to those of an independent rater, Blacks tended to over-estimate the lightness of their own skin (Anderson and

Cromwell 1977). Thus, even if we assume that the rising economic clout of Black consumers creates pressure to cast Blacks in commercials, there is an irony: if these consumers share the dominant cultural ideal, even ads targeted in whole or part at African Americans may reproduce a colour hierarchy.

Thus, research demonstrates the great cultural power attributable to the symbolic associations of skin colour. Scholarship also reveals that this cultural power translates into socio-economic capital. Several scholars find a strong relationship between skin colour and socio-economic success in the US (Hughes and Hertel 1990; Keith and Herring 1991; Seltzer and Smith 1991)—a clear monetary value that accrues to light skin colour. Although the correlation is obviously not perfect, African Americans with light skin tend to attain both higher status and higher incomes. Given advertisers' desires to associate their products precisely with higher status and income, we would expect at the minimum for skin colour to be a salient factor in the decisions of those who cast commercials. And systematic associations between skin colour and advertising would in turn reinforce the cultural hierarchy that establishes the market worth of lighter skin. In other words, the economic value of lighter skin colour would be simultaneously reflected and reinforced by the images of television advertising.

Therefore, we predict, advertisers will prefer lighter-skinned Black actors, particularly for products that are most likely to be pitched to audiences' fantasy, luxury, and ideal self-images: perfume, cars, credit cards. For the more mundane, the necessities of life, such as fast food, groceries, and pain relievers, darker-skinned Blacks will attain more prominence. Since lighter skin is empirically associated with higher-status occupations, and high status with attainment of US cultural ideals, we would expect Black actors playing characters of higher status to be lighter-skinned than those playing low-status roles. We also believe the impact of skin colour on females, both children and adult, will be greater than on men. Because women in ads are frequent carriers of symbolic associations with purity, safety, innocence, and beauty—and women in general must meet more rigid standards to attain physical attractiveness—advertisers' preference for lightness of skin will likely be more pronounced for females than males (Coltrane and Adams 1997). Finally, we note that most commercials featuring Blacks are in fact predominantly White. However, a small subset are all-Black, in this sample 15 of the 122 ads shown during one week of primetime advertising on a major network featured all-Black casts. Given the hypothesized potency of skin colour, we would expect light-skinned Blacks to predominate in all-Black ads. In integrated ads, Blacks typically play peripheral roles in which their presence can easily be overlooked (Entman and Rojecki 1997). Where advertisers go out on a cultural limb to employ all-Black casts, producing a commercial in which viewers cannot avoid noticing the Black actor(s), we believe, they will be especially likely to compensate by using those with lighter skin tones.

The five hypotheses are:

(1) The majority of Blacks appearing in primetime commercials will be light-skinned.
(2) Black women and girls in commercials are more likely to have lighter skin on average than their male counterparts.

(3) When a commercial makes occupations clear, the Blacks portraying higher-status roles will tend to be lighter-skinned than those playing lower-status characters.

(4) Commercials for luxury items or those relying upon appeal to fantasies of the ideal self will tend to use lighter-skinned Blacks.

(5) In commercials featuring Black actors exclusively, light skin will predominate.

Methods

Previous researchers have employed a variety of scales to assess skin colour. No single, standard scale has been adopted to classify skin colour, posing a challenge to the present study. From an attempt to use a three-part scale that included photographs of skin colours we considered dark brown, medium brown, and light brown (since in fact hardly anybody has literally black skin), we discovered that intercoder reliability was difficult to attain. The problem we had in establishing finer gradations of colour has theoretical significance. Most other multi-racial societies have developed words and thus visual acuity among their members for a variety of hues; in the US, the 'one-drop' rule classifying persons as Black if they have any African ancestry at all seemingly has hindered that development. Since skin colour perceptions are not as well developed in US culture, finding a reliable coding scheme was our first priority. To provide a confident basis for inference, this kind of content analysis must show reliability during repeated measures. We therefore enlisted thirteen independent student coders, who were asked to make a simple categorical judgement: was the skin colour of Blacks in a sample of TV commercials 'light' or 'dark'? Using this system, intercoder reliability (correcting for chance as recommended by Brennan and Prediger 1981), exceeded 0.9 among these independent coders. These results confirmed our decision that the best coding scheme would measure just two shades of definable Black skin colour—light and dark.

We coded a week (27 November–3 December 1996) of primetime advertising on one of the national networks, NBC. Initial coding was conducted as part of the Entman and Rojecki project (1997). During that week, a total of 408 commercials appeared. Racial composition was determined, and 122 ads (30 per cent) included at least one identifiably Black actor; 107 ads were integrated and 15 had exclusively Black casts. A total of 466 individual Black persons appeared in these 122 commercials. (Note that ads were coded each time they appeared; thus the figure of 122 represents that many showings of commercials, not 122 different ones.) The 466 Black actors broke down into five gender/age categories: male, female, male child, female child, and baby of unidentifiable gender. Males comprised 45.7 per cent, females 34.3 per cent, male children 12.7 per cent, female children 6.0 per cent, and babies 1.3 per cent.

Results

Considering skin colour for the sample at large, 44 per cent were classed as dark-skinned and 56 per cent as light-skinned. The difference was statistically significant (p<.01). This finding supports our first hypothesis, that a majority of Blacks employed by primetime advertisers would be light-skinned.

Cross-tabulating skin colour with gender reveals significant associations supporting our second hypothesis, that light skin shade would be more common among female actors. Removing six Black infants where the gender was not identifiable, and one Black actor whose skin shade could not be classified, the remaining N = 459. Of those, 41 per cent were females and 59 per cent males. Among the female actors, the vast majority were light-skinned—75 per cent. Lighter Black females constituted 55 per cent of the total light-skinned Black population even though females only made up just over 40 per cent of the actors in the study. The probability level of p<.01 is based on a one-way analysis of variance for significance of the difference between numbers of light- and dark-skinned females. As further evidence of the systematic preference for light-skinned Black females, the children in our commercials featuring Black actors and actresses were examined for skin colour. Even among children the preference for light-skinned females obtains (p<.01).

Our third hypothesis explores occupation or roles (when determinable in the commercial) as related to skin colour. We anticipated finding that Blacks portraying higher-status occupations/roles would tend to be lighter-skinned than those playing lower-status occupations/roles. We formed seven categories: parent, entertainer,

TABLE 14.1 Skin colour in TV advertisements by gender*

Gender	Light-skinned	Dark-skinned	Total
Females	141	47	188
Males	115	156	271
Total	256	203	459

* p < (.01)

Note: Statistical significance established by one-way analysis of variance of light- v. dark-skinned actors for gender category.

TABLE 14.2 Skin colour in TV advertisements by female categories

Category	Light-skinned	Dark-skinned	Total
Female Adults*	117	43	160
Female Children*	24	4	28
Total	141	47	188

* p < (.01)

Note: Statistical significance established by one-way analysis of variance of light- v. dark-skinned actors for adult and children categories.

athlete, business person, public servant, service worker and undetermined. The first thing to note is that the vast majority of Blacks appearing in primetime commercials were not linked to any identifiable occupational role (N = 362/78 per cent). But for the remainder, the data did not support the third hypothesis. We found a majority of those who were in identifiable occupations/roles were played by dark-skinned Blacks. The one category where dark-skinned Blacks did not outnumber the light-skinned Blacks was 'entertainer', and one role demonstrated a significant preponderance of dark-skinned Blacks—athletes. Arguably, this link of athleticism and darker colour accords with dominant cultural stereotypes that associate darkness with less refinement, less civility, more animal-like strength and quickness (see Rainville and McCormick 1977, on television announcing of football). This association was graphically conveyed by controversial film director and former Nazi propagandist Leni Riefenstahl (1974) in her book of photographs of the tribal Nuba of Sudan. Riefenstahl, an indubitable racist, nevertheless could celebrate Black aestheticism through her regard for Black athleticism. This example illustrates that racist ideology does not preclude establishing niches where the object of general scorn earns praise for a particular trait—one that ultimately confirms and justifies the ideology. Thus Riefenstahl's work on the Nuba has been criticized for objectifying and thus perpetuating the relationship between dark skin and animal-like characteristics (cf. Faris 1993). While Riefenstahl's photos were linked to her fascist ties, however, the same cannot be said of the general objectification of black males found in media portrayals (Rainville and McCormick 1977).

A partial explanation for the lack of association between higher-status occupation and lighter skin may be the predominance of Black *males* in depictions of identifiable occupations and roles. As noted, Black males on average exhibit darker skin tone than Black females in ads. Thus the gender bias (for showing male rather than female characters in job roles) partly obscures the skin colour bias. A previous study showed similar gender skew: women appearing in a sample of 1699 commercials 'were less prevalent, more likely to be shown in families, [and] less likely to hold jobs' (Coltrane and Adams 1997: 323).

Entman and Rojecki (1997) determined that Blacks were not represented as prominently in commercials for luxury/fantasy goods as for necessity items. In an effort to determine if skin colour was related to types of products, we explored the

TABLE 14.3 Skin colour in TV advertisements by occupations/roles

Occupations/roles	Light-skinned	Dark-skinned	Total
Parent	1	3	4
Entertainer	6	6	12
Athlete*	8	28	36
Business Person	8	10	18
Public Servant	2	3	5
Service Worker	12	17	29

* p < (.01)

Note: Statistical significance established by one way analysis of variance of light *v.* dark skinned actors for occupation/role category.

skin shade of Black actors appearing in fifteen categories of commercial products. Significant differences were found between numbers of light- and dark-skinned actors in five of the fifteen categories: entertainment, department/furniture store, snacks/soft drink, grocery/household, and apparel. Department/furniture store commercials were far more likely to use light-skinned Blacks (74 per cent). In the other four main categories, dark-skinned Blacks predominated: in entertainment commercials, 69 per cent of Blacks were dark-skinned; in snack/soft drinks/beer, 62 per cent; in grocery/household products, 75 per cent; and in apparel, 63 per cent.

The hypothesized link between lighter skin shade and luxury/fantasy product advertising did not appear consistently. One reason is that breaking a sample of just 122 commercials and 466 actors into 15 categories yields small numbers. A larger sample might yield more definitive results. However, two of the results clearly conform to expectations. There were dozens of ads in the department/furniture store category (N = 165). The majority touted clothing and gift items available at the stores; they tended to show the fantastic variety of goods they made available to satisfy everyone's longings. Typically, the commercials featured a rapidly edited montage of several (as many as ten or fifteen) different scenes of individuals or couples shopping or enjoying purchased goods. Almost every one of the commercials showed broadly smiling or laughing people laden with packages or surrounded by piles of goods, usually name-brand or designer-labelled, moderately upscale products. In this sense, the department-store ads quintessentially depict the American fantasy of consumer abundance. Incidentally, two companies accounted for over half of these ads, Sears (N = 57) and J.C. Penney (N = 27), most of

TABLE 14.4 Skin colour in TV advertisements by commercial product categories

Product	Light-skinned	Dark-skinned	Total
Public service announcement	0	1	1
Business service	27	22	49
Entertainment*	5	11	16
Appliance	2	1	3
Department store/furniture*	122	43	165
Snack/soft drink/beer*	17	28	45
Drugs	2	1	3
Fast food	25	27	52
Perfume	1	0	1
Jewels/female	1	1	2
Auto/truck	7	5	12
Charge cards	7	6	13
Grocery/household*	5	15	20
Apparel*	23	39	62
Other	16	6	21
Total	205	260	465

* p < (.01)

Note: Statistical significance established by one-way analysis of variance of light- v. dark-skinned actors for product category.

them constructed in this mode. In these fantasy-driven commercials depicting the cultural ideal, we would expect the finding that light-skinned Blacks predominated by a ratio of around 3:1.

At the other end of the spectrum are groceries/household goods. As Entman and Rojecki (1997) discovered, Blacks tend to be associated more frequently with the realm of everyday necessity. (It may also be that African Americans are proportionally heavier purchasers of certain products in this category, such as detergents or canned foods, although Blacks would still represent a minority of purchasers of such goods.) Thus the finding that dark-skinned Blacks outnumber light-skinned in this category by 3:1.

The significant presence of darker-skinned models in the other categories may be traceable to the dominance of a single product in the category. In this sense, the findings may be idiosyncratic. Thus 45 of the 62 apparel ads hawked Nike products, most of them showing dark-skinned Black athletes like Michael Jordan. Most of the Entertainment commercials (12 of 16) touted Blockbuster Video, and 9 of their ads featured a darker Black actor, 3 a lighter one. The snack/soft drink/beer category consisted entirely of 7-Up, Snickers, and Miller Beer commercials; the latter two used 4 light-skinned actors and 17 dark, whereas 7-Up used 11 light and 13 darker actors. Again, a larger sample would help provide a more definitive test of the hypothesis.

Our fifth and final hypothesis anticipated finding that commercials featuring only Black actors would include more light-skinned than dark-skinned Blacks. Since light-skinned Blacks outnumbered darker ones overall (56 to 44 per cent), the issue was whether the predominance of the light-skinned is more pronounced in all-Black than in integrated commercials. This was indeed the case, as the light-skinned outnumbered dark-skinned 4:1 in the all-Black ads, compared with about 1.3:1 in the integrated ones (p<.05).

Since there were only 15 all-Black commercials, it would not be proper to make too much of this finding. On the other hand, the fact that in a week of primetime network television only 15 all-Black commercials appeared is itself revealing; sampling four weeks of primetime yielded just 53 all-Black ads in the original study (Entman and Rojecki, 1997). As is true of all our results, more research is appropriate. We suspect that further sampling would confirm these initial findings.

TABLE 14.5 Skin colour in all-black advertisements *v.* multiracial advertisements

Type of Ad	Light-skinned blacks	Dark-skinned blacks	Total
All-Black*	12	3	15
Mixed-race**	248	202	450
Total	260	206	465

*p < (.05); ** < (.01)

Note: Statistical significance established by one way analysis of variance of light- *v.* dark-skinned actors for ad category.

Conclusion

Again, these findings are certainly not definitive. Not every difference we discovered between light- and dark-skinned models was significant, and not all the hypotheses we tested received support. Moreover, it is possible that the 56–44 per cent split in light- *v.* dark-skinned models represents the actual distribution of skin colour in the general African American population. Or perhaps dark shades are even over-represented in advertising, if it turned out that, say, only 30 per cent of African Americans would be considered dark by our two-category classification. This is not a possibility we can address definitively. However, it is our impression that a representative sampling of African Americans would yield a much higher proportion of individuals we would classify as dark skinned than of those falling into the light category. In addition, previous research buttresses the assumption that advertisers are highly colour- or race-conscious. (Besides works already cited, see on race and advertising Elliot 1995; Seiter 1995; Branthwaite and Peirce 1990; Zinkhan, Qualls, and Biswas 1990).

Assuming the basic finding that advertisers privilege lighter skin is plausible, we offer the following concluding observations. In a 'colourblind' society, skin shade would make no difference to cultural judgements of attractiveness, trustworthiness, competence, and other valued traits. But the US is not colourblind. Empirical research repeatedly finds that light skin conveys privileges in the culture and these in turn yield economic benefits in the market economy. At one time the colour hierarchy was so pronounced that even light-skinned Blacks were virtually absent from commercials. But the culture has been undergoing a transition over the past forty years or so. As a barometer of cultural change, advertising can tell us how far the transition has progressed. We now see African Americans in a high proportion of commercials. They are not randomly distributed in commercials, as they would be if the transition to colourblindness had been achieved. Instead there are clear relationships between race and a variety of measures of advertising texts.

In this essay we have tested and found considerable evidence for the notion that the acceptability of Blacks in advertising—and by extension in the culture—is calibrated in significant measure by the shade of their skin. Those Blacks with lighter skin, that is, whose appearance is closer to the White ideal, have greater cultural capital. They have more opportunities than their darker brethren to earn money by appearing in commercials generally, and in specific types of commercials. This advantage of light skin accrues with particular strength to Black females. Black males (like males of all ethnicities) enjoy a wider latitude of variation in physical traits that can be considered attractive. In addition, the symbolic associations of darkness with primitive strength and danger can sometimes even be an advantage, depending on the image an advertiser seeks to convey. An obvious example is athletics; African American sports heroes can be dark-skinned and still amass hefty advertising fees (Hoberman 1997). But in the main, although the results presented here are far from the final word, the data indicate that advertising reproduces the racial hierarchy and liminal status of African Americans rather precisely. The culture awards Blacks provisional acceptability, with a preference for those whose physical features place them closer to the dominant ideal. That cultural bias translates into greater upward mobility, easier social acceptance for African Americans with lighter skin. In this way advertising inscribes economic value, as it ascribes cultural value, to lightness of skin.

References

Anderson, C., and Cromwell, R. L. (1977). '"Black is beautiful" and the Color Preferences of Afro-American Youth'. *Journal of Negro-Education*, 46 winter: 76–88.

Branthwaite, A., and Peirce, L. (1990). 'The Portrayal of Black People in British Television Advertisements'. *Social Behaviour*, 5: 327–34.

Brennan, R. L., and Prediger, D. J. (1981). 'Coefficient Kappa: Some Uses, Misuses, and Alternatives'. *Educational and Psychological Measurement*, 41: 687–99.

Bristor, J. M., Lee, R. G., and Hunt, M. R. (1995). 'Race and Ideology: African American Images in Television Advertising'. *Journal of Public Policy and Marketing*, 14/1: 48–59.

Coltrane S., and Adams, S. (1997). 'Work-family Imagery and Gender Stereotypes: Television and the Reproduction of Difference'. *Journal of Vocational Behavior*, 50/2: 323–47.

Cunningham, M. R., Roberts, A. R., Wu, C. H., Barbee, A. P., and Druen, P. B. (1995). 'Their Ideas of Beauty Are, on the Whole, the Same as Ours: Consistency and Variability in the Cross-cultural Perception of Female Physical Attractiveness'. *Journal Of Personality and Social Psychology*, 68/2: 261–79.

Douglas, M. (1970). *Purity and Danger: An Analysis of Concepts of Pollution and Taboo*. New York: Penguin.

Elliot, M. T. (1995). 'Differences in the Portrayal of Blacks: A Content Analysis of General Media versus Culturally-targeted Commercials'. *Journal of Current Issues and Research in Advertising*, 17: 76–86.

Entman, R. M. (1992). 'Blacks in the News: Television, Modern Racism and Cultural Change'. *Journalism Quarterly*, 69/summer: 341–61.

Entman, R. M., and Rojecki, A. (1997). Advertising Boundaries: Race and Intimacy in Television Commercials, Paper presented at the 1997 annual conference of the International Communication Association, Montreal.

Faris, J. C. (1993). 'Leni Riefenstahl, and the Nuba Peoples of Kordofan Province, Sudan', *Historical Journal of Film Radio and Television*, 13/1: 95–7.

Gleiberman L., Harburg, E., Frone, M. R., Russell, M., and Cooper, M. L. (1995). 'Skin Color, Measures of Socioeconomic-status and Blood-pressure among Blacks in Erie County, NY'. *Annals of Human Biology*, 22/1: 69–73.

Goldman, R., and Papson, S. (1996). *Sign Wars*. New York: Guilford.

Hall, R. E. (1992). 'Race Differences and Experimenter Race Effect in Galvanic Skin Response'. *Research on Social Work Practice*, 2/4: 479–86.

—— (1995). 'The Bleaching Syndrome: African Americans' Response to Cultural Domination Vis-à-vis Skin Color'. *Journal of Black Studies*, 26/2: 172–84.

Hamm, N. H., Williams, D. O., and Dalhouse, A. D. (1973). 'Preference for Black Skin among Negro Adults'. *Psychological Reports*. 32/3, pt 2: 1171–5.

Hoberman, J. (1997). *Darwin's Athletes*. Boston: Houghton Mifflin.

Hughes, M., and Hertel, B. R. (1990). 'The Significance of Color Remains—A Study of Life Chances, Mate Selection, and Ethnic-consciousness among Black-Americans'. *Social Forces* 68: 1105–20.

Johnson, J. T. (1973). *A Study of Counselors' Galvanic Skin Responses to Video Taped Stimuli of Racial/Sex Pairings and Three Verbal Affect Situations*. Athens, GA: University of Georgia.

Keith, V. M., and Herring, C. (1991). 'Skin Tone and Stratification in the Black Community'. *American Journal of Sociology*, 97/3: 760–78.

Kern-Foxworth, M. (1994). *Aunt Jemima, Uncle Ben, and Rastus: Blacks in Advertising, Yesterday, Today and Tomorrow*. Westport, CT: Praeger.

Klag, M. J., Whelton, P. K., Coresh, J., Grim, C. E., and Kuller, L. H. (1991). 'The Association of Skin Color with Blood-pressure in United-States Blacks with Low Socioeconomic-Status'. *Journal of the American Medical Association*, 265/5: 599–602.

Messaris, P. (1997). *Visual Persuasion*. Newbury Park, CA: Sage.

Muller, R. (1993). *The Wonderful Horrible Life of Leni Riefenstahl* (film). New York: Kino Video.

Neal, A. M., and Wilson, M. L. (1989). 'The Role of Skin Color and Features in the Black Community: Implications for Black Women and Therapy'. *Clinical Psychology Review*, 9: 323–33.

O'Barr, W. (1994). *Culture and the Ad*. Boulder, CO: Westview Press.

Ogbu, J. (1978). *Minority Education and Caste: The American System in Cross-cultural Perspective*. New York: Academic Press.

Pieterse, J. N. (1992). *White on Black: Images of African and Blacks in Western Popular Culture*. New Haven, CT: Yale University Press.

Rainville, R., and McCormick, E. (1977). 'Extent of Covert Racial Prejudice in Pro-football Announcers' Speech'. *Journalism Quarterly*, 54: 20–6.

Riefenstahl, L. (1974). *The Last of the Nuba*. New York: Harper & Row.

Rojecki, A. (1996). 'Deadly Embrace'. Paper presented at the annual conference of the International Communication Association, Chicago.

Sciara, F. J. (1983). 'Skin Color and College Student Prejudice'. *College Student Journal*, 17/4: 390–4.

Seiter, E. (1995). 'Different Children, Different Dreams: Racial Representation in Advertising', in G. Dines and J. Humez (eds.), *Gender, Race and Class in Media: A Text-reader*. Thousand Oaks, CA: Sage, 99–108.

Seltzer, R., and Smith, R. C. (1991). 'Color Differences in the Afro-American Community and the Differences They Make'. *Journal of Black Studies*, 21/3: 279–86.

Stallybrass, P., and White, A. (1986). *The Politics and Poetics of Transgression*. Ithaca, NY: Cornell University Press.

Turow, J. (1997). *Breaking Up America*. Chicago: University of Chicago Press.

Williamson, J. (1978). *Decoding Advertisements: Ideology and Meaning in Advertising*. London: Marion Boyars.

Zinkhan G., Qualls, W., and Biswas, A. (1990). 'The Use of Blacks in Magazine and Television Advertising: 1946 to 1986'. *Journalism Quarterly*, 67: 547–53.

Chapter 15

Talking back to Calvin Klein: Youthful 'Targets' Confront Their Commercial Image

Lauren Tucker

For almost three decades, youthful sexuality has been the primary product promoted by Calvin Klein's marketing strategy. Since 1980, when Calvin Klein's 'Nothing comes between me and my Calvins' campaign titillated Americans with a sexy, 15-year-old Brooke Shields, media criticism of the fashion designer's marketing tactics has become a recurrent feature of news media discourse in the United States. In August 1995, however, Klein launched a $6 million advertising campaign for his *cK* jeans line that ignited a firestorm of criticism within the media community, eventually leading to the early withdrawal of the campaign. Accusing Klein's advertising of portraying sexually vulnerable young models in settings reminiscent of 1970s-style porn movies, the news media and the marketing trade press charged that the ads were more about kiddie porn than kiddie pants. While all but two of the models were between the ages of 18 and 25 (and the two models under 18 had parental consent), the media community expressed little doubt that Calvin Klein had breached the boundary between bad taste and criminality.

Klein's campaign, launched in a limited number of large, US metropolitan media markets, featured young models, male and female, who were either photographed or filmed against a backdrop of what the media community labelled 'a cheap, wood-panelled' room. The television campaign adopted the format of an audition and featured a male, off-camera gravelly voice that asked the models personal and provocative questions concerning how they felt about their bodies and what they would be willing to do in front of a camera. The models were scantily clad in a variety of denim fashions and underwear.

Due to limited media acceptance and placement of the campaign, most Americans did not see the ads until they were contextualized by the media discourse as 'kiddie-porn'. Early criticism of the campaign was limited to the activities of the American Family Association (AFA)—a conservative political action group headed by long-time family-values watchdog Donald Wildmon. Few Americans were aware of the campaign or the nascent controversy until mainstream news coverage brought the issue into the national spotlight. These conditions encouraged news audiences to 'buy' the kiddie-porn media frame that encouraged them to see Klein's models, and by extension Klein's youthful target market, as 'victims' of child abuse and sexual exploitation (Tucker 1998). Like Klein, the news media created an image of young people that would sell their product, news programming and copy. The news discourse worked in conjunction with Klein's campaign to commodify youth. The models and the young people they were intended to represent were transformed by the discourse from sexualized objects to victimized objects. This essay explores how young people negotiate their objectification within the narrow confines of a media discourse that leaves little room for them to define an identity independent of the media images created by and within commercial media culture.

The news discourse about the campaign constructed an image of an outraged 'public' that demanded the withdrawal of the campaign from the media (Tucker 1998). The discourse suggested that teens and young adults were willing victims of Klein's clever attempts to recognize and legitimize youthful sexuality in a world rife with paedophilia, teenage mothers and other social problems resulting from the irresponsible, and perhaps irrepressible, combination of youth and sex (Tucker 1998). According to this discourse, the public's outrage prompted the call for a criminal investigation of Klein for promoting child pornography. Yet, despite all its references to 'the public', the body of media discourse about the campaign allowed little space for 'the public voice', especially the voice of youth. In this essay I seek to open this space by examining how Klein's target of teenagers aged 12–17 and young adults aged 18–25 interpreted and evaluated the news discourse about the controversy.

Klein's 1995 *cK* Jeans campaign featured young models who were filmed and/or photographed against a 'cheap' wood-panelled backdrop. They were shown in Klein's denim-wear and underwear in various stages of dress. The campaign could be seen in a limited number of metropolitan broadcast television markets, cable channels (MTV), print (*Vanity Fair* and *YM*) and out-of-home media. The threat of an investigation by the Federal Bureau of Investigation (FBI), combined with increasing pressure from the media community and the conservative AFA, prompted Klein to take the unprecedented steps of prematurely withdrawing his campaign and offering a public apology. The FBI investigation was later dropped, and, as expected, Klein's jeans experienced robust sales among members of his target group.

Klein is a favourite of the youth market, which ranges in age from 12 to 25, and according to a 1996 *Youth Markets Alert* report, his brand ranks among the five 'coolest' brands in the teenage market ('Teens' Coolest Brands' 1996). While many advertisers have found the youth market to be 'elusive' and hard to reach, Klein's promotional strategies have been very successful in tapping into a market that commands more than $100 billion in consumer spending per year. The young are particularly receptive to advertising, but this does not mean that teens and young adults are naive about how advertising works. While cynical about brands built on hype, young buyers seem willing to pay for those items they believe express their lifestyle and taste (Brookman, 1996).

Dateline's report (NBC, 12 September 1995) by correspondent Dennis Murphy was typical of the news coverage about the controversy and was one of many sites offering audiences their first glimpse of Klein's campaign. *Dateline* anchor Jane Pauley introduced the report by reviewing Klein's past transgressions and his use of nudity and sexual innuendo. The intervention of the FBI, which Pauley described as 'one tough customer' was given as the justification for *Dateline*'s interest in the story. Pauley led the segment by telling the audience that 'questions persist about just what it was he [Klein] was really selling'. The news package began with a Klein television ad featuring a 20-year-old male model who was responding to questions from an off-camera voice. He shyly told the voice that he was from Kentucky and was wearing 'short shorts'. Murphy cut in with 'What do you think is for sale here? Jeans or young boys?'

Dateline's report featured interviews with Patrick Truman, an AFA lobbyist and former Justice Department prosecutor, and Barbara Lippert, a columnist for *Adweek*, who accused Klein of engaging in, at the very least, 'pseudo child pornography'. Truman and Lippert represented the unlikely alliance between media watchdogs and the media community whose combined voice defined Klein's advertising as kiddie porn (Tucker 1998). Murphy also interviewed Marjorie Hines, a legal representative of the American Civil Liberties Union, who seemed to provide an alternative view to the dominant perspective presented by this report. Hines told Murphy the FBI's interest in the case was bad law, bad policy, and bad politics, and argued that accusing Klein of child pornography trivialized a serious issue. Hines called the Justice Department action 'deplorable' and politically motivated. These were the 'public voices' representing the politics surrounding the controversy (Tucker 1998).

The *Dateline* report was one of the few sites to offer a glimpse of how teens and young adults felt about the controversy ('Teenagers wonder "What's the Fuss?"' 1995). While the subject of the segment concerned Klein's use of young models, emphasis was placed on the portrayal of the male models. Murphy interviewed 14-year-old Delancy, one of the male models. He admitted to Murphy that the campaign exploited the models' sexuality, but dismissed the accusation that the ads were abusive or pornographic. Delancy's father, interviewed with his son, expressed his support for Delancy's nascent modelling career and explained that his reservations about the content of the campaign were secondary to his interest in the economic potential of his son's 'beautiful body'.

Delancy was recruited for the campaign from a group of New York City teenagers who frequented one of the city's many parks. When Murphy interviewed these young people about the ads and their friend's participation in the campaign, he got a response similar to those given by Delancy and his father. Murphy underscored these interviews by mentioning that, despite Klein's withdrawal of his campaign, or perhaps because of it, the sales of *cK* jeans were brisk among young buyers.

Klein refused to be interviewed for this report. However, *Dateline* aired a 1987 interview in which he defended his portrayal of youthful sexuality in his advertising campaigns. Pauley closed the segment with an ominous announcement of the FBI's impending investigation into Klein's marketing tactics.

The media frame of kiddie porn employs specific stock phrases, catch words, and routine linguistic associations that resonate the culturally available, politicized language of the discourses of middle-class morality, patriarchy, and generation-gap conflict (Tucker 1998). These discourses mobilize specific sets of self-validating beliefs about the nature of youthful sexuality that cast Klein as a lecherous and cynical businessman 'who seduces children into a life of crime and social deviance' (Tucker 1998:7). Yet, the kiddie-porn frame and the news discourse in which it is embedded minimize the voice of youth within the discourse and marginalize the very group that the discourse claims to serve.

In this study I seek to understand how teens and young adults make sense of the complex public issue of their 'victimization' as promoted by the news media's frame of kiddie porn and how they negotiate the commodification of youthful sexuality within commercial media culture. Gamson (1992:4) asserts that people 'negotiate with media messages in complicated ways that vary from issue to issue'. The images of passivity and ignorance that often characterize the social science descriptions of 'the public' are challenged by Gamson's analysis of focus-group conversations in which members of the community were asked to talk about and respond to particular social issues made salient by the media. I argue that these images of passivity and ignorance are particularly pervasive in social-science literature about youth. Yet, Gamson makes the point, though mainstream social science often constructs the public as a collection of victims of the media, these self-same critics rarely give members of the public a voice within their critique:

The critics, of course, don't blame the people for their false consciousness and incomprehension. They are victims of a consciousness industry that produces and encourages a conveniently misleading and incomplete understanding of their world. The victims, in fact, make few appearances in analyses that emphasize the power of the sociocultural forces that put scales on their eyes. (Gamson 1992:5).

Likewise, the news discourse surrounding Klein's campaign, while claiming to be reporting on the 'public' outrage at the campaign, rarely gives a voice to members of the public, especially the members of the public who are also members of Klein's target group (Tucker 1998). Borrowing Gamson's approach, I shall analyse 'peer group conversations' of teenagers and young adults to understand how young people respond to media messages and public issues about them.

Peer groups are variations of the traditional focus group. They primarily consist of acquaintances recruited by a peer contact person who in this case did not participate in the group discussions. This approach assumes that the level of familiarity among peer group members encourages a freer exchange of ideas and opinions than would be the case among a group of strangers. Here again, Gamson's theory and method are instructive. He argues that the analysis of peer group conversations 'allows us to observe the process of people constructing and negotiating shared meaning, using their natural vocabulary' (Gamson 1992: 17). The analysis of peer group conversations enables the examination of 'sociable public discourse' (p. 20), a foundational element of public issue formation and negotiation. The interaction found in group conversation also allows for observing the processes by which the group gravitates to a shared structure of meaning.

Two groups of young people, one consisting of eight teenagers aged 12–17 and the other consisting of eleven young adults aged 18–25, were recruited for this study. Each member was invited to participate by a friend or acquaintance known through school or church. Both groups were shown the *Dateline* report on the controversy surrounding Klein's campaign. After viewing the report, I asked each group a series of questions designed to get their response to the *Dateline* report; to Klein's advertising campaign and marketing tactics; and to the controversy surrounding the campaign.

The initial reaction of both groups focused on the role *Dateline* played in extending the reach of Klein's advertising and his brand name. The consensus was that *Dateline* and Klein were motivated by the same commercial considerations, selling their respective products.

Jessica (White, female, seventh grade, aged 12–13): They're telling him [Klein] he gets too much attention for his ads and then they show them all over TV. . . . It's not much worse than what's already on television, what's on commercials. [General agreement from the group.] It's like free advertising, so he doesn't care.

To group members, the tone of *Dateline*'s report and the allegation that Klein might be guilty of child sexual abuse titillated rather than informed and served to enhance the marketing potential of *Dateline* and Klein's advertising.

Trellis (black, female, college junior, aged 21, psychology major): I think they were trying to call Calvin Klein a sexual . . . paedophile.

Jennifer (white, female, college senior, aged 21, marine science major): I feel that it was really negative. The whole way they represented everything, and they just wanted to get people stirred up and say this is a bad thing and Calvin Klein is.

Abby (white, female, college senior, aged 21, interdisciplinary studies major): But I think that's the typical attitude of *Dateline*. I mean it really is. It's typical of how they present all their issues. When they present something, they always want to present the thing that's most controversial, so that people watch the show.

Jay (white, male, college sophomore, aged 19, accounting major): This is what he [Klein] wants whether it's good or bad it's just still more publicity for him and him selling his jeans.

The participants seemed challenged by Klein's advertising. Members of each group struggled to define their feelings towards Klein's portrayal of youthful sexuality without necessarily endorsing *Dateline*'s kiddie-porn framework. Using terms like 'nasty' and 'bad taste', participants attempted to distance themselves from the young people depicted in Klein's ads.

Matt: (white, male, seventh grade, aged 12–13): Just don't like it. It's kinda nasty.

Facilitator: What do you mean, 'kinda nasty'? You don't like the *Dateline* segment, or you don't like the ads themselves?

Matt: I don't like the ads themselves.

Yet, in an effort to resist *Dateline*'s depiction of youth as a victimized class, participants dismissed the report's suggestion that Klein's campaign could be considered child abuse or illegal.

Facilitator: So you're saying it wasn't wrong . . .?

Walker (white, male, seventh grade, aged 12–13): It was wrong but not in the way they're saying.

Facilitator: Wrong in what way? Do you think it's illegal? Do you think it should be illegal? Or do you think it's just bad taste?

Walker: Bad taste. They make a thousand dollars a day just to pull off their clothes, make some money.

Matt: The idea of using minors for it. . . . It's stupid.

Katie (white, female, ninth grade, aged 14–15): I think the same thing. I don't think he should be allowed to use kids, I mean, it sells his stuff but I don't think he should be allowed to use kids for it. It's just, like, nasty.

Jessica: I definitely think it's nasty, but if the models want to bare all . . . that's their choice, not anybody else's. I think Calvin Klein draws attention for his ads but for the wrong reasons.

While the consensus among both groups was that many of the ads within the campaign crossed the border into 'bad taste,' when pressed for specifics, the participants struggled to define their attitude outside of the frame constructed by the *Dateline*. Hence, group members often relied on those indicators of bad taste identified by the report. These indicators included the campaign's low-budget setting, the appearance of the models, the vagaries of the models' ages and suggestions of homoeroticism:

Noy (asian, female, college sophomore, biology major, aged 20): That was probably bad taste, but that same advertisement in the same form, in the same layout of the models in a white room with windy curtains flying around nobody would have done anything. It's just the fact that it's bad taste in the background.

Facilitator: Let me ask you this—what makes it bad taste?

Noy: Well, in my opinion it looks like it's something. . . . The reason why people probably think it's something of a paedophile thought because it looks like a basement like the person said on TV. It looks like somebody just posing at home.

Facilitator: What do you think about the models?

Jennifer: They're not very attractive if they were wearing, you know, regular type of clothes. I don't think they're attractive.

Joe (white, male, college senior, hotel–restaurant–tourism major, aged 22–25): I think the actual scene of the man interviewing with the grungy old voice or whatever, and it seems like he's interviewing almost like a pornography movie. But the one guy that did do that interview was like 20 years old, he said, so that wouldn't be a problem at all.

Members of both groups grappled with defining their subjectivity within and against nexus of gender, age and lifestyle identities constructed by *Dateline* and Klein's campaign.

Katie: Well, I don't think there's anything wrong with it, that's not how the clothes are going to look like on *you*, I mean, you're not in that position . . . I mean, they're just showing the clothes, you just have to look . . . you're on the outside looking in.

Lisa: I think he uses average people to see, because he's not using, like I mean, like Kate Moss is a supermodel, but all the others aren't and I think he's also trying to get that point across. But I mean it's no worse than any other ads that are out there so if they're going to target him they need to target everybody else too, and I mean it's just one way of advertising and it works.

Some of the participants noted that the only positive statements about Klein came from the models and teenagers interviewed by Murphy. The participants did not consider the models or the teenagers to be representative of their own values and lifestyles.

Abby: Yeah, it seems like the only thing they had in his defence was the female attorney that they had toward the end of the segment, and besides that everything else was really against what he had to say with the exception of the group of kids who were 14–19 years old, and they only showed the segment from the one group, and I would say they didn't represent the majority of the population.

Kevin (white, male, college sophomore, aged 20, marketing/finance major): Yeah, that's the impression I got from that group of kids. Every other word was 'like' this and 'like' that from Jason [a 15-year-old model featured in the August campaign] . . . they did not seem to be . . . they were not well educated.

Confusion and contradiction characterized the attitudes of the participants when considering how they would feel about their children modelling in similar ads. While several participants expressed hope that their children would not choose to model in these types of ad, considerations of gender and commerce qualified their responses. The sexually vulnerable attitude of Klein's male models was a challenging image for group members struggling to define themselves as future parents. Participants said that they would allow their 15-year-old daughter to model in these ads, but not their 15-year-old son:

Abby: Just because you don't want people to think of your son like that or to think of a friend, I mean, if your son is gay or is whatever I guess that obviously they're going to think of him in that manner, but if your son is straight, I don't know, it's difficult . . . You don't want people to have a false impression of what type of child that you have no matter what the situation is. Girls have always been used, I mean, I know that's a bad way to put it, but they have always been used in modelling that way no matter what age. Once they get to be a teenager, they've always been used to sell things in a sexual fashion drawing attention to themselves as sexual people.

Joe: I mean they are playing off a homo thing, homosexual thing it seems like.

Yet, the consensus was that once a person was 18 years of age, he or she could do whatever they liked, especially if they were being paid 'good money'. The participants argued that young people should have the right to some degree of self-determination in their lives:

Michael (white, male, aged 16–17): I would hope that my child wouldn't want to do that but [One of the girls interrupts: 'Yeah exactly.'] I wouldn't, obviously, I'm not going to say, I mean, I'm almost 18 myself, I wouldn't want my mom saying, no, you can't do this, because I'm sure they make pretty good money doing things like that.

Discussion and conclusion

The central objective of this study is to understand how the participants made sense of the news discourse about the Klein campaign. Without a doubt, both Klein and *Dateline* exploited youth as a means of meeting their specific commercial objectives. While Klein's advertising marketed the sexuality and vulnerability of youth to sell jeans, *Dateline* and other news discourse used Klein's bad-boy image and the portrait of sexually exploited 'kids' to sell news content. *Dateline*'s use of the kiddie-porn media frame depended on Klein's sexual objectification of youth. Thus, the exploiter was exploited. At issue, however, is the insidious nature of a news discourse that claimed to serve the public interest by reporting on Klein's most recent breach of American moral standards. To reframe Jane Pauley's question, I asked the participants in the study to consider what it was that *Dateline* was really selling.

Certainly, the resistance to being characterized as hapless victims who needed the protection of concerned adults lay at the heart of many of the participants' responses. Throughout the conversations, the participants tried to put symbolic space between their social identities and the image of youth articulated by the kiddie-porn frame. One of the discursive strategies they used was to dismiss the impact of the news discourse about the issue. Central to this strategy was the assertion that Klein's campaign and *Dateline*'s subsequent exploitation of the controversy were 'typical', just business as usual. Group members recognized that *Dateline* and Klein operate within the same cultural space in the commercial media industry. This is a world of commerce in which profit motives belie the concern for young people. The participants were 'outside looking in' on this world as independent, media-savvy consumers. They were spectators who understood the game.

Participants also distanced themselves from the images portrayed by the frame by constructing Klein's models as 'the other'. The ads were considered 'nasty', the models unattractive, and, despite *Dateline*'s report stating that only two of the models were under the age of 18, the participants, like the news discourse, characterized all the models as 'kids'. The idea that these 'kids' were paid 'good money' to 'pull off their clothes' made the ads seem nasty and challenging. Unlike the participants, the kids in the ads willingly submitted to their own victimization, for the right price. To group members, this was not illegal, just disturbingly unrepresentative of their own values and lifestyles. As one participant said, 'I definitely think it's nasty, but if the models want to bare all . . . that's their choice, not anybody else's.'

The participants considered the models and the lifestyle they represented alien. Their assessment revealed much of the elite class bias articulated by the kiddie-porn frame. The models and the teenagers interviewed for the *Dateline* report were viewed as inarticulate, 'uneducated'. Against the middle-class backgrounds of both groups interviewed for this study, these characteristics indicated an image of youth that did not connect with their concepts of themselves or their peer groups.

The participants also used these discursive strategies to distance themselves from the images of young sexuality articulated by Klein's ads and the kiddie-porn frame. The news discourse invited them to confront the complex image of youthful sexuality that is so often defined between the narrow borders of sexual independence and sexual deviance. Members of both groups expressed qualms about Klein's portrayal of the young male models as sex objects, and they accepted, somewhat reluctantly, the portrayal of sexually vulnerable young women as an established custom in the world of fashion marketing for advertisers, media practitioners, media critics, and consumers. Perhaps inhibited by the conditions of the focus group structure or challenged by their own beliefs about the nature of female sexuality versus male sexuality, the participants reaffirmed dominant, heterosexual gender constructions.

This analysis also reveals just how difficult it was for the participants to define an image of youthful sexuality and lifestyle without 'buying' into the kiddie-porn frame that constructs them as victims and sex objects. Group members made liberal use of the framing elements, the stock phrases, key words and routine linguistic associations that structured the kiddie-porn frame. These elements articulate the nexus of the discourses of age, class, and gender that mobilized the images of sexual objectification and victimization within the frame. Hence, the kiddie-porn frame was inscribed on the peer group conversations as the participants' search for the shared vocabulary needed to conduct a 'sociable public discourse' about this issue.

While this study does not pretend to reflect a representative or an extensive sample of young people, it offers some insights into how young people negotiate with public discourse concerning them. As they worked to construct their own framework for understanding Klein's campaign and the controversy surrounding it, they mined the discursive field underlying the kiddie-porn media frame without necessarily adopting its specific structure. The lesson to be gleaned from this study and the work of Gamson is that journalists, social commentators, and social researchers would do well to reassess how they conceptualize the relationship between 'the public' and the media. More importantly, these self-proclaimed protectors of the people would do well to reassess the relationship between themselves and the publics they claim to serve.

References

Brookman, F. (1996). 'Teen Buying Power'. *Drug Store News*, 18: 11.

Gamson, W.A. (1992). *Talking Politics*. New York: Cambridge University Press.

'Teenagers wonder "What's the Fuss?",' (1995). *Advertising Age*, 4 September: 35.

'Teens' Coolest Brands'. (1996). *Youth Markets Alert*, 8: 4.

Tucker, L. R. (1998). 'The Framing of Calvin Klein: A Frame Analysis of Media Discourse about the August 1995 Calvin Klein Jeans Advertising Campaign'. *Critical Studies in Mass Communications*, 15: 1–15.

Part V

Politics, Citizenship, and Fragmentation

Introduction

As audience and consumer segmentation have developed into the dominant marketing strategies over the past few decades, scholars have argued that these commercial media practices have serious social and political implications. As the public
becomes more accustomed to messages targeted directly to its own interests and closely
defined needs, what becomes of its ability to communicate with and understand groups
outside each closely defined demographic category? What becomes of the ideal of
democratic citizenship in a heterogeneous society?

In 'Segmenting, Signalling, and Tailoring: Probing the Dark Side of Target Marketing',
Joseph Turow explores the geography of the targeted media landscape and maps a view
of future media configurations. He makes a distinction between segment-making media
and society-making media. He traces the historical development of targeted commercial
media strategies and their applications to new interactive technologies and the telecommunications superhighway.

In the political realm, with media-driven elections and targeted messages designed
from focus group research, Robin Andersen argues that the ability to conceive of and
engage in a more democratic discourse is severely hindered. In 'The Commercial Politics
of the 1996 US Presidential Campaign,' she explains how media strategies applied to
political discourse threaten our ability to articulate issues of common concern in order to
solve entrenched social and political problems, transform the nature of citizenship, and
place discursive practices of concession and compromise at risk. Targeting segmented
markets is the antithesis of leadership, as political messages are often contradictory
because they are tailored to win votes, not explain political philosophies.

Conceptions of citizenship often are formed in the schoolroom, hence the significance
of Margaret Cassidy's historical examination of media forays into American education,
'Commercial Media and Corporate Presence in the K-12 Classroom'. By comparing the
media's involvement with primary education in the 1920s and 1930s to the increased
penetration of highly commercial formats in the 1990s, she offers a better understanding
of the current situation and its possible trajectory into the future.

Class structure and class stratification have long been understood to pose obstacles to
democratic participation, and media commercialism has generally been thought to
reinforce class systems. In 'Commodity Fetishism: Symbolic Form, Social Class, and the
Division of Knowledge in Society', Paul Lippert argues that class divisions are as much a
product of inequalities in symbolic power as they are of economic and political control.
Tracing our contemporary dilemma back to the Renaissance, he describes how the commercial and communication revolutions have worked together to mystify social relations.

Chapter 16

Segmenting, Signalling and Tailoring: Probing the Dark Side of Target Marketing[1]

Joseph Turow

WITH the triumph of target marketing in the last decades of the twentieth century, the United States is experiencing a major shift in balance between society-making media and segment-making media. Segment-making media are those that encourage small slices of society to talk to themselves, while society-making media have the potential to get all those segments to talk to each other. In the ideal society, segment-making media strengthen the identities of interest groups, while society-making media allow those groups to move out of their parochial scenes to talk with, argue against, and entertain one another. They can lead to a rich and diverse sense of overarching connectedness or understanding: what a vibrant society is about.

The US has never enjoyed such a situation. It has been far too easy for both segment-making and society-making media to lapse into stilted stereotyping of many groups rather than to act out the complex, fascinating texture that is the United States. As marketers increase their ability to target desirable customers in media environments designed for them or people like them, though, even the possibility of the ideal is fading because of a profound movement by advertisers away from society-making media.

The hypersegmentation of consumers for separation into specialized media communities is accelerating through new methods of signalling to target audiences and tailoring content for them. These and related activities are beginning to transform the way television is programmed, the way newspapers are 'zoned', the way magazines are printed, and the way cultural events are produced and promoted. Advertisers' interest in exploiting differences between individuals is also woven into the basic assumptions about media models for the next century—the so-called '500-channel environment' or the future 'information superhighway'. In the next century, it is likely that media formats and commercials will act out a society so split up that it will be impossible to know or care about more than a few of its parts.

---

[1] Material from this article was published in the November 1997 issue of *American Demographics* titled, 'Breaking up America: the Dark Side of Target Marketing'.

The rise of targeting

What people now call target marketing goes back at least to the first quarter of the twentieth century. In an influential 1915 textbook called *The Business of Advertising,* Ernest Elmo Calkins showed clear awareness of the use of different periodicals to target various populations, including children, farmers, college students, and religious people, and of 'trade' or 'class' magazines such as those aimed at plumbers or Masons (see pp. 19–51). He appreciated the targeting value of a small-town newspaper, saying that it 'gives local influence to the advertisements which it carries' (p. 22). And he suggested 'canvassing consumers' (p. 185) in different cities around the country in order to gather information for an ad campaign.

Some media firms also noted social distinctions. In 1913, for example, the *Chicago Tribune*'s research department began a massive house-to-house survey in residential districts throughout the Windy City. Its report, released in 1916, presented figures on rents, buying habits, and the number of dealers for different product lines for each district (Strasser 1989: 151–2).

Then there was the introduction of Crisco Oil, carried out in 1912 by Proctor and Gamble with the help of the J. Walter Thompson ad agency. The campaign showed that both firms were well aware of the utility of markets, from railway chefs to immigrant Jewish kitchens to south-west American kitchens, that reflected lifestyles relevant to their product. They even practised what today would be called integrated marketing—encouraging a process that linked advertising activities with store promotions and public relations (Strasser 1989: 3–57).

These examples support social historian Susan Strasser's (1989: 14) argument that the seeds of 'market segmentation and targeted promotion' were sown in the first quarter of the twentieth century, as advertisers and their agencies looked for ways to expand their products' reach. It is, however, difficult to determine how frequently such activities were carried out by national advertisers.

We do know that from the late nineteenth century through the 1960s national advertisers were fixated on how they could sell to the largest number of people with the lowest cost in time and money. Ad practitioners considered the mass-circulation newspaper, magazine, and radio network to be people-delivery systems par excellence, and they played down their use of alternatives. They, and many scholars, accepted the idea that the transformation of radio and magazine into relatively targeted media were simply the result of the triumph of a new mass medium, television.

The problem with naming television as the cause of the rise of targeting in the magazine and radio industries is that it ignores the broad business forces that were moving the media inexorably in that direction. The basic change at work was product differentiation. It involved systematic attempts by manufacturers to create slightly different versions of the same products in order to aim at different parts of the marketplace.

Business historian Daniel Pope(1983: 259) traces the activity back to the early 1920s. By then, economies of scale had made it feasible for a manufacturer to differentiate its creations. General Motors, a troubled company with a confusing collection of car brands, was the leading edge of the change. Managed by Pierre Dupont and Alfred Sloan, the firm pulled out of its problems by reorganizing its auto-marketing strategy based on price segments. The different GM cars (Chevrolet, Pontiac, Buick, Cadillac) were priced differently and advertised to buyers with different incomes.

This sort of logic led manufacturers increasingly to support magazines and radio stations that reached the consumer segments that they coveted. Advertisers and their agencies also began in the decades following the Second World War to nurture research companies that allowed them to learn about the buying and leisure habits of listeners to particular stations and subscribers to particular periodicals. Researchers' statistical tools grew tremendously. In addition, the plunging cost of computer power made it economically feasible to merge large databases for marketing purposes and perform new kinds of number-crunching analyses on the newly merged files. That allowed them to find clusters of relationships among demographic, attitudinal, behavioural, and geographical features of a population that marketers hadn't noticed before.

It was in this manufacturing and marketing environment that widespread talk grew among marketers about using TV to reach different audiences in the same way that they were doing with radio and magazines. In the late 1970s, the growth of cable television in upscale suburbs and the rise of Home Box Office and the WTBS 'Superstation' spurred advertisers toward thinking about fundamental changes they would have to make in their approach to the home tube and its viewers. Although HBO refused to carry commercials, most marketers were sure this was just temporary and that the channel would provide great opportunities to target relatively wealthy homes. They also discussed the target-marketing potential presented by other cable channels, video tapes, personal computers, video games, and interactive TV technologies that had yet to appear.

Around that time, advertising and media executives adopted a view of American society that explained media fragmentation and justified their pursuit of smaller and smaller population segments. They advanced the notion that Americans were becoming more fractured, frazzled, self-indulgent, and suspicious than ever. US consumers were getting harder to reach and were sharing fewer common views of the world.

Ad people believed that these trends presented opportunities to create and sell new products. But this would work only if they understood the new social realities and if the media targeted the groups that marketers wanted. As a result, both marketing and media executives worked to develop a shared understanding of how America was splitting up and to make sure that changes in media would take place in ways that would help advertisers persuade their chosen segments as efficiently as possible. Advertising and marketing practitioners jockeyed to present their versions of the way men, women, Blacks, Hispanic Americans, suburbanites, seniors, and a wide spectrum of other groups were changing. Reaching the right groups efficiently became an important part of the marketing goal. Media formats that signalled an interest in people with specific backgrounds grew in popularity.

Building primary media communities

All this has meant that cutting-edge competition is no longer over the creation of mass-circulation media with huge audiences, as it had been for three-quarters of the twentieth century. The ultimate aim of the new phase of marketing is to reach different groups with specific messages about how certain products tie into their lifestyles. Target-minded firms are helping advertisers do that by building primary media communities. These are formed when viewers or readers feel that a magazine, TV channel, newspaper, radio station, or other medium reaches people like them, resonates with their personal beliefs and helps them chart their position in the larger world. For advertisers, tying into those communities means gaining consumer loyalties nearly impossible to establish in today's mass market.

Nickelodeon and MTV were pioneer attempts to establish this sort of ad-sponsored communion on cable television. While they started on particular media, they have transcended them. Owned by media giant Viacom, they are lifestyle parades that invite their target audiences (relatively upscale children and young adults, respectively) into a sense of belonging that ranges across a panoply of outlets, from cable to magazines, to books, video tapes, and outdoor events that their owners control or licence.

The idea of these sorts of 'programming services' is to cultivate a must-see, must-read, must-share mentality that makes the audience feel part of a family, attached to the programme hosts, other viewers, and sponsors. It is a strategy that is being launched off a wide spectrum of marketing vehicles, from magazines to catalogues, from direct mailings to online computer services, from outdoor events to in-store clubs. *Sports Illustrated* is a prime example of this approach. The name no longer signifies just a magazine. A key subsidiary of the Time Magazine, Inc. division of media conglomerate Time Warner, Sports Illustrated as a company places its name on videos, syndicated television programmes, college promotional events, a web site and a cable network, among other places. Sports Illustrated is now positioned as a cross-media brand that stands for a certain approach to life.

For executives at Sports Illustrated, MTV, ESPN, Nickelodeon, and other media firms, the mandate is to create a brand that is available to the consumer in a variety of manifestations, expose the brand to new target consumers and create added value for advertisers. Media executives and their sponsors understand that what makes these and other media brands distinctive is not necessarily the uniqueness of their content. Distinctiveness lies, rather, in the special character created by their formats: the flow and tone of their content, packaged to attract the right audience at a price that will draw advertisers.

Signalling and tailoring

But many media firms are coming to believe that simply attracting groups to specialized formats is often not enough. Making sure that people who do not fit the desired lifestyle profile are *not* part of the audience is sometimes also an aim, since it makes the community more pure and thereby more efficient for advertisers.

'Signalling' is one way that this is done. It involves the creation of media materials in ways that indicate to certain types of people that they ought to be part of the audience and to other populations that they do not belong. This activity has been going on for some time in the highly segmented magazine industry. A magazine cover is a touchstone for signalling points of distinction about the preferred audience. A key reason the cover is so important is that it reaches out to readers. Even executives whose periodicals rely mostly on subscription view the front of the magazine as crucial to attract single-copy purchasers who will replenish and augment subscription rolls.

The general feeling within the industry is that a cover must make the most of a very short instance of opportunity by telegraphing the right prejudices to the right targets. 'A magazine has three seconds' to grab the interest of a customer in a store, the design director for the magazine *Family Fun* asserted in an interview.[2] He and counterparts from other periodicals elaborated quite consistently on the way magazine designers, editors, publishers, and art directors work to communicate both blatant and nuanced notions about the race, income, age, and other features of the preferred audience during an era when advertisers expect periodicals to gather very specific types of people. They said they do it through photos, illustrations, typography, and cover lines, the come-on phrases that call out to the reader about the inside of the magazine. The cover planners insisted that even the smallest touches contribute to a magazine's ability to raise a mirror to its desired audience.

In the 1990s, this keen desire to signal to ever-narrower differences could also be found in electronic media from radio to the Internet. Using sound, moving pictures, or both, media people worked with ad people to make clear whom their formats were for, whom they weren't for, and what that meant. The feverish competition for their intended viewers, listeners, or 'users' led many executives toward promotional styles designed to call out to them loudly, even if the way it was done offended people who were not in the target audience.

Beavis and Butt-head filled this role for MTV during the mid-1990s, as did *The Howard Stern Show* for E! Entertainment Television. These were programmes with 'attitude', series with such a fix on separating their target audiences from the rest of the population that they sparked controversy among people who were clearly removed from their 'in' crowds. Executives involved with scheduling the shows hoped that controversies surrounding them would crystallize the channels' images and guarantee sampling by the people they wanted to attract. The executives

---

[2] Interview with Hans Tensma, design director of *Family Fun*, March 1995.

acknowledged that they also expected 'signature shows' would turn off viewers whom they didn't want in their audience.

An even more effective form of targeting, and one that doesn't bring with it the negative valence often associated with controversy, goes beyond chasing undesirables away. It simply excludes them in the first place. This activity is 'tailoring', the capacity to customize media content and ads to the backgrounds and lifestyles of particular individuals.

Melding new printing and electronic technologies with computer models based on zip codes and a variety of databases, it is becoming increasingly feasible to tailor materials for small groups, even individuals. That is already taking place in the direct-mail, telemarketing, magazine and Internet industries. 'Mass customization' is the term marketers use to describe the use of computers to send individually created messages efficiently to thousands, even millions, of people. Organizations in a wide range of media industries are working on mass-customization technologies with an eye toward attracting advertisers. For example:

(1) Magazine firms are using high-speed computer-controlled printing presses to direct messages to certain readers and not others. Two common approaches are 'ink-jet printing', in which the press sprays out messages to the subscriber, and 'selective binding', in which materials are inserted into an issue of the magazine depending on what the firm knows about the subscriber. The costs of these activities are still relatively high, and activities using them are still rather limited, though they are increasing. *Time* has used ink-jet printing to tell individuals about their Congressperson's voting record. *Sports Illustrated* has used selective binding technology to allow advertisers who want to reach golfers to sponsor a multi-page insert that reaches only those readers who fit the periodical's profile of golf enthusiasts.

(2) Many supermarket chains use the Catalina coupon dispenser, which prints customized coupons based on the products a person has bought; the purchase of hot dogs might yield a coupon for mustard. More high-tech are supermarket chains that use loyalty cards to track individuals' purchases. When used at the cash register to get discounts, the card registers the shopper's name and purchases into a database. The information collected in this manner allows the supermarket chain to programme coupon kiosks in the stores to give different types of discounts to different people depending on what their long-term purchasing patterns indicate about their lifestyles. Having long-range purchase data also allows supermarkets to send tailored advertising materials to people based on their shopping patterns.

(3) Marketers see the Internet, and especially the World Wide Web, as perfect for sophisticated tailoring of information and entertainment. The inherent two-way nature of the web leads users to provide immediate feedback to content providers about their choices. Volunteered personal information (often provided when 'registering' for a site), supplemented by 'clickstream' data about what the user has done at a particular site, is often stored in software called a 'cookie' on the user's computer. The cookie is read by the site's computer every time the user goes back to it, thereby allowing the site to create a customized face with specialized content for that particular individual.

(4) With certain forms of interactive cable television, it is technically quite possible (though still relatively costly and rare) to use computers to insert commercials and even programmes aimed at selective audiences. Through such 'digital insertion' activities, audiovisual materials can be sent to only the particular neighbourhoods, census

blocks, and households that advertisers want to reach. Interactive TV navigators are also technically possible—and, executives assert, will be necessary when people start receiving hundreds of channels. An interactive TV navigator stores a viewer's stated interests, keeps track or his or her programme routines, and then suggests a menu of viewing options for different times of the day.

The growing use of the terms 'mass customization', 'digital insertion', 'clickstream', 'web cookies', and 'interactive TV navigators' by executives and the trade press reflects their awareness that the long-term trajectory of media and marketing is towards customizing the delivery of content as much as possible. Although costs are high in some cases, technical advances are driving them down. Key to the diffusion of these tailoring tools is an increasingly widespread conviction in marketing that being able to speak to consumers on a one-to-one basis will be crucial in the decades to come.

Proponents of these technologies argue that, while consumers may use mass-market vehicles such as network television in their everyday activities, they identify more strongly with the worlds portrayed in formats specifically aimed at them and people like them. Media technologists argue that when advertisers piggyback on personalized news, entertainment, and information, the advertisers become an ongoing part of their customers' lives. The advertisers can also track potential customers' activities, shadow their purchases and reward the 'proper' ones with reinforcing notes and discounts. In an era in which consultants such as Don Peppers and Martha Rogers have helped make the word 'relationship' a mantra in all sorts of selling, executives are quite aware of the utility of creating individualized and lasting bonds with desirable customers. Repeat purchasers can be much more lucrative than continually hunting for first-time buyers. 'Not all customers are equal,' said a consultant in 1994, 'You have to put golden handcuffs on your very best customers' (Raphael 1994: 118–20).

Because of the relatively high costs involved, tailoring is now used mostly to pursue and keep upscale individuals. Media firms and marketers are together encouraging consumers into media worlds that reward their distinctive lifestyles by reflecting the lifestyles back at them. With just a little effort (habit, actually), they can listen to radio stations, read magazines, watch cable programmes, surf the web and participate in loyalty programmes that parade their self-images and clusters of concerns. With no seeming effort at all, they receive offers from marketers that complement their lifestyles. And with just a bit of cash, they pay for technologies that can further tailor information to their interests—through, for example, highly personalized news delivery.

Eye on the future

The heads of major technology firms, media corporations and marketing companies point out that these activities are primitive compared to the tailoring activities that are coming down the road. The high cost of introducing interactive television in the mid-1990s derailed the plans of some companies and caused sceptics to argue that high-tech scenarios wouldn't ever come to pass. But the competition to develop interactive technologies has not faded, despite the changing strategies of particular firms.

Momentum toward creating targeted spaces for increasingly narrow niches of consumers is both national and global. All signs are that in the next century print and electronic technologies will allow media firms to bring to the spaces the efficient conduct of three activities that marketers covet. One is selectability—an ability to reach an individual with entertainment, news, information, and advertising based on knowledge of the individual's background, interests, and habits. The second is accountability to advertisers—an ability to trace the individual's response to a particular ad. The third is interactivity—the ability to cultivate a rapport with, and loyalty of, individual consumers over time.

Privacy may seem an issue likely to derail the most sophisticated collaboration of target marketing and target media. It almost surely will not, however. In response to advocacy groups in the US and laws in Europe, privacy regulations and self-regulations will probably require marketers to tell consumers more than they do now about the information firms collect about them and how they use it. Yet marketers will probably encourage consumers to believe that what companies know about them will enable them to enjoy the warm attention, discounts, and specialized content that they can get in exchange for allowing firms to track their movements within and across web sites and interactive TV channels.

Such rifle-shot power will be hard to turn down in favour of mass-market tactics, which will appear inefficiently scattershot in comparison. Certainly, there will be companies that want to get their brands out to the broad population as quickly as possible and so will find mass-market media useful. They will support the presence of billboards, supermarket signs, and TV shows such as the Super Bowl, the World Series and the Miss America Pageant that are designed to grab millions of viewers in a short period. That kind of programming will help create immediate national awareness, and maybe word-of-mouth, for a new car model, a new athletics shoe, or a new computer to as many people as possible.

An impulse toward mass-market media will probably also exist side by side with targeted signalling and tailoring in the interest of economic efficiency. To recoup the high production costs for a TV movie about the Chernobyl nuclear disaster, Warner Brothers Television might try to reach as many people as possible by targeting their personal TV navigators with plot descriptions that are tailored to their backgrounds. Different descriptions might be written for people old enough to remember the incident, for people interested in science, for people who have a habit of viewing films starring the lead actor, and so on. As another example, NBC might set up its election coverage so that it can be tailored to viewers with different interests. People who care especially about foreign affairs, people specializing in agricultural issues, people who want to know about environmental issues on a state-by-state basis: they and others may be given the option of choosing versions of the network feed that supply experts in their interest areas in addition to generic NBC coverage.

But this desire to combine production efficiencies of mass marketing with the audience draw of tailored materials may end up pushing separation over collectivity.

Over and over again, the different versions of news will act out different social distinctions for different people. And even when the content is the same for the various segments (as in the Chernobyl movie), producers will promote the films differently to different types of people, or certain media communities, will encourage the perception that the viewing experience in America is an enormously splintered one.

It is likely that producers of news and information will be able to customize content to a greater range of demographic, psychographic, and lifestyle choices than will those who create expensive movies. The reason is simply that, at present at least, it is less expensive to customize news and information programmes than top-of-the-line entertainment. From an economic standpoint, shopping, video games, light entertainment, and many sports are closer to news and information than to high-cost films. It seems likely that they will become major platforms for tailored TV and online materials in the years to come. That will drastically splinter audio-visual choices.

The individual and the society

It will take time, possibly decades, for the full effects of the emerging media world to take shape. Even when the new media environment does crystallize, segmentation and tailoring are not likely to be total. Consumers will still be able to seek media not directed at them, and they will probably even be able to block direct-marketing offers from reaching them, if they choose.

Increasingly, though, the easiest path will be to go with the customized flow of media and marketing paraphernalia. In fact, for you and me—individual readers and viewers—this segmentation and targeting can portend terrific things. If we can afford to pay, or if we're important to sponsors who will pick up the tab, we will be able to receive immediately all the news, information, and entertainment we like. In the face of daily tensions of work, family, and immediate community, who would not welcome media and sponsors that offer to surround us with exactly what one wants when one wants it?

But while we as individual consumers benefit from targeted media and marketing, that isn't the same as benefiting society. It is likely that the United States as an entirety will suffer when there is no hope of a balance between segment-making media and strong society-making. The many demographic and lifestyle labels that marketers acted out during the 1990s extend the portrait of America as splintered by distinctions. Doing that, they have signalled that people should find their own kind in media communities designed for them. They also signalled the irrelevance of many geographic relationships. In an era of satellites, physical distance is becoming less and less a concern for media companies. Huge media firms interested in target marketing increasingly find it far more useful to distribute materials for far-flung consumers with similar tastes than to produce entertainment, news, or information for audiences in relatively narrow geographical areas who have little in common.

These far-flung groups of people may be more like one another in their backgrounds and lifestyles than the people who live in neighbourhoods two miles away. People may increasingly feel that links to individuals in their immediate space and time—people they work with, see in stores or on the streets—are not nearly as important as their far-flung virtual communities. News about their own neighbourhoods will probably draw people who care about schools and property values. Beyond those tangibly important concerns, though, they may not care to learn about people who live close to them—in the same or nearby neighbourhoods—but whom they consider substantially different. Links between suburbs and cities, already tenuous, will likely become even thinner.

Given the chance to separate themselves electronically from types of people they believe are threatening their well-being, media users are likely to do so. Keeping 'different' people out of mind when they don't have to deal with them may become as important as keeping them out with gates. Those who can afford it will deal with the fear of going out by dialling into malls set up for individuals like them. Media firms will customize e-mail, interactive games, and online chat rooms to create virtual communities of people from around the world who have similar interests, and attract similar advertisers.

Eventually, it may well be that children growing up in the hyper-segmented environment will see the pictures of division as reflecting the real thing. Compared even to today, the media of the future will be far more fragmented, with hundreds of market-driven options targeted and tailored to carefully calibrated types. While that may engender a tight sense of community among people who share similar backgrounds, it could also reinforce suspicion, lack of empathy, and alienation between people of different backgrounds, income classes, and lifestyles. Primary media communities—image tribes—will guide consumers' sense of social separation by helping them understand whom to label as 'not like them'.

In that kind of environment, it is easy to imagine critics worrying that the absence of strong collective media poses a threat to democracy. Society-wide debate will be harder and harder to sustain. People who fundamentally disagree may simply not argue with one another; key political and social issues may not be thrashed out as well as they should. With people so accustomed to their own image tribes, they may be unwilling to connect in debates with people outside their circles. And advertisers, traditionally wary of controversy, certainly won't encourage it.

It is difficult to come up with ways to solve the problem of this fractured media world. One problem is that the emerging world seems to be in sync with the fractured way in which Americans and their leaders view their worlds beyond the media. But marketers and media practitioners have a special responsibility for reinforcing this widely felt sense of fragmentation, since they are building it into the very content and structure of the media system.

Is it too idealistic to hope for a concerted effort by marketing and media leaders to bolster society-making media and slow down the frantic slicing and dicing of populations? That would be an important first step towards building a balance between individual community and the collectivity that is the hallmark of a healthy society.

References

Culkins, E. E. (1915). *The Business of Advertising.* New York: D. Appleton.

Pope, D. (1983). *The Making of Modern Advertising* . New York : Basic Books.

Raphael, M. (1994). 'Supermarketing Yesterday, Today and Tomorrow'. *Direct Marketing,* July: 118–20.

Strasser, S. (1989). *Satisfaction Guaranteed.* New York: Pantheon.

Chapter 17

The Commercial Politics of the 1996 US Presidential Campaign

Robin Andersen

Eᴀʀʟʏ in the 1996 presidential campaign the candidates from the two major parties, on separate occasions, sat down with their wives and talked to Barbara Walters in the intimate, celebrity interview that is her trade mark. The Clintons told Barbara they liked to stay home, eat popcorn, and watch movies. Bob and Elizabeth Dole, on the other hand, preferred to go out to the movies.

Acting on the advice of friend and political adviser William Bennett, one of the movies the Doles saw was *Independence Day*, the summer blockbuster of 1996 that featured enemy spacecraft, each ten miles across, that loomed over Los Angeles, New York, Washington, and all Earth's other major cities. Upon emerging from the cinema, Bob Dole reportedly said, 'Bring your family. You'll be proud of it. Diversity. America. Leadership' (Menand 1996: 6).

Even though *Independence Day* turned into one of the largest grossing movies of the summer, movie critics Jean Siskel and Roger Ebert, gave it a rating of two thumbs down. They said the plot was unoriginal, the aliens were stale clones of past aliens, and even though it had nonstop special effects, that's all it had.

How could the Doles have enjoyed such a movie? In *Independence Day* the White House and the Capitol are blown to bits. Well-known buildings in New York and LA are zapped by alien invaders using weapons that send huge fireballs through city streets wiping out whole urban centres. Even though 'a nightmare of depravity' is how Bob Dole described a typical Hollywood movie in the 1995 version of his Hollywood speech, both Dole and William Bennett say they liked the film.

Aligning himself with a movie that featured the President as a former fighter pilot in the Gulf war was a fortuitous association for a presidential candidate. In the movie the presidential hero is forced to rally a rag-tag team and once again become the Top Gun who saves the world. But we must wonder what the Doles thought of the black single mother, the girlfriend of the character played by Will Smith. She has the sense to save herself and her son as a fireball sweeps through a tunnel, killing just about everyone in LA. She then commandeers a huge city truck and makes her way to safety, gathering up the wounded and saving them too. But this character works as a stripper to support her little boy. She is not married but lives with her boyfriend, who is not her son's father. She is the antithesis of the Republican moral agenda that champions 'family values'.

Mr Bennett pointed out to the *New York Times* (Menand 1996: 6) that he liked the movie because in the end all the couples are reunited (read 'married') with one exception. Unfortunately the First Lady doesn't make it. (And that may be why the Republicans liked the movie. The destruction of American cities, in which millions perished, was not necessarily all bad, as Dole's senior California adviser, Ken Keachigain, explained to reporters, hopefully tongue in cheek, since most of the people who live in big cities are liberals.)

Campaign discourse became comical under the influence of *Independence Day*, which was itself a filmic comic book. Almost half the movie was filmed inside a computer in what is known as 'digital special effects'. The technique combines actual footage of real places with simulated images of mayhem and destruction. 'The general idea is to make what is essentially a comic book look like a movie, that is, to manipulate realistic people and things in order to make them behave as though they were in a cartoon.' (Menand 1996: 4). The marketing practices and wham-bang special effects targeted at fourteen-year-old boys trivialize movie content, and when employed in a political campaign they trivialize political discourse as well.

As a summer blockbuster, the movie itself was the quintessential commercial vehicle (Bart 1999). It was a composite of recycled images and plots from old 1970s disaster films like *Towering Inferno* and other old movies like *The War of the Worlds* and *The Right Stuff*. This was patched together with fragments from TV series like *The X-Files*. Like the other summer hit of 1996, *Mission Impossible*, it appealed to babyboomers while also attracting their kids. Its inspiration was based in marketing, not originality, and it garnered a mass audience.

The real reason Bob Dole and his advisers liked the movie was revealed by Bennett when he said that *Independence Day* was a 'movie that has been ratified by the American people', and 'a movie that the American people love' (Menand 1996: 6). And so the candidates must love it too. If they do they hope to garner this huge constituency that has already voted with their $7 for the movie. Candidate Dole was attempting to play the same chords that had already resonated with a huge part of the media market, and turn that mutual sympathy into votes. In an election campaign, reaching audiences has become the substitute for what used to be called garnering constituencies. Just as advertisers sell products to audiences, political consultants market candidates to those same audiences. In contemporary media-driven elections, programme, advertising, and film audiences become targeted markets of voters. In the larger sense, citizens are transmuted into consumers, connecting with a media product instead of a political platform.

The ability to appropriate movie themes and transform them into campaign slogans is a type of intertextual political shorthand that does not reflect the candidate's politics. Diversity, an *Independence Day* theme pointed out by Dole, is of course an important issue for the Republicans. Columnist Bob Hurbert wondered in the *New York Times* what Colin Powell must have thought at the Republican convention, looking out over a crowd that was 90 per cent white and only 3 per cent African American. Almost 20 per cent were millionaires, not a diverse crowd. When political consultants align candidates with popular media themes, the process bypasses the recognition of actual political platforms, reconfiguring them with the already commercialized themes of media culture.

Candidates, popular culture, and media resonance

Inserting candidates into the landscape of popular culture is done through a variety of intertextual strategies. While both candidates struggled to achieve this goal, Bill Clinton was far more successful than Senator Dole. After all, Clinton had already perfected those strategies during his 1992 race against George Bush. The babyboom theme song of the 1992 Democratic convention, 'Don't Stop Thinking about Tomorrow', was a stroke of intertextual genius and his adaptation of the testimonial style of warmth and redemption garnered him the nickname, in some corners, of the 'talk-show President' (Andersen 1995).

In 1996 Dole endeavoured to strike the chords of media resonance as well. When the Republicans introduced advertisements castigating teenage drug use, for example, Dole's message was enhanced using the theme song to the TV show *Cops*, which was played at the candidate's campaign stops. His other attempts to appropriate popular music met with less success. The Dole camp had to stop using its unofficial theme song, 'Dole Man', altered from 'Soul Man', after the owner of the 1967 motown hit threatened to sue for copyright infringement. This attempt at 'diversity' failed.

While Bob Dole's references to popular culture resulted in such gaffes as uniting Brooklyn and the Dodgers, a team and city that have not been together for thirty years, it was Elizabeth Dole who successfully connected with the media. Mrs Dole triumphantly rode on the back of Jay Leno's motorcycle and onto the set of *The Tonight Show* after a rally of 'Bikers for Bob'. Taking her cue from Bill Clinton, she also used the talk-show format successfully at the Republican convention, and at other appearances, as she descended from the stage talking to the audience up close and personal.

These are but a few illustrations of the persistent bonds forged between candidates and entertainment formats. Even as Republicans criticized the commercial values embedded within the media, both campaigns aspired to profit from their successes. The party conventions may be the best illustrations of the media-driven presidential race of 1996. Their successes at adopting commercial media techniques and values undoubtedly spurred the campaigns to continue crafting such strategies.

The conventions

Walter Goodman (1996*a*: 8) of the *New York Times* opened his commentary about the Republican convention with the words 'Television news met its enemy this week, and it was television'. Everyone knew that the media consultants producing the conventions would deliver carefully scripted entertainment spectacles, but, according to Goodman, no one foresaw how effectively this would be done. Convention producers had so skilfully poached the human-interest appeal of commercial television that news purveyors and pundits had no political controversy or political debate to disseminate. When Congresswoman Molinari delivered the keynote address at the Republican convention, her story about her immigrant grandparents and the American dream was carried by all the networks right up to 11 p.m., leaving no time for political analysis. These human-interest stories of heroic actions in the face of adversity, of success based on hard work and American greatness, are the stuff of TV news and entertainment genres. ABC television anchorman Ted Koppel left the floor of the convention in protest.

Mr Dole had won respect over the years for not putting his severe war wound to political service. But in 1996 it became a major campaign theme, beginning at the convention. As one journalist pointed out, 'It's touchy to observe that Bob Dole's famous war wound is less relevant to his current quest for the presidency than his long record in the Senate, which went uncelebrated in his acceptance speech' (Goodman 1996b). In his five-minute human-interest commercial it featured heavily, complete with pictures of his struggle for rehabilitation after returning home from the war.

At the Democratic convention, campaign media managers also flaunted their mastery of primetime know-how. Human-interest videos and the appearance of Christopher Reeve in his wheelchair presented dramatic media events with little political substance. The human-interest stories are effective at taking the focus away from what they covered up. The conventions were once vibrant, contentious policy-making political rituals. After the smoke cleared, resolutions were either passed or not passed and one candidate emerged to represent the party. What the political media consultants have achieved is the transformation of an event as unmanageable as a convention, complete with a cast of thousands, and held for an historically important political purpose, into a series of slick infomercials. Gary Smith, who produced the convention for the Democrats, defended the practice by asking, 'What's wrong with an infomercial? It's not as if it's an infomercial for hot dogs' (Goodman 1996b: A13).

Infomercials are the result of 1980s media deregulation; previously, there were restrictions on the number of commercials that could be aired in any single hour of television programming. In the absence of any restrictions programmes can contain as much promotion as the market will bear. Thus, the infomercial was born. The ethos of persuasion, once largely restricted to advertising strategies, is now being effectively incorporated into the world of entertainment. And politics is embedded within this same commercial media culture. The boundaries between politics and promotion have all but disappeared.

The Dick Morris sex scandal erupted toward the end of the Democratic convention and added some spontaneity to an otherwise strictly formatted media spectacle. While it emphasized personal scandal, the news coverage contained political revelations as well. That this same consultant, whose lack of personal virtue was now suffering intense public exposure, had been the very one who advised President Clinton to push for school uniforms offered some insights into the manufactured nature of political proposals. This uncontrolled news contrasted heavily with the pretences of the convention spectacle.

Conventions of the future will remain highly choreographed, slick infomercials. In the absence of any authentic political activity or discourse at national conventions, viewers have tuned out and networks have threatened to reduce convention airtime greatly.

Seinfeld

An example of the debasing of electoral politics by media marketing and promotional strategies can be found in what one columnist refers to as President Clinton's Seinfeldian style. When *New York Times* columnist Maureen Dowd (1996: A23) criticized the Clinton presidency for trivializing politics (by using free-call numbers to solve pressing social issues) she remarked, 'He's only reflecting trivial yuppies used to a world not of heroic proportions but of Seinfeldian proportions, a world defined not by a battle between good and evil but a choice between skim or whole, caf or de, foam or no foam, carbonated or still, lemon or lime.' What Dowd was describing, as she blamed 'yuppie' audiences, was consumer media culture. *Seinfeld* is trivial because it is a programme-length commercial. It is the banter over products that is Seinfeldian. It is a show about products, their slogans, and the many ways all that can be worked into funny scripts that mimic the world of advertising to which it is so closely tied. This trivialization reflects TV marketing strategies and the trivialities of commercial culture.

Dowd levelled another criticism against Clinton, this time for his personality, which she complained was 'conciliatory', 'malleable', 'eager to please', 'but under the tutelage of Dick Morris, he became completely reactive, learning to mirror the mood of the country, and to back issues that would appeal to the most people in the most important groups' (Dowd 1996: A23). What she observed was not Clinton's personality, but the consequences of sophisticated marketing strategies that sell politicians to the voting public by reflecting back to them their own opinions, ideas, and desires. Clinton is 'The Man in the Mirror' because his political platform has been so carefully constructed through the use of marketing strategies. Through sophisticated research, pollsters determine the opinions, interests, and mood of the country and then fashion slogans, taking care to appeal to the most important voting segments. This discourse can indeed be described as malleable and eager to please.

In the age of media marketing the contemporary face of persuasion has been transformed. It no longer has the Herculean task of convincing everyone of the same thing through political rhetoric and leadership. Instead, persuasive strategies, selling either products or politicians, target key messages at highly defined consumer and opinion groups. Those targeted segments are voting groups, some of them important 'swing voters', and adding them up results in enough votes to get elected. But this is not political consensus. It's the sum of an often very disparate set of promises, values, and ideologies. Any attempt at majority consensus can only be achieved through the most vague and meaningless metaphorical phraseology such as 'bridge to the twenty-first century'. Of course Dole's failed attempt at consensus was the promise of a 15 per cent tax cut, a proposal that most found implausible, for reasons discussed below. Such strategies reverberate through the political arena in very destructive ways. Let's take a look at some of the advertising strategies, the centrepieces of both campaigns during the 1996 presidential race.

The drug ads

The long-awaited attack ad aired nationally with such frequency—the image of Clinton saying he would smoke marijuana again if he could—will be seared into American culture for years to come. Doctored to give the clip a grainy appearance, and presented in black and white, the video fragment from MTV was a national embarrassment (a portent of much worse things to come). Undoubtedly, most Americans had never seen the clip of then presidential candidate Clinton, especially with those production qualities.

How could Clinton have said such a thing? Did he really want to try again in 1992? That is highly unlikely. He was aggressively courting the youth vote in 1992. His remark is a consequence of a political strategy that targets segments of the voting public with singular political messages that speak specifically to that segment's interests and sensibilities. Clinton's claim on MTV that he would-again-if-he-could in hopes of winning over that youthful target audience was little more than campaign bluster. Most Americans never knew he said such a thing because most Americans don't watch MTV. It is a narrowcasted market of music/advertising. But Bill Clinton certainly could not defend himself later by arguing that he did not mean what he said. He only said it to win votes.

Nor did media stories or commentaries argue that Clinton's remarks were part of a campaign strategy. For that would discredit a system of which they are very much a part. Instead, the media took both Clinton and Dole's political rhetoric at face value.

This example illustrates one of the main problems with media-driven campaign strategies. Just like product advertising, campaign media buys are designed to target audiences by age and other demographics and often by region and states. In politics, these targeted audiences are also voters. And the swing voters are especially important. They are usually members of politically unsure, or unaffiliated, or cross-over groups whose votes come to determine who will win or lose an election.

Soccer moms

In 1996 political analysts defined white suburban females as important swing voters, a group that could have a significant effect on the outcome of the election. The shorthand phrase of political consultation seeped into public discourse, and 'soccer moms' became the au currant media construct of the electioneering. The embarrassing clip of Clinton undoubtedly played to that group.

In addition to national advertising, both campaigns designed specific appeals to key constituencies in battleground states. Most voters do not hear different regional ads. This allows candidates to say one thing to one target audience, and something completely different to another.

'Mediscare'

Clinton's MTV remarks did not play well to a national audience, but Bob Dole also had problems with targeted messages. The Dole campaign ran ads carefully tailored to elderly voters in Florida and Arizona. In promising to put money in the pockets of pensioners, the ad promised to increase federal spending by 14 per cent, to help support Social Security and Medicare. Other Republican commercials not targeted to seniors said exactly the opposite. They claimed Dole would reduce federal spending. As the *New York Times* pointed out, 'the Dole commercial, in aiming specifically for the votes of the elderly, makes claims that might sit poorly' with other Republicans, 'particularly younger conservatives looking for a smaller federal government' (Bennett 1996: A19).

The Clinton/Gore camp ran ads pointing out some of Dole's contradictory statements. One commercial opened with Mr Dole accepting the Republican presidential nomination: 'I will be the president who preserves, and strengthens, and protects Medicare.' The ad then showed Mr Dole speaking to the American Conservative Union in 1995 saying, 'I was there, fighting the fight, voting against Medicare, one of twelve, because we knew it wouldn't work.'

Marketing segmentation, a key advertising strategy, now used in politics to target key votes, requires candidates to make a variety of claims that often contradict what they've said to another group. The formulation of coherent political platforms is lost to these techniques. Nor can a candidate keep all the promises he has made to all the different groups once he gets into office. Instead of leadership and coherence, political discourse descends to manipulation and clutter.

Will the real candidate please stand up

A disturbing aspect of the 1996 campaign was the way in which both candidates underwent significant political transformations early on. After campaigning turns to governing, candidates often become unrecognizable, unable to fulfil promises designed specifically to attract votes. In 1996 however, as commercial media techniques escalated, both candidates became almost unrecognizable as soon as the race began, strangely detached from their own histories and political philosophies. They were recontextualized into media themes past and present as they became the political products of media intertextuality.

Morning in America II

As the challenger in 1992, Clinton criticized President Bush for his failure to understand the economic insecurity felt by most Americans. For candidate Clinton it was 'the economy, stupid', and his platform promised the creation of new jobs, the end of wage stagnation, overwork, and unemployment, and sweeping transformation in health-care delivery.

For the 1996 campaign, Democratic pollster Stan Greenberg was commissioned by the AFL–CIO trade-union federation to do extensive focus-group research to determine the key issues and attitudes of the American working class. The results of that research were astonishing when compared to the discourse of economic prosperity so prevalent in the media. Greenberg (1996) found that Americans were still suffering from underemployment, overwork and low wages. They were working harder just to stay afloat. To make ends meet, most had to work at more than one job. Greenberg's findings are borne out in the realities of the American economy. Wages have been ratcheting down for twenty years as full-time jobs with benefits have been replaced with low-wage, part-time jobs. The share of income collected by 80 per cent of American households fell from 59.5 per cent in 1968, to 51.3 per cent by 1994, while the top 20 per cent enjoyed an 8 per cent increase (Brouwer 1997). Just 1 per cent of the population owns 46 per cent of the wealth (Brouwer 1997: 10) in the USA, which by the 1990s was the country with the largest gap between the rich and the poor of any of the industrial democracies. Robert Reich (1999), Secretary of Labor during Clinton's first term, continues to point out in public forums and published material that the wealth gains of the 1990s bull market have benefited the few wealthiest Americans, 85 per cent of market gains going to the 10 per cent at the top. While wages at the bottom have started to rise slowly, it will take years for working Americans to achieve the standard of living enjoyed during the 1970s. The wealth gap is the largest it has been for a century.

Not surprisingly, Greenberg found that prosperity was not part of the lexicon of this significant sector of blue- and white-collar workers. In addition, he found that they mistrust government and feel that no one in politics represents their interests. They rely instead on their own hard work, responsibility, and personal virtue. They look to their families for support and security. This research demonstrated that for most working Americans the economy was still the most significant factor in their lives.

But while issues of employment and economics had not changed significantly by 1996, Clinton's electoral strategy certainly had. Clinton the incumbent was to be a very different candidate. As Ed Rollins (1996) revealed at a Press Club luncheon, the Clinton team visited the Ronald Reagan archives in Bethesda, Maryland, and scoured Reagan's material, scrutinizing every detail of the strategy. Reagan's 1984 'Morning in America' campaign became the model for Clinton's electoral strategy: in 1996 voters lived through Morning in America II. The Clinton campaign painted a picture of economic well-being and future glory.[1] He took credit for the creation of 10.5 million new jobs, even though those replacement jobs were not high-paying, full-time jobs with benefits like the ones lost over the last two decades.

Unable to ignore Greenberg's findings of the level of economic hardship faced by a majority of Americans, politicians used some of them to shape political messages. The non-college-educated working class dream of improving their prospects by going to school or starting their own small business. Into this dream stepped President Clinton. He offered tax deductions for college education and the assurance that workers would not lose health-care benefits if they changed jobs. Such carefully crafted proposals spoke to the reality of individual hardship while actually doing very little to improve the economy for the majority. Interestingly, it was the Republican camp that recognized the policies for what they were, referring to them as 'itty-bitty, teeny-weeny' policy proposals.

Fifteen per cent

The story of a place called Hope worked so well for Mr Clinton in 1992 that by 1996, during the Republican convention, it had become a long way from Russell, Kansas, to San Diego for Bob Dole. Dole's metamorphosis was unstable and ineffective from the start. His decision to quit his job as Senate majority leader to run for president as 'Just a Man' (itself a commercial tag line) was the first sign that his campaign would attempt to ignore the last thirty-five years of the candidate's professional life. As a senator Dole had debated, written, and voted on every major piece of legislation during the past three decades. But telling the story of thirty-five years of law-making takes time. Legislative intricacies must be explained and many specific votes must be justified. Obviously, commercial rhetoric is the worst vehicle with which to lay out such a complicated narrative.

In addition, focus-group issues did not work well with Mr Dole's record. He voted against family leave and drug-free school zones, and he put his name to legislation that would have cut social programmes from education to health care.

Dole had the credentials to run as a pre-eminent senator with wisdom and integrity. Instead, he gave up his political identity for a promotional façade that, in his case, did not work. Dole's transformation was too transparent (Weisberg 1996). His entire career was based on fiscal responsibility and conservatism, making his 15 per cent tax cut so implausible that it revealed itself as a marketing strategy. It was not so much that the American public did not believe Dole; they trusted the judgement of the real Bob Dole, the one who would never propose such a plan, not the marketing product who tried to bribe them for votes. The Dole campaign

---

[1] In 1984, Ronald Reagan was the incumbent running against challenger Walter Mondale. In Reagan's first term certain economic indicators had improved. Reagan's enormous military budget expanded the economy, even as it created the deficit we live with today. But the stagflation of the 1970s under Carter was ended. Reagan's successful campaign, known as, 'Morning in America', was singularly positive (see Rollins 1996).

demonstrated the limits of the political sell. Such a strategy cannot work if it reveals itself to be arrogant commercial persuasion.

The decision to 'go negative' at the second debate and in the follow-up stump speeches and in ads came on the heels of an 'extraordinary public, week-long discussion of how ferociously he should attack Mr Clinton'. As one of Clinton's ad team put it, 'It was the first time that the American people got to sit in on a strategy meeting.' He called it a 'horrible strategy'. The chilling moral of this story is that the American people must at all costs be kept in the dark about campaign strategy. If we know too much, we may no longer be the easily manipulated consumers that political strategists need us to be. We were expected to believe that Bob Dole attacked the president's ethics in a spontaneous burst of moral obligation, not in a last-ditch effort to boost his numbers.

But nothing Dole said or did had any significant impact on the polls; not retiring from the Senate, not proposing a 15 per cent tax cut, not choosing a life-long enemy, Jack Kemp, as a running-mate, not telling kids, 'Just don't do it', and not going negative, because Mr Dole had lost all authenticity. After thirty-five years as a respected legislator, Dole's entire personal and political identity was reduced to a marketing nonentity, an advertising façade searching in vain for any persuasive issue to 'boost his numbers'. Dole was unable to present himself as anything but an also-ran. The failure of his campaign does point to the limits of promotional discourse and to the impact of media scrutiny and exposure of marketing techniques.

Election discourse as advertising

The merger between political and advertising rhetoric took a large step forward on 18 September, when Bob Dole rolled out his anti-drug slogan 'Just Don't Do It.' Dole hoped the Nancy Reagan– Nike promotional hybrid would be a focal point of his campaign. In fact, Nike resented its priceless trademark being transfigured into an anti-drug slogan. As Jim Small, a Nike spokesman, said, the slogan is 'cemented in consumers' minds as a rallying cry to get off the couch and play sports. We're uncomfortable entering the political arena' ('Just Don't Say It, 1996: 40). As a political message, the negative transmutation of the ad phrase is meaningless, yet as a symbolic marker it is suffused with significance. With the phrase, American political language openly embraced the ethos of advertising and marketing persuasion.

The advertising, the miscontextualized soundbites with production qualities that make candidates appear far less than presidential, have become the primary modes of public address in election campaigns. The ads have also changed the language of politics. Bob Dole is 'about' various things. 'About' is a word that has been tried and found effective in advertising. Politicians used to 'address' issues, a term that implies solutions. Talking in soundbites is also common: as one commentator pointed out, Mr Dole sometimes answered Barbara Walters in what sounded like lines from his advertisements.

Neither did the highlight of Dole's campaign, his endorsement by Colin Powell, make any political sense. On issues such as welfare, affirmative action, immigration and abortion, Powell's political sensibilities are quite distinct from those of the candidate he was endorsing. Powell's speech at the Republican convention would have found more common ground at the Democratic convention. But in the age of marketing politics, Powell's support of Dole did not represent political cohesion; rather, it mirrored the persuasive strategies of commercial endorsement, the associations that couple celebrities with products. The celebrity endorsement is a strategy so common in advertising that it does not draw attention to itself when applied to this new geography of commercial politics. Like Michael Jordan endorsing Coke, Powell became the celebrity spokesperson for Dole (Weisberg 1996).

Politics is now utterly subsumed within an entire complex of commercial media culture. In this unified discourse the characteristics that separated candidates from celebrities and celebrities from hucksters are the quaint distinctions of a past era. Like Dan Quayle, who endorsed WavyLays after losing his bid for re-election as Vice-president in 1992, Bob Dole went on to advertise Visa Card, using his lost identity as a commercial theme. Possibly in an attempt to become the celebrity spouse of the first woman presidential candidate, Elizabeth Dole in 2000, by 1999 a humble but sincere Bob Dole was educating men about erectile dysfunction in commercial spots on primetime television.

Debates

The debates between candidates did not offer a solution to these problems. Even though the televised debates were live and the candidates themselves spoke, their words cannot be considered spontaneous utterances. Both candidates had rehearsed 'zingers', or soundbites, before the debates. Clinton managed to use the carefully crafted phrase 'drive-by deliveries', aimed at the women's vote, twice. And Dole himself helped expose the ludicrous nature of focus-group politics and marketing speech when he uttered the code-words 'soccer moms' during the last debate. Nor did the press provide commentary independent of the persuasive techniques and advertising ethos that dominated the campaign.

For days leading up to the first TV debate we were bombarded with seemingly endless replays of video clips of the most dramatic one-liners from past televised debates. Good-natured Ronald Reagan saying, 'There you go again.' Vice-presidential candidate Lloyd Bensen telling Dan Quayle, 'Senator, you're no Jack Kennedy.' Bernie Shaw asking Michael Dukakis what he would do if his wife were raped and murdered. In fact, it started to become clear that these singular soundbite moments were the sum total of the media's history of presidential TV debates.

These frozen moments were the subject of so much talk that the different types of one-liner and gaffe were meticulously defined and categorized. There were policy gaffes that took time to be realized, like Gerald Ford insisting that Poland was not under the domination of the Soviet Union. Then there were non-verbal gaffes that were immediately judgeable, Richard Nixon sweating off his layers of 'lazy shave' make-up, and President Bush looking at his watch.

Into this 'historical' perspective came countless predictions of gaffes which might occur on Sunday night. If Bob Dole appeared mean, or if Clinton appeared unpresidential, they would both falter. What would Clinton do if Dole called him a liberal?

According to Jack Kemp, what Bob Dole had to do was look directly at the cameras, and convince the American people he was going to give them a tax cut. What Clinton had to do was remain presidential. But Dole's positive message would not be enough. He would also have to cast doubts on Clinton's character. He must put him on the spot about the possible presidential pardon of people involved in the Whitewater scandal.

But as important as being able to deliver a punchy rhetorical line, like 'Are you better off now than you were four years ago?' just at the right moment, was the ability to respond well under attack. The worst thing about 'Senator, you're no Jack Kennedy' was that Quayle had no good comeback.

These TV commentaries were giving viewers a framework for judging the outcome of the debate. And all criteria were theatrical. All the preparatory TV talk revolved around the candidates' performance as entertainers. They were telling us what to look for and creating a sense of anticipation. How would the candidates conduct themselves? Could they pull it off? Would they look nervous? How would they appear and be perceived? What rhetorical devices would they use? We were to look for calmness, reserve, warmth, and sincerity, against a background of drama and anticipation. We would all be sitting expectantly waiting for the dramatic surprise announcement, or the gaffe that would become the future video clip.

While we were all becoming sophisticated theatre and media critics, almost no one was talking about the issues that might be debated. No context was offered within which to evaluate the content of what the candidates said. Would campaign finance reform be brought up? If not, why? What questions would Jim Lehrer ask on PBS's *The Newshour*? How were the questions and rules for debate being determined? Could Bob Dole reconcile his history of fiscal conservatism with his newfound embrace of supply-side growth? Would questions about the American economy be formulated so that Clinton's rehearsed Morning in America II campaign would stand out as political packaging? Most in the media asserted that TV debates were not true debates. CBS anchor Dan Rather insisted on calling them joint appearances, and on ABC Sam Donaldson's term was 'parallel press conferences'.

Surveys showed that the public wanted to see interaction between the candidates. They wanted point and counterpoint. They wanted genuine dialogue in which each candidate must respond directly to the other, defending their respective positions. They wanted authenticity. But rules were established that did not allow the candidates to address each other directly. And Lehrer was not allowed to ask follow-up questions. Everything the candidates were going to say had been carefully moulded and shaped, checked and double-checked for thematic content anyway. All controversy had been avoided wherever possible. Any unavoidable negatives were carefully predicted and given predetermined responses. As CBS's Rita Braver joked about the president, 'White House aides tell us he's been hard at work preparing those clever one-liners. You know, the ones that are supposed to sound like ad-libs.'

But even as the media admitted the inauthentic nature of the event, all were hoping that something unrehearsed might actually occur. That could happen only if one of them were to make a performance error. The content was so carefully controlled that the only thing left to evaluate was the acting. But this process was legitimized. As Phil Jones said on CBS, 'The bottom line in this debate is not about substance. It's about performance. And Bob Dole needs the best performance of his political life.'

After watching we had our answers. New York's Channel 4 had a focus group on hand. One young woman said that over the course of the debate she had begun to focus on the issue of education. And so when, in closing, Bob Dole addressed his remarks to the young, she thought he might speak to her about education. Instead, she said incredulously, he told me, 'Just don't do it.' She would now be voting for Clinton. The example illustrates the nature of the borrowed advertising phrase. It provides the appearance of addressing the issue while actually doing very little. It is insulting to the intelligence of the American voter, as was the entire campaign.

Conclusion

Commentators, researchers, and the public considered the campaign dull, boring, and even sad. This was because both campaigns were driven by focus groups, advertising slogans, tales of human interest, and all the other commercialized marketing practices that trivialize media discourse and obfuscate political issues.

The 1996 election campaign was the most media-driven election in history, costing upwards of $1 trillion. So-called 'soft money' from political party fundraisers paid for a staggering number of advertisements for both candidates. Reporting on questionable fundraising consumed much of the post-election discourse. These campaign contributions funded an advertising and marketing structure that served to mould campaign discourse in a broad sense, by establishing themes and slogans that influenced 'free media' coverage as well. There is a connection between the huge price tag in the 1996 election and the lack of substance. Legal and illegal fundraising is used to finance the rising costs of media-driven elections. Advertising strategies helped the candidates and their handlers control the public dialogue, avoiding pressing issues and sidetracking insightful journalistic commentary.

The merger between media culture and politics, which began in earnest with the birth of TV, is now nearly complete. Political strategists learned from advertising experts how to market a product on television. The results are the infomercials disguised as political conventions, and the commercial tag lines the candidates use to define themselves, like 'Just don't do it', or 'Building a bridge to the twenty-first century'. The political campaign, like the advertising campaign, is now a scientific process based on polling and focus groups. In addition, campaign managers fashioned their candidates so that they would resonate with existing commercial media formats, the themes and attitudes from films, advertising, and TV shows.

In September 1996, during the presidential race, the Media Studies Center together with the Roper Center conducted a survey of 1,000 registered voters. Voters rated live debates, with little interference from journalists, their best source of information. The Media Studies Center's executive director, Nancy Woodhull, concluded from these findings that 'voters are looking to see the candidates through the candidates' eyes' (Media Studies Center 1996: 1) Given the larger media context, encompassing advertising strategies, marketing practices and 'intertextual resonance', we must ask if it is possible for candidates to 'speak in their own voices'.

The Dole campaign demonstrated that selling candidates like products has its limits. Practices of persuasion, as they become more extreme, sometimes also become more transparent. But that is certainly not to say that the candidate who won was any more authentic, only that his marketing was more sophisticated. Finding a pathway to a different political discourse for the future must include campaign finance reform. The enormous amounts of money injected into the American electoral process subvert democracy as they help degrade political discourse. Political advertising and the marketing practices that propel elections are expensive. Placing limits on spending would do much to lessen their influence in shaping the candidates and the subjects they address. Free airtime for candidates is also essential. At present, only those politicians with enough campaign funding can enter the political arena. These reforms would begin to reinject citizens back into the electoral process.

References

Andersen, R. (1995). *Consumer Culture and TV Programming*. Boulder, CO: Westview Press.

Bart, P. (1999). *The Gross: The Hits, the Flops—The Summer that Ate Hollywood*. New York: St Martin's Press.

Bennett, J. (1996). 'Using Televised Ads as Rifles, Campaigns Aim at the Elderly'. *New York Times*, 9 October: A19.

Brouwer, S, (1997). *Sharing the Pie*. New York: Metropolitan Books.

Dowd, M. (1996). 'The Man in the Mirror'. *New York Times*, 12 September: A23.

Goodman, W. (1996*a*). 'For the Networks, This was the Week that was Mostly Forgettable'. *New York Times*, 17 August: A8.

—— (1996*b*). 'Blending Disability with Celebrity to Lure Viewers'. *New York Times*, 28 August: A13.

Greenberg, S. (1996). 'Private Heroism and Public Purpose'. *The American Prospect*, September–October 34–40.

'Just Don't Say It' (1996), *New York Times*, 20 September: 40.

Media Studies Center (1996). 'Voters to Media: Let the Candidates Talk'. *Communique*, fall: 1.

Menand, L. (1996) *New York Review of Books*, 19 September: 4, 6.

Reich, R. (1999) *Marketplace*, National Public Radio, 15 March.

Rollins, E. (1996). National Press Club luncheon remarks. New York, 2 October.

Weisberg, D. (1996). 'Dole's Commercial Campaign'. Unpublished manuscript, Fordham University, Department of Communication and Media Studies, New York.

Chapter 18

Commercial Media and Corporate Presence in the K-12 Classroom

Margaret Cassidy

A WALK round a typical American elementary or secondary school reveals a wide array of commercial materials in use or on display. Perhaps a nutrition poster, provided free by a cereal company, hangs in the hall. A walk past a classroom may provide a view of children watching a commercial cable TV programme, or a pair of students navigating their way past advertisements on a web site. This is a time when commercially sponsored educational media are proliferating; there is an endless array of sponsored media and materials, provided free or at low cost to schools, intended to establish brand loyalties or to promote goodwill towards organizations of sometimes questionable reputation. For the most part, these materials are accepted by educators whose schools cannot afford other materials, or who accept commercial media as a given in American society.

Commercial media institutions, and corporate interests more generally, tried to find their way into schools for most of the twentieth century. Their attempts to bring their messages to school children have varied somewhat over time, as has the attitude of the American public to those attempts. Although there always have been—and continue to be—critics of commercialism in schools, the general climate in the United States has moved away from one that encourages or accepts such criticism.

In order to understand the current climate better, it can be helpful to step outside it by looking at an earlier time and examining its events and characteristics. In this case, a look at commercial involvement in educational radio in the 1920s and 1930s offers an interesting comparison to the 1990s. Some of the struggles of those educators may sound familiar, at the same time as their belief that they could take on commercial media institutions may seem woefully naive to a contemporary reader.

Educational radio and commercial broadcasters

1920—the year that radio broadcasting fever spread across the United States. RCA was only a year old, and acronyms like NBC, CBS, and FCC were yet to be imagined. Radio was in its infancy, and, while it was not at all clear what it might become, there were strong feelings that this was a powerful new medium destined to enlighten all Americans and to promote democracy and citizenship.

It was in 1920 that two stations, one in Pittsburgh and one in Detroit, first broadcast educational programmes. By 1921, the Radio Counsel of the Payne Fund had met with the US Bureau of Education to propose national radio programmes for broadcast in public-sector schools. By 1922, sixty educational institutions were broadcasting educational programmes. Many universities were giving extension courses via radio, and some universities were planning to install loudspeakers in classrooms so lectures could be conducted by one professor for many audiences.

Some educational broadcasting ventures involved collaboration between educators and commercial broadcasters, the latter claiming to be sincerely interested in donating free airtime to educators. When NBC first went on the air in 1926, the general belief was still that profits were to be made in selling radio sets, not in selling airtime, and the Radio Act of 1927 emphasized the obligation of broadcasters to the public they served. So while it may sound idealistic today to think that commercial broadcasters would willingly give anything away to educators, keep in mind that they probably did not yet realize the value of their donations; moreover, they may genuinely have felt some degree of obligation to the public they served—at least for a little while.

In the late 1920s, the Payne Fund approached NBC, CBS, and the Crosley stations. All indicated that they would donate their services and their airtime, free of charge, to educational broadcasting (Perry 1929: 7). Given that the profit to be made by selling that time to advertisers was already substantial, some people questioned how willing broadcasters really would be to make such a donation. But 'each of these three great broadcasting companies assured representatives of The Payne Fund that money making was not the primary object of its activities. The officials are interested in the cause of public education' (Perry 1929: 21). When an NBC representative was asked what would happen if an advertiser wanted a slot allocated for educational broadcasting badly enough to make a tempting offer, 'the reply was that the Company would not sell the free time assigned to an educational program at any price, and that it would not even shift a program from one hour to another in order to make room for a commercial program' (Perry 1929: 21).

And yet, as early as 1929, educators were noticing that advertisers were encroaching on time slots previously promised to educators:

While educators are making progress in the use of radio, and in some cases rapid progress, business concerns are moving still more swiftly. Daylight hours, once so little sought by advertisers that it seemed as though they might always be available for school programs, are now being filled rapidly with programs advertising department stores and other business concerns. In some cases educational programs that were well established after years of effort have been crowded out by advertising programs [Perry 1929: 75]

Commercial broadcasters moved educational broadcasts out of profitable slots, or shortened the length of programmes, or tried to exert greater influence on the content of the programmes, convinced that only highly entertaining programming would attract big audiences. Directors of educational programming for major networks had once occupied positions equal in importance to executives for commercial programming, but their departments were scaled back and their positions diminished in authority and influence. Columbia University began an experiment with NBC in 1927 on a series of Home Study courses, but abandoned the project because they felt that NBC and the Federal Radio Commission were putting commercial interests ahead of educational ones (Davis 1934: 4).

Meanwhile, there were educators who believed deeply in the potential of radio, and who wanted to use it both for adult education at home, and for instructing children in the classroom. Some educators believed that the only way to proceed was to do it themselves, that commercial broadcasters would always put their own interests first, and that this made it impossible to engage in any meaningful collaboration. Others, however, argued that the partnership could be successful, and that, in any event, it was necessary. The commercial broadcasters had the powerful stations, the good frequencies, the studios, the writers, the talent. Educational broadcasts by educators had an amateurish quality that lessened their effectiveness and displeased their audiences.

The lack of consensus among educators on the question of whether commercial broadcasters could be trusted in schools led educational-radio advocates to split into two organizations with incompatible goals. The National Advisory Council on Radio in Education, an organization consisting of educators and commercial broadcasters, took the position that the only way for educational radio to survive was to work with commercial broadcasters. On the other hand, the National Committee on Education by Radio, consisting only of educators, pushed for educational radio to be entirely separate from commercial radio. They believed that the National Advisory Council, formed at the behest of the chairman of the board of RCA, was being used by powerful commercial interests to promote their own ends.

The National Committee on Education by Radio also believed that allowing commerical broadcasters into education would promote a damaging trend in American cultural life and in the growth of American media institutions. They were critical of what they saw as a growing equation of the American idea of progress with material progress, and with 'the complete surrender of the public interest in radio to private ownership' (Benner 1934: 14). Instead, they believed that 'education by radio should be the objective of national planning, not the incidental by-product of private enterprise' (Moyer 1934: 16). They pushed for the reservation of 15 per cent of the broadcast spectrum for educational use, arguing that the Federal Radio Commission was not doing enough to further the cause of educational broadcasting. Although they were unsuccessful in that venture, they did succeed in protecting some educational stations that were put in jeopardy by the actions of the FRC and/ or commercial stations (Hill 1942).

So there grew some serious animosity by the early 1930s—some teachers thought they'd be selling out if they allowed children to be exposed to commercial programmes in the classroom, which sometimes included advertising for the sponsors of the programmes. On the other hand, some teachers thought it excessive to object to a little commercial sponsorship, arguing that children live in a commercial world anyway, that it doesn't really affect them, and that this was the only way for educational radio to survive. And then there were the broadcasters, who had come to feel that sceptical teachers were just jealous of commercial radio programming because they wished they could get the kind of attention from kids that radio could.

There *were* some commercial radio ventures that were well received by teachers. The most influential was *The NBC Music Appreciation Hour*, hosted by Dr Walter Damrosch, conductor of the New York Symphony Orchesra. It went on the air on NBC's Blue Network in 1928, and became simply the *Music Appreciation Hour* when NBC sold the Blue Network in 1942 (Atkinson 1942: 22). It is estimated that some six million children listened to these broadcasts in school at the height of the programme's popularity.

CBS attempted an even more ambitious venture in 1930 with its School of the Air, later the School of the Air of the Americas when it expanded its reach into Latin America. They offered weekly series in news, civics, literature, music appreciation, history, geography, drama, and other subjects. By 1942, twelve state education departments had officially adopted the School of the Air of the Americas for use in their schools, and it had the endorsement of the National Catholic Education Association (Atkinson 1942: 96).

These efforts of NBC and CBS were openly commercial programmes with an eye to profits—the *Music Appreciation Hour* was created to boost sales of RCA radios, and the CBS School of the Air was meant to be a sales incentive for Majestic radios. But the programmes themselves were highly regarded by many teachers, and few people objected to their use in schools. As long as the *content* of the programming was commercial-free, educators tended not to perceive a conflict between the purposes of broadcasters and the purposes of teachers.

And then there were Schools of the Air founded by universities, the most notable being the Ohio School of the Air. It began broadcasting on 7 January 1929; by April that year, it had an audience of more than 100,000 students in twenty-two states. It broadcast lessons from Monday to Thursday, taking Fridays off 'in deference to [the] splendid R.C.A. Educational Hour conducted by Walter Damrosch each Friday at 11 A.M.' (Perry 1929: 18). However, despite its warm welcome into many classrooms, the Ohio School of the Air was off the air by the late 1930s, primarily due to its inability to keep the programming funded.

Generally, educational radio—at least for classroom use—was over by the 1940s, mainly because of funding problems. It was not profitable enough for commercial broadcasters, at least not in the way educators wanted it done. In most cases, there were too many conflicts of interest to make for an easy relationship between teachers and broadcasters. However, educational institutions did not have the financial resources or the talent to operate apart from the commercial broadcasters.

Advocates of non-commercial educational radio came to realize that the broadcasting industry was headed in a direction that would not include them. As one such advocate wrote of the early efforts to reserve frequencies for education, 'Whatever may now be thought of the wisdom of that proposal, it did not seem so drastic in 1931 as it would seem to most Americans today. Broadcasting was then about ten years old. The system of supporting it by advertising was not so old' (Hill 1942: 53). By the early 1940s, the American public had already come to take for granted the commercial sponsorship of media. Now, several generations later, the acceptance of commercial media—and of their presence in schools—seems to be even less subject to questioning or criticism by most Americans.

Contemporary commercialism in American schools

Before coming back to an examination of the situation today, consider the follow-ing scenario, imagined by Arthur E. Morgan (1934: 81–2).

Suppose our public schools had been established on a purely commerical basis. . . . the teaching staff might be supplied by the toothpaste manufacturers or patent medicine manu-facturers . . . and they would have textbooks describing the values of toothpaste or patent medicine. . . . The schools would be furnishing what the public wanted, and the one that furnished the most habit-forming drink would be in greatest demand, and the one that had the most salacious movies would have the patronage.

   If the public schools for a century or for a generation had happened to grow up in that way they would represent vested interests, and any effort to change them to another basis would be looked upon as an interference of the government in business. It would be looked upon as improper. Fortunately, our public schools have been saved from that fate . . .

Would that he were alive today—there are certainly people who would want to take him up on his plan! He might also be dismayed to find that he so accurately prophesied the current frame of mind that *does* tend to see the criticism of com-mercialized education as unAmerican, or at least as unrealistic.

   One of my clear (and fond) memories from my elementary-school days is of a particular day in each school year when our school nurse would come to class with a canister of free gifts for each of us. As I recall, the canister contained a toothbrush, a sample of Colgate toothpaste, a pamphlet on dental hygiene, a coupon for Col-gate, and—the big crowd-pleaser—a couple of red tablets which, when chewed, stained any part of your teeth that you weren't brushing properly.

   At the time, it did not occur to me to wonder why Colgate should be so generous. I cannot remember the nurse or any teacher making any point of talking about the source of these gifts. Nor did anyone ever engage us in a discussion of who pro-duced the pamphlets on nuclear energy, the filmstrips on food-processing, or the ever-popular 'mother–daughter film' that revealed to us the workings of the pubes-cent female body. I cannot say for sure whether those materials swayed my opinions or fostered brand loyalties in me or my classmates. But I am inclined to believe that they did have some effect on us—not uniformly, and not absolutely, but enough to keep businesses interested in getting their messages into the classroom.

   Commercial presence in American schools takes a greater variety of forms these days than it did in the 1920s and 1930s. Today, sponsored materials available to schools range from television broadcasts to computer software to pamphlets to posters to free product samples, produced by a company or an organization seeking to advertise or publicize itself in schools. On the surface, some of these materials seem like generous gifts. However, they—along with the climate that makes them possible and acceptable—warrant closer investigation.

Channel One television

One of the most unabashed recent examples of commercialism in schools is Channel One Television, the idea of entrepreneur Chris Whittle. Before Channel One, Whittle was best known for his ability to create not advertising itself but vehicles for advertising, such as posters for school use that had something educational on them, along with ads for the sponsors of the poster. For example, one of his posters, called 'The Beat of Life', showed how the heart works, and had ads for junk food across the bottom of it. Whittle did so well with these ventures that in 1989 he tried something bigger. He introduced a deal whereby he would provide a school with a satellite dish, VCRs, monitors, and some other related equipment at no charge to the school, provided that 90 per cent of the children in the school watched a twelve-minute, Whittle-produced news programme every day. The funding for all this came from advertisers, whose commercials would be shown during that news programme. Teachers were not permitted to edit out the commercials, or to interfere in any way with children's viewing of them.

Channel One was met with outrage by many organizations, including the American Federation of Teachers, the National Education Association, the National PTA, the National Associations of Elementary and Secondary School Principals, and the National Association of State Boards of Education. Some states, notably New York and California, banned Channel One outright. Many people were infuriated by the prospect of making children a captive audience, sold to advertisers in what they believed should be a protective environment. They urged schools to adopt instead a service like Cable in the Classroom, in which major cable networks like C-Span, Bravo, Nickelodeon, and the Weather Channel provide commercial-free programming for school use.

Whittle responded by claiming that the effect of the advertising on children was only 'incidental'. But when pitching Channel One to advertisers, he described it as a 'direct pipeline' to the teenage market, a perfect opportunity to 'establish brand loyalties and perceptions that will last a lifetime' (Molnar 1996: 66). The fact that advertisers were willing to pay $200,000 for a thirty-second spot suggests that the ads' effects were probably more than merely incidental. Studies of children in Channel One schools found that they often believed the advertised products were good for them because the ads were shown in school (some Channel One advertisers: Burger King, Frito-Lay, M&M/Mars, Taco Bell). Studies have also shown that students were rarely able to do more than simply name the stories in the news broadcasts, not discuss details of the stories (Knupfer and Hayes 1994), so this was purely a case of creating a vehicle—the news programme—for the important part—the advertising.

Many educators claimed that they agreed to Channel One contracts in order to have audiovisual equipment that their schools could not otherwise afford. However, they had been somewhat misled. First of all, schools were only given the wiring; all other equipment had to be returned when the Channel One contract was terminated. Additionally, the borrowed equipment had fairly limited uses. The satellite dish was fixed to the Channel One station and could not be used to receive other programmes; classrooms had monitors, not independent television sets; and only one VCR was provided per school, to be used to tape the Channel One broadcast (Barry 1994: 110). Teachers often found that the uses to which they wanted to put the equipment would require the purchase of additional equipment, such as editing-bays. In other words, the argument that the commercial broadcast was but one small part of a wide array of experiences a student might have in a Channel One school was seriously flawed. The primary purpose around Channel One, the one around which all other aspects of the deal were organized, was to deliver a carefully targeted teenage audience to advertisers.

McCurriculum

The purpose behind a television broadcast with recognizable commercials is obvious enough. On the other hand, there are many curricular materials, activity kits, and teaching aids that are not as obviously commercial in nature, but that primarily serve the purpose of advertising a product or building a positive image for an organization. The examples from my own childhood were not unique to that era; if anything, there are more of these materials available now than ever before. Lest my nostalgic examples seem dated, here are a few current ones.

General Foods produces a 'Gushers Wonders of the World' package for science teachers. The letter to teachers reads:

They are the Earth's great geothermic 'gushers': volcanoes, geysers and hot springs. For centuries, humans have been fascinated by these 'wonders of the world.' Now, your students can share in this fascination. Lifetime Learning Systems, in cooperation with General Mills, Inc., maker of GUSHERS fruit snacks, is pleased to present you with this free educational program, GUSHERS WONDERS OF THE WORLD, along with free samples of GUSHERS for your students to enjoy [Molnar 1996: 33]

Teachers are encouraged to have their students bite into the candy and compare the sensation to a geothermic eruption.

Pizza Hut has sponsored the BOOK IT! National Reading Incentive Program for ten years, with 22 million children enrolled annually. Children are rewarded with Pizza Hut 'personal pan' pizzas when they reach monthly reading goals (DeVaney 1994: 115). If a whole class meets certain goals, they get a pizza party. In other words, children are taught that the greatest reward for reading is pizza. Rush Limbaugh, an American radio host and author famous for his right-of-conservative views, called the programme 'bribes for books'—that is, until he realized it was a Pizza Hut project, and, having done Pizza Hut ads himself, decided to endorse it (Molnar 1996: 45).

Philip Morris Companies, Inc. released a package in 1991 called 'The Bill of Rights: Protecting Our Liberty'. It contained no cigarette ads, and had no overt messages about smoking, but used a variety of techniques to suggest 'an implicit link between First Amendment freedoms and the freedom to smoke' (DeVaney 1994: 115–16).

The situation is made even more complicated today by complex webs and pyramids of media ownership, which make it difficult to know who, exactly, is sponsoring a particular message and how that message may, therefore, be distorted. A good example of how media ownership tends to affect media content is a shift that occurred in *Weekly Reader*, a weekly newsletter provided free to schools. After being purchased by K-III Communications, which, in turn, is a major shareholder in RJR Nabisco (a major cigarette manufacturer), the tobacco-related *Weekly Reader* articles changed dramatically in tone. The number of articles containing an anti-smoking message dropped from 65 per cent to 24 per cent. It was easy enough to see what Joe Camel was about; it's not as obvious when you don't know exactly who the source of the message is, or what their agenda might be. Incidentally, K-III Communications also owns Channel One Television; Whittle sold Channel One to K-III in 1994.

New media, new commercial opportunities

Commercialism in schools is not limited to print and broadcast media. The growing interest in the educational uses of digital media is producing its own particular brand of publicity stunts. Apples for the Students is a programme in which a school collects receipts from sponsor stores and trades them in for Apple computers; $500,000 in receipts gets you only about $3,000 worth of computers. Better yet is a programme created by a company called Computers for Education. They claim that this programme not only gets computers into classrooms, but also teaches children important writing skills. Children are asked to write six letters to relatives asking them to subscribe to magazines. The suggested letter is provided to them, and it goes like this (Molnar 1996: 23)

Dear Grandma,
My school needs more computers for our classrooms. You can help us by ordering some new magazines or extending your current subscriptions at this time.
    You'll save money with the school prices and your magazine orders provide more 'hands on' computer training for me. Order by the prize deadline and I can earn a school crew shirt.
    Please help me if you can.
        From: Amy
        P.S. I love you.

Most recently, ads for a programme called ZapMe! have been appearing in ed-tech publications. The ad reads: 'We'll give you a free lab of computers for your school. Here's the catch: You have to let your students use them.' It goes on: 'The ZapMe! Knowledge Network, a private enterprise coalition of leading technology companies and education professionals, will begin its national launch of FREE computer labs and its private, high-speed (2Mbps), Internet-based educational network this fall.' What the ad does not explain is that the company selects and reviews all content supplied to the schools through this network, and it requires that 'some pages on the network must carry corporate information' ('ZapMe!' 1998: 10).

Schools also have to enter into a contractual agreement to use the network at least four hours a day. ZapMe! is funded by corporate sponsors who pay for the right to deliver their brand image and educational content over the network to schools. Although its developers claim that the programme is not primarily about advertising, many educational organizations (many of the same ones that condemned Channel One Television) have opposed this programme, arguing that children should not have to be delivered to advertisers in order to have the instructional media or materials that they deserve.

There *are* strong arguments in favour of using computers for various purposes in schools, and the reality is that computers are expensive, and that most schools are having a hard time funding new technology initiatives. So it might seem that the only way to move ahead is to seek the help of corporations willing to supply materials and services at little or no monetary cost. At the same time, it seems that a great deal of the current hysteria about getting computers into every classroom, in getting schools wired to the Internet, and in teaching whatever is meant by 'computer literacy' is more about business than it is about the education of children. First, schools are a huge market that a lot of people want to tap into, regardless of the educational value of the technology they are selling. And, second, businesses that require their employees to have computer skills want schools to provide that training so that employers don't have to do it. This is a climate of aggressive implementation of new technology, not implementation that permits school districts to make careful plans about integrating new technology into their curriculum, staff development, and assessment measures. As such, it needs to be watched very carefully. Unfortunately, this does not appear to be a time when most people see the corporatization of the classroom as an unwelcome change; although there are some professional organizations whose members openly criticize or condemn these developments, they are not representative of the overall climate in the US today.

The underlying climate

In 1983, the publication of a National Commission on Excellence in Education report called *A Nation at Risk* prompted the business community to begin to exert greater influence on education. Nowhere in the report was there any explicit argument that business should exert a stronger influence in schools. What the report did express was the sentiment that schools aren't tough enough, that standards aren't high enough, and that graduates of American public schools aren't up to par. It named learning as 'the indispensable investment required for success in the "information age" we are entering' (National Commission on Excellence in Education 1984: 7), and expressed alarm that the deficiencies in American schools 'come at a time when the demand for highly skilled workers in new fields is accelerating rapidly' (p. 10).

This report contributed to a conservative turn in conceptions of American education, whereby business and industry began to exert their control over schools. In the process, a new way of thinking about schools emerged: 'the value of education is reduced to economic utility . . . Other goals—such as critical understanding, political literacy, personal development . . . self-esteem, and shared respect—are seen as beside the point or "too expensive"' (Apple 1994: 175).

We have reached a point where it is largely taken for granted by many people that schools are more accountable to business than they are to children. Of course schools have to be concerned about the employability of their graduates, but that is different from making job readiness a central purpose of education. Consider the following excerpt from a report called *Ten Years After 'A Nation at Risk'*, prepared by the Conference Board, an organization interested in fostering connections between school and business: 'Business needs to remember its role as a consumer of the "goods" of the education system and hold school systems, as "vendors," accountable. . . . Over the past decade, business has become much more effective in its rightful role as the customer of the education system. The role of any customer is to define the needs and then work in partnership with the organization to determine ways those needs can be met' (Lund and Wild 1993: 25). Keep in mind that the 'goods' which schools deliver to their business 'customers' are children—human lives which (some would still argue) deserve to be treated as something more than a product to be manufactured and handed over by school-'vendors' to business-'clients'.

In a climate that is capable of producing ideas like the one I just quoted, I think it is crucial that we try to be more thoughtful about the proper place of all commercial interests in schools. As early as the 1920s, people involved in educational radio and film were calling for school districts and professional organizations to develop guidelines that would regulate the interaction of business and schools, and that would establish policies for the use of sponsored media in schools. But as far as I have been able to determine, it is still highly unusual for a district to have any such policy.

In 1929, the Committee on Propaganda in the Schools presented its report at the annual meeting of the National Education Association. They had surveyed schools to determine the extent of the presence of sponsored materials in classrooms. One New England school identified eighty-two items in just one classroom, from insurance to cereal companies (Harty 1979: 99). The committee recommended that state departments of education set up guidelines to evaluate sponsored materials, and for teacher education to address this issue more. They called for careful selection, not exclusion, of sponsored materials, recognizing that the only way to eliminate them would be to fund schools adequately, an unlikely alternative.

Since then, there have been some efforts to establish policies to guide the selection and use of commercial media and sponsored materials in schools. For example, the Association for Curriculum and Supervision Development published *Using Free Materials in the Classroom* in 1953, and the American Association of School Administrators published *Choosing Free Materials for Use in the Schools* in 1955. More recently, media literacy organizations have offered guidelines on using sponsored media. However, I do not get the impression that this issue is a priority for most teachers, or that their own education raises the issue very much at all. It is ironic that in one study of teacher, parent, and student reactions to Channel One, it was *teachers* who had the fewest concerns about the broadcasts as a whole, and about the advertising in particular (Knupfer 1994). This is not to argue that teachers should be blamed for the absence of criticism of commercialism in schools; until American teacher education incorporates these ideas into the preparation of elementary and secondary teachers, teachers cannot be expected to be much aware of the issues in question. Young teachers today are generations removed from a time when commercialism was more openly questioned, so it is not surprising if they do not give the issue much attention.

Conclusion

When the new medium was radio, commercial messages in schools were called 'propaganda'. Over the decades, the terminology has changed, and now they're called 'free and inexpensive educational materials'. We have clearly lost the opportunity to keep private industry and schools separate; for that matter, it is possible that the opportunity never really existed. Such a separation is hardly a popular idea right now, and the chances are that pushing for it would be unsuccessful. At the same time, it is important to keep working at countering the ever-increasing commercial presence in schools, so that commercial entities are forced to take the interests of educators seriously, and so that educators remain vigilant about holding such entities accountable for any promotions that are launched in schools.

References

Advisory Committee on Education by Radio. (1930). *Report of the Advisory Committee on Education by Radio.* Columbus, OH: F. J. Heer Printing Co.

Apple, M. W. (1994). 'Whittling away at Democracy: The Social Context of Channel One', in A. DeVaney (ed.), *Watching Channel One: The Convergence of Students, Technology, and Private Business.* Albany, NY: State University of New York Press, 167–88.

Atkinson, C. (1942). *Radio Network Contributions to Education.* Boston, MA: Meador Publishing Company.

Barry, A. (1994). 'Advertising and Channel One: Controversial Partnership of Business and Education', in A. DeVaney (ed.), *Watching Channel One: The Convergence of Students, Technology, and Private Business* (pp. 102–36). Albany, NY: State University of New York Press.

Benner, T. E. (1934). 'Radio and the Cultural Depression', in T. Tyler (ed.), *Radio as a Cultural Agency: Proceedings of a National Conference on the Use of Radio as a Cultural Agency in a Democracy.* Washington, DC: National Committee on Education by Radio, 10–14.

Davis, J. (1934). 'The Radio, a Commercial or an Educational Agency?', in T. Tyler (ed.), *Radio as a Cultural Agency: Proceedings of a National Conference on the Use of Radio as a Cultural Agency in a Democracy.* Washington, DC: National Committee on Education by Radio, 3–10.

DeVaney, A. (1994). Introduction, in A. DeVaney (ed.), *Watching Channel One: The Convergence of Students, Technology, and Private Business*. Albany, NY: State University of New York Press, 1–19.

Harty, S. (1979). *Hucksters in the Classroom: A Review of Industry Propaganda in Schools*. Washington, DC: Center for Study of Responsive Law.

Hill, F. E. (1942). *Tune in for Education: Eleven Years of Education by Radio*. New York: National Committee on Education by Radio.

Knupfer, N. Nelson (1994). 'Channel One: Reactions of Students, Teachers, and Parents', in A. DeVaney (ed.), *Watching Channel One: The Convergence of Students, Technology, and Private Business*. Albany, NY: State University of New York Press, 61–86.

Knupfer, N. Nelson, and Hayes, P. (1994). 'The Effects of the Channel One Broadcast on Students' Knowledge of Current Events', in A. DeVaney (ed.), *Watching Channel One: The Convergence of Students, Technology, and Private Business*. Albany, NY: State University of New York Press, 42–60.

Lund, L., and Wild, C. (1993). *Ten Years after A Nation at Risk*. New York: The Conference Board.

McCarty, H. B. (1934). 'The Wisconsin Radio Plan in Practise', in T. Tyler (ed.), *Radio as a Cultural Agency: Proceedings of a National Conference on the Use of Radio as a Cultural Agency in a Democracy*. Washington, DC: National Committee on Education by Radio, 18–23.

Molnar, A. (1996). *Giving Kids the Business: The Commercialization of America's Schools*. Boulder, CO: Westview Press.

Morgan, J. E. (1934). 'A National Culture: By-product or Objective of National Planning?', in T. Tyler (ed.), *Radio as a Cultural Agency: Proceedings of a National Conference on the Use of Radio as a Cultural Agency in a Democracy*. Washington, DC: National Committee on Education by Radio, 23–32.

Moyer, J. A. (1934). 'Adult Education by Radio', in T. Tyler (ed.), *Radio as a Cultural Agency: Proceedings of a National Conference on the Use of Radio as a Cultural Agency in a Democracy*. Washington, DC: National Committee on Education by Radio, 14–18.

National Commission on Excellence in Education (1983). *A Nation at Risk: The Imperative for Educational Reform*. Washington, DC: US Government Printing Office.

Perry, A. (1929). *Radio in Education: The Ohio School of the Air and Other Experiments*. New York: The Payne Fund.

'ZapMe! Offers Free Intranet Computers in Exchange for Ads Aimed at Kids.' (1998) *eSchool News*, 1/5: 10.

Chapter 19

Commodity Fetishism: Symbolic Form, Social Class, and the Division of Knowledge in Society

Paul Lippert

Today's postmodern mentality is most confusing—or, to some, most confused—in the attitude it takes toward the relation between the world of symbolic social constructions and the world of material reality. Ever on the offensive against vulgar materialistic opponents, real or imagined, 'critical' thought has drifted drastically toward an idealist extreme. An unfortunate consequence of this has been the reduction of epistemological arguments to a remarkably simple-minded either/or form: either symbols reflect reality, or they do not. That the relation between words and things is complex and intellectually difficult to formulate is a point that emerges quite prominently out of the two-millenium-old tradition of Western philosophy and especially out of the modern philosophical tradition of scepticism (see Scruton 1995; Russell 1945). Key insights into that relation are provided by an intellectual tendency to see technology in general and the means of economic production in particular as the primary determinants of social relations and ideology, as in the works of Karl Marx (for example, 1976) and even, one could argue, in those of media theorists such as Harold Innis (1950, 1964) and Marshall McLuhan (1962). In this scheme, the analysis of industrial commodity production is essential to an understanding of how consciousness emerges out of the material conditions of contemporary society.

While deconstructionists and others base cultural analyses on studies of language and other symbolic activity, this symbolic base, which is itself a cultural product, is left to float ethereally, groundless, at the whim of the political preference of the pundit. This tendency is the target of Marx's critique of Hegel as well as that of idealism generally. On the other hand, scholarship in a more modernist vein, such as James Beniger's (1986) recent study of the 'control revolution', looks to the material needs arising out of the conditions of industrial production in accounting for the emergence of new forms and patterns of communication. Beniger draws on the work of Max Weber (1930) and Emile Durkheim (1947) in order to describe Weber's concept of rationalization and Durkheim's concept of anomie as semantic phenomena which respond to a societal loss of control caused by rapidly expanding networks of industrial production and distribution. As workers' lives are rationalized, or adapted to fit the logic and procedures of an impersonal, technical industrial system, they experience anomie, which involves a loss of meaning and social identity. Both these concepts refer specifically to the type of refiguration of knowledge which is attendant upon what Saint-Simon saw as a move 'from the government of men to the administration of things' (cited in Beniger 1986: 15). In other words, material production processes determine a social division of labour which determines forms of knowledge and thus states of mind.

In addition to its value as an example of scholarship which grounds developments in knowledge and communication in concrete historical contexts, Beniger's work is significant because it describes a process whereby workers are systematically alienated from the material contexts of their life situations. In both these aspects, it is conspicuous for its rarity these days. How can this be? How can social theory have drifted so far from the material world both in its own frame of analysis and in its image of its subjects' lives? And, given this situation along with the general state of contemporary capitalism, what hope is there for these subjects?

At this point it might seem odd for me to point to a Jesuit scholar whose major works emanate from the study of post-medieval logic as the person to clarify the problem and set Hegel back on his head where he belongs. But in many ways, I believe that Walter Ong's work, in particular his study of the social and historical functions of the work of the sixteenth-century philosopher Peter Ramus (Ong 1958), is well suited to advancing our understanding of the evolving role of technology in reflecting and shaping our responses to historical contexts, even those responses through which we ignore or are alienated from those contexts.

The contemporary relevance of Ong's study of Ramus is evidenced in a remark Beniger (1986: 26) makes about modern digitalized electronic information systems; he characterizes them as 'only the most recent stage in a growing systemness of world society dating back at least to the Commercial Revolution of the fifteenth century'. For Ramus, working at the centre of the Western intellectual tradition and responding to the main social currents of his time, was the granddaddy of all systematizers. In his quest for dialectical method, he crystallized certain habits of thought that have proven especially congruent with the distinctive features of modern society, serving as a formative influence on the thought of both Bacon and Descartes. For the transition from medieval to modern—or from chirographic to typographic—thought consists not in a change from deductive to inductive modes of reasoning or from an emphasis on the subjective to one on the objective, as has often been argued. The significant characteristic shared by rationalist and empiricist alike is one that derives from the same source as Ramus's interest in systems and method and which passes directly from Ramus's work into the mainstream of modern philosophy: a visual phenomenological bias.

What is immediately striking about this characteristic is how little it has to do with anything explicit in Ramus's thought. He was exposed as an incompetent philosopher in his own day, and mainstream interest in his own works dried up shortly after his death. Rather, Ramism is significant precisely for what it left implicit, for what the climate of the times was beginning to allow or even encourage people to assume without even being aware of it, much like the implicit assumptions held in discourse today, such as that involving deconstruction and computers. Ramism, in other words, was a near-ideal though unwitting exemplar of this bias in knowledge through its interest in systems and method, which was to have a great influence on educational theory and practice, as well as philosophy and thought generally. And yet to Ong Ramus was not really the driving force behind the events that his work helped to set in motion; he was just an ambitious academic hustler who took advantage of an opportune situation.

Behind Ramism and its aftermath, Ong's study reveals the influence of three much more pervasive factors: the institutional problems and expediencies of mass pedagogy, the phenomenological shifts encouraged by print technology, and the social and material conditions of the Commercial Revolution. Of these three factors, it is the influence of the Commercial Revolution that is fundamental, not only in affecting Ramism but as the underpinning for the other two factors. The dawning mass production of knowledge, in terms of both the printed book and the increasing scale of university and other school enrolment, was greatly influenced by the new mass-market orientation of society in general. And Ramism, according to Ong (1961: 173), represented a 'tendency to reduce knowledge to something congenial to the artists' and burghers' commercial views. . . . what can legitimately be called a kind of intellectual commercialism'. It was developed in the atmosphere of a university system that Ong (1961: 173) argues took on the qualities of a 'consumer culture', where complex, troubling intellectual problems were glossed over in favour of a smoother, more efficient means of transmitting knowledge in a form that appealed to the taste and convenience of students. In addition, the development of the printing industry, which Ramus was to utilize as no one before in developing and revising successive editions of his logic textbooks, 'brought the crafts and commerce into direct contact with the world of learning more than ever before' (Ong 1961: 182). For just as 'the logicians wanted to hypostatize discourse in order to subject it to formal analysis, the merchants were willing to hypostatize expression in order to sell it' (Ong: 1961: 183). What is the common element here?

The homologous relation between the historical events of the Commercial Revolution, the mechanical and symbolic features of printing, the organizational practices associated with teaching, and the epistemic characteristics of Ramist method is embodied by a visual, spatial model of thought, communication, and reality. It is a phenomenological model through which the subjective, symbolic, and objective realms are all conceived in terms of the visual tendency to perceive objects situated in spatial relations to one another. For Ong (1958), this phenomenological model emerges in response to specific historical conditions and has a pervasive influence on thought and perception. It is a model by means of which both the mental and the material world take on the qualities of neutral spaces in which chunks of stuff are discreetly assembled and moved around from box to box, rather like the parts of machines or commodities in an inventory. The concept of a system, which as originally popularized in the work of Copernicus referred specifically to the physical motion of material objects in space as observed visually (like the orbits of planets seen through a telescope), came quickly to be generalized to the point where just about anything could be thought of along these lines. Charts and diagrams in printed books began to represent as 'systems' of visual objects in spatial patterns concepts and phenomena that had never before been thought of in these terms. Human discourse, traditionally thought of in terms of living dialogue and the aural phenomenology of voice, came to be seen as systems of stuff that were to be structured for transmission to a receiver in mechanistic fashion. This massive reification of both objective and subjective phenomena had the effect of allowing anything that did not lend itself to being viewed as an object to drop out of consciousness. This, Ong (1958) argues, is what became of the remnants of scholastic predication theory, which during the time of Thomas Aquinas had dealt ambitiously with metaphysical issues concerning knowledge and reality but virtually disappears with Ramism. For predication is more than a visual figuration of an entity or event; it involves an ontological judgement about it, an assertion, a call, ultimately, a cry, which is best conceived in terms of the phenomenology of sound.

And, in spite of the many conscious philosophical and scientific achievements that have been made since then, these visual, spatial habits of thought persist today, encouraged more than ever by the mechanistic, object-oriented economic base that was just beginning to take form in Ramus's time. These days it is deeply ironic to hear deconstructionists and other postmodernists decry the tendency of some scientists not to take adequate account of the subjective factors involved in the symbolic construction of reality, while they themselves fail to take account of the objective factors involved in the practical construction of texts and other cultural phenomena. The scientist tends to underplay the extent to which raw experience is shaped by interpretation, while the humanist tends to ignore the external phenomena that interpretations are constructed from. Yet although the deconstructionist and his supposed target seem to inhabit opposite sides of the Cartesian divide—with one seeing an objective world made up of things and the other seeing a subjective world made up of words—each conceives of his own half in terms of almost identical visual, spatial models: reifying referents in one camp, reifying symbols in the other. This tendency to conceive both worlds in mechanistic terms led Ramus to confuse word and thing in his textbooks on method. Today it permits otherwise intelligent people to speak about one world or the other as if it existed alone as a closed system, whether by treating thought as if it were a system of building blocks out of which physical-like structures are constructed or by treating experience as if it came preconceptualized in neatly objectified essential categories. And these visual, spatial models, which derive from neither the objective nor the subjective world in abstract isolation but from the particular historical dialectic between the two which constitutes industrial commodity production, provide the basis for what I believe to be the unacknowledged philosophical common ground shared by the postmodernist rebel, the logical positivist technocrat, and the Ramist as well: instrumentalism, which in crude terms amounts to the tendency to grant truth status to whatever serves one's particular purposes.

In this light, the triangular love affair between postmodernists, technocrats, and computers becomes easy to understand. For the computer, in essence, is the ultimate mechanical juggler of categories: fast, accurate, and compliantly mute in regard to the coherence or truth status of the conceptual marbles that it endlessly rearranges. In terms of how the machine operates, what it is mathematically manipulating need not even be conceptual at all: it could be merely tallies of unidentified objects being sorted to keep track of them, like inventories, or patterns of nonrepresentational electromagnetic signals. Its epistemic bias is toward quantitative relations between discrete entities, such as could be readily represented by visual objects in spatial arrangements. Looking back on his studies, Ong (1958: viii) remarks on the 'resemblance of Ramus' binary dichotomized charts . . . to digital computer programs,' arguing that, '[t]he quantifying drives inherited from medieval logic were producing computer programs in Ramus' active mind some four hundred years before the computer itself came into being'. Philip Leith (1990: 73) calls Ramus 'the first [computer] programmer'. In a chapter devoted to explaining similarities between Ramism and programming logic, he concludes, 'It is striking that the method of logic programmers is identical to that of Ramus,' for in both cases, 'the epistemological foundations were entirely *ad hoc*' (Leith 1990: 80). No wonder, then, that both technocrats and postmodernists see computers as their ultimate tool. The technocrats seek to control society through a process of rationalization which ignores the existential questions raised by the anomie that it causes: people are treated like mechanical cogs in a machine. The postmodernists seek ultimate liberation through cyberspace fantasies which are untroubled by the tragic limitations of an abrasive material world: their ideas seem real enough to them. Neither group has much genuine scepticism about or much desire to revise and improve their understanding of the actual nature of the entities they are dealing with. The satisfaction of their own intentions suits them. In both cases, the technology and the habits of thought it fosters serve to insulate concepts from their material referents, and thus from any possibility of refutation leading to revision.

At this point, I would like to interject the question 'How does this all affect average people?' (You know, those of us who are neither technocrats nor postmodernists—and I hope not Ramists!) For, all too often, it is they who are the final material referents of the conceptual schemes cooked up by industrialist and academic alike. They are the ones who have to live with the very real consequences of the 'information society'. There is a weakness in the contemporary literature on the effects of computers on modes of thought in that these effects are rarely seen to vary greatly between different social classes. Perhaps this is an intellectual habit carried over from the study of the social effects of print, which consisted in large part of a massive facilitation of social mobility and the creation of at least the ideal of a universal symbolic competence: social literacy. But as Ong (1967, 1971, 1977, 1982) continually reminds us, the achievement of anything close to this ideal outside typographic society is extremely rare in the history of literacy. Instead, most societies that have utilized writing have been characterized by what he calls 'media interface', which involves the interaction between literate elites and residually oral masses. In other words, there is a division of modes of knowing and knowledge in a society which corresponds to the division of labour in that society. The domination of one class by another is maintained not merely through physical possession of industrial plant and material forms of wealth but through what Harold Innis (1950, 1964) has called 'monopolies of knowledge', by means of which control of technology, wealth, and other aspects of society is achieved and legitimized.

In their struggle to 'rationalize' and thus control society, Beniger (1986) has shown how elites make efficient use of digital information-processing technology.

But, as is everywhere apparent, average people use computers outside their jobs almost exclusively through the mediation of graphic user interfaces. Increasingly, their dealings with computers, like their dealings with television and other electronic media, involve the use of pictures rather than words. Instead of the neo-Gutenbergian revolution predicted by populist advocates of the personal computer, most people today use the computer to consume mass-produced images rather than to produce their own discourse. The popularity of Web TV and other Internet access devices that are sold without even a keyboard or memory—to say nothing of video games—is eloquent testimony to the fact that, although the computer as used by the elite can be said to share and massively build upon the digital symbolic biases of the printed book, as marketed to average people it is being adapted to the symbolic biases of such analogic media as television.

In addition, just as the massive routines of industrial production are alien to the life experiences of the worker, so does the imagery of the consumer culture emanate from a source other than the everyday life of the consumer. But, on the other hand, it is perhaps the greatest advance of twentieth-century capitalism that it has developed the art of marketing to such an extent that people now embrace industry's products—both material and ideal—as if they were their own. In this respect, one can say that the media of the consumer culture are dealing quite effectively with the problem of anomie.

In Ongian terms (1971, 1977, 1982), a conceptual framework for understanding these phenomena is suggested by the term 'secondary orality', which refers to the re-emergence of oral cultural (tribal) characteristics in a form mediated by electronic mass media, which in turn, of course, are controlled by literate elites. Within this framework, Ong's studies of the characteristics of oral, as contrasted with literate, culture prove an invaluable guide in the interpretation of new developments in popular culture. And yet, since primary oral cultures are free of the influence of literacy, their study provides little insight into the questions of control and alienation which apply to secondary oral culture. Somewhat more insight into these political issues is provided, however, by Ong's (1967, 1971, 1977) studies of the media interface dynamics that developed in chirographic cultures, such as ancient Rome and medieval Europe, as well as by other studies of orality–literacy interactions, such as those of Harold Innis (1950, 1964) and the anthropologist Jack Goody (1986).

Primary orality is a cultural form that can be evaluated only by its own standards. In its own context, it is neither inferior nor superior to literate culture, which is judged by entirely different standards of its own. Yet literate culture never entirely replaces oral culture; rather, it grows out of it and is added onto it. Writing visualizes speech, thus subjecting it to analysis and control. Oral culture never disappears, but it is changed by the new cultural context and standards created by literacy. Specifically, it is subjugated, as literate elites develop economic, political, and religious institutions based on the written word to rule over and control the residually oral masses. In this context, rhetoric develops as a communication medium of social control and class domination by which literate resources are used to exploit and manipulate oral sensibilities. The dynamic between these media/culture/classes is what Ong calls media interface. Chirographic cultures—which lack the techno-logical means and political will to pursue the goal of universal social literacy as typographic cultures do—are the classic embodiment of such media interface. Their study can teach us a lot about the role of orality, literacy, and media in class struggle.

Our modern electronic media culture—although it grows out of the typographic culture with its universalist and egalitarian ambitions—can also be studied in terms of such media interface dynamics, as secondary orality grows among the bulk of the population and what I have called 'technoliteracy' is concentrated within the elite. Once we begin to look at the influence of communication media such as computers and television not in isolation as closed systems but in the historical context of a society shaped by materially determined class structures, the very different sym-bolic forms found at the sending and receiving ends of these media begin to take on immense cultural and political significance. At one end, they cultivate the abstract reasoning characteristic of literacy and digital symbolic forms; at the other, they cultivate the allegorical cast of mind characteristic of oral culture, of the kind of people whom Eric Havelock (1963) called 'image thinkers'.

In traditional societies, the oral mind's tendency toward concrete as opposed to abstract forms of thought and expression was appropriate in its cultural context. Such local, interpersonal, non-technological (*gemeinschaft*) cultures kept their knowledge 'close to the human lifeworld', as Ong (1982) has described it, through image-evoking narrative which appealed to values that are quite different from those which emerge with literacy. But the secondary orality of modern society exists in a cultural context which is not of its own making and which is governed by literate standards. This is not to say that oral cultural values necessarily disappear or are totally devalued: they may even be romantically embraced by the literate elite to some extent. But still, to the extent that literacy changes society, it changes the intellectual traits necessary for the attainment of power in society.

For example, economic production and many other social functions take place on a scale and level of abstraction far beyond the lifeworld of the individual in modern society. Social processes are fragmented, few workers are directly involved in manufacturing, and home and community have become primarily sites of con-sumption. Under these conditions, the down-to-earth concreteness of oral forms of expression are ill suited to empowering people whose lives are no longer grounded by direct participation in a local, organic culture. And not only has the production of narrative been taken out of people's hands and industrialized itself; like another rust-belt industry, it seems to be withering away. In its place we find a proliferation of elaborate imagery which issues not from concrete experience but from the abstract, rational calculations of marketers, and which exists not in the living world of human dialogue but in the decontextualized visual spaces of the screen.

All this leaves people in the secondary oral culture in a semantic environment filled with disembodied images which, while quite concrete and lifelike in visual form, lack the depth and grounding of the lived experience of material contexts. Under these circumstances, tangible commodities take on a dual role. On one hand, they serve as signifiers of cultural ideals. On the other, they are the last remaining socially shared objects of experience. These roles complement one another, since the former assures the significance of the latter and the latter assures the realness of the former. In traditional societies, the fetish is a powerful form of symbolism through which the realness and significance of a concept is assured by the signifier's physical form. In a society where the 'relations between objects take on the nature of relations between people and relations between people take on the nature of relations between objects,' Marx (1976: 165) identified a 'fetishism of commodities' in which people whose lives are alienated turn to commodities as expressions of human values. That this emerges in industrial society is a sign of the epistemic desperation—dare I say intellectual proletarianization—of the culture of secondary orality.

The poverty of the discourse by and about commodities becomes obvious when considered in the historical context of what it is replacing: the traditional organic culture of preindustrial society. The transition is one from an environment in which oral modes of thought are appropriate for effective praxis (an oral cultural environment) to one in which oral sensibilities are exploited and manipulated (by means of literate cultural resources). As knowledge plays a central role in economic production and political power, different symbolic forms—like different technologies—facilitate different forms of production as well as different forms of knowledge appropriate to them. The alienation of the proletariat from the production process involves not only a lack of possession of machinery but a lack of intellectual participation as well. Just as scientific management, or Taylorism, is a technique for removing the worker from any creative input in the industrial process, so is the discourse by and about commodities a technique for alienating the consumer from any source of cultural values that is independent of the increasingly monopolistic marketplace. Again, to assert the superiority of literacy as an intellectual tool and the value of the forms of knowledge traditionally associated with literate elites does not imply any sort of abstract or absolute comparison between oral and literate cultures considered separately and as wholes. What it does implicitly compare is the relative efficacy of oral and literate modes of thought and expression within the specific historical context of an industrial market culture and with regard to specific political questions of power and control. And when one considers that what is happening is a substitution of objects and images not merely for the written and printed word but, to a large extent, for interpersonal spoken dialogue as well, it becomes a comparison between the relative worth of the word and the image in this situation. An examination of the historical relationship between printing, Protestantism, and capitalism is illuminating in this regard (Eisenstein 1980; McLuhan 1962; Weber 1930).

And yet, the materiality of the commodity fetish is significantly different from that of other forms of fetish in one respect. Unlike the sexual fetish, which, according to Freud (1950), is related to its referent only accidentally, or the fetish found in primary oral culture, which is related allegorically, the commodity fetish is the direct material as well as symbolic product of the technological forces and social relations which dominate the culture. Marx (1976) cautioned that although they embody these forces and relations, they are 'enigmatic' since their appearance in the marketplace masks their social origins. But unlike pure images, which are seamless in this respect, physical commodities to some extent bear the stamp of their manufacturedness, which appears in the course of exercising their use value as technologies (as opposed to their market value as commodities). Like a written work which will always bear the traces of a human voice—'the jinnee in the well-wrought urn', Ong (1954) calls it—though mere objects, commodities hold within them the marks of the human activities that made them. Whatever other ideational content they may be used to signify, their material structure always holds the potential to be read as symptomatic of the historical, technological, and social conditions which have figured in their creation. This is because that structure is a concrete manifestation of the logic used in responding to those conditions in order to manufacture the commodity. As such, it is a concretized illustration of the abstract logic of typographic culture. Though fragmentary, the insights afforded by such illustrations have historically been a means for working people to ground their lives in a sense of 'how things work'. Think of the fascination that working-class men in particular have traditionally had for machines—for building them, fixing them, operating them. Think of the type of guy who would get more satisfaction out of repairing a television set than watching one. Think of how mastery over a small part of the technological culture can serve as a foothold in the attempt to grasp the meaning of the whole culture in the terms of those who control it.

And yet today, as manufacturing jobs disappear and products increasingly are sealed in plastic so as to conceal their mechanisms, this kind of concretized, technical reading of commodities must surely be an uphill struggle. (Think of how difficult or impossible it has been made to fix one's own car, for example.) Whether the symbolic competence to do this reading can be cultivated within the culture of secondary orality or whether it would require the adoption of another symbolic mode is a question of the utmost historic importance. Either way, it would require a major reversal of the tendency passively to accept the commodity as fetish. It would require the adoption of the viewpoint not of the tribal fetishist but of the archaeologist of industrial culture. One model of such archaeology can be found in a poem by Robert Pinsky.

Shirt

The back, the yoke, the yardage. Lapped seams,
The nearly invisible stitches along the collar
Turned in a sweatshop by Koreans or Malaysians

Gossiping over tea and noodles on their break
Or talking money or politics while one fitted
This armpiece with its overseam to the band

Of cuff I button at my wrist. The presser, the cutter,
The wringer, the mangle. The needle, the union,
The treadle, the bobbin. The code. The infamous blaze

At the Triangle Factory in nineteen-eleven.
One hundred and forty-six died in the flames
On the ninth floor, no hydrants, no fire escapes—

The witness in a building across the street
Who watched how a young man helped a girl to step
Up to the windowsill, then held her out

Away from the masonry wall and let her drop.
And then another. As if he were helping them up
To enter a streetcar, and not eternity.

A third before he dropped her put her arms
Around his neck and kissed him. Then he held
Her into space, and dropped her. Almost at once

He stepped to the sill himself, his jacket flared
And fluttered up from his shirt as he came down,
Air filling up the legs of his gray trousers—

Like Hart Crane's Bedlamite, 'shrill shirt ballooning.'
Wonderful how the pattern matches perfectly
Across the placket and over the twin bar-tacked

Corners of both pockets, like a strict rhyme
Or a major chord. Prints, plaids, checks,
Houndstooth, Tattersall, Madras. The clan tartans

Invented by mill-owners inspired by the hoax of Ossian,
To control their savage Scottish workers, tamed
By a fabricated heraldry: MacGregor,

Bailey, MacMartin. The kilt, devised for workers
To wear among the dusty clattering looms.
Weavers, carders, spinners. The loader,

The docker, the navvy. The planter, the picker, the sorter
Sweating at her machine in a litter of cotton
As slaves in calico headrags sweated in fields:

George Herbert, your descendant is a Black
Lady in South Carolina, her name is Irma
And she inspected my shirt. Its color and fit

And feel and its clean smell have satisfied
Both her and me. We have culled its cost and quality
Down to the buttons of simulated bone,

The buttonholes, the sizing, the facing, the characters
Printed in black on neckband and tail. The shape,
The label, the labor, the color, the shade. The shirt.

Pinsky uses poetic imagery and association to evoke the concrete experience of the shirt, to analyse it, to reconnect it to the social and material world, to connect consumer with producer. It is one attempt to help us all to read our way back from consumption to production, from viewing back to speaking.

References

Beniger, J. R. (1986). *The Control Revolution: Technological and Economic Origins of the Information Society.* Cambridge, MA: Harvard University Press.

Durkheim, E. (1947). *The Division of Labor in Society.* Glencoe, IL: The Free Press.

Eisenstein, E. L. (1980). *The Printing Press as an Agent of Social Change: Communications and Cultural Transformations in Early Europe.* New York: Cambridge University Press.

Freud, S. (1950). *Totem and Taboo; Some Points of Agreement between the Mental Lives of Savages and Neurotics.* London: Routledge & Paul.

Goody, J. R. (1986). *The Logic of Writing and the Organization of Society.* New York: Cambridge University Press.

Havelock, E. A. (1963). *Preface to Plato.* Cambridge, MA: Belknap Press of Harvard University Press.

Innis, H. A. (1950). *Empire and Communications.* Oxford: Clarendon Press.

—— (1964). *The Bias of Communication.* Toronto: University of Toronto Press.

Leith, P. (1990). *Formalism in AI and Computer Science.* New York: Ellis Horwood.

Marx, K. (1976). *Capital; A Critique of Political Economy,* vol. i. New York: Penguin.

McLuhan, M. (1962). *The Gutenberg Galaxy; The Making of Typographical Man.* Toronto: University of Toronto Press.

Ong, W. J. (1954). 'The Jinee in the Well-wrought Urn'. *Essays in Criticism* (Oxford), 4: 309–20. Reprinted in *The Barbarian Within* (1962), 15–25.

—— (1958). *Ramus, Method, and the Decay of Dialogue; From the Art of Discourse to the Age of Reason.* Cambridge, MA: Harvard University Press.

—— (1961). 'Ramist Method and the Commercial Mind'. *Studies in the Renaissance,* 8: 155–72. Reprinted in *Rhetoric, Romance, and Technology* (1971), 165–89.

—— (1962). *The Barbarian Within: And Other Fugitive Essays.* New York: Macmillan.

—— (1967). *The Presence of the Word: Some Prolegomena for Cultural and Religious History.* New Haven, CT: Yale University Press.

—— (1971). *Rhetoric, Romance, and Technology: Studies in the Interaction of Expression and Culture.* Ithaca, NY: Cornell University Press.

—— (1977). *Interfaces of the Word: Studies in the Evolution of Culture and Consciousness.* Ithaca, NY: Cornell University Press.

—— (1982). *Orality and Literacy: The Technologizing of the Word.* London: Methuen.

Pinsky, R. (1990). *The Want Bone.* New York: Ecco Press.

Russell, B. (1945). *A History of Western Philosophy, and its Connection with Political and Social Circumstances from the Earliest Times to the Present Day.* New York: Simon & Schuster.

Scruton, R. (1995). *A Short History of Modern Philosophy: From Descartes to Wittgenstein* (2nd edn). New York: Routledge.

Weber, M. (1930). *The Protestant Ethic and the Spirit of Capitalism.* New York: Charles Scribner's Sons.

Part VI

Resisting Persuasions

Introduction

WE would like to offer in this final section, a few examples of alternative practices and strategies designed to counter the influences of a media environment controlled and dominated by a few corporate conglomerates with primarily commercial interests.

One example of community resistance to imported commercial culture is documented in 'KFC into India: a Case Study of Resistance to Globalization Discourse', by Melissa Wall. She also compares US news coverage of actions taken against McDonald's to European reporting, demonstrating the ways in which US press reports borrowed from the company's own public relations discourse. In doing so she illustrates the ways in which increased commercialization distorts news reporting of American companies abroad.

The media literacy and community media movements have grown dramatically in the UK, Canada and the United States over the last twenty years. They provide examples and pathways to articulating and developing alternative media practices. Activities by community organizations, grass-roots activists, media literacy advocates, university educators, and alternative media producers provide a wealth of diverse perspectives. The philosophies and debates within these movements are articulated by Norman Cowie in 'Media Literacy and the Commercialization of Culture'. Current debates revolve around the degree to which media literacy can remain critical in a cultural environment dominated by corporate influences, or whether it is destined to become a practice aimed simply at creating more sophisticated consumers. Cowie addresses the issues raised as the movement expands, offering strategies aimed at retaining a critical alternative perspective.

In 'The Public Interest in the Twenty-first Century', the Reverend Everett Parker brings the logic and language of the historic public-interest mandate to life once again. Drawing on a rich history of US telecommunications regulatory policy, he articulates the concerns of scholars, analysts, and media observers, presenting a timely discussion of the present regulatory debates and solutions offered by community and public-interest organizations.

Chapter 20

KFC into India: a Case Study of Resistance to Globalization Discourse

Melissa Wall

WHEN India's first KFC (Kentucky Fried Chicken) opened in 1995, its arrival sparked immediate controversy, ranging from local government charges that the restaurant sold carcinogenic foods to tens of thousands of farmers protesting against a suspected takeover of the locally based agricultural system. This essay is concerned with how Western media are representing the process of economic globalization, which is carried out almost entirely by Western multinationals. This media coverage of the KFC controversy reflects more than simply reporting on the travails of doing business in countries with newly 'reformed' economies; it constitutes a critical case study of how the dominant, Western media are covering resistance to the largest and most far-reaching economic change in this century: the globalization of the world's economy.

One of the main trends affecting the world since the end of the Cold War, globalization is allowing a relatively small number of companies to control much of the world's economy (Tehranian 1993; Brecher and Costello 1994). According to some critics, this trend threatens to create a global 'monoculture' of consumerism, or what Shiva, Jaffri, and Bedi (1997: 5) call a globalization of 'maldevelopment' based on the spread of a 'nonsustainable Western industrial paradigm'. Pathy (1995: 30) argues that globalization in general 'substantially erode[s] the economic sovereignty, cultural identity, legitimate political strength, and even the territorial integrity of the nation'. Whatever the impact, these immense changes have gone largely unexamined and unexplained by the mass media, which have tended to follow the discourse of the 'political arena' which 'remains rooted in the paradigm of nation-based economies' (Brecher and Costello 1994: 67; see also Mander 1996). Stories rarely connect specific events with the overarching picture of this major change in the world economy, and, given the dominance of Western news sources, often rely on the point of view of those who benefit from globalization rather than those who are hurt by it (Brecher and Costello 1994; Mander 1996). Assadi (1996: 181) says opposition to KFC 'should not be viewed in isolation. Rather it has to be linked to the larger strategy of international capitalism entering India in recent years.' Observers note that coverage of this resistance by American media has been 'cynical' and mocking even though the United States is India's largest trading partner (McKibben 1996: 11; Narasimhan 1996).

How globalization is reported in the Western media has become particularly important because it potentially represents a new means of interpreting events around the world since the end of the Cold War. The media are one of the important sites for the struggle to define globalization. In this essay I seek to take a first step in explaining how globalization works by analysing coverage of resistance to Indian opposition to this economic process in elite American publications and European wire services.

The framework for analysis

This essay is operating from the premiss that news is a socially constructed product, determined in part by the routines of news institutions and norms of newsworkers who follow certain prescribed processes in selecting, gathering, and producing news stories (Tuchman 1978; Gans 1979). News is not merely what has happened; rather events are selected and assigned particular meanings, providing news consumers with 'maps of the social world' (Hall *et al.* 1978: 54). These maps are constructed by including certain information and leaving out other information, even though the news item will imply that its version of reality is the accepted consensus of that society (Gitlin 1980). These choices of selection and presentation are so important because they often represent the only information many audience members will ever receive about an event. Though various names are given to this process, I shall here call it 'framing' (Goffman 1974; Gitlin 1980; Entman 1991, 1993).

Framing does not mean a news organization simply reproduces the ideology of its owner (Hartley 1982; Hallin 1987). Instead, the media are independent of direct political control, and ideology is 'embedded in practices and routines' (Hallin 1987: 11). Thus framing represents a subtle process in which the news is a negotiation among editors, reporters, and sources. Reporters may be exposed to various discourses representing a range of opinion, which are woven into the story. Even though a news story allows for oppositional information to be presented, it does so in such a way that the dominant interpretation, usually provided by powerful institutions in a society, is made to appear the accepted or real explanation (Gitlin 1980). Even when reporters might not support the dominant forces in a society, they are likely to report challenges to the status quo negatively. Hallin (1987) argues this is what happened with American news media coverage of Central America in the 1980s. Coherent statements about alternatives to the status quo rarely appear because most reporters have a 'preference for order' (Hallin 1987: 19).

In addition to general ideas about news as a social process, two other areas of research have influenced this analysis. The first focuses on international news norms, including collection and distribution of news about international events. The second area concerns the commodification of news as well as the growth of media conglomerates and monopolies.

International news norms
Most international news is collected by a small number of Western news organiza-

tions such as the Associated Press, the New York Times News Services, and Reuters. Despite supplying much of the world with its news, these agencies have been accused of concentrating their personnel in the Northern hemisphere to the exclusion of poorer Southern-hemisphere countries (Rosenblum 1979; Hachten 1992). Because they disseminate news not only to other Western countries but back to the Southern countries as well, South to South news flow continues to be the exception rather than the rule (Hachten 1992; Frederick 1993; Righter 1978). Another problem with international reporting involves a tendency to 'parachute' journalists into whatever country happens to be experiencing the crisis of the moment. The journalists often know very little about the country in which they have arrived and rarely speak the language (Rosenblum 1979, 1993).

In addition to these constraints, the international news that does get collected has little chance of appearing in print. Critics see a paucity of international news in US publications because of market concerns: American newspaper editors believe there is no audience for international news, and the increasing emphasis on profit ensures that commercial concerns outweigh any need to educate the public (Hoge 1997). The news that does run fits within a very narrow range of topics, more likely to be determined by the closeness of the new item's relationship to US political and business concerns than by concern about public education (Cohen 1963; Gans 1979; Shoemaker, Danielian, and Brendlinger, 1991; Hess 1996). Galtung and Ruge (1965) found that the following attributes of international events helped determine whether they received coverage or not: frequency, amplitude, clarity, cultural proximity, consonance, continuity, elitism, personalization, and negativity. The more of these criteria that an event met, the more likely it was to be covered. Others have suggested foreign news is covered when it falls into a category that Rosenblum (1979) calls 'coups and earthquakes.' That is, unusual and often negative events are more likely to be reported, especially when the country is not Western. This argument, combined with concerns about the dominance of news flow by a small number of Western agencies, became part of the debate over the New World Information Order voiced in the 1970s and 1980s (Masmoudi 1981).

Other criticism has particularly focused on the role of Western government sources in influencing international news. Various studies have posited that the presentation of international news is shaped by the concerns of the US government, which guides news selection and framing of the stories that do get covered (Cohen 1963; Herman and Chomsky 1988). What is important for researchers today is to remember that these assertions were made when the Cold War was still a dominant lens for interpreting world events. With the end of the East–West competition, some argue that no new central organizing frame has emerged to guide reporters on how to cover international news (Hallin 1992; Halliday, Jansen, and Schneider 1992).

Commercialization and conglomerate control
The US news media have always been commercially oriented, tending to ignore the role of big business in influencing political and economic decision-making (Schudson 1995). Yet recent years have seen a disturbing growth in emphasis on news as a product which must be managed by marketing experts (Underwood

1993). In addition, fewer and fewer companies control more and more of the world's media outlets, a trend that has affected European media as well (Bagdikian 1996, 1997). For media industries, the mantras of the 1990s have been: privatization, deregulation, and expansion (Schiller 1996). The global media that have emerged are missionaries of 'the ideology of global corporate capitalism' (Herman and McChesney 1997: 38). News has been homogenized and commercialized (Bagdikian 1996). Consumerism promoted by the media has resulted in the takeover of meaningful political concepts, turning them into vapid choices among commodities rather than anything substantive (Goldsmith, Heath, and Smith 1991). The result of these processes has been corporate censorship of news as well as a dearth of news frames critical of these very business practices (Andersen 1995; Jensen 1997).

Methods

This analysis has been guided by the recommendations of Hall (1975) concerning textual analysis as well as the more recent work of Gamson (1992) and Entman (1991, 1993) on frame analysis. Hall (1975) describes a textual analysis as one in which appropriate examples are selected and examined in detail, indicating why one reading is more plausible than another. More specific directions for textual analysis have been created by various researchers employing what has come to be known as frame analysis (Gamson 1992; Gamson and Modigliani 1989; Gamson and Lasch 1983; Pan and Kosicki, 1992; Entman 1991, 1993). This type of analysis also examines the text of news stories in depth, but attempts to define a precise set of attributes to study.

Gamson and Modigliani (1989: 3) characterize news stories as interpretative packages that 'give meaning to an issue'. The package consists of an internal frame, within which other condensing devices help shape the perspective being presented. These are divided into framing devices and reasoning devices. To clarify further the process of framing, Entman (1993; 52) provides this definition: 'To frame is to select some aspects of a perceived reality and make them more salient in a communicating text'. Like Gamson, Entman also notes that a frame will consist of certain rhetorical and semantic devices, which he lists as keywords, stock phrases, stereotyped images and sources of information. These will make salient certain problems, causes, and solutions (Entman 1991).

Although multiple frames may be found in a story, Gamson (1992: 135) believes that '[s]ome frames have a natural advantage because their ideas and language resonate with a broader ... culture. Resonances increase the appeal of a frame making it appear natural and familiar'. He further notes that, while frames may represent the points of view that various sources are contributing to a story, certain frames are created by the journalists. In their attempts to present the news in terms that their audience will understand and find appealing, reporters rely on inter-textual references. They 'invent their own clever catchphrases, and metaphors, drawing on a popular culture that they share with their audience' (Gamson 1992: 24).

This essay employs a frame analysis of print news media coverage of globalization, examining in depth one case: coverage of the opposition to KFC in India. The case study consists of 36 news reports that ran from the opening of the first KFC in June 1995 to one year later, June 1996. This includes all staff-written stories that ran during that period in the following elite American publications: *New York Times*, *Los Angeles Times*, *Chicago Tribune*, and *Time* (international and domestic editions). Also examined were wire-service stories from Reuters World Service, Agence France-Presse and Deutsche Presse-Agentur. All stories were retrieved from the Lexis electronic database. American elite coverage was selected because of its acknowledged potential impact on not only elite audiences but on other media. The other news services were selected to contribute an elite European point of view. Differences in coverage might be due in part to the format of wire reports, which focus on breaking news, versus the more feature-oriented staff-written reports which made up the American stories.

Each story was closely read to determine patterns found in the coverage, focusing systematically on framing devices (metaphors, exemplars, catchphrases, depictions, and visual images) as well as reasoning devices (causes, consequences, and moral claims). Also, as Entman (1993) noted, sources of information can influence what sort of frames are employed. In order to recognize the link between sources and certain ways of presenting information, a matrix was created for better displaying the source of certain recurring framing and reasoning devices. This matrix consisted of a list of all possible sources of information that appeared in the stories: KFC representatives; activists opposed to KFC and other multinational corporations; government representatives; politicians/political party representatives; other media; other; no source (in some stories information was provided without discernible attribution.) Sources were listed at the top of the matrix. Running vertically were the following four subjects: KFC actions; activists' actions (including environmentalists, farmers, animal rights activists, trade unions etc.); political opposition's actions; government (at all levels) actions. This matrix isolated which sources, for example, were characterizing opposition to KFC as unfair, nationalistic, and so on.

Background

The groundwork for the arrival of the American-based multinational corporation had been laid four years earlier in 1991 when India undertook vast economic restructuring. That year, the Gulf war brought a large drop in remittances from the Middle East. Pereira and Seabrook (1994) argue that at roughly the same time India was deemed uncreditworthy by Western banks. In order to restore its creditworthiness, the government agreed to adopt an International Monetary Fund–World Bank structural adjustment programme (SAP), which required India to devalue its currency and drop many of its barriers to foreign trade (Pereira and Seabrook 1994). Previously, India had followed a policy of limiting foreign investment in order to pursue economic self-reliance. Though supported by Prime Minister Rao of the Congress Party, the change in economic policies has been far from universally accepted across the country, as they were never based on popular mandate (Bhambhri 1996). Some observers believe that the economic changes have primarily benefited the elite and worsened the living conditions of the poor (Bidwai 1995; Patnaik 1994, 1996–7; Bhambhri 1996). Indeed, critics have declared that 'structural adjustment and trade liberalization measures are becoming the most serious threat to survival of the people' (Shiva, Jaffri, and Bedi 1997: 5). Such policies have led to dominance by multinational corporations, which destroys cultural heritage and eliminates the need for local skills and production (Bagchi 1994).

In June 1995, KFC, a subsidiary of PepsiCo, joined a number of other foreign companies entering India. Its first restaurant opened in the southern city of Bangalore, where multinational computer and other high-tech firms had begun to locate. Situated in a ritzy area of town, the fast-food outlet's intended market was a group of people Vandana Shiva (1996) identified as 'a very tiny elite' who could afford their food. The cost of eating at KFC—a little over a $1 for a piece of chicken—was more than the average daily per capita income in India (Narasimhan 1996).

Two months later, in August, opposition groups warned KFC to leave India. Among those opposing KFC were the Karnataka Rajya Ryota Sangha (KRRS), a farmers' union led by M. D. Nanjundaswamy, which was spearheading resistance to KFC as part of a strategy of opposing foreign firms whose products they believed threatened the livelihood of the nation's millions of agriculturists. Animal and environmental rights activists led by Maneka Gandhi, daughter-in-law of the late prime minister Indira Gandhi and a former environmental minister, accused KFC of being unhealthy, a threat to the environment and to animals because of its factory farming methods. Other opponents included consumers, doctors, people concerned about Indian culture, and politicians from all shades of the political spectrum (Vandana Shiva 1996).

At the beginning of September, the Bangalore city authorities threatened KFC with closure for serving more than the allowed amounts of monosodium glutamate (MSG) in their food. Indian health laws limit the amount of this ingredient in food because the government believes it to be carcinogenic. Following the threat of closure, KFC successfully appealed to the Indian courts to allow it to stay open. The corporation also set in motion its public relations defence of KFC, calling press conferences to defend its presence in India. At the end of the month, the farmers' union staged a protest against KFC in Bangalore, which was attended by at least 25,000 people.

In November, KFC opened its second restaurant in India's capital, New Delhi. Less than three weeks later, local authorities closed it down, too. Reports of why the restaurant was closed varied, but all mentioned health-code violations: too much MSG, the presence of too much sodium phosphate, and an unclean kitchen, which some reports said was based on the presence of two flies in the kitchen. The restaurant remained closed for three weeks, then was reopened by court order. In December 1995, the Indian government changed the permissible level of MSG, and the restaurant was no longer in violation of the health codes (Vandana Shiva 1996; 'Kentucky Fried Chicken Protests' 1995).

In January 1996, the farmers again protested in Bangalore, this time entering the restaurant and breaking equipment. Their leader, M. D. Nanjundaswamy, despite the fact that he was not present at this protest, was arrested in connection with it. In June 1996, PepsiCo announced the opening of its first Pizza Hut. The multinational is continuing with its plans for more KFC outlets in India.

Findings and discussion

Having systematically looked for framing and reasoning devices as described by Gamson, but also keeping in mind Entman's argument that sources are important to frames, four frames were located in the coverage of Indian opposition to KFC.

(1) *The Saga of Colonel Sanders' Indian Travails*, which relies on a personification of Colonel Sanders and satire of all opposition. The primary sources of this frame were the reporters covering the story, including Indian reporters whose stories served as sources for Northern reporters.
(2) *KFC is Wrongfully Vilified*, which presents the multinational as a harmless free-market player persecuted by illegitimate lawbreakers. The primary source for this frame was KFC itself.
(3) *All Opposition is Die-hard Nationalism*, which labels opposition to multinationals as strictly nationalists out to protect their own investments. The primary sources of this frame were the reporters and proponents of free-market trade.
(4) *KFC is Harmful to India*, which suggests that this American fast-food corporation is a threat to India's agricultural and cultural systems as well as to its people's health. The primary sources of this frame were the activists opposing KFC.

Some frames were much more prominent in certain stories than in others. For instance, the Colonel Sanders frame was seldom found in the European coverage, but figured prominently in the American stories. This may reflect the fact that American business's role often goes largely unnoticed by the media and that pro-business attitudes among US media have become particularly prevalent with the emergence of media conglomerates in the 1990s (Schudson 1995; Jensen 1997).

The Saga of Colonel Sanders' Indian Travails

This frame identifies the primary problem as Indian opponents overreacting to the arrival of a harmless American fast-food restaurant as personified by the kindly old Colonel Sanders. The cause of the overreaction was Indian backwardness. This frame occured mainly in the coverage by American media, where it appeared to be the dominant frame. It was characterized by adopting the Kentucky Fried Chicken marketing terminology, and by relying on hyperbole and satire to portray opposition as ludicrous and comical, implying that this was not a story to take seriously. Thus, it linked news audiences to American cultural knowledge.

How can anyone condemn good old Colonel Sanders? Colonel Sanders was talked about as if the white-haired Southern 'gentleman' were literally back in the kitchen, running the restaurants in question. The *Los Angeles Times* reported that 'South Indian Farmers Tell Colonel Sanders to Get out of Town', while later noting that the local government and KFC are playing 'a high-stakes game of chicken . . . and Col. Sanders could be the loser' (Dahlburg and Sharma 1995). The *New York Times* weighed in with its observation that 'the travails of Colonel Sanders' beachhead in the land of tandoori chicken' had been the source of a 'brouhaha' (Burns 1995*b*: A4). *Time* reported on the conditions of the 'Colonel's kitchen' (Spaeth 1995: 23)

Stories also dropped bits and pieces of the fast-food restaurant's own marketing language into stories. All the marketing slogans that follow were underlined by the author. *Time* noted that 'Colonel Sanders' secret recipe has brought down the shutters' (Spaeth 1995: 23). Agence France-Presse reported that government health tests found KFC's 'finger-lickin' good' chicken contained double the allowable amount of MSG (Chanda 1995). Another *Time* story noted that 'KFC PepsiCo Inc. which had hoped to have a good number of Indians licking their fingers by now, is instead licking its wounds' (Spaeth 1995: 23), while the *Los Angeles Times* wrote about 'Col. Sanders' hot & spicy seasoning' (Dalhburg and Sharma 1995). These word choices were intended to resonate with readers and authors long exposed to KFC's sales strategies. They also implied a familiarity with the restaurant that would keep those with whom it resonates from condemning a product so familiar. In essence, it implied an acceptance and support of the restaurant.

The frame further implied that this was not a story to take seriously based on its commercial and market dominance in the wider media frame. Quite noticeable in the American coverage of the resistance to KFC was an apparent inability to consider seriously any of the opposition claims. Instead, reporters used the protests and accusations as fodder for writing stories that fell far outside typical hard news discourse. By choosing to present the opposition in terms of hyperbole and satire, coverage implied that these were silly and unbelievable charges. For example, the *Chicago Tribune* reported that 'government officials . . . acted swiftly last month to save Indians from the dangers of that potential scourge of the West, Kentucky Fried Chicken' (Brandon 1995). The *New York Times* noted that 'wags here have a name for the episode: The Tale of Two Flies' and that some local newspaper columnists had called the opposition the 'Chicken War' (Burns 1995*b*: A4). Then there was this lead from the *Chicago Tribune* (Brandon 1995):

At long last someone has tackled India's biggest threat to public health and safety. It is not the contaminated water disguised as 'nutritious' spring water and sold in re-sealed plastic bottles. It is not driving conditions, where a combination of narrow highways and daredevil truckers reduce all rules of the road to one basic premise: 'Might is right.' It is not what people airily call the 'Killer Red Line,' the bus system in Delhi, so named because its drivers regularly run down cars and passengers that interfere with a prompt arrival at the next stop. Nor is it the disease potential posed by open sewers, meat carcasses hanging in 90-degree heat, or urban encampments consisting largely of plastic sheeting, sold in stores as 'Calcutta-style tent homes.' It is Colonel Sanders.

The reporters chose not to believe the charges against KFC. Instead, they expressed utter scepticism and what seemed almost like delight in this story. As the *New York Times* reported, 'this is no year and New Delhi no place, to be trumpeting the superior virtues of tandoori restaurants, at least from the standpoint of hygiene'. The article went on to report a four-month-old story about an Indian politician killing his wife and attempting to burn her body in a tandoor oven. 'For several months after the episode, tandoori restaurants in the city reported a sharp falloff in trade' (Burns 1995*b*: D5). Clearly, this story (the *Chicago Tribune* also reported the incident in its KFC coverage) had no relationship to the opposition to KFC, but was intended to denigrate that opposition and suggest that Indian people are barbarians indeed.

Compared to the other four main frames used to talk about Indian opposition to KFC, this one relied on noticeably fewer sources of information. Much of the commentary was unattributed. It appeared that reporters were casting the events within self-devised frames clearly drawn from the world of marketing and advertising, tapping into slogans and metaphors that would likely be familiar to most American readers.

KFC is wrongfully vilified

This frame represents KFC as a legitimate business concern with a generous investment programme for India which had been undermined by lawbreakers. However, because KFC is a law-abiding company, it would fight to the end these false claims and unfair opposition to its entry into India. Their reasons included the fact that KFC was in many other countries, so it should be in India too; India was filthy and had no room to criticize the 'modern' practices of KFC; customers liked it, so it must be OK; and opponents were vandals and so their views did not count. The primary source of this frame was KFC and its spokespeople, who held news conferences and made themselves available to reporters. Their interpretation of events remained consistent throughout the various moves to stop the restaurant. Another key element to this frame is the directly negative characterization of India, which was implied in some of the other frames. This frame is found in both American and European coverage, though it is strongest in the American coverage.

KFC is everywhere; therefore, why shouldn't it be in India? A common argument in stories was reflected in the Reuters lead, 'Kentucky Fried Chicken has discovered that serving its standard fare in some 9,400 outlets worldwide is fraught with challenge and opportunity when it comes to India' (Madhavan 1995*b*). This statistical data was included by Reuters, Agence France-Presse, the *New York Times* and *Time*. A KFC manager told the *New York Times*, 'KFC is a responsible, internationally renowned company serving meals to 7 million people daily' (Burns 1995*a*: A4) When *Time* reported that in India MSG is believed to cause cancer, in the next sentence it noted that the US Food and Drug Administration had found no such link, implying that it must not be unhealthy: 'In a land where food adulteration is rampant, there was little alarm over a touch of sodium phosphate, an ingredient in baking soda, approved within limits by the World Health Organization and the U.S. Food and Drug Administration' (Spaeth 1995: 23). When Reuters too reported that sodium phosphate was an ingredient in baking soda, it did include its source of information: Sandeep Kohli, managing director of KFC in India (Madhavan 1995*a*). Agence France-Presse quoted Kohli at a press conference: 'MSG is a flavouring agent in Europe, the United States and other countries and nobody has a problem' (Chanda 1995).

India is a filthy country and has no room to criticize KFC's standards. This idea was presented in stories that talked about India's overall dirtiness, as well as in stories that focused on the fly issue that developed around the closure of the Delhi restaurant. Some stories juxtaposed opposition based on hygiene and healthiness with descriptions of India as a dirty country. The *Chicago Tribune* noted: 'In a country where sanitation is so poor that people routinely die of diarrhea and outbreaks of plague still occur, reports now chronicle with considerable license the potential health hazards presented by Western fast food' (Brandon 1995). Agence France-Presse quoted a KFC manager claiming that the restaurant was the '"cleanest" restaurant in India and was equipped with an air-conditioned kitchen' (Chanda 1995). The *New York Times* too reported the 'cleanest' restaurant claim (Burns 1995*a*: A4).

Though some stories also reported that health officials had charged that the products sold contained harmful and possibly carcinogenic ingredients, reporters often did not seek out expert scientific opinion to help readers understand this matter. Instead, many stories chose to focus on the issue of flies in the Delhi KFC's kitchen. *Time* reported that the Delhi KFC was closed because of two flies found in the kitchen, and the reporter noted this was 'evidence that KFC was running one of the cleanest kitchens around' (Spaeth 1995: 23). The *New York Times* told its readers that 'the fly has never been hard pressed in India. The Indian restaurant has been something of a home away from home for flies' (Burns 1995*b*: A4). Reuters provided this quote: '"They found two flies," a KFC spokesman said dryly' (Madhavan 1995*b*). Agence France-Presse also reported on the Delhi closure, noting that 'one of the reasons given for the closure of the restaurant was the alleged discovery of two flies in the kitchen' ('Kentucky Fried Fights' 1995).

KFC is popular with customers; therefore, it is good for India. The *New York Times* noted that the restaurant was serving 1,500 customers a day in Bangalore and later reported that the 'middle classes ... flocked' to KFC (Burns 1995*a*; 1995*b*: D5). Reuters headlined a story this way: 'Politicians bait KFC, but customers aren't chicken' and went on to report that 'customers didn't seem to care about criticism' (Madhavan 1995). Agence France-Presse quoted Kohli explaining that 'the health aspect was never in doubt in the minds of the seven million customers we serve daily' (Chanda 1995). The *Los Angeles Times* quoted a KFC manager as suggesting India should 'let the customer decide' (Dalhburg and Sharma, 1996).

Opponents were outside the law, so their claims didn't deserve to be acknowledged. Agence France-Presse reported a KFC manager's quote: '"We will not negotiate with vandals"' ('Security for Foreign', 1995). Reuters too quoted a KFC manager labelling the protest an '"act of vandalism" ... In a democracy, such acts are unjustified and cannot be considered to be a substitute for legitimate means of protest' ('Indian Farmers Ransack' 1995).

All opposition to KFC is based on nationalism

In this frame, opposition was presented as having very little to do with KFC and much more with rampant nationalism in India. Nationalism was sometimes equated with socialism, both of which were portrayed as barriers to joining the modern world and participating in the global economy. The frame worked by suggesting that Indian nationalism came from inherent xenophobia and backwardness, that nationalism was the opposite of modernity, and that nationalists represented an irrational threat to the legitimate foreign business concerns who only wanted to invest in India. This frame featured much more in the American coverage of events, and its primary source was the reporters and those Indians who promoted free-market trade (investment officials and politicians).

Opposition comes from India's xenophobia. Opposition was simply irrational anti-foreigner hatred. A *Time* headline read, 'American Firms Face an Anti-foreign Backlash', while within the story we read of 'anti-foreigner furor', 'anti-foreign agitation could spin out of control' and 'anti-American' furor (Greenwald 1995: 92). Not only did stories stress the anti-foreign attitudes of Indians, but they also suggested that anti-foreign sentiment was especially anti-American, such as when the *Los Angeles Times* reported that 'in recent years other large U.S. companies including Cargill, Inc., Du Pont Co., Enron Corp. and Coca-Cola Co. have been targets of protests and opposition' (Dahlburg and Sharma 1995). *Time* chalked up the opposition as a continuation of 'proud anti-colonial traditions' (Greenwald 1995: 92), while Agence France-Presse quoted what it called a 'U.S. educated' politician who called the KFC controversy ' "insincere, jingoistic talk" ' (Chanda 1995).

Opposition comes from nationalists who oppose modernity. Although the Indian government chose to move forward when, as the *New York Times* noted, it 'broke the tablets of socialism' (Burns 1995*b*: D5), many noted that inflexible people clinging to passé traditions continued to oppose KFC. Yet the multinational's representatives told Agence France-Presse that opposition stemmed from 'ignorance' and opponents needed to be 'educated' ('Closure of Kentucky Fried', 1995). Coverage implied that these were not flexible people whose minds could easily be changed. Reuters called them 'die-hard nationalists who cannot stomach its [KFC's] presence' (Madhavan 1995), while Agence France-Presse labelled opponents 'traditionalists' ('Indian Activists Arrested' 1996).

A *Time* headline reads, 'No Passage to India', a play on the E. M. Forster novel and movie about colonial India. In the same *Time* story, an investment banker, Barton Biggs, explained that this was 'typically Indian. For every three steps forward, they take two steps backward', while the reporter noted that the country had long been 'a black hole for foreign investors', and ended his story with a warning that 'nationalist outbursts threaten to stall India's effort to become an Asian tiger' (Greenwald 1995: 92).

Indian nationalists represent a violent threat to harmless multinationals who only want freedom of the marketplace to do business. The *New York Times* described KFC's entry into Delhi as 'challenging the lion in its den' (Burns 1995*b*: D5). In describing the KFC shutdown in Bangalore, *Time* wrote of '[s]haken KFC managers' (Greenwald 1995: 91), while Reuters reported KFC's assertion that it was a 'legitimate investor' in India ('Indian Farmers Ransack' 1996). Continuing its characterization of KFC and other corporations as victims, *Time* later wrote of the 'assault on multinationals' (Spaeth 1995: 23).

KFC is a Threat to India

Much of the colourful writing that characterized some of the other frames was missing in this one. There were fewer commercially inspired metaphors and other framing devices. This frame presented the argument that KFC was not merely a harmless restaurant but might in fact be damaging to the environment, represent an economic threat, and serve unhealthy food that was culturally inappropriate in a land with a strong history of vegetarianism. This was the frame where the opposition was given room to articulate its grievances. Unlike the other frames, reporters relied almost entirely on attributed information in this frame. The primary sources used were the activists who opposed the entry of KFC and other multinationals into India. This frame was stronger in the European stories than in the American ones. Although American reporters included some of the same information, they tended to present the opposition arguments more quickly and succinctly in such a way that they were much less of a focus than the concerns of KFC. The European coverage tended to allow the opposition more room to voice their complaints. In addition to patriotism, this would appear to reflect the increasingly favourable coverage of business in the American press as a consequence of commercialism.

KFC's entry into India represents an economic threat. This argument was more prominent in the European wire stories, which usually sourced the information to the farmers' opposition group. Deutsche Presse-Agentur noted that opponents believed that KFC would 'take away jobs from Indians and drive out local businesses' ('Police Guard Pizza Hut' 1996), a claim Agence France-Presse also reported by quoting farmers' union (KRRS) leader M. D. Nanjundaswamy's assertion that corporations such as KFC 'would force poor agriculturists through economic muscle to grow chicken fodder instead of vital crops' (Indian activists arrested, 1996). The same activist told Reuters that KFC and other fast-food restaurants would 'divert food grains from human consumption. "It directly affects Indian agriculture"' (Madhavan 1995b). Both *Time* and the *New York Times* reported the opposition slogan which supports foreign high technology firms, but not those of the food and beverage industries: 'Microchips, yes! Potato chips, no!' (Greenwald 1995: 92; Burns 1995b).

KFC's food is unhealthy. One of the most common criticisms of KFC was that its food is not healthy. With the exception of *Time* and the *Chicago Tribune*, all the news organizations ran at least one story calling KFC's fare 'junk food', a term that was usually attributed. The *Los Angeles Times* also quoted Nanjundaswamy's remark that the children of overseas Indians who consume American fast food 'look like broiler chickens themselves' (Dahlburg and Sharma 1995). More serious charges by activists were also quoted. The Deutsche Presse-Agentur quoted Nanjundaswamy's claims that the US Senate had ordered a report that found Americans contracted cancer 'every seven seconds' and the 'main culprits were identified as processed meats and chicken in the junk food industry' ('Du Pont and Kentucky Fried Chicken' 1995), while Reuters carried a darkly satirical quote by a politician who told a rally, 'A poison like Kentucky Fried Chicken will only help in controlling the country's population boom as it would lead to more deaths' (Samath 1995). The *Chicago Tribune* reported one leader's characterization of KFC restaurants as '[d]eath chambers' (Brandon 1995).

KFC could wreck Indian culture. Some reports characterized the arrival of KFC in terms of a generic threat, such as *Time*'s reporting that some Indians saw it as part of a 'cultural invasion' (Greenwald 1995: 92). More specifically, the arrival of KFC was linked with the destruction of India's religious reverence for cattle (some activists charged that the restaurant was using beef in its food). Deutsche Presse-Agentur reported that 'farmer activists urging "Let us drive out foreign meat industry" say KFC, McDonalds and Pizza Hut should be banned in India to save the country's cattle wealth' ('Security to be increased' 1996). Agence France-Presse quoted Nanjundaswamy saying, 'We will seize the calves which the multinationals take out to slaughter for export and rear them in our farms. This is the only method to prevent them from extinction' ('Indian farmers' group' 1995).

Those opposing KFC represent the will of the people and the country's best interests. Reuters reported that Nanjundaswamy called his movement's opposition to KFC a *satyagraha*, Gandhi's form of non-violent protest used to fight British colonial rule (Madhavan 1995b). Deutsche Presse-Agentur reported also that activist leaders saw their opposition as democratic 'direct action' ('India's First KFC Outlet' 1995). Agence France-Presse quoted opposition leaders claiming that 'There is no other way out. People have to resort to direct democracy. This is the only way to educate the people's representatives, the judiciary and the media and consumers about these companies' ('Indian farmers' group' 1996).

Conclusion

As Amiya Kumar Bagchi (1994) argues, globalization represents not a historical inevitability, but rather a choice. While multinationals and others who benefit from their presence may choose to allow them to enter places where they are not wanted or needed, other people can choose to oppose them. One of the most important sites for battle between those who have chosen globalization and those who are opposed to it is the media. This is especially true in the rich Northern countries where the media are sometimes our only sources of information about the consequences of globalization, a process often carried out by corporations based in the North, in other parts of the world. Equally important, but beyond the scope of this essay, are the ways globalization is portrayed to those in the South, who are usually the most negatively affected by it. Although I have considered only Western coverage of this event, it is likely that the equivalent, elite Indian press's coverage was similar. This press in India tends to consist of English-language publications which are heavily influenced by advertisers, supportive of economic privatization policies, and aimed at the middle class—who also happen to be KFC's intended audience (Bathla 1998; Singh 1992; Parthasarathy 1989; Mukerjee 1996; Ghosh 1996; Assadi 1996).

This study found four distinct frames in the coverage of Indian opposition to the arrival of the multinational food and beverage corporation restaurant, KFC, in India. *The Saga of Colonel Sanders' Indian Travails* relies on personification of Colonel Sanders and satire of the opposition. The primary sources were the reporters covering the story, including Indian reporters whose stories served as sources for Northern journalists. This frame was found almost exclusively in the American coverage. *KFC is Wrongfully Vilified* presents the multinational as a harmless free market player persecuted by illegitimate lawbreakers. Its primary source was KFC itself. This frame was found in both American and European stories, although primarily in the America reports. *All Opposition is Die-hard Nationalism* leaves little or no room for any other types of opposition. The primary sources of this frame were the reporters and proponents of free-market trade. This frame was particularly strong in the American coverage. *KFC is Harmful to India* suggests that this fast-food corporation is a threat to India's agriculture and cultural systems as well as to its people's health. The primary sources of this frame were the activists opposing KFC. This frame was much stronger in the European coverage than in the American.

Because this essay is only one case study of such opposition, we must use some caution in talking about these results; media coverage of other acts of resistance may be different. However, we can talk more generally about the characteristics of the frames found in this analysis. It appears that we were seeing one of the results of the end of the Cold War. Previously, most foreign news had been interpreted by US government sources. Yet the American government, while supportive of multinational business operations, was not portrayed as directly involved in this story. The Indian government, while involved, did not represent a major voice in many of the stories (especially the American ones), perhaps reflecting India's own internal dissent concerning this economic process. Instead, one of the primary sources was KFC, an American-based multinational. Thus, rather than patriotic slogans about our allies and enemies as we might have seen with the Cold War, we got news reports that spoke the language of American consumer culture. The American stories repeatedly used the marketing slogans of KFC, transferring meanings and values from commercials and advertisements to news coverage, thus ultimately obscuring the real issues about power in the globalization process. The language of KFC marketing was re-encoded in this process to be representative of American values. This transfer of meanings works so well for a multinational like KFC because most Americans are not familiar with India, but they do know KFC advertising language. Thus, what may likely resonate with readers will be these very familiar phrases and symbols, lessening their interest in and sympathy with the opposition to KFC.

One of the ways KFC was able to influence coverage was by holding press conferences and repeatedly presenting their point of view, which was reported in every publication. That viewpoint was concise and delivered almost every time by one or two company representatives who presented reporters with facts and statistics such as the number of customers served, or the numbers of restaurants all over the world. KFC depicted themselves as the victims and their opponents as violent 'vandals', working against India's best interests. One of the other tendencies presented all opposition as based on nationalism. While certainly some of the opposition in this case was based on nationalism, to label all opponents nationalists was to oversimplify the complex political processes occurring in India. Such generalizations also allowed reporters to overlook the local level where often the real grassroots opposition was operating. Again, this frame was more prominent in the American coverage than in the European.

There was some criticism of KFC and the globalization pattern that it represents, but this frame was much weaker in the American coverage than in the European stories. In the European wire stories, it seemed the norms of objectivity were followed, allowing opposition points of view to be included. Although the European media have been following a trend toward privatization, they have not experienced the level of merger mania that has swept through the American media, which became increasingly commercialized and business-oriented in the 1990s. Not surprisingly, the Colonel Sanders frame was so strong in the American stories that all other frames were barely discernible.

While this might suggest that oppositional discourses will simply be marginalized in the process of creating the news, the media in fact 'show discursive openings, inconsistencies and contradictions' in their reports which can be used to insert alternative viewpoints (Bruck 1989: 113). Identifying those discursive openings can help us make concrete suggestions for opposition movements to locate 'opportunities and margins for change' (Bruck 1989: 113). How might the hegemonic marketing frame have been resisted in the coverage analysed here? One tack taken by the activists was to use humour or satirical language, such as when M. D. Nanjundaswamy was quoted describing the children of overseas Indians as looking like broiler chickens. Such language could be even more effective if more specifically linked with Western, especially American, concerns about healthy foods. In this way, Indian opposition could portray itself as having not just a sense of humour but values in common with average Westerners. A second way that activists seemed more effective was when they were able to use positive cultural symbols, such as when they linked their opposition to Gandhi's *satyagraha*. Perhaps this strategy could be made even more compelling by linking Indian cultural symbols with Western news values. In particular, because the US coverage of the resistance was much less positive, this study recommends tapping into some of what researcher Herbert Gans (1979) has found to be 'enduring news values' in American media. Those values that appear to be relevant to this study include: small-town pastoralism and the virtue of smallness; individualism; responsible capitalism; and altruistic democracy. For example, activists could link their emphasis on Gandhi to the American values of democracy and of smallness.

As for the media, reporters should remember that, while using such frames may create colourful copy, they do a disservice to the people and issues involved. Reporters should take more pride in their writing by creating their own evocative language rather than relying on that of marketing agents. Journalists need to be aware that the press in countries such as India speaks for an elite minority and should not be seen as representative of the point of view of the average Indian. If they are logistically limited to relying on other media, they should make an effort to seek out alternative publications that include different points of view from the mainstream, commercial media. In addition, journalists should make an effort to expand their range of Indian sources. Local think-tanks and academics could be called upon to provide context and explain cultural nuances. To avoid reliance on elite classes, reporters could seek to build networks of contacts among indigenous NGOs and people's organizations.

Overall, the findings in this study suggest that the European wire-service stories gave space to the claims of the proponents and opponents, while the overwhelming frame in the American coverage was one that mocked and belittled Indian opposition to a multinational company that millions of farmers and other concerned citizens saw as a threat to their livelihoods and culture. It is possible that this occurred because the wire stories were shorter and written in a hard-news format, while the American stories were more feature-oriented. Yet this does not fully account for the level of satire and marketing language employed in the American stories. It appears that the media are presenting serious challenges to globalization and consumerization as comical quibbles with American popular culture. Instead of Cold War rhetoric, we might now need to be aware that American marketing language will be adopted and employed to help cover up the sometimes violent effects of economic globalization.

References

Andersen, R. (1995). *Consumer Culture and TV Programming*. Boulder, CO: Westview Press.

Assadi, M. (1996). '"Chickens", "Greens", and "Ragi Balls": A Discourse on Kentucky Fried Chickens [*sic*] (KFCs)'. *Social Action*, 46/April–June: 179–91.

Bagchi, A. K. (1994). 'Globalising India: The Fantasy and the Reality'. *Social Scientist*, 22/7–8: 18–27.

Bagdikian, B. H. (1996). 'Brave New World Minus 400', in G. Gerbner, H. Mowlana, and H. Schiller (eds.), *Invisible Crises: What Conglomerate Control of Media Means for America and the World*. Boulder, CO: Westview Press, 7–14.

—— (1997). *Media Monopoly*. Boston: Beacon Press.

Bathla, S. (1998). *Women, Democracy and the Media: Cultural and Political Representation in the Indian Press*. New Delhi: Sage Publications.

Bhambhri, C. P. (1996). 'New Economic Policy: Indian State and Bureaucracy'. *Social Scientist*, 24/1–3: 44–58.

Bidwai, P. (1995). 'Making India Work—for the Rich'. *Multinational Monitor*, July–August: 9–14.

Brandon, K. (1995). 'Fast Food Runs Afowl of Indian Culture'. *Chicago Tribune* (Lexis), 12 October.

Brecher, J., and Costello, T. (1994). *Global Village or Global Pillage: Economic Reconstruction from the Bottom Up*. Boston, MA: South End Press.

Bruck, P. (1989). 'Strategies for Peace, Strategies for News Research'. *Journal of Communication*, 39/1: 108–29.

Burns, J. (1995a). 'Indian Nationalists Oppose Presence of U.S. Chains'. *New York Times*, 13 September: D5.

—— (1995b). 'New Delhi Journal: Fowl Fight over Flies Sends India into a Stew'. *New York Times*, 25 September: A4.

Chanda, A. K. (1995). 'Kentucky Fried Chicken Vows to Stay on in India'. Agence France-Presse (Lexis), 13 September.

'Closure of Kentucky Fried Chicken's Second Outlet Draws Nearer' (1995). Agence France-Presse (Lexis), 9 November.

Cohen, B. (1963). *The Press and Foreign Policy*. Princeton, NJ: Princeton University Press.

Dahlburg, J.-T., and Sharma, A. (1995). 'KFC Outlet Ordered Closed in India'. *Los Angeles Times* (Lexis), 7 November.

'Du Pont and Kentucky Fried Chicken under Attack in India' (1995). Deutsche Presse-Agentur (Lexis), 1 August.

Entman, R. (1991). 'Framing US Coverage of International News: Contrasts in Narratives of the KAL and Iran Air Incidents'. *Journal of Communication*, 41/4: 6–27.

—— (1993). 'Framing: Toward a Clarification of a Fractured Paradigm'. *Journal of Communication*, 43/4: 51–8.

Frederick, H. (1993). *Global Communication and International Relations*. Belmont, CA: Wadsworth Publishing.

Galtung, J., and Ruge, H. (1965). 'The Structure of Foreign News'. *Journal of Peace Research*, 2: 64–91.

Gamson, W. (1992). *Talking Politics*. Cambridge: Cambridge University Press.

Gamson, W., and Lasch, K. E. (1983). 'The Political Culture of Social Welfare Policy', in S. E. Spiro and E. Yaar (eds.), *Evaluating the Welfare State*. New York: Academic Press, 397–415.

Gamson, W. A., and Modigliani, A. (1989). 'Media Discourse and Public Opinion on Nuclear Power: A Constructivist Approach'. *American Journal of Sociology*, 95/1: 1–37.

Gans, H. (1979). *Deciding What's News*. New York: Pantheon.

Ghosh, S. (1996). *Mass Communication Today: In the Indian Context*. Calcutta: Profile Publishers.

Gitlin, T. (1980). *The Whole World is Watching: Mass Media and the Making and Unmaking of the New Left*. Berkeley, CA: University of California Press.

Goffman, E. (1974). *Frame Analysis: An Essay on the Organization of Experience*. Boston, MA: Northeastern University Press.

Goldsmith, R., Heath, D., and Smith, S. (1991). 'Commodity feminism'. *Critical Studies in Mass Communication*, 8: 333–52.

Greenwald, J. (1995). 'No Passage to India: American Firms Face an Anti-foreign Backlash in the World's Largest Democracy'. *Time*, 18 September: 91–2.

Hachten, W. A. (1992). *The World News Prism*. Ames, IA: Iowa State University Press.

Hall, S. (1975). 'Introduction', in A. C. H. Smith (ed.), *Paper Voices: The Popular Press and Social Change, 1935 to 1965*. Totowa, NJ: Rowan and Littlefield, 11–24.

Hall, S., Critcher, C., Jefferson, T., Clark, J., and Roberts, B. (1978). *Policing the Crisis: Muggings, the State, Law and Order*. Basingstoke: Macmillan Education Ltd.

Halliday, J., Jansen, S. C., and Schneider, J. (1992). 'Framing the Crisis in Eastern Europe', in M. Raboy and B. Dagenais (eds.), *Media, Crisis and Democracy: Mass Communication and the Disruption of the Social Order*. Newbury Park, CA: Sage, 63–78.

Hallin, D. (1987). 'Hegemony: The American News Media from Vietnam to El Salvador: A Study of Ideological Change and its Limits', in D. L. Paletz (ed.), *Political Communication Research: Approaches, Studies and Assessments.* Norwood, NJ: Ablex Publishing, 3–25.

—— (1992). 'The Passing of "High Modernism" of American Journalism'. *Journal of Communication,* 42/3: 14–25.

Hartley, J. (1982). *Understanding News.* New York: Methuen.

Herman, E., and Chomsky, N. (1988). *Manufacturing Consent: The Political Economy of the Mass Media.* New York: Praeger.

Herman, E., and McChesney, R. (1997). *The Global Media: New Missionaries of Global Capitalism.* London: Cassell.

Hess, S. (1996). *International News and Foreign Correspondents.* Washington, DC: Brookings Institution.

Hoge, J. F. (1997). 'Foreign News: Who Gives a Damn?'. *Columbia Journalism Review,* November–December: 48–52.

'Indian Activists Arrested for Wrecking Kentucky Fried Chicken Outlet' (1996). Agence France-Presse, (Lexis), 3 February.

'Indian Farmers Group to Target McDonalds Next' (1996). Agence France-Presse (Lexis), 1 February.

'Indian Farmers Ransack Kentucky Fried Chicken Shop' (1996). Reuters World Service (Lexis), 30 January.

'India's first KFC Outlet will be Driven Out, Activists Warn' (1995). Deutsche Presse-Agentur, 14 September.

Jensen. C. (1997). *20 Years of Censored News.* New York: Seven Stories Press.

'Kentucky Fried Chicken Protests in India' (1995). *The Ecologist,* November–December. World Wide Web. http://www.mcspotlight.org/media/press/kentucky.html.

'Kentucky Fried Fights Closure' (1995). Agence France-Presse (Lexis), 28 November.

McKibben, B. (1996). 'Chicken Sutra'. *Utne Reader,* September–October: 11–12.

Madhavan, N. (1995*a*). 'Indian Leftists Campaign against Pepsi'. Reuters World Service (Lexis), 15 October.

—— (1995*b*). 'Politicians Bait KFC, but Customers Aren't Chicken'. Reuters World Service (Lexis), 13 November.

Mander, J. (1996). 'The Dark Side of Globalization; What the Media are Missing.' *The Nation,* 15–22 July: 9–14.

Masmoudi, M. (1981). 'The New World Information Order', in J. Richstad and M. H. Anderson (eds.), *Crisis in International News: Policies and Prospects.* New York: Columbia University Press, 77–96.

Mukerjee, H. (1996). Foreword, in S. Ghosh, *Mass Communication Today: In the Indian Context.* Calcutta: Profile Publishers.

Narasimhan, S. (1996). 'Tandoori vs. Kentucky Fried'. *Multinational Monitor,* January–February: 8–9.

Pan, Z., and Kosicki, G. M. (1993). 'Framing Analysis: An Approach to News Discourse'. *Political Communication,* 10: 55–75.

Parthasarathy, R. (1989). *Journalism in India: From the Earliest Times to the Present Day.* New Delhi: Sterling Publishers Private Ltd.

Parthy, J. (1995). 'The Consequences of the New Economic Policies on the Peoples of India: A Sociological Appraisal'. *Sociological Bulletin*, 44/1: 11–32.

Patnaik, P. (1994). 'Notes on the Political Economy of Structural Adjustment'. *Social Scientist*, 22/9–12: 4–17.

—— (1996–7). 'Trade as a Mechanism of Economic Retrogression'. *Journal of Peasant Studies*, 24/1–2: 221–5.

Pereira, W., and Seabrook, J. (1994). *Global Parasites: 500 Years of Western Culture*. Bombay: Earthcare Books.

'Police Guard Pizza Hut Outlet in Indian City' (1996). Deutsche Presse-Agentur (Lexis), 10 June.

Righter, R. (1978). *Whose News? Politics, the Press and the Third World*. New York: Times Books.

Rosenblum, M. (1979). *Coups and Earthquakes: Reporting the News for America*. New York: Harper & Row.

—— (1993). *Who Stole the News?* New York: John Wiley & Sons.

Samath, F. (1995). 'Kentucky Fried Chicken Undeterred by Possible Bombay Ban'. Reuters (Lexis), 4 October.

Schiller, H. I. (1996). 'Information Deprivation in an Information-rich Society', in G. Gerbner, H. Mowlana, and H. Schiller (eds.), *Invisible Crises: What Conglomerate Control of Media Means for America and the World*. Boulder, CO: Westview Press, 15–26.

Schudson, M. (1995). *The Power of News*. Cambridge MA: Harvard University Press.

Seabrook, J. (1995). 'Cultural pollution'. *Third World Resurgence*, May: 38–9.

'Security for Foreign Firms' (1996). Agence France-Presse (Lexis), 31 January.

'Security to be Increased' (1996). Deutsche Presse-Agentur (Lexis), 1 February.

Shiva, V., Jaffri, A., and Bedi, G. (1997). *Ecological Costs of Economic Globalization: The Indian Experience*. New Delhi: Research Foundation for Science, Technology and Ecology.

Shoemaker, P., Danielian, L. H., and Brendlinger, N. (1991). 'Deviant Acts, Risky Business and U.S. Interests: The Newsworthiness of World Events'. *Journalism Quarterly*, 68/4: 781–95.

Singh, S. N. (1992). *Your Slip is Showing: Indian Press Today*. New Delhi: UBS Publishers.

Spaeth, A. (1995). 'Battle of the Chickens'. *Time*, 27 November: 23

Tehranian, M. (1993). 'Ethnic Discourse and the New World Dysorder: A Communitarian Perspective', in C. Roach (ed.), *Communication and Culture in War and Peace*. Newbury Park, CA: Sage, 192–215.

Tuchman, G. (1978). *Making News: A Study in the Construction of Reality*. New York: The Free Press.

Underwood, D. (1993). *When MBAs Rule the Newsroom: How Marketers and Managers are Reshaping Today's Media*. New York: Columbia University Press.

'Vandana Shiva on McDonald's, Exploitation and the Global Economy' (1996). RealAudio Interview. World Wide Web. http://www.mcspotlight.org/people.

Chapter 21

Media Literacy and the Commercialization of Culture

Norman Cowie

I. 'Hello? It's Free.'[1]

In the United States, proponents of media literacy have come to an uneasy consensus around the following definition: the ability to ' "access, analyze, evaluate and produce" media in a variety of forms' (Tyner 1998: 129). Although this definition has served as a rallying cry for media literacy advocates, there is a decided lack of agreement around its politics and practices. While some argue that media literacy must be seen as a critical response to commercial culture, and one that potentially integrates analysis, production, and activism, others argue against taking such positions and making such connections (see Lewis and Jhally 1998; Hobbs 1996, 1998). This raises a number of questions for people interested in promoting media literacy, and points to a long-standing struggle over definitions and strategies, which today might be articulated as follows: how should media literacy analyse and respond to the expansion and consolidation of commercial culture in the deregulatory, depoliticized, 'we won' era that is ours?

For many, the term 'media literacy' evokes a call to 'read and write media' with the new imaging tools of our image-driven age. But while most practitioners agree that media literacy should incorporate analysis and production, they hold a variety of opinions about the form and content of the analysis, the relative importance of production and what it should consist of, and how to teach a field that is premised on the integration of theory and practice. They also differ on other substantive issues, including where media literacy should be taught, who its constituency should be, what its goals are, how it should be funded, and whether it can be realized in the absence of struggles for democratic change within institutions of education and culture (see Tyner 1998; Hobbs 1998).

That these tensions are active and unresolved can be read in various ways. However, at the present moment there seems to be a preferred reading against which

The author would like to thank the following people for their comments on drafts of this article: Robin Andersen, Ron Clark, Steve Goodman, DeeDee Halleck, Anahid Kassabian, Cara Mertes, Branda Miller, Allan Siegel, and Anne Cowie Wilson.

[1] This section of this essay is drawn in part from an unpublished paper given at a 1996 Alliance for Community Media regional conference in Burlington, VT: 'Media Literacy: From the Creation of Critical Consumers to the Formation of (Radical) Political Subjects.' The title of this section is from a recent series of Disney ads promoting ABC's nightly television schedule.

others are measured, one that privileges pluralistic vigour, but only for approaches it deems pragmatic (Hobbs 1996, 1998). This reading fails to question its own relationship to the needs and demands of commercial culture, and considers unrealistic any approach that might seek to challenge prevailing relations of power and authority. Yet such concerns have played a formative role in the history of Western media education.

In the United Kingdom, long considered an international leader in the field, the shape of media education has been deeply influenced by progressive discourses on politics, culture, and education (see Masterman 1985; Alvarado and Boyd-Barrett 1992). Australian and Canadian educators have sought to build on this tradition, and popularize critical concepts drawn from media and cultural studies (see Duncan 1992). However, in the US, such discourses are routinely delegitimized, thanks in part to the relative absence of progressive perspectives in the mass media, and the dominance of ones that are thoroughly commercialized (see Bagdikian 1997). Colleagues in other countries take pains to point out that the largest media producing and exporting country in the world lags decades behind their own in terms of developing and implementing a coherent and critical approach to media education.

Of course the reasons for the USA's relative impoverishment and lack of national initiatives are complex. Commentators have pointed to a legacy of 'top down' efforts marked by little teacher involvement or popular support, local resistance to federal educational policies, and institutional prejudices against teaching about media, and teaching about media with media in schools (Tyner 1998; Kubey 1998; S. Goodman, personal communication, 10 October 1998). Others note that media literacy's failure to gain academic respectability has contributed to uneven and inadequate levels of funding, while a preoccupation with the media component of media education at the expense of the educational component has contributed to media literacy's ineffectiveness within schools (Desmond 1997, cited in Tyner 1998; Tyner 1998). Tyner further suggests that media literacy's protectionist past—the attempt to protect or inoculate children against purportedly negative media effects—and its avoidance of critical and materialist approaches to culture have constrained its pedagogical potential.

Media literacy in the United States is truly underdeveloped, with the limited definitions of its terms and practices serving to benefit the powerful and the privileged, including the media industries themselves.

Background

In a useful introductory article, media literacy proponents Kathleen Tyner and Deborah Leveranz (1992; see also Tyner 1998) point out that what we now call media literacy in the United States grew out of political pressures concerning the effects of television on social behaviour in the 1970s. In the wake of a 1972 surgeon-general's report, substantial federal funding was allocated for the development of 'critical viewing skills curricula' that were designed 'to protect children from television, as though it represented an electronic form of toxic waste' (Tyner 1998: 136).

At the same time, the introduction of media production in the classroom was spurred by the interests of video manufacturers (D. Halleck, personal communication, 15 October 1998), institutional priorities and equipment purchases, and the hiring of artists to teach media-making in the schools. This was accompanied by the elaboration of a new media arts field that brought together federal and foundation funding to support regional media arts centres and independent media production.

Tyner and Leveranz (1992) argue that the conservative 'back-to-basics' movement in schooling nearly killed media literacy efforts in the early 1980s, but that a variety of new initiatives developed in the 1990s, many linked to the school reform movement and its emphasis on interdisciplinary, democratic, student-centred and inquiry-based forms of learning. In their analysis of the field in 1992, Tyner and Leveranz note that the lack of consensus regarding the terms and practices of media literacy in the US stemmed from the enduring tensions between proponents of critical viewing and media production, and the absence of forums devoted to bridging these oft-separated domains. They suggest that media literacy could become a viable movement if it were to become a grassroots effort involving teachers and citizens, and embrace Len Masterman's (1985) goal of achieving democratic citizenship in our media culture by training people to become critically autonomous in relation to any media representation that they may encounter in the future.

Today, media literacy in the US is underfunded, conceptually diffuse and politically disorganized. There is limited independent financial support for the field; little federal, state, or foundation funding for school or community-based projects. There are few incentives for teachers outside the academic world to study or teach the media, or to explore innovative pedagogies using media. Splits among and between proponents of critical viewing and media production have become institutionalized in many educational settings, and continue to inform media literacy's ambivalent response to commercial culture. The dislocation of the 'media literacy movement' from progressive movements for education, culture, and social change, coupled with the failure of many progressives to link 'media issues' to their own struggles—such as the need for a democratic media system, or a concern with 'the politics of representation'—have made it difficult for media literacy practitioners to follow Masterman's (1985, 1990, 1997) lead and develop critical democratic approaches to media education.

Advocates of media literacy's critical viewing mission have typically come from the ranks of government, consumer groups, high schools, and academia, and their goals vary widely. While some continue to embrace protectionist ideologies, others seek to create discriminating consumers, or citizens who will be liberated from the seductions of commercial culture. Still others celebrate the pleasures of those seductions. With the exception of hard-core protectionists, however, most allow that media meanings are the result of an active process of encoding and decoding by producers and interpreters of media texts. While this has been a critical insight in moving away from reductive conceptions of media effects and audience subjectivities, proponents of critical viewing often focus their attention on the signifying operations of commercial texts, the savvy of individual decoders, and the plurality of their readings. In so doing, they risk neglecting the formative role played by 'institutional, cultural and economic conditions' (Lewis and Jhally 1998: 111) in limiting the production of textual meaning, and the rich history of experimental, alternative, community-based, and student-produced work that questions the logic and representations of commercial culture (see Boyle 1997; Goodman 1994; Halleck 1991; Juhasz 1996).

Advocates of media production have largely come out of a different tradition, that of the media arts centre movement and its ties to the cultural upheavals of the 1960s. Despite oft-expressed anxieties associated with teaching production, that 'practical work' (Hobbs 1998: 20) might be used to reproduce rather than critically engage mass culture, many media educators who teach production have shown that it can also be an empowering form of subjective expression and cultural resistance (see Goodman 1994). Others consider production to be an integral part of critical pedagogies that seek to cultivate student-centred, collaborative, and inquiry-based forms of learning (see Tally 1994; Goodman 1996a, b). Most educators who teach production within a media literacy framework agree that training students to deconstruct mass media texts and institutions is essential. However, they argue that the ability to construct and distribute alternative representations is equally vital, both as a way to envisage alternative and public cultures, and to extend agency to those who wish to produce media of their own. In this sense, many advocates of media production see their goal as not simply creating opportunities for creative self-expression, but laying the groundwork for the realization of a democratic culture.

Such a position is marginalized within dominant definitions of media literacy, many of which seem to imply (in relationship to television, for example) that we can change the channel or our viewing habits but not TV itself (see Goodman 1996a; Cowie 1995). Of course this reflects the interests of the media industries and their support for ideologies that dissuade us from developing and implementing critiques of commercial culture. In our society, where, as Robert McChesney (1997: 44) notes, 'the ideology of the market is a civic religion', the organization of culture by the interests of capital confronts us as a foregone conclusion, while critiques of the social effects of such organization remain largely invisible, except in so far as they can be appropriated by dominant interests. Critics have argued that the anticommunist crusades against organized labour and the political and cultural left after the Second World War, the steady commercialization of public expression, and the media's ability to normalize social inequalities and manufacture consent have played a decisive role in this process (Schiller 1989; Herman and Chomsky 1988).

Funding for projects that seek to challenge these assumptions has been shrinking, as commercial and conservative interests have effectively targeted efforts that seek to expand democratic conceptions of education, culture and citizenship. In the schools, splits between advocates of production and critical viewing are reinforced by a lack of resources and institutional prejudices that have traditionally defined production as vocational training, and dismiss media study as something tainted and banal. At a time when education has become synonymous with traditional curricula and a preoccupation with standards, many teachers lack the support they need to challenge such assumptions or to experiment with new initiatives. While they recognize the need to develop thoughtful responses to the ways that commercial culture educates their students, they are rarely encouraged to do so, or to develop curricular materials of their own.

Outside the schools, there are a variety of initiatives that seek to train people in media literacy, some of which are extremely interesting and successful.[2] Those that are most visible, however, are often supported by the media industries, and promote a paternalistic feel-good, family-friendly attitude towards mass culture. Few creatively interrogate the dialectic between how commercial culture constructs meaning and subject positions for interpretation, and how audiences negotiate meaning. Few actively train people in the technologies of media production, or work to create citizens or publics who will demand complex and compelling forms of non-commercial media. Although many practitioners agree that media literacy projects should ally themselves with public access centres which are mandated to provide production training and programming opportunities to community residents, few projects actually make this connection, and the idea of public access remains largely discredited in public discourse.

Without countervailing efforts, media literacy may too simply become known as a novel idea, or an appendage of the consciousness industry, uniquely suited to the needs of discriminating capitalists . . .

The American agenda

In the mid-1990s, ABC's *World News Tonight* ran an 'American Agenda' segment on media literacy. After a lengthy series of commercial breaks, Peter Jennings introduces the report:

We suggested that you watch all of those commercials because in the 'American Agenda' tonight we have put teaching teenagers to think critically about the commercials they see on television as our principal report. In Canadian and British schools children take mandatory classes in how to watch and dissect the media. In the United States the quest to demystify the subliminal messages of television commercials is just beginning. A lesson in media literacy from our agenda reporter . . .[3]

The segment follows Bob McCannon, director of the New Mexico Media Literacy

[2] Two notable projects that focus on integrating production and criticism include Appalshop in Whitesburg, Kentucky, and the Educational Video Center in New York City. For accounts of both projects, see Tyner (1998: 231–54). For an account of Educational Video Center's inquiry-based approach to video production and media analysis, see Tally (1995). For an account of EVC's portfolio review process, see Goodman and Tally (1993).

[3] A video clip of Peter Jennings' introduction is posted on the web site of the New Mexico Media Literacy Project (www.nmmlp.org/), under the heading 'Sample Deconstructions'. This is at least the second 'American Agenda' segment that ABC News has produced on media literacy. A segment that highlighted Canadian accomplishments was broadcast in the early 1990s (Duncan 1992).

Project, an initiative whose goal is 'to make New Mexico the most media literate state in the U.S.' (from its web site). In the segment, we see McCannon lecturing to students and teachers as he presents media literacy workshops that focus on the deconstruction of ads. We also hear from various people who comment on why media literacy is important.

Towards the end of the segment, a reporter interviews the state school super-intendent, and introduces him with the following voice-over:

Reporter: 'State education officials see the project as a way to make New Mexico's 350,000 school children smarter and more attractive to potential employers.'

NM state school superintendent: 'They help define that in terms of kids who are able to think more critically, to examine information, and separate fact from fiction. Media literacy helps us do that.'

Dissolve to: two Hispanic youths sitting on a couch watching TV. One of them is waving a remote and talking in a low voice: '. . . the way they use celebrities to promote their products . . .'

Reporter (voice-over): 'Those that have had training, like sixteen-year old Max Rodriguez, say that it has changed the way they see what they watch.'

Close-up Max: 'People think, ooh, it's backed by the sciences, it's got to be good.'

Reporter (voice-over, over image of Max watching TV): 'They are trying to develop skills useful for any consumer, or employee, or citizen; discernment, judgement, informed choice.'

This segment tells us much about the ways that media literacy is conceptualized by media corporations, and the ways that representations of media literacy are being integrated into hegemonic discourses. The news story suggests that media literacy *is* critical viewing, that its goal is to create discriminating consumers, and that it is best realized within a banking model of education (Freire 1981), where figures of social authority deposit knowledge into students and 'viewers like us'.

The segment also constructs a story in which the interests of media literacy are made equivalent to those of the state of New Mexico, corporate America, high-school students, and ABC's television audience. The viewers were addressed as 'Americans, consumers, employees, and citizens', different subject positions which they can all presumably recognize themselves in, and which allows them to 'make sense' of the story as viewers. However, part of the submerged sense of the story is the subordination of these subject positions to others who are apparently exempt from the needs of media literacy (such as business tycoons, politicians, teachers, or reporters), and the neutralization of social antagonisms which could contribute to democratic change through political struggle (such as the tension between the role of employee and employer, citizen and politician, student and teacher, or audience and reporter).

In addition to ratifying existing social hierarchies, the story suppresses differ-ences of race and ethnicity that are embedded within it. It suggests that media literacy is necessary for 'us', but it makes this appeal over the image of Max Rodriguez, a non-white subject against whom a seemingly conflict-free 'we' is constituted. And while the story suggests that the subject positions constructed are universally available and equivalent, it fails to acknowledge that racial and ethnic identities are unequally articulated in a society structured by racism and economic injustice.

So what media literacy skills are viewers told that 'we' need?

'Critical thinking', 'discernment', 'judgement', and 'informed choice'.

But how 'critical' would the state of New Mexico, and corporate America, like people to be? Presumably not too 'discerning'. At least not discerning enough to critique their construction of a unified public sphere, untroubled by hierarchies of power embedded in late capitalism. A project that taught such critical thinking might enable 'judgement' and 'informed choice' against such structures; it could well disrupt the effort to win the consent of 'consumers, employees or citizens' through 'a lesson in media literacy'.

Media literacy and cultural politics

Given this history, and the particularities of national circumstances, what can media literacy mean in a severely depoliticized culture such as the USA? Can it mean something more than accommodation to the terms of commercial culture? Clearly it already does. However, in the absence of struggle it is easy to imagine the emergence of a dominant definition that will march alongside a Disney footsoldier, a Time Warner division, or a News Corporation satellite armada.

But how can compelling, alternative visions of media literacy be developed and explored at a time when support for such visions can barely be heard? Perhaps one way would be to insist that media literacy become a part of a cultural politics that advocates change in the ways that the media are taught, conceptualized, and experienced in the United States, as a way to expand and deepen democratic discourses, and reconstruct public life (Giroux 1992). Such a progressive pedagogy would necessarily focus on analysis, production, and activism, and align itself with the interests of those who seek not simply to study culture, but to change it.

In the eyes of some media literacy proponents, such work is becoming increasingly necessary. We feel that media literacy cannot simply remain a defensive, reactive project, and that it must make an attempt to transform those institutions and practices that it seeks to critique. However, this position is rarely represented in the media literacy mainstream, and there is little organized support for media reform in the United States. As McChesney (1998: 28) notes, 'at present, media control and support for a truly democratic public media system are not on the political agenda. This is the immediate core problem—the problem that is nowhere being addressed, much less solved'.

How might a progressive media literacy play a role in addressing this problem? I think there are two interrelated struggles that we must focus on—ideology and organizing. Media literacy must be concerned with the commercialization of culture and the need for alternatives, but it can only do this work if it is defined in ways that support such concerns. Part of establishing such a definition will be the ability of media literacy advocates simultaneously to embrace progressive conceptions of education (in Henry Giroux's (1992: 10) terms, 'the engagement of a language of critique with a language of possibility'), cultural analysis (where media texts and institutions are situated within relations of power that are, as Justin Lewis and Sut Jhally (1998: 109) remind us, 'neither inevitable nor irreversible'), and media production (which can be, as Steve Goodman (1994: 8) suggests, a 'public space for authentic youth art, critical inquiry and dissent'). However, media literacy advocates must also work to build a diverse constituency that can articulate the need for a democratic communications system, and link their concerns with other democratic struggles for equality and social change.

Historically, media literacy has been defined as a practice of empowerment and critique, pitting rational, centred citizens against the machinations of the culture industries. However, Stuart Hall (1982, 1996) and others (Giroux 1992) suggest that such visions need to be complicated and reformulated. They argue that cultural theory must account for the complex pleasures that people derive from media consumption, the contradictory readings and subject positions that media interpretation engenders, and the ways that de-centred social subjects are positioned by and can reposition ideological discourses which seek to contain difference and oppositionality.

Such definitional shifts have important implications for considering media literacy as a form of cultural politics. For if media literacy abandons its rationalist, individualistic framework, how should it formulate its appeals? If it acknowledges the centrality of pleasure in mass media consumption, how should it formulate a politics that seeks to transform the commercial and ideological frameworks within which such pleasure is experienced? If it leaves behind essentialized identities, whether individual or collective, how should it think about agency and change? And here we might ask a question that links itself to McChesney's concern, and to Enzensberger's (1970) call to action some thirty years ago: how can the need for a democratic media system mobilize citizens to action?

The work of Chantal Mouffe (1988, 1993) on hegemony is suggestive in this regard. She argues that, although there is no reason to assume that citizens will become politically active in the absence of social antagonisms, such antagonisms are structured into the fabric of capitalist society, and today include the subjection of citizens to the commodification of social life, to mass culture's enforced codes of uniformity, and to the bureaucratic character of the state. Mouffe argues that social antagonisms can lead to political struggle when individuals and groups that have been structured in subordinate, essentialized, and commodified identities take up the claims of the liberal democratic tradition, demand that equal rights and individual liberties be democratically distributed, and develop a politics of solidarity based on the equivalence of this demand (Mouffe 1988).

Mouffe's arguments for radical democracy suggest that media literacy can become an effective form of cultural politics when its struggles against the culture industries can be made equivalent to 'the democratic demands found in a variety of other movements: women, workers, black, gay, ecological, as well as a variety of other "new social movements"' (Mouffe 1993: 70). She argues that such formulations are essential for addressing the complex way that social subjects are discursively positioned, and that these efforts will produce new collective identities and forms of democratic citizenship, and could 'provide the vehicle for the construction of a radical democratic hegemony' (Mouffw 1993: 73).

To me, Mouffe's framework implies that media literacy advocates who seek a democratic media system must work to organize people—to construct a new 'we' against which social differences can be deconstructed, and to develop new 'global and local' forms of 'critical solidarity' (Ferguson 1998: 17). To do so, we must attempt to link popular sentiments towards the uniformity of mass culture to progressive agendas and struggles, reorient the critical viewing tradition away from a protectionist stance towards a transformative one, insist on the inseparability of media education and educational change, and work closely with teachers. We must also resist the efforts of global media corporations to commodify the channels of public expression, contest their ability to secure consent for definitions that support prevailing relations of power, create new opportunities for citizens to use the media to represent their interests and publicize their demands, and strengthen public access and community-based media centres involved in outreach, education, production training, and distribution.

Henry Giroux (1992: 135) has argued that Mouffe's position implies 'a pedagogical task that has to be taken up and argued for by all cultural workers who take a particular political stand on the meaning and importance of radical democracy as a way of life'. As a cultural politics and a pedagogy of culture, media literacy would be uniquely positioned to take on such a task, which would be aimed at challenging the terms and conditions of commercial culture itself.

II. Media piracy manifesto[4]

Given the corporate configuration of the communications industries, and their everyday practice of shaping public discourse on social and political issues, a number of media artists have sought to take matters into their own hands, ripping corporate images and slogans out of their bedrocks of common sense and mass-mediated nature by theft and appropriation. I, too, have become a media pirate over the years, in an effort to inform, agitate, and entertain. Following many artist-educators, my ultimate goal is to foster a more media-literate and activist public, and to contribute to building a more democratic communications system.

However, to accomplish such a goal at a moment when the conditions that have given rise to the realization of such projects in the past are being dismantled, requires new strategies, alliances and coalitions. This dismantling includes, among

[4] This section of the paper is based on a talk and screening given at *Visible Evidence, V* at Northwestern University in 1997. By 'media piracy' I mean to invoke a low-budget, critical strategy of media appropriation and production which is often referred to as 'culture jamming' (see Dery 1993; Tyner 1998: 149–52). My argument is essentially pedagogical; I do not mean to suggest that original non-pirated work should not be created or supported. For other interpretations of media piracy as it relates to contemporary media, see the web sites of Radio Free Berkeley (www.freeradio.org), Paper Tiger Television (www.papertiger.org), Phil Patiris (www.moderntv.com), and Craig Baldwin's film *Sonic Outlaws*.

other things, renewed assaults on disenfranchised communities, drastic cuts in education and social services, the gutting of the field of independent media, and the drive to commercialize the Internet. At a time when the corporate voice, as Herb Schiller (1996: 36) exclaims, 'booms across the land', public dissent is muted and diffuse, while the spaces for dissent are shrinking and being absorbed by ever-expanding media conglomerates.

Meanwhile, within our media culture, we remain largely positioned as con-sumers, a site that celebrates the privatization of social experience, and where participatory democracy is always a spectacle. We live in a society permeated by ads, and corporate messages of all kinds, and, as we well know, these representations have consequences. Stuart Hall (1997) has suggested the need to denaturalize mass media representations, and 'render their ideological meanings uninhabitable'. Others stress the need to produce alternative representations, to provide emancipa-tory visions of the possible. Still others stress the need to build a democratic communications infrastructure, so that such representations might actually be seen.

Obviously, these are all critical areas for intervention within any media education project, and for me they all imply the need to integrate production within media education curricula.

Enter media piracy, an active practice of deconstruction and reconstruction, that's cheap, easy and fun! Media piracy sets out to take apart mass-media texts, and recombine their signifying elements (while sprinkling in a few new ones), all in the spirit of producing new and unexpected meanings and pleasures for readers who are already fluent in the modes of address of mass culture. Poised, as we all are, in the everyday effluent of consumer society, what could be a better place from which to dress down the images and slogans that threaten to drown us? And if one is blessed with the ability to operate a VCR, one can make repeated unauthorized tape withdrawals from the twenty-four-hour-a-day archives of television, straight from the image banks of our culture.

While some may shy away from media piracy because it seems too crass and vulgar, they should know that it comes with the best modernist and postmodern credentials. You can virtually take your pick: from Dadaism and Surrealism to Situationism and beyond. Moreover, it's a practice that has been perfected by the media industries themselves. For, as Martha Rosler (1987) reminds us, the culture industries have always used visual strategies perfected on the margins to re-energize the mainstream, so why not the other way round?

Can image-bank heists and manipulations achieve the goal of creating a more media-literate and activist public? Perhaps not. However, I think it's a good place to start for a variety of reasons. First, media piracy immediately calls into question issues of cultural ownership, First Amendment freedoms, and political authority, which are central concerns for any media literacy pedagogy. As Marita Sturken (1996: 2) notes, 'Television is the image without an original, for which the status of the copy is ultimately irrelevant'. Such sentiments coincide with those of media pirates, and are a healthy antidote to an academic obsession with copyright law that has discouraged the production of media appropriation critiques. Piracy can also raise questions about the relationship between the state and the culture industries. In an age when corporations routinely invoke the First Amendment to protect their right to sell anything to anyone in any place at any time, media piracy asks about protection for citizens who wish to speak back using the same languages. In an age of deregulation, when giant media transnationals are commercializing and privatizing public spaces everywhere, we may one day invoke the notion of media piracy to talk about the absence of protection for those of us who wish to speak at all.

Second, media piracy can be used to focus attention on media institutions and the imperatives of a market economy. Pirates typically pay attention to what they steal, and it doesn't take long for certain patterns to emerge, such as the frequency of ads, the redundancy of programmes, the replication of channels, and the commonality of stories. They *see* the invisibility of whiteness, class, and heterosexuality, and the symbolic annihilation of people of colour, lesbians and gays, the poor, and working people. These patterns bleed into the consciousness of pirates in ways that provoke questions and reflection. They take the invitation to 'follow the money' literally, tracing the effects of commodification as it courses through their veins. They walk the streets with new eyes, seeing circuits of meaning and pleasure tied to structures of privilege and power, where previously they only saw signs.

Third, media piracy can foster a sophisticated understanding of media rhetoric, in the deconstruction and reconstruction of mass-media texts. Pirates relish the opportunity to take apart these texts, and to reinvest their signifying elements with new meanings. They stalk corporate representations with relentless care, waiting patiently for just the right capitalist nugget to crack. They can think of nothing better than using the signifying arsenal of corporate America against itself, and calling attention to its ideological underwear. While you may wonder how smart such a strategy is in the present day—whether one can use the emperor's clothes to critique the emperor—these pirates take seriously the postmodernist invocation that the image is everything. They recognize that the field of the visible is deeply structured (Butler 1993), that politics is largely conducted in a symbolic realm (Jhally 1990), and that the struggle over cultural meaning is never secure (Hall 1982).

Finally, media piracy is uniquely positioned to exploit the cracks and fissures in the New World transnational order. Like the disembodied voice-overs that haunt our everyday media experiences, pirates can exist everywhere and nowhere simultaneously. In fact, one well-known pirate resides only in cyberspace, where s/he deploys cryptic greetings that can scramble Chrysler's global positioning system as it seeks to triangulate children and parents into loyal consumers. In the US, some pirates salivated at the convergence of the so-called conservative and digital revolutions, tipping their hats to technologies that made it easier and cheaper to skewer their prey at faster speeds and better resolutions. Personally, I've been investigating the next great technological wave of freedom, interactive television, which threatens to keep those with disposable incomes off the streets for ever.

In a provocative essay, Michael Nash has argued that video art is dead because the material and social conditions that gave rise to its funding have been destroyed, and because its effectiveness as televisual critique has been muted by television itself. He also suggests that media artists must seize the moment prior to the consolidation of our digital future to seek out new sources of funding and distribution in the competing multiplicity of commercial cable outlets, direct broadcast cable systems, and the digital servers of our interactive dreams. He asks that media artists be realistic and 'accept who television audiences are, how television distribution works, and how it will be radically altered in the next two decades' (Nash 1996: 394).

Despite the collapse of the media arts field, and most funding for video art, such pills are still hard to swallow. For as Gregg Bordowitz (1996: 177) reminds us, 'video is a medium, but television is a situation'. And here we must ask whether television's situation, as a culture industry, has changed dramatically since the 1960s, or will change in the foreseeable future. And in response, we might venture to say that the social conditions which politicized video art in the first place, and led a number of artists to practise image theft and appropriation, have not disappeared, and that, rather than 'getting realistic' about television, we should continue to work on ways to change its situation, and make *it* a democratic medium. Perhaps then, and only then, will some of us say that video art and alternative media have truly died.

Until that moment, media pirates will scavenge the borders of capitalist media, breaking up images and breaking down tales.

References

Alvarado, M., and Boyd-Barrett, O. (eds.) (1992). *Media Education*. London: British Film Institute.

Bagdikian, B. (1997). *The Media Monopoly*. Boston, MA: Beacon Press.

Bordowitz, G. (1996). 'Operative assumptions', in M. Renov and E. Suderburg (eds.), *Resolutions: Contemporary Video Practices*. Minneapolis: University of Minnesota Press, 173–84.

Boyle, D. (1997). *Subject to Change: Guerrilla Television Revisited*. New York: Oxford University Press.

Butler, J. (1993). 'Endangered/Endangering: Schematic Racism and White Paranoia', in R. Gooding-Williams (ed.), *Reading Rodney King; Reading Urban Uprising*. New York: Routledge, 15–22.

Cowie, N. (1995). 'The Future of Media Literacy in the Age of Corporate Sponsorship'. *Video and Learning*, summer–fall: 5–6.

Dery, M. (1993). *Culture Jamming*. Westfield, NJ: Open Magazine Pamphlet Series.

Desmond, R. (1997). 'Media Literacy in the Home: Acquisition vs. Deficit Models', in R. Kubey (ed.), *Media Literacy in the Information Age*. New Brunswick, NJ: Transaction, 323–43.

Duncan, B. (1992). 'Surviving Education's Desert Storms: Adventures in Media Literacy'. *English Quarterly*, 25/3–4: 14–18.

Enzensberger, H. M. (1970). 'Constituents of a Theory of the Media', in Enzensberger, *The Consciousness Industry*. New York: Seabury.

Ferguson, R. (1998). 'Global Interculturalism and the Dilemmas of Universalism: Teaching the Media after 2000'. *Mediacy*, 20/3.

Freire, P. (1981). *Pedagogy of the Oppressed.* New York: Continuum.

Giroux, H. (1992). *Border Crossings, Cultural Workers and the Politics of Education.* New York: Routledge.

Goodman, S. (1994). 'Reframing the Picture: Youth Media and Culture'. *Immediate Impact,* 2/2: 8.

——(1996a). 'Media Education: Culture and Community in the Classroom', in S. Cahan and Z. Kocur (eds.), *Contemporary Art and Multicultural Education.* New York: Routledge, 18–23.

——(1996b). 'Media, Technology and Educational Reform'. *Video and Learning, fall/winter:* 1–2.

Goodman, S., and Tally, B. (1993). 'The Tape's Great, but What did They Learn?'. *The Independent,* August–September: 30–3.

Hall, S. (1982). 'The Rediscovery of "ideology": Return of the Repressed in Media Studies', in M. Gurevitch, T. Bennett, J. Curran, and J. Woollacott (eds.), *Culture, Society and the Media.* London: Routledge, 56–90.

——(1996). 'The Meaning of New Times', in D. Morley and K. Chen (eds.), *Stuart Hall: Critical Dialogues in Cultural Studies.* London: Routledge, 223–37.

——(1997). 'Representation and the Media'. Videotaped lecture produced by the Media Education Foundation, Northampton, MA.

Halleck, D. (1991). 'Watch Out, Dick Tracy! Popular Video in the Wake of the Exxon Valdez', in C. Penley and A. Ross, (eds.), *Technoculture.* Minneapolis: University of Minnesota Press, 211–29.

Herman, E., and Chomsky, N. (1988). *Manufacturing Consent: The Political Economy of the Mass Media.* New York: Pantheon.

Hobbs, R. (1996). 'Media Literacy, Media Activism'. *Telemedium, The Journal of Media Literacy,* 42/3.

—— (1998). 'The Seven Great Debates in the Media Literacy Movement'. *Journal of Communication,* 48/1, 16–32.

Jhally, S. (1995). 'Image-based Culture: Advertising and Popular Culture', in G. Dines and J. Humez (eds.), *Gender, Race and Class in Media,* London: Sage 77–87.

Juhasz, A. (1996). *AIDS TV: Identity, Community and Alternative Video.* Durham, NC: Duke University Press.

Kubey, R. (1998). 'Obstacles to the Development of Media Education in the U.S.'. *Journal of Communication,* 48/1, 58–69.

Lewis, J. and Jhally, S. (1998). 'The Struggle over Media Literacy'. *Journal of Communication,* 48/1, 109–20.

Masterman, L. (1985). *Teaching the Media.* London: Comedia.

—— (1990). 'Media Education's Eighteen Principles'. *Strategies for Media Literacy,* 2/2: 8.

—— (1997). 'A Rationale for Media Education', in R. Kubey (ed.), *Media Literacy in the Information Age.* New Brunswick, NJ: Transaction, 15–68.

McChesney, R. (1997). *Corporate Media and the Threat to Democracy.* New York: Seven Stories Press.

—— (1998). 'The Consolidation of Corporate Media'. *Community Media Review*, 21/1: 28.

Mouffe, C. (1988). 'Hegemony and New Political Subjects: Toward a New Concept of Democracy' , in C. Nelson and L. Grossberg (eds.), *Marxism and the Interpretation of Culture.* Chicago: University of Illinois Press, 89–102.

—— (1993). 'Democratic Citizenship and the Political Community', in *The Return of the Political.* London: Verso, 60–73.

Nash, M. (1996). 'Vision after Television: Technocultural Convergence, Hypermedia, and the New Media Arts Field', in M. Renov and E. Suderburg (eds.), *Resolutions: Contemporary Video Practices.* Minneapolis: University of Minnesota Press, 382–99.

Rosler, M. (1987). ' "Video art," its audience, its public'. *The Independent,* December: 15.

Schiller, H. (1989). *Culture, Inc.: The Corporate Takeover of Public Expression.* New York: Oxford University Press.

—— (1996). 'Data Deprivation', in D. Hazen and L. Smith (eds.), *Media and Democracy.* San Francisco: Institute for Alternative Journalism.

Sturken, M. (1996). 'The Politics of Video Memory: Electronic Erasures and Inscriptions', in M. Renov and E. Suderburg (eds.), *Resolutions: Contemporary Video Practices.* Minneapolis: University of Minnesota Press, 1–12.

Tally, B. (1994). 'Inquiry Learning through Video Production: Lessons from the Educational Video Center'. *News from the Center for Children and Technology,* 2/5: 1–6.

Tyner, K. (1998). *Literacy in a Digital World.* Mahwah NJ: Erlbaum.

Tyner, K., and Leveranz, D. (1992). 'Inquiring Minds Want to Know: What is Media Literacy?'. *The Independent,* 16/7: 21–5.

Chapter 22

The Public Interest in the Twenty-First Century

Everett C. Parker

I N modern, industrialized societies, the communication systems are the lifelines of social, political, and economic well-being. Totalitarian leaders understand this and carefully restrict access to the printed press, broadcasting, and the World Wide Web, using all these media strictly for propaganda and sanitized entertainment. Even telephone calls are monitored.

But in a democracy, multiplicity of sources and diversity of views are vital to public life. In the USA we have largely delegated the tasks both of informing and of influencing the public to the mass media—particularly television. Therefore, mass communication is indissolubly married to the public interest. The social responsibilities of the media are very great, because the electronic communication entities are so pervasive and dominant a force in the life of the nation. There is no possibility that we will change our policy of having our regulated electronic media operated by private interests for profit; nor is there any pressure for such change. On the other hand, no other major nation has allowed its communications policies, as the USA has, to be shaped wholly by these same private entrepreneurs, for the sole purpose of wringing maximum profits from the communications system.

On the other hand, there is a long historical tradition and public policy, mandated by Congress, that these privileged private entrepreneurs are public trustees and are required to operate 'in the public interest, convenience, or necessity'.

A trustee supposedly is a person or organization of proven probity. Yet as far back as 1966, former Chief Justice Warren Burger, in his landmark decision giving standing to the public to intervene in affairs of the Federal Communications Commission, was so exasperated by the callous attitude of broadcasters to their public-interest responsibilities that he wrote: 'After nearly five decades of operation the broadcast industry does not seem to have grasped the simple fact that a broadcast license is a public trust subject to termination for breach of duty' (*Office of Communication*, 1966: 13).

The consciences of many of the powerful men who control broadcasting and other vital communications industries have not been sufficiently touched to this day! Examples abound.

Localism and universal service are basic principles of US communications policy, embodied in the Federal Communications Act of 1934. Congress, in legislating rules to govern telephone usage, mandated that telephone service should be made available to all who wanted it, regardless of remoteness of location or ability to pay.

Broadcasters were permitted to be private entrepreneurs, but Congress stressed the need for the widest possible dissemination of radio signals. Therefore, the Act provided for the creation of radio stations in as many local communities as possible, and in larger towns and cities a multiplicity of stations, each operated by an independent licensee. No operator was permitted to hold two or more licences in the same community.

As frequency modulation (FM) came into general use, a single broadcaster was allowed both an AM and an FM radio station, and, later still, a television station in a single community. Total station ownership country-wide was limited by the FCC, first to five each of AM, FM, and TV stations; then to seven; then to twelve. In recent years, prodded by both broadcasters and Congressional regulatory committees, the FCC has virtually abandoned ownership restrictions for radio stations. Individual corporations are permitted to own as many radio stations as they can borrow money to buy, running into hundreds of licences. The largest radio chains, such as Infinity, owned by CBS, are able to buy up enough stations in a single community to dominate the radio market there. (In New York City, CBS/ Infinity owns both the bellwether twenty-four-hour news stations, WCBS and WINS.)

On 1 March 1999, officials from thirty radio stations in nine states filed comments with the Federal Communications Commission objecting to pending regulations that would require them to continue to provide equal employment opportunities for minorities and women. Diversity in a station's workforce is expected to encourage diversity in programming, and thus better service to the community of licence. Not so, say these officials, in part because so few of their programmes originate locally. Reported local origination of programmes ranged from a low of 4 per cent to 6 per cent, 9 per cent, 10 per cent, and for one station, 15 per cent–20 per cent.[1]

Television viewers fare no better as far as local control is concerned. The FCC has permitted multiple television station owners to acquire as many stations as they can finance, up to the point where their potential coverage equals 25 per cent of the total television audience. All four of the full-time television networks and several other corporate multiple station owners have reached this quasi-monopolistic status. Even at market levels lower than the 25 per cent of audience cap, absentee corporate ownership of commercial television stations is the rule.

Up to September 1999, the FCC has held to its rule that no licensee may own more than one TV station in a community. However, the stronger operators have got round this rule by creating what are called local market agreements (LMAs). Under an LMA, the most successful station in a community becomes partners with one or more of its weaker competitors, sharing sales, marketing and programming facilities. This practice further erodes diversity in local programming. Objections to it have led to an industry effort to have Congress, by legislation, or the FCC, by

---

[1] Comments of Haley, Bader & Potts before the Federal Communications Commission in the Matter of Review of the Commission's Broadcast and Cable Equal Employment Opportunity Rules and Policies and Termination of the EEo Streamlining Proceeding, MM Docket No. 98–204, 1 March 1999.

rule-making, to 'grandfather' at least current LMAs (that is, to allow existing functions to continue).

Late in 1999 the FCC bowed to pressure from the powerful broadcasting lobby and permitted duopoly ownership of television stations in single markets. The dominant corporations, such as the networks, that own stations in multiple communities have moved quickly to acquire second stations in their communities of licence. This absentee ownership/monopoly problem grows ever more complicated—and dangerous—as new communications technologies shoulder aside the traditional media, and both old and new strive mightily for maximum control of the market.

For more than thirty years ABC, CBS, and NBC enjoyed a virtual monopoly of the television audience; then were sent reeling by competition from cable TV and later from the upstart Fox network. Now all four networks are faced with steadily eroding audiences, plus the heavy costs of converting to digital TV. In their efforts to hold on to viewers and advertising dollars, the four networks have allowed programme costs to skyrocket far above what they can afford to pay. The three traditional networks allowed Fox to outbid them at a heretofore unheard-of figure for the National Football League Sunday games, counting on the fact that the prodigious outlay would put Fox (and its parent News Corporation) deeply in debt. The three realized their miscalculation when Fox began raiding their affiliated stations. Armed with the most popular sports programming available, Fox easily persuaded major multiple station owners in the nation's most populous markets to switch their network affiliations. In a significant number of markets ABC, CBS, and NBC lost affiliated VHF stations and were forced to switch to ultra-high-frequency outlets.

Entertainment programming quickly followed sport into the cost stratosphere. When *Seinfeld* left the air, NBC agreed to pay $13 million an episode to keep ER in an effort to retain its audience lead in network nighttime programming.

The networks are still indispensable to advertisers who must have access to a mass audience for their products, the network audience still being significantly larger than that garnered by all the other electronic media combined. Nevertheless, nothing tried so far has stopped the erosion of network audiences, and there is genuine fear about the future of the services. Therefore, the industry, following its time-honoured custom, is turning to its benevolent Uncle Sam for relief. A forceful campaign is afoot to get the federal government to sanction ownership of multiple television stations by a single licensee covering up to 50 per cent of the nation's television homes, in addition to permitting ownership of more than one station in a community of licence. Should this effort succeed, only a handful of the most affluent broadcasting corporations could finance the jump from the present 25 per cent cap to 50 per cent, and thus to control of virtually all over-the-air television programming. The reach for the 50 per cent cap immediately follows Congress's greatest ever giveaway of valuable public resources, the spectrum needed so that current broadcasters may introduce digital TV. Congress has condoned the assignment of a second frequency to each commercial television licensee (and also to each current public broadcasting station) to produce high-definition digital programming, and to no one else, thus for now cutting out all other individuals and entities with the will and the resources to enter the broadcasting universe of the future.[2] This universe will not be the high-definition television (HDTV) promised years ago. Early on broadcasters complained to the FCC about the costs of producing true HDTV. The Commission, also worried about the spectrum width needed for an analogue HDTV signal, reduced both signal quality and band width requirements to fit something called Advanced TV. But scientists persevered. Today a digital signal of the highest necessary quality can be compressed into the band width of a standard analogue station; so the second frequency assignment to each licensee is smaller than expected. As a consequence, if there is continuous, unyielding public pressure, the FCC may be able to find room in the spectrum for new digital licensees.

The networks and some other broadcasters have already built digital transmitters and begun broadcasting programmes in a few of the larger markets; but penetration of the new service may be slow. Current costs of sets—$3,000 to $12,000 in 1999—are a deterrent to widespread sales. But between 20,000 and 25,000 have been reported sold, about the same number as went into bars and pubs in the earliest days of colour TV. Set prices will come down as demand increases. Industry analysts believe it should not be hard to switch a nation that already spends $80 billion a year on consumer electronics to a really desirable new TV service by 2006. That is a deadline year mandated by Congress, when 85 per cent of US households must have access to over-the-air digital television service.[3] Set manufacturers are betting they can meet the deadline, but at the moment there are potential roadblocks, not the least of which is the slowness with which broadcasting companies are getting their digital stations up and operating. They are reluctant to lay out the necessary development costs, just as they were when radio was king and they were converting to television. And they are wrestling with real technical problems, such as mastering new equipment and even building new plants in communities that are loath to sanction more towers.

In a lapse of oversight (that is, regulatory) responsibility, the FCC has failed to adopt an established single technical standard for digital broadcasting. As a consequence, individual broadcasting corporations have adopted differing technologies with the video signal ranging from 750 to over 1,000 lines an inch. The pictures being shown may not be as vivid and the sound as crystal clear as true HDTV, but they are a significant improvement over what we see now from our analogue stations.

All the broadcasters will break up their new frequencies into four or five channels, a mini cable system. One channel will be devoted to today's type of

[2] This strictly political decision will work particular hardship on women and minorities who are now woefully underrepresented as owners of television and radio stations.

[3] An important part of the digital TV deal between Congress and the broadcasters was that all current licensees would be wholly digital by 2006, and would turn back to the government their analogue assignments valued at $4 billion. The FCC would then sell off this spectrum to help reduce the then current deficit. As soon as the new digital spectrum assignments were made, industry spokesmen made it clear to Congress that the economics of the switch to digital were such that the analogue stations would still be needed and the spectrum could not be returned then, if ever, a stand that public groups had predicted would be taken.

programming. The rest will be used for data transfer, pay-per-view, or other forms of subscriber supported programming.[4]

Having received their spectrum assignments, valued in billions of dollars, broadcasters are resisting efforts of the FCC to have them adopt and adhere to public interest responsibilities in their digital programming. Public groups strenuously demanded public-interest guarantees to the extent that a Governmental Advisory Commission was formed to recommend specific public interest requirements to the FCC. Leslie Moonvees of CBS was named chair and a majority of the members were drawn from the broadcasting industry, with only two or three from the public sector. Not surprisingly, the recommendations were minimal and cambric-tea-weak, and have been ignored.

In the interests of brevity, I have limited to broadcasting examples of how the public interest is disregarded—even trampled on—by our powerful communications entities. They could easily have been drawn from any, or all, of the electronic or print technologies. Every assigned broadcasting spectrum creates a monopoly on that frequency. Every cable system is a monopoly. So is every local telephone exchange for residential and small business users. National and regional newspaper chains constrict the abilities of local communities to exchange ideas and deal with local issues. These conditions pose fundamental ethical policy questions for our elected representatives, governmental regulators, and members of the public.

Central to the public interest is the hand-in-glove relationship between the Congress and the communications industries. Years before they passed the Federal Communications Act of 1934 members of Congress realized how helpful it might be to re-election efforts if they could frequently speak and be heard over local radio stations. No reporter to filter ideas and statements through; no editor to slant stories or editorial writer to criticize; just a speaker-to-audience relationship! Soon station licensees and their members of Congress were bosom buddies. Today, even more than in the past, each sees that the other gets what he or she wants. A vast percentage of campaign expenditure goes to broadcasting and cable companies, a great boon to their profitability. There is a general belief that no one can be elected without widespread media exposure, preferably on television. Conversely, electronic outlets favour incumbents and contribute to their campaigns. Why chance an outsider, when the incumbent is your staunch friend and protector?

Equal to political bias in favour of industry as a threat to US democratic institutions is the concentration of control of mass communications in a handful of all-powerful corporations. Since the mid-1980s, mergers and acquisitions have been a way of life for American business—especially the Fortune Five Hundred companies—and the government has done little to discourage them, using the anti trust laws. For communications, the way was opened for unlimited consolidation by a law that, on paper, was meant to discourage it. The Telecommunications Act of

---

[4] Congress has ordered that a 2 per cent tax be levied on these so-called ancillary services. Broadcasters have strongly opposed such a tax, but seem to be willing to compromise, since the National Association of Broadcasters has proposed that there be at least a two-year fee-free period to let the pay channels get started.

1996 was supposed to open local telephone servers, such as the Bell operating companies, to competition while giving them the opportunity to get into long-distance; encourage cable-TV and telephone companies to get into each other's businesses; and provide consumers with enhanced services at lowered costs.

It has done none of the foregoing. Long-distance rates have risen steadily. No local telephone company has opened itself to competition. Instead, the regional Bell telephone companies have been merging, Bell Atlantic with NYNEX and GTE for example, creating a monopoly in the Middle Atlantic and New England states, among the nation's heaviest telephone users. Similar consolidation of the former REBOCS has taken place in the Middle West and on the West Coast.

The 1996 Act also lifted caps on premium cable channels, effective in March 1999, leaving operators free to charge subscribers what they will.

Monopoly is the game for mass communication. Even before the 1996 Act was promulgated, corporate consolidation of programme control was in full swing. During the Reagan administration General Electric was allowed to reacquire NBC, of which Herbert Hoover forced the company to divest itself. By 1995, Disney had acquired ABC, giving it control of films (including TV programme production), broadcasting, newspapers, publishing, and its burgeoning theme parks, among other properties. Fox network weighed in with a movie studio, cable properties, newspapers, international satellite-to-home broadcasting, and so on. Westinghouse bought CBS and Infinity Radio, which in turn put the venerable electric company and its ambitious chairman out of business. Time Warner is a major player in print, movies, cable, and video (HBO), everything but over-the-air broadcasting.

In 1999, AT&T acquired TCI, number two in size but the most aggressive cable company. Object: sell local telephone service to TCI's millions of subscribers. Large cable operators are buying out their fellows. Regional telcos are buying into cable. Cable companies have assiduously acquired regional sports franchises covering basketball, hockey, baseball, and boxing to the point where they nearly have the monopoly they are seeking. Cable is preparing to offer Internet access to its subscribers. TCI already offers a successful entry system, @Home.

All these mergers and acquisitions and the new services being prepared or already being offered to consumers require enormous capital outlays. In 1999 AT&T announced the largest capital borrowing in history. Companies such as Time Warner and Viacom are labouring under debt loads they may never be able to shed, and there is speculation that Rupert Murdoch's News Corporation may be in the same circumstances.

New communications services are aimed only at individuals that can pay for them. And little, if any, attention is being paid to the responsibilities of the corporate gatekeepers to meet the needs of consumers for vital communications services, such as news and information, regardless of profitability. The Supreme Court has held, unanimously, that the First Amendment rights of the public to access to the media and receipt of vital information come before those of media owners (*Red Lion Broadcasting v. Federal Communications Commission,* 1969). But today's media moguls, almost without exception, are reaching out to control not only the means of production and distribution of content, but also what content we are allowed to see and hear.

Small wonder that Leo Bogart (1996: 20), a powerful champion of the First Amendment and citizens' rights under it should ask: '[I]s profitability the only proper measure of a firm that deals in the facts that shape history and the fictions that represent a nation's collective dream?'

The danger of communications monopolies and the practices that stem from them has also caught the attention of Rep. Edward J. Markey, ranking Democrat on the House Subcommittee on Telecommunications and Finance. In a 21 January 1999 letter to William E. Kennard, chairman of the FCC, he wrote: 'It is with growing concern that I note the emergence of broadband networks—most notably in the cable industry—that are designed to reintroduce bottlenecks to competition, choice and innovation. Many cable companies are bundling proprietary Internet content—a WWW channel such as @Home—with their broadband transmission facilities. The end result of such an offering may be to allow the owners of that transmission facility to significantly alter the nature of the Internet experience for consumers and businesses.'

Similar bottlenecks also exist in monopoly control of sport and entertainment programmes; restricting of sources of news and information; sale of political time to those who can most afford to pay for it; and failure to cover significant segments of society and broad divergence of views. Especially unfortunate is the inability of the public to prise open the secrecy that surrounds the policies and practices of the communications industries. Our main source of news is not over-anxious to lay bare its own foibles.

It would be unpropitious for the future of our society if electronic media monopolies were able to control what pills or toothpaste we should use or never hear of. But this is our basic communications system that we most depend on to set tastes and sell products. Above all, it must report events, accurately and in detail; articulate ideas; present conflicting points of view; and expose politicians to the electorate, if the USA is to remain a working democracy.

Our society is constantly becoming more complex. The range of information needed for surviving is burgeoning. With most new communications technologies and facilities also becoming more complex and expensive than the older forms, we are faced with a pressing ethical question: how can we keep the gap between the information-rich and the information-poor from widening perilously as we move into the digital era and cyberspace?

The American people can get whatever it wants when it sets its mind to it, especially when its conscience is awakened to a need whose fulfilment is for the good of all. Witness the growth and coming to power of the environmental movement; the cessation of nuclear power plant construction; motor car safety trends; the almost universal commitment to Social Security and Medicare/Medicaid. There is a much broader understanding than some politicians like to contemplate that government exists to serve the electorate, not to control our lives. Given a mandate and a clear directive, with no meddling by allied political and special-interest forces, government can protect wide public interests well. The federal government has been successful in dealing with monopolies in the past; it can be so now.

The Federal Communications Commission is in place to wrestle with this problem in communications. It is not there to put any corporation or individual out of business or narrow the scope of any medium. It can rightfully be the arbiter between greed for the highest possible profits and the loftier necessity for communications entities to respect the First Amendment rights of others than themselves, to give voice to the whole public, and to operate in such a manner that their services shall be universally available and affordable.

Such an end can be achieved only through a determined citizen movement with clear objectives and the will to see them carried out. The people of Virginia by vigorous public outcry recently prevented New York City from dumping garbage in their state. The same dogged action can prevent the dumping of garbage at exorbitant fees from our television sets and computers.

Any US reader of this book can initiate a citizen movement on behalf of public-interest issues in his or her community, or to foster fair employment opportunities for minorities and women in communications entities. Legal power is available because of Chief Justice Burger's decision, cited earlier, giving standing to the public to participate in the activities of the FCC. Citizens have the same right to participate in decision making by their state regulatory agencies.

Citizen groups probably will not have the close personal relationships that may exist between their representatives in Congress and the suave Washington lobbyists from the media with their deep pockets, but they have a potent weapon, nevertheless—numbers. A well-thought-out presentation about communications needs and policies, made to a senator or representative in her or his local office by an impressive delegation representing local churches, civic groups, educational interests, civil rights, labour, and business organizations will receive respectful attention.

Local organizations can also get advice from experienced organizations that are veteran defenders of the public interest in communications: the Washington public interest legal consultants, Media Access Project and Minority Media and Telecommunications Council, Office of Communication, Inc. of the United Church of Christ, the Communications Commission of the National Council of the Churches of Christ in the USA, American Civil Liberties Union, National Latino Telecommunications Task Force, Puerto Rican Legal Defense and Education Fund, National Association for the Advancement of Colored People, and the Women's Institute for Freedom of the Press are a few of the bodies that are ready to help.

References

Bogart, L. (1996). 'What does it all Mean?' *Media Studies Journal*, 10/2–3: 15–27.

Federal Communications Commission in the Matter of Review of the Commission's Broadcast and Cable Equal Employment Opportunity Rules and Policies and Termination of the EEo Streamlining Proceeding, MM Docket No. 98–204, (1 March 1999).

Office of Communication of the United Church of Christ v. Federal Communications Commission, US Court of Appeals, DC Circuit, No. 19,409 (25 March 1966).

Red Lion Broadcasting Co. v. FCC, 395 US 367, 89 S. Ct. 1794, 23 L.Ed.2nd 371, United States Supreme Court (1969).

About the authors

Craig Allen is an associate professor and the coordinator of broadcast news at the Walter Cronkite School of Journalism and Telecommunication at Arizona State University. He has written extensively on mass media history and television news and was one of the first to expose the role of consultants and applied research in the news process. Prior to receiving his Ph.D. at Ohio University in 1989, he was a reporter on the *Oregon Journal* in Portland and a news director and producer at television stations in Denver, Colorado Springs, and Spokane.

Robin Andersen is associate professor in the Department of Communication and Media Studies and director of the Peace and Justice Program at Fordham University, New York. She is the author of *Consumer Culture and TV Programming*, and her numerous articles appear in books and scholarly journals such as *The Media Reader; Journalism and Popular Culture; Media Culture and Society; Communication Ethics and Universal Values; Latin American Perspectives; Social Text; EXTRA!*; and *The Humanist*. Her current research includes the environmental impact of consumer culture.

Constance Ledoux Book is an assistant professor of Mass Communication at Meredith College. Her research interests include cable television policy, the implementation of new technology and consumer response, and she is currently involved in several research projects related to the transition to digital television in the US.

Margaret Cassidy is an assistant professor of Communications at Adelphi University. Her research and writing focus on the use of media in K-12 education; she is currently working on a book that examines the history of educational media in American public education, and working with elementary and secondary schools on technology evaluation and staff development activities.

Norman Cowie is an assistant professor of Communication and Media Studies at Fordham University, New York, an independent producer, and a board member of Manhattan Neighborhood Network, Manhattan's public access cable TV facility. He was co-director of *Signal to Noise: Life with Television*, a three-hour media education series produced for PBS in 1996. From 1994 to 1997 he was the director of the Five College Summer Institute in Media Literacy in Amherst, MA, a teacher-training project that sought to integrate concepts from media studies with video production and issues of school reform.

Robert M. Entman is professor of Communication at North Carolina State University. He is currently completing books on media and race relations and media and US defence policy; and is the author of *Democracy Without Citizens*.

Katherine Fry is an assistant professor in the Department of Television and Radio at Brooklyn College of the City University of New York. Her research interests are in news and advertising analysis, and in media and cultural geography. Recent publications include 'The Case of Germany (ALMANAC), A Cultural Geography of Lake Wobegon' (*Howard Journal of Communication*) and a chapter entitled, 'Regional Consumer Magazines and the Ideal White Reader: Constructing and Retaining Geography as Text (The American Magazine: Research Perspectives and Prospects)'. She is currently working on a book about natural disaster news and the Midwest heartland.

Delicia Harvey is a public relations professional for the Alley Theatre in Houston.

Sut Jhally is professor of Communication at the University of Massachusetts at Amherst, and founder and executive director of the Media Education Foundation. He has written broadly on popular culture and advertising and is author of *The Codes of Advertising*, co-author of *Enlightened Racism*, and producer and director of the videotapes *Dreamworlds II: Desire/Sex/Power in Music Video* and *Advertising and the End of the World*.

Paul Lippert is professor of Communication at East Stroudsburg University. He is currently working on a book about Walter Ong's orality–literacy theory and mass communication.

Matthew P. McAllister is an associate professor of Communication Studies at Virginia Tech. His research interests include advertising criticism, popular culture, and economics of the mass media. He is the author of *The Commercialization of American Culture: New Advertising, Control and Democracy*, which was named an Outstanding Academic Book of 1996 by *Choice* magazine. He has also published in *Critical Studies in Mass Communication*, *Journal of Communication*, *Journal of Popular Culture*, and *Journal of Popular Film and Television*.

Robert W. McChesney is a research associate professor in the Institute of Communications Research and the Graduate School of Library and Information Science at the University of Illinois at Urbana-Champaign. He is the author of *Rich Media, Poor Democracy: Communication Politics in Dubious Times*; *Global Media: The Missionaries of Global Capitalism* (with Edward S. Herman); *Corporate Media and the Threat to Democracy*; and *Telecommunications, Mass Media, and Democracy: The Battle for the Control of U.S. Broadcasting, 1928–1935*; and is editor of *Last Rights: Revisiting Four Theories of the Press* (with John C. Nerone); *Ruthless Criticism: New Perspectives in U.S. Communication History* (with William L. Solomon); and *Capitalism and the Information Age: The Political Economy of the Global Communication Revolution* (with Ellen Meiksins Wood).

Marshall McLuhan was professor of English and director of the Centre for Culture and Technology (now known as the McLuhan Center) at the University of Toronto, as well as holding Fordham University's Schweitzer Chair in the Humanities 1967–8. He is the author of *The Mechanical Bride*; *The Gutenberg Galaxy*; *Understanding Media*; *The Medium is the Message* (with Quentin Fiore); *Through the Vanishing Point* (with Harley Parker); *War and Peace in the Global Village* (with Quentin Fiore); *The Interior Landscape*; *From Cliché to Archetype* (with Wilfred Watson); *Culture is our Business*; *Take Today: The Executive as Dropout* (with Barrington

Nevitt); *Laws of the Media* (with Eric McLuhan); and *The Global Village* (with Bruce Powers). His writings have also been collected in *Marshall McLuhan: The Man and his Message* (edited by George Sanderson and Frank Macdonald); *Media Research: Technology, Art, Communication* (edited by Michel A. Moos); and *The Essential McLuhan* (edited by Eric McLuhan and Frank Zingrone).

Nancy Morris teaches in the Department of Broadcasting, Telecommunications and Mass Media at Temple University. She is the author of *Puerto Rico: Culture, Politics, and Identity*.

Rev. Everett C. Parker is a senior research associate in the Donald McGannon Communication Research Center, which he founded in 1984, and adjunct professor of Communication and Media Studies at Fordham University. From 1954 to 1983, he was director of the Office of Communication of the United Church of Christ (UCC), through which he conducted an advocacy programme on behalf of minorities, women, and consumers to ensure access to broadcasting and other electronic media, and to make the media accountable to the public. This effort resulted in several landmark federal court decisions that guaranteed standing to the public before federal regulatory agencies, protected access and employment rights, and caused the Federal Communications Commission to issue fair employment practices rules. He is the author of numerous books and articles on communications subjects, and producer–director of numerous prize-winning television series, including *Off to Adventure*, the first religious TV programme for children; *Tangled World*; and on PBS *Six American Families*.

Neil Postman is University Professor, the Paulette Goddard Professor of Media Ecology, and chair of the Department of Culture and Communication at New York University. He is the author of twenty books including *Teaching as a Subversive Activity* (with Charles Weingartner); *Crazy Talk, Stupid Talk*; *Teaching as a Conserving Activity*; *The Disappearance of Childhood*; *Amusing Ourselves to Death*; *Conscientious Objections*; *Technopoly*; and *The End of Education*.

Anthony Smith is president of Magdalen College, Oxford, a former director of the British Film Institute, and a former board director of Great Britain's Channel Four Television. He is the author of *The Shadow in the Cave*; *The Newspaper: An International History*; *Goodbye Gutenberg*; *The Geopolitics of Information*; *Books to Bytes: Knowledge and Information in the Postmodern Era*; *The Age of the Behemoths*; *The Oxford International History of Television*; and *Software for the Self*.

Lance Strate is associate professor and chair of Fordham University's Department of Communication and Media Studies. He is the editor (with Ron Jacobson and Stephanie B. Gibson) of *Communication and Cyberspace: Social Interaction in an Electronic Environment*. He is currently working on a book entitled *Understanding Media Ecology* and on two anthologies, *Cybertheory: The Ecology of Digital Media* (with Susan Barnes); and *The Legacy of McLuhan* (with Edward Wachtel). He is the supervisory editor of the Media Ecology Book Series for Hampton Press (Cresskill, NJ), founding president of the Media Ecology Association, and a past president (1998–9) of the New York State Communication Association.

Lauren R. Tucker is an associate professor of Mass Communication at the University of South Carolina.

Joseph Turow is professor of Communication at the Annenberg School for Communication, University of Pennsylvania. He is the author of *Media Today: An Introduction to Mass Communication*; *Breaking Up America: Advertising and the New Media World*; *Media Systems in Society: Understanding Industries, Strategies, and Power*; *Playing Doctor: Television, Storytelling, and Medical Power*; *Media Industries: The Production of News And Entertainment*; *Entertainment, Education, and the Hard Sell: Three Decades of Network Children's Television*; and *Getting Books to Children: An Exploration of Publisher–Market Relations*.

Melissa A. Wall is a doctoral candidate in the School of Communications at the University of Washington. Her international media work includes conducting research on a township magazine in Zimbabwe and training journalists in Ethiopia. Her published research focuses on Western media coverage of non-Western countries, while her dissertation examines the emerging transnational NGO communications sphere.

Dan Weisberg is an associate editor of *Beyond Computing* magazine.

Index

Note: References to foot notes are indicated by the letter 'n' after the page number.

A. C. Nielsen Company 42–3
ABC 104, 105, 110, 118–19
   news 12, 14, 314
   sport 64, 108, 111–12, 115, 326
advertising 1, 5, 8, 111–12, 190
   agencies 181, 240
   American 40–6
   development of 28–9, 31–2
   exoticism in 173–5, 176, 177
   exploitation of nature
      imagery 158–64
   skin colour in 214–23
   spending on 104–6
AFA (American Family
   Association) 225, 227
AFL-CIO trade union
   federation 257
Agence France-Presse 295– 303
   passim
Akre, Jane 11, 12
Allen, Craig 84–99
Altman, Robert 206
American Association of
   School Administrators 273
American Civil Liberties Union
   227, 331
American Management
   Association 193
American Society of
   Newspaper Editors 8
Amnesty International 168
Andersen, Robin 1–19, 147,
   158–70, 250–63
AOL (America Online) 15–18
Apples for the Students 271
AR&R (Audience Research and
   Development) 85–6, 90,
   94, 96
ARI (Audience Research Inc.)
   41–2
Aronson, Steven 205
Assadi, M. 291
Associated Press 293
Association for Curriculum and
   Supervision Development
   273

AT&T 19, 60, 67, 68, 69, 329
Atkinson Research 95
Australian media 94

Bagchi, Amuja Kumar 296,
   303
Bagdikian, Ben 102
Barber, Benjamin 7
Barrett, Edward 86
Barrett, Marvin 87
Battista, Tom 95
Baudrillard, J. 209, 210
Bayer, Sam 191
BBC 51, 73, 82, 89, 90, 91, 94,
   98
   pronunciation policy 127
   radio 128–9
Bedi, G. 291, 296
beer, advertising of 145–56
Bellafante, Ginia 207
Beniger, James 276, 277, 280
Bennett, William 250–1
Bensen, Lloyd 260
Berger, W. 111
Berkowitz, Dan 88
Berlusconi 72
Bertelsmann 59, 65
Bewkes, Jeffrey 62
Bewley, Ed 95
Bhambhri, C. P. 296
Bidwai, P. 296
Biggs, Barton 301
Blockbuster 5, 65, 66, 221
Bogart, Leo 330
Book, Constance L. 214–23
books 51–2, 62–72 passim 109
Boorstin, Daniel 180, 184, 208,
   209
Bordowitz, Gregg 321
Bourdieu, Pierre 176–7, 181
Boylan, David 11
Bradsher, Keith 168
brand recognition 188
Braver, Rita 261–2
Brazilian media 94
Brecher, J. 291

British media 65, 67, 72–3, 82,
   90–1, 92, 94, 127–42: see
   also BBC
Broadcasting Research Unit 82
broadcasting and education
   264–7
Brubach, Holly 211
Brunei media 94
Burger King 105, 117, 269
Burger, Warren 324, 331
Bush, George 37, 261
Business Week 188
Butler, J. 320

Calkins, Ernest Elmo 240
capitalism 28
CARE 182
Case, Steve 16
Cassidy, Margaret 264–74
CBS 108, 326, 325, 328
   cross promotion 105, 106
   educational broadcasting
      265
   Infinity Radio 325, 329
   news programmes 9, 116
   Schools of the Air 267
   Westinghouse 5, 9, 60, 329
censorship 8–9, 11–12, 17–18, 169,
   170
Center for Science in the Public
   Interest 148
Channel One Television
   269–70, 271, 274
Chevron 168–9
Chicago Tribune 240, 295–303
   passim
Chrysler Corporation 8–9
church and state 10–12, 102
Clinton, Bill 168, 195, 250–61
   passim
CNBC 70, 116
CNN 5, 62, 86, 207
Coleman, Richard 88
Columbia 60, 109
Columbia Journalism Review 14
Columbia University 265–6

Columbian media 94
Comedy Central 62, 66, 106
Commercial Revolution 277, 278
commercial television 47–53
Committee on Propaganda in the Schools 273
Commoner, Barry 35
communications, public interest in 324–31
Compaq 194
Computers for Education 271
Conference Board 273
corporate ownership 9–10
corporate synergy 5–7, 57, 68, 108–10, 114, 116
Costello, T. 291
Cowie, Norman 310–21
Cronkite, Walter 12, 84, 86, 99
cross-promotion 102–3, 105, 109, 110, 113, 117–18
culture
  advertising 27–30
  commercialization of 310–18
Czech media 90, 93–4, 95

Damrosch, Walter 267
Dateline 116, 226–7, 228–9, 230, 232, 233
DC Comics 62, 109
Deeb, Gary 86
Department of Health and Human Services 146
deregulation 76–7, 320: see also regulation
Deutsche Presse-Agentur 295, 302, 303
digital special effects 251
digital television 327 & n.
Diller, Barry 69
Disney 5, 6, 59, 61, 63–4, 104, 105, 106, 115, 119, 329
  corporate synergy 108, 109, 110
Dole, Bob 250–62 passim
Dole, Elizabeth 250, 252, 260
Donaldson, Sam 261
Douglas, Mary 146, 214
Dowd, Maureen 254
Downing, Kathryn M. 13
drink driving 167
  beer advertising 145–56
Drucker, Peter 148

Dukakis, Michael 260
Dupont, Pierre 241
DuPont-Columbia University organization 87
Durkheim, Emile 276
Dutch media 65, 94, 97

E! Entertainment Television 69, 243–4
Ebert, Roger 250
e-business 192–3
e-commerce 15–16, 18–19
education 264–74
Edwards, Karen 188
Ehrenreich, Barbara 33, 34, 38
Eisner, Michael 7, 63, 64, 67
ElHassan, L. 3
Ellul, Jaques 186, 196, 197
entertainment marketing 102–19
entertainment programming 326, 330
Entman, Robert 214–23, 219, 221, 294, 295
environmental issues 35–6, 163–6, 168–70
Enzensberger, H. M. 317
ER 108, 111, 116, 326
ESPN 64, 101, 106, 108, 115, 242
European Community cultural policy 74
event entertainment 110–11

Faludi, Susan 205
fashion 203–8
FBI (Federal Bureau of Investigation) 226
FCC (Federal Communications Commission) 88, 324–31 passim
Federal Communications Act (1934) 324–5, 328
film studios 62, 64, 70, 106
Financial Interest and Syndication Rules 118
Finnish media 94
Ford, Gerald 260
Ford, William Clay, Jr. 170
Fox 12, 112, 119
  news 11, 68, 69
  sport 68, 69, 108, 118, 326
Frank N. Magid Associates 85–6, 88, 90, 92, 94, 95, 98

Frankola, K. 88
FRC (Federal Radio Commission) 266
Freedman, Rita 210
French media 65, 72
Freud, Sigmund 283
Fruit of the Loom 118–19
Fry, Katherine 173–84

Galtung, J. 293
Gamson, W. A. 228, 294
Gandhi, Maneka 296
Gans, Herbert 305
Garfield, Bob 191
General Electric (GE) 9, 60, 69, 70, 116, 329: see also NBC
  advertising spending 104
General Mills, Inc. 105, 270
General Motors (GM) 105, 118, 241
German media 65, 90, 91–2, 94, 95, 96
Giroux, Henry 317, 318
Glaser, Milton 8, 9
globalization 14, 291–306
  ethics of 71–83
  media giants 59–70
Goodis, Jerry 32
Goodman, Amy 169
Goodman, Steve 317
Goodman, Walter 252
Gramsci, Antonio 38
Greek media 90, 92–3, 95
Greenberg, Stanley 88, 98, 257
Gross, Michael 205
Grove, Andy 186, 196
Grove, Lloyd 86
Gruntman, Marion 96
Gumpert, Gary 209

Hall, R. E. 215
Hall, Stuart 294, 317, 319, 320
Hallin, D. 292
Harmon, Mark 87
HarperCollins 68, 109
Harvey, Delicia 203–11
Havelock, Eric 282
HBO (Home Box Office) 1, 5, 9, 62, 241, 329
Heilbroner, Robert 36
Heineken 114
Hersant 72
Hewitt, Don 13

'high concept' entertainment 110–11
Hines, Marjorie 227
Hoffman, Peter 89
Honey, J. 140
Hoover, Herbert 50, 329
Hurbert, Bob 251
Hyperion Press 64, 109

IBM 192–3
Independence Day 250–1
independent TV companies 72–3
Indian media 94
Indonesian media 94
Infinity Radio 325, 329
infomercials 189–91, 253, 262
Innis, Harold 276, 280
Insurance Institute for Highway Safety 168
International Monetary Fund 295
Internet 15–19, 60–1, 106, 186–98, 281, 329, 330
  censorship 17–18
  supermodels on 208
  target marketing 243, 244
ITN (Independent Television News) 90, 94, 96
Itochu 61
ITV 89–90, 95

Jacobs, J. 88
Jaffri, A. 291, 296
Jaquet, Janine 10
Jennings, Peter 314 & n.
Jhally, Sut 27–38, 112, 317, 320
Jollymore, Nicholas 10
Jones, Clive 96
Jones, Phil 262
journalism 8–9, 10–15, 305–6

Karnataka Rajya Ryota Sangha (KRRS) 296, 302, 303
Keachigain, Ken 251
Kemp, Jack 261
Kennard, William E. 330
Kent, Arthur 10–11
KFC (Kentucky Fried Chicken) 291–300
Klein, Calvin 225–33
Kleinsteuber, Hans J. 141
Kohli, Sandeep 299–300

Koppel, Ted 13, 253

Lauren, Ralph 205
Lee, C. C. 97
Lehrer, Jim 261
Leith, Philip 280
Leveranz, Deborah 311, 312
Levin, Gerald 67
Lewis, Justin 317
licensing rules 324–7, 328
Liebow, Victor 30
Lifetime Learning Systems 270
Limbaugh, Rush 270
Lippert, Barbara 227
Lippert, Paul 276–86
Lippmann, Walter 79
literacy 51–2, 270, 310–18
Littlefield, Warren 11
LMAs (local market agreements) 325–6
local radio 127–42
Los Angeles Times 13, 295, 298, 300, 301, 302
Lost World 4, 105, 108, 113, 117
Luxembourg media 65
Lynch, Merrill 69

magazines 8–9, 65, 68, 51, 103, 109, 116, 205: *see also* *People; Time*
  Advertising Age 60, 63, 106
  Sports Illustrated 62, 64, 242, 244
  Sunset 173–4, 178–9
Magid *see* Frank N. Magid Associates
Magid, Brent 95–6
Magid, Frank 89, 90
Malaysian media 94
Malone, John 67, 69
Mandala, Mark 110
Manes, Stephen 191
Marine Broadcasting (Offences) Act 129
marketing
  entertainment 102–19
  news 12–14
  politicians 250–63
  targeting 240–8
Markey, Edward J. 330
Marx, Karl 27–8, 37, 49, 276, 283
mass customization 244–5
Masterman, Len 312

Matsushita 68, 70
Maxwell, Robert 71
MCA Inc. 70, 104
McAllister, Matthew 101–19
McCannon, Bob 314–15
McChesney, Robert 110, 313, 316
McCrum, Robert 206
McHugh & Hoffman 85–6, 87, 89, 90, 93, 94, 96
MCI Communications Corp. 118, 186, 187, 191
McKibben, Bill 35
McLuhan, Marshall 40–6, 149, 161, 276
media conglomeration 5, 7
media deregulation 253
media literacy 310–18
media monopoly 81–3
media piracy 318–21
Medicare 256
Meehan, Eileen 98, 109
Meister, M. 165
Men in Black 4, 114, 117
Mercedes-Benz 105, 113
Microsoft 62, 70, 190, 191
Miller, Ray 88
Mills, C. Wright 209
minority tv 73–4
Mizrahi, Isaac 207
Modigliani, A. 294
Molinari, Susan 116 & n. 252–3
Monsanto 11
Moonvees, Leslie 328
Morgan, Arthur E. 268
Morning in America 257–8, 261
Morris, Dick 253, 254
Morris, Nancy 127–42
Motion Picture Association 74
Mouffe, Chantal 317–18
MSNBC 70, 86, 116
MTV 66, 207, 242
Mulder, Karen 208
Munro, Charles 95
Murdoch, Rupert 12, 67, 71, 82
Murphy, Dennis 226, 227
Murrow, Edward R. 86
music 62–70 *passim* 109, 207–8, 266, 267

Nanjundaswamy, M. D. 296, 297, 302, 303
Nash, Michael 320–1

National Advisory Council on Radio in Education 266
National Association of Broadcasters 328n.
National Catholic Education Association 267
National Commission on Excellence in Education 272
National Committee on Education by Radio 266
National Education Association 269, 273
National Highway Traffic Safety Administration 168
Naughton, James 13
NBC 62, 70, 104, 105, 106, 108, 112, 326, 329: *see also* *Dateline*
   educational broadcasting 265–6
   news programmes 10, 115–16
   Seinfeld 101, 116, 254–5
New Mexico Media Literacy Project 314–16
New York Times News Services 293
New York Times, on oppositon to KFC 295–302 *passim*
news consultancy 84–99
News Corporation 12, 59, 61, 62, 63, 67–8, 69, 82, 329: *see also* Fox
   advertising spending 104
   corporate synergy 108, 109
   newspapers 51, 64, 65, 68, 82: *see also* KFC
   news programmes 9, 12, 14, 116, 314: *see also* Dateline
   news reports 9–10, 12–15, 51, 292, 293, 294–5, 297–306
New Zealand media 94, 95, 97
Nickelodeon 66, 242, 269
Nielsen, Arthur C. 42–3
Nike 9, 259
Nixon, Richard 261
Norwegian media 94
NRI (Nielsen Radio Index) 43

Olympics 104, 108, 115
Ong, Walter 277, 278–9, 280, 281–2, 284
Oracle Corporation 195–6

Overholser, Geneva 12
Ozzard, Janet 207

Paramount 65, 66, 110
Parent'Hood 114–15
Parker, Everett C. 324–31
Parthy, J. 291
Patnaik, P. 296
Pauley, Jane 226–7
Payne Fund 265
Peale, Betsey 87
People 62, 101, 116
PepsiCo 106, 113, 117, 296, 297
Pereira, W. 295
Philip Morris Companies, Inc. 270
Philips Isis 193–4
Philips WebTV 189–92
Pinsky, Robert 284–6
Pipher, Mary 211
pirate radio stations 128–9, 140
Pitock, Todd 193–4
Pizza Hut 270, 297
Poffenberger, A. T. 44
political campaigns 252–3, 260–2
Polygram 106
Pope, Daniel 240
Postman, Neil 47–53
Powell, Colin 260
Powers, Ron 84, 86, 87
PrimeStar 62, 69
product placement 2–5, 8, 113–14, 115, 117
Project Censored 168
Project on Media Ownership 10
PSAs (Public Service Announcements) 112
Public Broadcasting System (America) 51
Puerto Rican media 94

Quayle, Dan 260
Quick, Terence 92, 93

Rabine, Leslie 204
Radio Act (1927) 265
radio broadcasting 64, 65, 137, 138, 264–7
   British 127–42
Ramism 277–8, 279
Ramus, Peter 277, 278, 279, 280
Rather, Dan 261

Reagan, Ronald 257, 258n. 260
Red Lion Broadcasting 329
Redstone, Sumner 65–6, 67
regional accents 127–8, 130, 132, 137–8, 141–2
regulation 77–81: *see also* deregulation
Reich, Robert 257
Renick, Ralph 88
Retallack, S. 165
Reuter, Vic 96
Reuters 293, 295, 299, 300, 301, 302–3
Riefenstahl, Leni 219
Rojecki, A. 219, 221
Rollins, Ed 257
Romanian media 94
Roseberry, William 179
Rosenberg, Scott 191
Rosenblum, M. 293
Rosie O'Donnell Show 2–3
Rosler, Martha 319
RTNDA (Radio-Television News Directors Association) 87, 88, 97–8
Ruge, H. 293
Russian media 95

Sachs, Aaron 168
Saint-Simon 277
Schatz, T. 6
Schiller, Herb 319
Schools of the Air 267
Schultz, Howard 180, 181–4
Schwartz, Tony 149–50
Scitovsky, Tibor 32
Seabrook, J. 295
Seagram 60, 68, 70, 105, 110
Seinfeld 101, 116, 254–5
Sellers, Len 190, 191
sexuality in advertising 225–33
Shapiro, Andrew 18
Shaw, Bernice 260
Shiva, Vandana 291, 296
Sierra Club 170
Singapore media 94
Siskel, Jean 250
sitcoms 101, 108, 109, 113
Sloan, Alfred 241
Slovenian media 94
Small, Jim 259
Smith, Anthony 71–83
Smith, Gary 253

Soloski, John 12
Sony 60, 68, 101, 104
Soros, George 37
South African media 95
South Korean media 94
sponsorship 28–9, 87
sport 63, 64, 101, 106, 111–12, 115,
    242, 330
  programming 108, 326
spot advertising 1–2, 5, 7
Starbucks Corporation 173–84
Steinhem, Gloria 30
Strasser, Susan 240
Strate, Lance 145–56, 203–11
Sturken, Marita 319
Sudjic, Deyan 205, 206, 208–9
supermodels 203–11
SUVs (sport utility vehicles)
    158–70

talk shows 101
Taylorism 283
TBS (Turner Broadcasting
    System Inc.) 5, 62
TCI 60, 67, 68, 69, 329
technology, advertising of
    186–98
Télé Luxembourg 74
Telecommunication Act (1996)
    18, 19, 328–9
telephone services 64, 76, 117,
    118, 324, 329
Télétel 72
Television Without Frontiers 74
Television: Europe – Its Peoples
    and Their Cultures 74
Tensma, Hans 342 & n.
Thatcher, Margaret 32–3
Thatcher government, media

privatization White Paper
    89
theme parks 6, 64, 66, 70
Tiegs, Cheryl 205
tie-ins 6, 105, 110, 115, 117
tight diversification 5, 17
Time 62, 109, 116, 186, 244
  fashion 205, 207
  on opposition to KFC
    295–303 passim
Time Warner 5–6, 10, 19, 59,
    61–3, 66, 69, 116, 242, 329
  advertising spending 104, 105,
    106
  corporate synergy 5–6, 108,
    114, 116
  Entertainment Weekly 101,
    109, 116
  news reporting 14–15
  People 62, 101, 116
Tocqueville, Alexis de 48–9
Toshiba 61
Toy Story 106, 118–19
Trudgill, Peter 137
Truman, Patrick 227
Tucker, Lauren 225–33
Tunstall, Jeremy 130
Turner, Ted 67
Turow, Joseph 239–48
TV shows 110, 115, 118–19, 251:
    see also ER
Tyner, Kathleen 311, 312

Ukranian media 94, 95
Union of Concerned Scientists
    36
Universal 60, 70, 105, 110
UPN 108, 112
Urry, John 175, 177–8

US Food and Drug
    Administration 11n. 299
US voice-overs 130, 131, 133–7,
    139, 140–1

Viacom 5, 6, 9, 59, 63, 65–6, 108,
    242, 329
  advertising spending 104, 106
videos 66, 68, 106, 107, 110
video art 320–1

WABC-TV 93
Wall, Melissa 291–306
Warner Bros 5, 6, 63, 104, 109,
    114–15, 118, 119
WCBS 325
Weber, Max 276
Weekly Reader 271
Weisberg, Dan 186–98
Wernick, Andrew 179–80, 183
Whittle, Chris 269, 271
Wildmon, Donald 225
Willes, Mark H. 13
William Morris talent agency
    113
Williams, Maslyn 175–6
Wilson, Steve 11, 12
WINS 325
Wolf, Naomi 210
Woodhull, Nancy 263
World Bank 295
World Health Organization 299
WTBS 'Superstation' 241
WTVJ 88

Y2K problem 196–8
You've Got Mail 16–18

'ZapMe' 271–2

DATE DUE

HIGHSMITH #451